TRAVELLERS
IN THE
THIRD REICH

THE RISE OF FASCISM
THROUGH THE EYES OF
EVERYDAY PEOPLE

Julia Boyd

First published 2017 by
Elliott and Thompson Limited
27 John Street
London WC1N 2BX
www.eandtbooks.com

This paperback edition first published in 2018

ISBN: 978-1-78396-381-2

Copyright © Julia Boyd 2017

PICTURE CREDITS: pages 10–11: JP Map Graphics Ltd

PLATE SECTION: Page 1: (top) Reproduced by kind permission of the Farrington Historical Foundation, (bottom) Everett Collection Historical / Alamy Stock Photo; page 2: (top) Private collection, (bottom) Reproduced by kind permission of the Thomas Cook Archives; page 3: Reproduced by kind permission of the Thomas Cook Archives; page 4: Reproduced by kind permission of the family; page 5: (top) Swim Ink 2 LLC, Getty Images, (bottom) Hulton Deutsch, Getty Images; Page 6: private collection; page 7: (top) mauritius images GmbH / Alamy Stock Photo, (bottom) © SZ Photo / Scherl / Bridgeman Images; page 8: (top) Cambridge University Library N8259 and N8260, (bottom) Hulton Deutsch, Getty Images.

TEXT PERMISSIONS: Ida Anderson, permission granted by George Watson's College, Archive. Samuel Beckett, German Diaries, by kind permission of The Estate of Samuel Beckett, The Beckett International Foundation/The University of Reading, Suhrkamp Verlag AG and Faber & Faber. Bridget von Bernstorff, permission granted by the author's estate. W. E. B. Du Bois, W. E. B. Du Bois papers, permission granted by The Permissions Company Inc., on behalf of the David Graham Du Bois Trust. Ivan Brown, permission granted by Lake Placid Olympic Museum. Arthur Bryant, permission granted by the Trustees of the Liddell Hart Centre for Military Archives. Victor and Thelma Cazalet, permission granted by the authors' estate. Manning Clark, permission granted by the author's estate. Geoffrey Cox, permission granted by the author's estate. Sibyl Crowe, permission granted by the author's estate. Admiral Sir Barry Domvile, permission granted by the author's estate. Ursula Duncan-Jones, permission granted by the author's estate. Eric Fenn, permission granted by the author's estate. Martin Flavin, permission granted by the Special Collections Research Center, University of Chicago Library. Louis MacNeice, extract from Autumn Journal, IV (Faber & Faber), printed by permission of David Higham Associates Limited. Princess Margaret of Hesse, permission granted by the authors' estate. Barbara Pemberton, permission granted by the author's estate. Barbara Runkle, permission granted by the author's estate. Stephen Spender, permission granted by the author's estate. Lady Margaret Stirling, permission granted by the author's estate. Joan Tonge, permission granted by the author's estate. Antony Toynbee, permission granted by the author's estate. Lady Mairi Vane-Tempest-Stewart, permission granted by the author's estate. Bradford Wasserman, permission granted by Virginia Historical Society.

Every effort has been made to trace copyright holders of material used within this book. Where this has not been possible, the publisher will be happy to credit them in future editions.

9 8 7 6 5 4 3 2

A catalogue record for this book is available from the British Library.

Typesetting: Marie Doherty
Printed and bound by CPI Group (UK) Ltd, Croydon, CR0 4YY

One of the *Daily Telegraph*'s Best Books of 2017

ur

bh

e

our
d

ew

ies
e
ant

full

hed

day when strong leaders are again all the rage' – Professor David Reynolds, *The Long Shadow: The Great War and the 20th Century*

'Drawing on the unpublished experiences of outsiders inside the Third Reich, Julia Boyd provides dazzling new perspectives on the Germany that Hitler built. Her book is a tour de force of historical research' – Dr Piers Brendon, author of *The Dark Valley: A Panorama of the 1930s*

'What was Nazi Germany really like in the run up to the Second World War? Julia Boyd's painstakingly researched and deeply nuanced book shows how this troubled country appeared to travellers of the 1920s and 1930s. A truly fascinating read' – Keith Lowe, *Sunday Times* bestselling author of *The Fear and the Freedom*, *Savage Continent* and *Inferno*

'To a younger generation it seems incomprehensible that after the tragic Great War people and political leaders allowed themselves to march into the abyss again. Julia Boyd's book, drawing on wide experience and forensic research, seeks to answer some of these questions' – Randolph Churchill

'Engrossing … skilfully woven together to create a three-dimensional picture of Germany under Hitler that has many resonances for today' – *The Bookseller*

'A glorious read for anyone with an interest in the history of the twentieth century' – Sir Christopher Mallaby, former ambassador to Germany and France

'Unique, original and engagingly written. This account of visitors and tourists to Germany brings to life these difficult decades in a most refreshing way [and] should attract a wide circle of readers' – Dr Zara Steiner, author of *The Lights that Failed: European International History 1919–1933* and *Triumph of the Dark: 1933–1939*

'An entertaining popular history … a fascinating book. Boyd lets the voices from the past speak to us … often at odds with or in more depth than many standard histories … very readable' – Paul Burke, nudge-book.com

For

Mackenzie, Harrison, Bella,
Robbie, Edie, Sebastian,
Matthew, Zoe, Jemima,
Clio and Kit

Contents

Introduction

Imagine that it is the summer of 1936 and you are on honeymoon in Germany. The sun is shining, the people are friendly – life is good. You have driven south through the Rhineland, admiring its castles and vineyards, and have watched fascinated as the huge, heavily laden barges ply their way slowly up the Rhine. Now you are in Frankfurt. You have just parked your car, its GB sticker prominently displayed, and are about to explore the city, one of the medieval architectural gems of Europe.

Then, out of nowhere, a Jewish-looking woman appears and approaches you. Radiating anxiety, she clutches the hand of a limping teenage girl wearing a thick built-up shoe. All the disturbing rumours you have heard about the Nazis – the persecution of Jews, euthanasia, torture and imprisonment without trial – are at that moment focused on the face of this desperate mother. She has seen your GB sticker and begs you to take her daughter to England. What do you do? Do you turn your back on her in horror and walk away? Do you sympathise but tell her there is really nothing you can do? Or do you take the child away to safety?

I first heard this true story from the daughter of the English couple, as we sat in her tranquil Cambridge garden sipping lemonade one hot summer afternoon. When Alice showed me the photograph of a smiling Greta holding her as a baby, confirming the remarkable and happy outcome of this particular traveller's tale, I tried to place myself in her parents' shoes. How would I have reacted had I found myself in the same situation? It took only seconds to conclude that, however touched by the woman's plight and no matter how appalled by the Nazis, I would almost certainly have opted for the middle course. But although it is easy enough to *imagine* our response in such circumstances, do we really know how we would react? How we would interpret what is going on right in front of our eyes?

～

This book describes what happened in Germany between the wars. Based on first-hand accounts written by foreigners, it creates a sense of what it was actually like, both physically and emotionally, to travel in Hitler's Germany. Scores of previously unpublished diaries and letters have been tracked down to present a vivid new picture of Nazi Germany that it is hoped will enhance – even challenge – the reader's current perceptions. For anyone born after the Second World War, it has always been impossible to view this period with detachment. Images of Nazi atrocities are so powerful that they can never be suppressed or set aside. But what was it like to travel in the Third Reich without the benefit of post-war hindsight? How easy was it then to know what was really going on, to grasp the essence of National Socialism, to remain untouched by the propaganda or predict the Holocaust? And was the experience transformative or did it merely reinforce established prejudices?

These questions, and many others, are explored through the personal testimony of a whole range of visitors. Celebrities like Charles Lindbergh, David Lloyd George, the Maharaja of

Patiala, Francis Bacon, the King of Bulgaria and Samuel Beckett passed through, to name just a few. But also ordinary travellers, from pacifist Quakers to Jewish Boy Scouts; African-American academics to First World War veterans. Students, politicians, musicians, diplomats, schoolchildren, communists, poets, journalists, fascists, artists and, of course, tourists – many of whom returned year after year to holiday in Nazi Germany – all have their say, as well as Chinese scholars, Olympic athletes and a pro-Nazi Norwegian Nobel laureate. The impressions and reflections of these assorted travellers naturally differ widely and are often profoundly contradictory. But drawn together they generate an extraordinary three-dimensional picture of Germany under Hitler.

Many people visited the Third Reich for professional reasons, others simply to enjoy a good holiday. Yet more were motivated by a long love affair with German culture, family roots or often just sheer curiosity. Against a background of failing democracy elsewhere and widespread unemployment, right-wing sympathisers went in the hope that lessons learned from a 'successful' dictatorship might be replicated back home while those subscribing to a Carlylean worship of heroes were eager to see a real *Übermensch* [superman] in action. But no matter how diverse the travellers' politics or background, one theme unites nearly all – a delight in the natural beauty of Germany. You did not have to be pro-Nazi to marvel at the green countryside, the vineyard-flanked rivers or the orchards stretching as far as the eye could see. Meanwhile, pristine medieval towns, neat villages, clean hotels, the friendliness of the people and the wholesome cheap food, not to mention Wagner, window-boxes and foaming steins of beer, drew holiday-makers back year after year even as the more horrific aspects of the regime came under increasing scrutiny

in their own countries. It is, of course, the human tragedy of
these years that remains paramount, but the extraordinary pre-
war charm of such cities as Hamburg, Dresden, Frankfurt or
Munich, highlighted in so many diaries and letters, serves to
emphasise just how much Germany – and indeed the whole
world – lost materially because of Hitler.

Travellers from America and Britain vastly outnumbered
those from any other country. Despite the Great War, a large
section of the British public considered the Germans close
kin – in every way more satisfactory than the French. Martha
Dodd, daughter of the American ambassador to Germany,
expressed a common view when she remarked, 'Unlike the
French, the Germans weren't thieves, they weren't selfish and
they weren't impatient or cold or hard.'[1] In Britain there was
also growing unease over the Treaty of Versailles, which, as
many then considered, had given the Germans a particularly
raw deal. Surely the time had come to offer this reformed
former enemy support and friendship. Furthermore, many
Britons believed that their own country had much to learn
from the new Germany. So, even as awareness of Nazi barbarity deepened and spread, Britons continued to travel to the
Reich for both business and pleasure. According to the American
journalist Westbrook Pegler, writing in 1936, the British 'have
an optimistic illusion that the Nazi is a human being under his
scales. Their present tolerance is not acceptance of the brute
so much as a hope that by encouragement and an appeal to
his better nature, he may one day be housebroken.'[2] There was
much truth in this.

By 1937 the number of American visitors to the Reich
approached half a million per annum.[3] Intent on enjoying their
European adventure to the full, the great majority viewed political issues as an unwelcome distraction and so simply ignored

them. This was easy to do since the Germans went to great lengths to woo their foreign visitors – especially the Americans and the British. There was another reason why American tourists were reluctant to question the Nazis too closely, particularly on racial matters. Any derogatory comment regarding the persecution of Jews invited comparison with the United States' treatment of its black population – an avenue that few ordinary Americans were anxious to explore. Most tourists, looking back on their pre-war German holidays, genuinely believed that they could not have known what the Nazis were really up to. And it is true that for the casual visitor to holiday hotspots like the Rhineland or Bavaria, there was limited overt evidence of Nazi crime. Of course, foreigners noticed the profusion of uniforms and flags, the constant marching and heiling but wasn't that just the Germans being German? Travellers frequently remarked with distaste on the abundance of anti-Semitic notices. But, however unpleasant the treatment of Jews, many foreigners considered this to be an internal matter and not really their business. Moreover, as they were so often themselves anti-Semitic, many accepted that the Jews did indeed have a case to answer. As for newspaper attacks on the Reich, these were often discounted since everyone knew journalists' penchant for sensationalising the least little incident. People also remembered how German atrocities reported in the newspapers during the early weeks of the First World War were later deemed to have been false. As Louis MacNeice put it,

> But that, we thought to ourselves, was not our business
> All that the tripper wants is the *status quo*
> Cut and dried for trippers.
> And we thought the papers a lark
> With their party politics and blank invective[4]

While much of the above may have been true for the average tourist, what of those who travelled in the Third Reich
for professional reasons, or who went specifically to explore
and understand the new Germany? In the early months of
Nazi rule, many foreigners found it difficult to know what
to believe. Was Hitler a monster or a marvel? Although some
visitors remained agnostic, the evidence suggests that, as the
years went by, the majority had made up their minds even
before they set foot in the country. They went to Germany (as
indeed they did to Soviet Russia) intent on confirming rather
than confronting their expectations. Surprisingly few, it would
seem, underwent a change of heart as a direct result of their
travels. Those on the right therefore found a hard-working,
confident people, shaking off the wrongs they had suffered
under the Treaty of Versailles while at the same time protect-
ing the rest of Europe from Bolshevism. To them, Hitler was
not only an inspirational leader but also – as one enthusiast
after another was so keen to state – a modest man, utterly
sincere and devoted to peace. Those on the left, meanwhile,
reported a cruel, oppressive regime fuelled by obscene racist
policies using torture and persecution to terrorise its citizens.
But on one aspect, both could agree. Adored by millions, Hitler
had the country totally in his grip.

Students form a particularly interesting group. It seems
that even in the context of such an unpleasant regime, a dose
of German culture was still considered an essential part of
growing up. But it is hard to find an explanation for why so
many British and American teenagers were sent off to Nazi
Germany right up until the outbreak of war. Parents who
despised the Nazis and derided their gross 'culture' showed
no compunction in parcelling off their children to the Reich
for a lengthy stay. For the young people in question, it was to

prove an extraordinary experience, if not exactly the one originally proposed. Students certainly numbered among those who, on returning from Germany, tried to alert their families and friends to the lurking danger. But public indifference or sympathy with Nazi 'achievements', cheerful memories of beer gardens and dirndls, and, above all, the deep-seated fear of another war, meant that too often such warnings fell on deaf ears.

Dread of war was the most important factor in many foreigners' responses to the Reich but this was especially acute among ex-servicemen. Their longing to believe that Hitler really was a man of peace, that the Nazi revolution would in time calm down and become civilised and that Germany's intentions were genuinely as benign as its citizens kept promising, resulted in many of them travelling frequently to the new Germany and offering it their support. The possibility that their sons would have to endure the same nightmare that they had, against the odds, survived makes such an attitude easy to understand. Perhaps, too, Nazi emphasis on order, marching and efficiency was innately appealing to military men.

The spectacular torchlight processions and pagan festivals that formed such a prominent feature of the Third Reich were naturally much remarked on by foreigners. Some were repelled but others thought them a splendid expression of Germany's new-found confidence. To many it seemed that National Socialism had displaced Christianity as the national religion. Aryan supremacy underpinned by *Blut und Boden* [blood and soil] was now the people's gospel, the Führer their saviour. Indeed numerous foreigners, even those who were not especially pro-Nazi, found themselves swept up in the intense emotion generated by such extravaganzas as a Nuremberg rally or massive torchlight parade. No one knew better than the

Nazis how to manipulate the emotions of vast crowds, and many foreigners – often to their surprise – discovered that they too were not immune.

All travellers to the Reich, no matter who they were or what their purpose, were subjected to constant propaganda: the iniquities of the Versailles treaty, the astonishing achievements of the Nazi revolution, Hitler's devotion to peace, the need for Germany to defend itself, retrieve its colonies, expand to the East and so on. But arguably the Nazis' most persistent propaganda message, and the one that they initially felt certain would persuade the Americans and British to join forces with them, concerned the 'Bolshevik/Jewish' threat. Foreigners were lectured incessantly on how only Germany stood between Europe and the Red hordes poised to sweep across the continent and destroy civilisation. Many became inured and stopped listening. Indeed, trying to figure out the precise difference between National Socialism and Bolshevism was for the more questioning traveller a confusing matter. They knew, of course, that the Nazis and communists were the bitterest of enemies, but what exactly was the difference between their respective aims and methods? To the untrained eye, Hitler's suppression of all personal freedom, control of every aspect of national and domestic life, use of torture and show trials, deployment of an all-powerful secret police and outrageous propaganda, looked, superficially at least, remarkably similar to Stalin's. As Nancy Mitford frivolously wrote, 'There's never been a pin to put between Communists and the Nazis. The Communists torture you to death if you are not a worker and Nazis torture you to death if you are not a German. Aristocrats are inclined to prefer Nazis while Jews prefer Bolshies.'[5]

Until 1937, when the anti-Nazi chorus grew much louder, it was the journalists and diplomats who, with some obvious exceptions, emerged as heroes. Travelling widely all over the country in their efforts to present an accurate picture, these men and women consistently tried to draw attention to Nazi atrocities. But their reports were repeatedly edited or cut, or they were accused of exaggeration. Many worked long years in Germany under nerve-racking conditions and, in the case of the journalists, with the knowledge that at any minute they might be expelled or arrested on trumped-up charges. Their travel accounts are very different from the joyous descriptions so often found in the diaries and letters of the short-term visitors who much preferred to believe that things were not nearly as bad as the newsmen made out. While it is natural that informed residents should perceive a country differently from the casual tourist, in the case of Nazi Germany, the contrast between the two viewpoints is especially striking.

From a post-war perspective, the issues confronting the 1930s traveller to Germany are too easily seen in black and white. Hitler and the Nazis were evil and those who failed to understand that were either stupid or themselves fascist. This book does not pretend to be a comprehensive study of foreign travel in Nazi Germany, but it does, through the experiences of dozens of travellers recorded at the time, attempt to show that gaining a proper understanding of the country was not as straightforward as many of us have assumed. Disturbing, absurd, moving and ranging from the deeply trivial to the deeply tragic, these travellers' tales give a fresh insight into the complexities of the Third Reich, its paradoxes and its ultimate destruction.

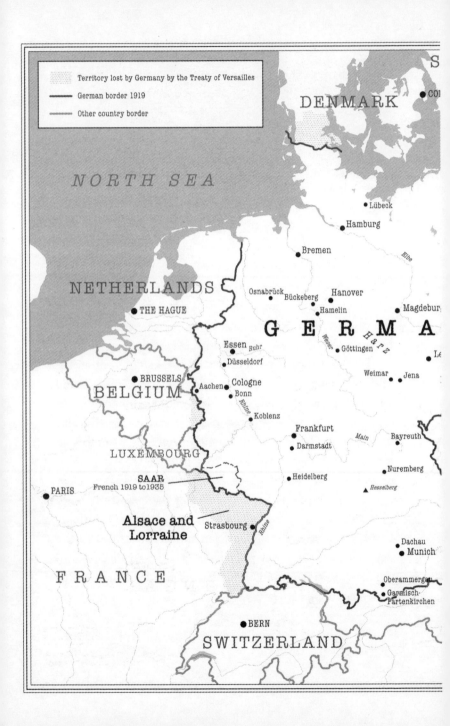

SWEDEN

COPENHAGEN

BALTIC SEA

Memel

LITHUANIA

Neman

Königsberg

East Prussia (German)

Danzig

Danzig Corridor

Tannenberg Memorial

Wisla

BERLIN

WARSAW

P O L A N D

ourg

Leipzig

S i l e s i a

Breslau

Dresden

S u d e t e n l a n d

Gleiwitz **Upper Silesia**

Marienbad

PRAGUE

C Z E C H O S L O V A K I A

Danube

VIENNA

BUDAPEST

Berchtesgaden

H U N G A R Y

A U S T R I A

100 miles

Lambert Conformal Conic Projection.
North at the top of the page.

1

Open Wounds

'GERMANY *invites* YOU' announces the title of a travel brochure aimed at American tourists. On its cover a young man in lederhosen, a feather in his hat, is pictured striding above a wooded ravine. Over him towers a gothic castle; behind him snow-covered mountains gleam enticingly. The hiker, bursting with vigour, gestures welcomingly to an inset panel showing a liner docked at New York harbour where the sun – rising behind the Statue of Liberty – heralds a bright new future.

All very beguiling, but it is the date of the leaflet that makes it so striking. Printed only months after the end of the First World War, it was a brave attempt by Germany's leading hotels (among them the Hotel Bristol in Berlin and the Englischer Hof in Frankfurt) to stimulate tourism. Naturally its few pages give no hint of the horror that had so recently consumed Europe and for which Germany was widely held responsible. Yet much of the leaflet's upbeat message was true for, despite the war, Germany's landscape was still beautiful and largely unspoiled. Because the fighting had taken place beyond its borders, most of Germany's towns – physically at least – had emerged unscathed. The brochure highlights twenty cities but only in its description of Essen ('once the world's greatest arsenal but now a centre for the production of implements of peace') is there any reference to the war. Appealing to the nostalgia of Americans who had known the country in happier times, it conjures up a returning traveller 'in whose breast there rises the joyous wave of recollection' of a romantic and poetic Germany; of its cathedrals and castles, of its art treasures, and of Bach, Beethoven and Wagner.

One such returning American was Harry A. Franck. Only twenty-seven, he was already an established travel writer* when in April 1919 (just five months after the Armistice) he set out to explore unoccupied Germany east of the Rhine. It was a bold venture for behind the brochure's alluring vision there lay a grim reality. The youth on the cover may never have experienced a trench or seen his friends blown apart by an exploding shell, but for those who had, and for Germany's millions of hungry citizens, the brochure's cheerful propaganda must have seemed nothing more than a bad joke. While Franck could anticipate his travels with all the enthusiasm of a healthy young man, ordinary Germans – those with whom he so eagerly sought contact – had little to look forward to in the aftermath of war, but grief, hunger and uncertainty.

When representatives of the two-day-old Weimar Republic signed the Armistice on 11 November, Germany's new leaders faced the nightmare of both external and internal collapse. Even before the war ended, revolution triggered by a naval mutiny in Kiel had spread rapidly across the country, bringing

* By 1918 Franck had published five travel books, of which the best known is *A Vagabond Journey around the World* (New York: Century Co., 1910).

in its wake strikes, desertions and civil war. Pitted against each other were, on the one hand, the Spartacists (their name derived from the rebel gladiator, Spartacus), who soon formed themselves into the German Communist Party, and, on the other, the Freikorps, right-wing militias intent on destroying Bolshevism. The Spartacists (led by Rosa Luxemburg and Karl Liebknecht) stood little chance against the well-disciplined paramilitary bands of demobilised soldiers and by August 1919 the revolt was crushed, its leaders dead. However, with unrest still simmering across the country, even those not directly caught in the crossfire of the post-war violence faced a miserable future. They had lost faith in their leadership, dreaded communism and, with the wartime blockade still firmly in place, continued to starve. Far from being the alluring holiday destination as promised by the brochure, Germany in 1919 was a bleak and desperate place.

Germany's new leader was the Social Democrat Friedrich Ebert. The son of a tailor and himself a saddler by trade, he could scarcely have presented a greater contrast to Germany's former head of state – Wilhelm II, Emperor of Germany, King of Prussia, grandson of Queen Victoria. However, although the coarse-featured, thickly built Ebert lacked sophistication, foreigners at once warmed to his straightforward manner. One British observer noted how his 'shrewd beady eyes twinkled with honest good humour'.[1] On 10 December 1918, he had stood before the Brandenburg Gate in Berlin to greet the returning regiments of the Royal Prussian Guard. Lorenz Adlon, founder of the famous hotel that bears his name, had watched from a balcony as the soldiers responded to the order: 'eyes right'. For monarchists like him, it was a bitter moment. No longer did the soldiers' gaze fix upon the Kaiser resplendent in uniform and mounted on a fine horse, but on the squat

figure of the Chairman of the Committee of the People's
Representatives (as Ebert was then), standing on a podium, in
black frock coat and top hat. Nevertheless, even the staunchest
monarchist must have taken heart on hearing Ebert cry out to
the soldiers: 'You have returned undefeated.'[2]

This conviction that the German army remained
undefeated was deeply rooted – as foreigners soon discovered. Before Franck set out on his own travels, he had served
as an officer with the American Expeditionary Forces (AEF)
on the Rhine at Koblenz. His duties involved interviewing
scores of German soldiers who, to a man, he reported, believed
that in terms of military prestige they were unquestionably
the victors. It was only the treacherous politicians in Berlin
who had stabbed them in the back, together with the lack of
food caused by the cowardly Allied blockade that had forced
Germany to surrender. Franck heard this argument repeatedly,
as well as from his cousins in the northern city of Schwerin.
'England starved us otherwise she would never have won,'
they told him. 'Our brave soldiers at the front never gave way.
They would never have retreated a yard but for the break-
down at home.'[3] Franck could detect no sense of guilt. Indeed,
he could not recall a single German ever expressing remorse:
'They seemed to take the war as a natural, unavoidable thing,'
he wrote, 'just a part of life, as the gambler takes gambling,
with no other regret than it was their bad luck to lose.'[4]

Franck's German roots made him particularly sensitive to
the humiliations imposed on civilians by the military occupation of the Rhineland. 'Occupation means a horde of armed
strangers permeating every nook and corner of your town,
your house, of your private life,' he wrote. 'It means seeing
what you have hidden in that closet behind the chimney; it
means yielding your spare bed ... it means subjecting yourself,

or at least your plans, to the rules, sometimes even to the whims of the occupiers.'[5] He recorded that Germans were not allowed to travel, write letters, telephone, telegraph or publish newspapers, without American permission. Nor were they permitted to drink anything stronger than beer or wine, or to gather in a café unless given written consent. Regulations such as the rule compelling householders to keep their windows open at night were a reminder of just how deeply the occupation affected the most intimate details of civilian life.[6] And in case anyone in Koblenz still needed reminding who was in charge, a colossal Stars and Stripes could be seen for miles around, floating above the Ehrenbreitstein Fortress that stands so commandingly above the east bank of the Rhine. It was 'quite the largest flag in the Occupation',[7] one British colonel's wife remarked tartly, a blatant standard of triumph.

In the countryside, roads became 'rivers of Yankee soldiers', their military vehicles displaying the motif of a German helmet sliced through with an axe. Everywhere small boys in cut-down uniforms proffered souvenirs – a belt buckle inscribed *Gott mit uns* [God with us] or a spiked helmet. Young men in tattered grey uniforms were to be seen once more in the fields, loading wagons with the fat, misshapen turnips that for much of the war had been all that stood between the Germans and starvation. If the roads were crowded with military traffic, the Rhine now swarmed with pleasure boats full of Allied soldiers turned day-trippers, singing anti-Boche songs as they cruised past the Rhine's most famous landmark – the Rock of the Lorelei. 'Baedeker himself', commented Franck, 'never aspired to see his land so crowded with tourists and sightseers as in that spring of 1919.'[8]

Another American officer, Lieutenant Truman Smith, who had seen much action in the war, and who like Franck subsequently served with the AEF, thought the Rhine 'gloriously beautiful' but also 'dark and weird' with its pine-clad hills, vineyards and ruined towers.[9] A few weeks after the Armistice he wrote to his wife in New England, 'I suppose you want to know all about the "Huns", the feeling of the people etc. This is a difficult matter. One doesn't know.'[10] But he was soon describing the Germans as 'Sphinx-like and proud', observing how quickly they had reverted to their traditional industriousness despite their lack of proper tools. Smith also noted that, although they seemed to accept the American occupation without question, they regarded their new republic with deep cynicism, adding that 'they live in deadly fear of Bolshevism'.[11]

Smith would certainly have endorsed the remarks made by another (anonymous) American observer who suggested that 'the longer one remains in Germany the more one is astonished at the simplicity (sometimes pathetically naïve, sometimes exasperatingly stupid) and the friendliness of the people'. The unexpected human warmth puzzled this writer until a German woman living in the British sector in Cologne offered an explanation:

Before the English came we starved. Now there is money in circulation and the shops are filled with foodstuffs and even dairy products brought from England, France and Scandinavia. Many of the English officers and men we have found friendly. I have married one. I had two English officers billeted in my house. They invited some others to spend the evening and I made some punch. One of the guests tasted the punch and said he would not leave Cologne until I agreed to marry him. It was just like that.[12]

In the American sector there was a much stricter policy of non-fraternisation than in that administered by the British. However, this was difficult to enforce, as so many 'doughboys' (soldiers) were themselves of German stock. At the outbreak of war around 8 million Americans had German parents or grandparents. Although these young soldiers had been willing to fight the German state, they had no quarrel with its people. How could they when German housewives washed their clothes and baked them cookies just like their own mothers? As for girls, 'the ordinary soldier doesn't care whether she is a Mamselle or Fraulein', commented Smith. 'He just wants to carry her off and then go home.'[13]

The complexities of relations between the victors and the occupied fascinated Violet Markham, arch-liberal and granddaughter of the architect and gardener Sir Joseph Paxton. In July 1919 she accompanied her colonel husband on his posting to Cologne. She too was astonished by 'the civility of these Germans among whom we live as conquerors ... how can they, outwardly at least, bear so little grudge against the people who have beaten them?'[14] Nor could she understand the 'Boche' habit of turning up in large numbers to every military event held by the English on the Domplatz, from which, she noted, the cathedral rose 'grim and protesting' above a sea of Allied khaki. 'Can we imagine', she wondered, 'a German parade held in front of Buckingham Palace to which the inhabitants of London would flock?' One such occasion was particularly poignant. On 11 November 1919, the first anniversary of the Armistice, she stood in the biting cold as trumpeters stepped forward on the cathedral steps and in a silence 'broken only by the moaning of the wind', played the Last Post.[15]

The home in which she and her husband were billeted was comfortable (like many others in Cologne, it was centrally heated), and, as time elapsed, relations with their 'Frau' grew increasingly friendly, although life below stairs was a different matter: 'Gertrude, the cross cook, is a lump of respectability and virtue,' commented Markham. 'She hates the English with a complete and deadly hatred, hence a series of feuds with a succession of soldier servants.'[16] Gertrude's views were perhaps more commonly held than the likes of Markham were prepared to acknowledge. The writer Winifred Holtby certainly thought so. In a letter to her friend Vera Brittain, she described Cologne as 'a heart-breaking city' where

> Tommies march up and down, looking very gay, friendly and irresponsible. Their canteens are in the best hotels, and a lovely building down by the Rhine. Outside are great notices "No Germans allowed." The money for their food is all paid from German taxes, and the German children crowd round their brightly lit windows, watching them gobble up beefsteaks. It is one of the most vulgar things that I have ever seen.[17]

It is surprising that, so shortly after the war, soldiers like Franck and Smith should have made it clear how much they preferred Germany to France. Not only were the towns cleaner, the people more diligent and the plumbing better, in their view, but prices were also lower and, as Smith remarked, 'one isn't robbed'.[18] In March 1919, he wrote to his mother-in-law:

> I think that the vast majority of American soldiers are leaving France hating and despising her. It is a fact that they dislike the French attitude to monetary matters and they have been uncomfortable nearly all the time in France.

> Americans feel that they've been cheated right and left. All
> France's destroyed churches and towns do not make half
> the impression on the doughboy as the charge of 15 francs
> for a handkerchief. And somehow or other in Germany
> Americans aren't over-charged even where military control
> is loose.[19]

Given all that France had suffered at the hands of Germany
this is a curious statement. Yet it was by no means unique.
Such anti-French bias is a recurring theme in accounts of travel
in Germany between the wars, and one repeated by commentators of every class and political hue.

Smith was soon recording his admiration of German efficiency. 'There is very little old world charm here,' he wrote to
his wife. 'One feels one is face to face with an energetic, hairy-
nation, once arrogant and overbearing, now bewildered and
wrestling with anarchy.'[20] Germany may have been crushed by
defeat, he went on, 'but one can feel the strength and vitality
in the air'.[21] This was no doubt true in the relatively prosperous Allied-occupied Rhineland, but in the rest of Germany it
was a different story, as Harry Franck was about to find out.

Bored with life in the AEF, he was impatient to shed his
uniform and set off on his own. But, having at last received permission, he was to find entry into unoccupied Germany every
bit as difficult after the Armistice as before. Thanks, however,
to a mixture of luck, bravado and pure guile, Franck found himself on 1 May 1919, dressed in an ill-fitting Dutch suit (he had
travelled by train into Germany via Holland), standing on the
platform of Berlin's Anhalter station eager to begin his adventure. With its cathedral-like arches and soaring vaults, the station
was a dramatic introduction to Germany's capital, exuding all
the power and confidence of a great city. And in that respect,

superficially at least, Berlin seemed to Franck little changed since his last visit a decade earlier. True, the Reichstag appeared to him 'cold and silent' and the Kaiser's palaces now like 'abandoned warehouses', but the massive statues of his Hohenzollern ancestors still flanked the Siegesallee in the Tiergarten; shops were adequately stocked, people appeared well-dressed and the city's numerous places of entertainment were full.[22]

Franck was not the only traveller in Germany during the immediate post-war period to be struck by this outward normality. But, as the defence minister, Gustav Noske (a former master butcher), explained to Lieutenant Colonel William Stewart Roddie, they were deceived in the same way that 'a hectic flush gives the appearance of health to a patient who is in fact dying of galloping consumption'.[23]

Stewart Roddie had been sent to Berlin by the War Office in London to report on precise conditions in Germany. Given his fluency in the language (he had been partly educated in Saxony) and his affinity for both the country and its people, he was well suited to the task. 'There was not a stratum of life into which we did not penetrate in order to satisfy ourselves that we were not forming a one-sided and biased opinion,' he wrote. 'Nowhere were we treated with anything but tolerance and courtesy.' Stewart Roddie, who was to spend much of the next seven years travelling around Germany on various army assignments, went on: 'It is perhaps a curious fact that although I had duties to perform which might, naturally enough, have made me an object of hatred and detestation to the Germans, I cannot recall one occasion on which I received rudeness or insult from them. Difficulties – yes. Obstruction – yes. Stupidity – yes. But never incivility – and never servility.'[24]

Like Stewart Roddie, Franck was also surprised at the tolerance Berliners showed their conquerors and at the way

Allied soldiers were able to wander freely about the city unconcerned for their safety. 'Doughboys were quite as much at home along Unter den Linden as if they had been strolling down Main Street in Des Moines,' he wrote. However, the anti-communism and anti-Semitism that were to become such hallmarks of Germany's inter-war years were already much in evidence. On every available wall were plastered virulently coloured posters warning of the blood-curdling deeds Bolshevism would inflict on the population should it ever succumb. A plea was made for volunteers and funds 'to halt the menace that is already knocking at the eastern gates of the Fatherland'. Such messages resonated with Berliners since memories of the violent Spartacist uprising were still fresh in mind. Stewart Roddie had arrived at Berlin's Potsdam railway station in the middle of it all: 'The rattle of a machine-gun unpleasantly near caused me to hesitate for a moment as I stepped on to the platform.'[25] Nor can he have been reassured when his cab driver informed him that the man firing the gun from the top of the Brandenburg Gate was one of 'Roger Casement's Irishmen' who had come to Berlin to fight with the Red Army.

After the terms of the Versailles treaty became public in May 1919, Franck noticed even more vitriolic posters. He kept one bearing a typical message:

END OF MILITARISM
BEGINNING OF JEW RULE!

Fifty months have we stood at the Front honourably and undefeated. Now we have returned home, ignominiously betrayed by deserters and mutineers! We hoped to find a free Germany, with a government of the people. What is offered us?

A GOVERNMENT OF JEWS!

The participation of the Jews in the fights at the Front was almost nil. Their participation in the new government has already reached 80 percent! Yet the percentage of Jewish population in Germany is only 1½ percent!

OPEN YOUR EYES!

COMRADES, YOU KNOW THE BLOODSUCKERS!

COMRADES, WHO WENT TO THE FRONT AS VOLUNTEERS?

WHO SAT OUT THERE MOSTLY IN THE MUD? WE!

WHO CROWDED INTO THE WAR SERVICES AT HOME?

THE JEWS!

WHO SAT COMFORTABLY AND SAFELY IN CANTEENS AND OFFICES?

WHICH PHYSICIANS PROTECTED THEIR FELLOW-RACE FROM THE TRENCHES?

WHO ALWAYS REPORTED US 'FIT FOR DUTY' THOUGH WE WERE ALL SHOT TO PIECES?

Comrades, we wish as a free people to decide for ourselves and be ruled by men of OUR race! The National Assembly must bring into the government only men of OUR blood and OUR opinions! Our motto must be

GERMANY FOR GERMANS!

DOWN WITH JEWRY!

As well as the ubiquitous posters, Franck also recorded newspaper advertisements, many of which illustrated the thriving barter economy: 'A pair of cowhide boots will be swapped for a Dachshund of established pedigree' or 'Four dress shirts will be exchanged for a working-man's blouse and jumper'.[26]

But, as Franck and Stewart Roddie soon discovered, there was really only one issue that mattered to Berliners in 1919, and that was food. Any conversation quickly reverted to this topic, which, with the exception of profiteers and the very rich, permeated every aspect of everyone's life. People were hungry all over Germany but in Berlin the situation was especially dire. Despite posters everywhere carrying the warning 'DON'T GO TO BERLIN!' the authorities could do little to stop people crowding to the city in search of work.

Because the Allies wanted to keep an arm lock on the Germans until the peace treaty was signed, the blockade imposed since 1914 remained rigorously in place – a cause of deep bitterness throughout the country. When Franck first crossed the border, he had witnessed the skill with which Dutch officials ferreted out foodstuffs no matter how meagre or ingeniously hidden. One woman even had her modest lunch confiscated. As she sat hunched in a corner of the compartment, silently weeping, two men, once safely into Germany, retrieved their respective contraband. The first drew a sausage out of a trouser leg while the second produced a tiny package of paper-soap leaves each no bigger than a visiting card. 'He pressed three or four of them upon his companion. The latter protested that he could not accept so serious a sacrifice. The other insisted, and the grateful recipient bowed low and raised his hat twice in thanks before he stowed the precious leaves away among his private papers.'[27]

To foreign eyes, Berliners were at once identifiable by their prominent cheekbones, sallow colour and loose-fitting clothes. Nor was it just the poor who went hungry; for once the middle classes were equally affected. Stewart Roddie described

how the market places had been converted into public kitchens where thousands of people from every class of society
were fed daily. 'Hunger is a great leveller. The rag-picker stood
cheek by jowl with the professor. And what an extraordinary appearance they presented – miserable, gaunt, emaciated,
shivering.'[28] Comments such as 'Why, how thin you are!' were
taboo, while in the schoolroom, Franck observed, 'there
were not enough red cheeks to make one pre-war pair, unless
the face of a child recently returned from the country, shining
like a new moon in a fog, trebled the pasty average'. Such was
the general sensitivity to food, or rather lack of it, that meals
could no longer be enacted on the stage as 'the pretence of
one was sure to turn the most uproarious comedy into a tear-
provoking melodrama'.[29]

Franck found the musty-smelling 'war' bread particularly
repellent, 'half sawdust and half mud, heavier and blacker than
an adobe brick'. 'Yet on this atrocious substance', he wrote,
'the German masses had been chiefly subsisting since 1915.
No wonder they quit!'[30] Even the occasional smear of turnip
jelly or ersatz marmalade did little to improve it. And because
such food contained so little nourishment, people's ability to
put in a full day's work became seriously compromised. Nor
was just food ersatz. Everything from rope to rubber, shirts to
soap was an imitation, occasionally ingenious but more often
useless. Germany, newspapers proclaimed, had become an
ersatz nation.

Help was at hand, however. On Easter Sunday 1919, two
trucks that had been allowed through the blockade arrived in
Berlin. Their cargo consisted of unheard-of luxuries – blankets,
beef dripping, condensed milk, cocoa, nappies and nightgowns.
To each parcel a note was attached bearing the message: 'A
gift of love to the hungry babies and their poor mothers from

the Society of Friends in England and their supporters.'[31] Three months later, on 5 July, four 'rather bewildered' English Quakers (two men and two women) stood on a platform at Anhalter Station. There was no one to meet them and they had nowhere to go. Nor did they dare approach anyone for fear of drawing attention to themselves.[32] But faith moves in mysterious ways and by nightfall it had installed them in the splendid, if un-Quakerish, residence of the last pre-war ambassador to London, Prince Lichnowsky. Joan Fry, the most prominent figure among the four, whose Bloomsbury Group brother, Roger Fry, had been a close friend of Princess Lichnowsky, recorded that their first action was to hold a Meeting in one of the Princess's sumptuous bedrooms. For a woman who until she was forty-five had never left home unchaperoned or even been to the theatre (she was descended from eight generations of Quakers on both sides of her family), Fry appeared remarkably undaunted by their mission: to mitigate the suffering caused by the Allied blockade, and to demonstrate Quaker empathy with an utterly demoralised people.

The immediate aftermath of the First World War was not the best time for foreigners to be wandering around Germany. But for the few who, like Franck, Stewart Roddie, Smith and Fry, did manage to roam outside the occupied sectors, the experience was profound, often moving. They carried away memories of a proud, diligent people confronting their unhappy fate with characteristic stoicism – if not acceptance.

2

Deepening Pain

The Quakers wasted no time. Within days of arriving they hosted a picnic at a hospital where delicacies such as 'Red Cross Glaxo, Miss Playne's chicken jelly and a bunch of Dorothy Perkins [grapes]' were dispensed. 'It was delightful to ply them with thick slices of bread and margarine and lots of treacle,' remarked one of Fry's colleagues.[1] A much larger party of American Quakers also arrived in Berlin to spearhead the 'Child Feeding', an aid programme supported by Herbert Hoover that at its peak provided nourishment for some 1.75 million children.

Joan Fry and her little band did not linger in Berlin. On 28 July 1919, just one month after the Treaty of Versailles was signed, she wrote home describing a journey to Essen and Düsseldorf, where they had been to investigate the shortage of coal. They were not encouraged. 'The coal question meets us at every turn with a terrible insistence,' Fry reported back to London. Lack of fuel meant that the hopelessly overcrowded trains on which they travelled often stopped for hours on end. 'What can you expect?' a stationmaster said to her. 'When the French and the English take away the coal we can't run trains.'[2] Delays were not the only reason journeys were fraught. There was almost nothing to eat, carriage seats had long since been stripped of their plush covering to be recycled into clothing, while the windows, shorn of their leather straps, were jammed or broken. The Quakers were indefatigable travellers and this expedition was just the first of countless such journeys Fry and her companions were to undertake over the next seven years from their base in Berlin – organising relief work, attending conferences and spreading their message of peace and reconciliation to anyone who would listen.

For the few civilian foreigners who, like Joan Fry and Harry Franck, were travelling east of the Rhine during the summer of 1919, the shock and despair felt by ordinary people in the wake of the Treaty of Versailles (signed on 28 June) was impossible to ignore. Firm in the belief that they had been honourably defeated and confident that President Wilson would guarantee them fair treatment, most Germans were quite unprepared for the humiliation it imposed on their country. Germany was to lose all its colonies (the most significant lay in Africa), its most productive industrial areas were to be under foreign control for at least fifteen years, and it would have to pay an unimaginable sum in compensation. Its army was to be reduced to 100,000 men and its navy also decimated. In order to give Poland access to the Baltic, the port of Danzig was to come under Polish control (although its population was predominantly German) and the 'Polish corridor' was to be created, thus dividing the bulk of Germany from the province of East Prussia. Furthermore, Germany had to sign the 'guilt clause' accepting responsibility for starting the war. But many people found the most degrading demand of all (in the event it was never met) the provision that the Kaiser and 1,000 prominent figures should be handed over to the Allies and tried for war crimes.

The conversations Franck and Fry held with their fellow rail passengers that summer were especially revealing. One old lady explained to Joan that, although she had felt no hatred during the war, the peace treaty aroused intense resentment: 'To be treated as outcasts, as individuals with whom no relations are possible, is even worse than hunger or constant anxiety.' Another woman stated how much in normal times she would have enjoyed speaking English, 'but now a broken people does not want to hear it'.[3] The women, Franck noted, were the most vitriolic against the Treaty in general while the old men minded most about the loss of colonies: 'We would rather pay any amount of indemnity than lose territory ... The Allies are trying to Balkanise us ... they want to *vernichten* us, to destroy us completely ... we believed in Wilson and he betrayed us.' More ominously, others expressed their dread of the future: 'Now we must drill hatred into our children from their earliest age, so that in thirty years, when the time is ripe....'[4]

Having lived among the Germans in the months after the Armistice and come to admire their virtues, Stewart Roddie and Truman Smith sympathised with these sentiments. Smith blamed the French for the harshness of the Treaty: '... certainly mercy and the future of the world cannot be expected from France. So we too must drink the bitter cup of despair. I had hoped a better era might be on the horizon and that our labour, sacrifices and separations from those dear to us might bear fruit in a "large" peace.'[5] Stewart Roddie, writing later, believed that the Allies' greatest mistake was letting fourteen months elapse between the Armistice and ratification of the Treaty in January 1920:

> The right moment for the passing of the Allied verdict upon Germany had long passed. Germany had had time

to sit in judgment upon herself and her former leaders, and had decided that the worst she and they could possibly have been charged with was manslaughter – but that was not admitted – and here she was accused, found guilty of, and punished for murder and robbery with violence.[6]

But, in the midst of all the gloom, there was the occasional glimpse of a brighter world. Joan Fry recalled the sight of nine teams of horses ploughing a single field as she journeyed across the great cornfields of Mecklenburg, and of the setting sun reflected in the vast stretches of water that lie north of the Elbe estuary. Nor would she ever forget – at a time when the 'tiny shrunken limbs and old, ashen grey faces of starving babies'[7] were an all too familiar reminder of human misery – the evening she sat under the stars, listening to her friend Albrecht Mendelssohn* playing his grandfather's music on the piano. Violet Markham remembered the Rhineland as a 'garden of enchantment', delighting in the vivid green of the fields, the yellow splashes of mustard, the varied tints of tree, and bush, and blossom 'all melting and glowing together in the clear sunlight'.[8]

* Grandson of the composer Felix Mendelssohn, Albrecht Mendelssohn Bartholdy (1874–1936) was a professor of international law and an active pacifist. In 1912 he was appointed to a committee seeking better relations between England and Germany. In 1920 he was made Professor of Foreign Law at Hamburg University and in 1923 he set up the Institute for Foreign Policy – one of the first research institutes for peace studies ever founded. After Hitler came to power in 1933 Mendelssohn was forced to resign all his academic positions. In 1934 he went to England, where he was elected a senior research fellow of Balliol College. He died in Oxford in November 1936.

Franck, too, had halcyon memories. Having decided to spend six weeks walking from Munich to Weimar, he spent the first night at an inn in the small village of Hohenkammer: 'I cannot quite picture to myself', he wrote, 'what would happen to the man who thus walked in upon a gathering of American farmers, boldly announcing himself a German just out of the army, but something tells me he would not have passed so perfectly agreeable an evening as I did in the village inn of Hohenkammer.'[9] The following day, in perfect weather, he set out across

> gently rolling fields deep-green with spring alternating with almost black patches of evergreen forests, through which the broad, light-gray highroad wound and undulated as soothingly as an immense ocean-liner on a slowly pulsating sea. Every few miles a small town rose above the horizon, now astride the highway, now gazing down upon it from a sloping hillside. Wonderfully clean towns they were, speckless from their scrubbed floors to their whitewashed church steeples, all framed in velvety green meadows or the fertile fields in which their inhabitants of both sexes plodded diligently but never hurriedly through the labours of the day. It was difficult to imagine how these simple, gentle-spoken folk could have won a world-wide reputation as the most savage and brutal warriors in modern history.[10]

On 28 February 1923, Violet Bonham Carter, accompanied by her maid, boarded a train at Liverpool Street Station in London. Daughter of Herbert Asquith (British prime minister, 1908–1916) and shortly to be elected chairman of the National Liberal Federation, she was bound for Berlin.

Her purpose was to investigate the French occupation of the Ruhr – an act she regarded as one of 'dangerous insanity'. On 11 January 60,000 French and Belgian troops had marched into Germany's industrial heartland intent on extracting the coal that their countries had been promised by the Treaty of Versailles but which Germany was failing to deliver. In Bonham Carter's view, the reparations policy insisted on by France (by 1923 Germany's debt to the Allies stood at £6.6 billion, the equivalent of £280 billion in 2013) was morally unjust and politically mad. Many in Britain and America agreed, believing that Germany's economic collapse would only result in victory for the communists.

The journey to Berlin was unpleasant. The train was grubby and crowded. And because the coal was of such poor quality, it was also frustratingly slow. At the border, Violet experienced her first encounter with German inflation – soon to be hyperinflation. She received 200,000 marks for £2, 'great bundles of paper-chase money which I could hardly carry' and was not amused by '3 intolerable and grotesque Music Hall Americans' who thought the exchange rate a huge joke ('5,000 marks, that's a nickel'). However, she enjoyed her chat with an Aberdeen fish merchant on his way to Germany to buy a German boat and to hire a German crew because, he explained, they were so superior to anything he could find at home. 'I'm pro German now,' he told her, 'we all are.'[11]

At 10.30 p.m. on 1 March, after fifteen hours' travelling, they arrived in Berlin and drove straight to the British Embassy, where Violet had been invited to stay with the ambassador, Lord D'Abernon, and his wife, Helen. 'It was divine to arrive dirty and exhausted at the cleanliness and comfort of the Embassy,' Violet wrote in her diary. 'Dear Tyler opened the door and I was told Helen had gone to bed after the ball last night but that Edgar was up and alone. It was the greatest fun finding him in a big delightful room. The ballroom is yellow brocade with a lovely bit of tapestry hung over some hideous German embossments.'[12] The Embassy, on the Wilhelmstrasse, was imposing if uninspiring. The front faced directly on to the street while towering over it at the back was the gloomy Adlon Hotel.

Lord D'Abernon, Britain's first post-war ambassador to Germany, had been *en poste* since October 1920. Over six foot tall and Olympian in manner, he looked every inch an ambassador. His job may have been difficult but it was a good deal easier than that of the French ambassador, Pierre de Margerie, who, along with his fellow countrymen, faced social ostracism after the occupation of the Ruhr. The restaurant at the Adlon was the only one in Berlin still prepared to serve the French and Belgians. In almost every other shop window appeared the notice: *Franzosen und Belgier nicht erwünscht* [French and Belgians not wanted]. According to Bonham Carter, the situation was particularly painful for de Margerie, who had arrived in Berlin only weeks before 'longing to be loved'.[13]

Lady D'Abernon, one of the great beauties of her generation, was also courageous, having worked as an anaesthetist nurse in France during the war. She was under no illusion as to the task in Berlin. 'To try and re-establish relatively pleasant normal relations will require a mountain of effort and of persevering goodwill,' she wrote in her diary on 29 July 1920. As she disliked Germany, and all things German, her role was to remain one of duty rather than pleasure. Whatever other attractions the city may have offered its visitors, charm was not high on the list. There were, in Lady D'Abernon's words, 'no narrow streets, no changes of level, no crooked passages, no unexpected courts and corners'.[14] She did, however, take pleasure in the sight of horse-drawn sleighs gliding across the snow in the Tiergarten:

> The horse is always covered with little tinkling bells and the harness is crowned by an immense panache of white horsehair, like the plume of a Life Guardsman's helmet, only much larger. Frequently the sleighs are painted scarlet or bright blue and the occupants, who are often smothered in furs, contrive to look picturesque and rather French *dix-huitième siècle* [eighteenth century].[15]

Despite her personal reservations, Helen D'Abernon was to prove an astute observer. 'In Berlin it is the fashion to make a parade of poverty and retrenchment,' she wrote after meeting the foreign minister and his wife for the first time, 'so in order to be in harmony with the prevailing atmosphere, I attired myself in a demure dove-coloured frock of Puritan simplicity.'[16] Nonetheless, she abandoned all austerity for their first diplomatic reception, determined that the British Embassy should appear as splendid and dignified as it had before the war. The ballroom overflowed with flowers. The servants went about their duties resplendent in buff and scarlet liveries. Two pre-war retainers, Fritz and Elf, in cocked hats and long gold-laced coats, stood at the entrance, holding elaborate staves (surmounted with the royal coat of arms) in outstretched arms. These they thumped three times on the arrival of an important guest. Afterwards, Lady D'Abernon claimed that she 'had not exchanged ten words of interest with anyone except a Bolshevist from the Ukraine' whose political creed, she observed, 'had in no way hindered his enjoyment of an *ancien régime* party'.[17]

She was not a sentimental woman and for the most part remained unmoved by German pleadings of hardship. Joan Fry failed to impress her. 'Miss Fry is all self-sacrifice and burning enthusiasm,' she noted, 'but her compassion seems to be reserved almost exclusively for Germans. She shys [sic] away from any allusion to suffering and privations in Great Britain.'[18] Nor did Lady D'Abernon leave Violet Bonham Carter in any doubt as to the true state of affairs in Germany: 'Believe me,' she told her, 'the Germans are *not* suffering as they say. There is no great poverty here. 95% are living in plenty, 5% are starving.' After visiting Berlin's poorest district herself, Violet tended to agree, having seen 'nothing one could *compare* to our slums. All the streets are wide, the houses big and built with windows the same size as the Embassy ones.'[19]

For Violet, as for so many other observers of inflation-ridden Germany, it was the plight of the middle classes that aroused her greatest sympathy. As no one could any longer afford their professional services, and as inflation had destroyed their capital, many were reduced to total penury. Within their neat, clean and respectable homes, Violet was informed, 'terrible quiet tragedies' were taking place each day. Having sold their last possessions, many of them, including doctors, lawyers and teachers, preferred to swallow poison rather than suffer the shame of starvation.[20] When hyperinflation reached its peak in November 1923, even the sceptical Lady D'Abernon was moved at the 'distressing spectacle of gentlefolk half hidden behind the trees in the Tiergarten timidly stretching out their hands for help'.[21] Violet Bonham Carter found this dismal state of affairs hard to reconcile with the jewels, furs and flowers she saw in the expensive shops on Berlin's smartest streets. But, as Lady D'Abernon explained, it was only the *Schiebern* [profiteers] – living like 'fighting cocks' in all the best hotels – who could afford such luxuries. She also pointed out how 'their women wear fur coats with pearls and other jewels on the top of them, the effect of which is further emphasized by the surprising addition of high yellow boots'.[22]

The communist and British trades unionist Tom Mann was quick to spot the profiteers when he visited Berlin for a party conference in the spring of 1924. He noted 'their typical bourgeois appearance and behaviour in eating heavy meals, smoking fat long cigars and generally behaving as though they had tons of cash'. But even more distressing for Mann was the worrying rift between the 'young militants' and the 'old reactionary trades union officials'. He reported that the Communist Party was expecting to increase its members in the Reichstag from fifteen to fifty at the next election. He did not, he told his wife, think much of the general political confusion in Berlin – 'Such a mix there is, no less than 15 political parties or sections running candidates.' Much more satisfactory was the evening he spent at a performance of Die Meistersinger. 'Betimes I thought the old cobbler had too much to say for himself,' commented Mann, 'but it was wonderfully well done … they had about 250 on a very large stage, not crowded, with the banners and regalia – and the chorus was grand.'[23]

He was certainly not the only foreigner to notice just how much music meant to ordinary Germans. 'Music is their finest and most potent medium of expression in moments like this,' wrote Violet Bonham Carter, 'one can't imagine any political demonstration in England opening with a very long string quartet.'[24] After attending one such event herself, she returned to the Embassy to find Lady D'Abernon 'nobly entertaining thirty English wives of Germans – such pathetic creatures'. One woman lived in a single room with her husband who had not spoken to her for a year. However, breezily sweeping aside her fellow countrywomen's miserable predicament, Violet reported that 'they were all much cheered when Colonel Roddie played the piano and sang, and they all had tea'.[25] At dinner that evening she was placed next to Germany's second president, Field Marshal Paul von Hindenburg. She was not impressed. 'I sat between Hindenburg – rather a little man who I disliked – and an insignificant Italian.'[26]

~

In 1920 Stewart Roddie was appointed to the Military Inter-Allied Commission of Control (headquartered in the Adlon) whose task it was to disarm Germany. But, judging from his memoir, *Peace Patrol*, he spent as much time comforting distressed members of the former imperial family as in tracking down illicit weapons. With his Rupert Brooke looks and sympathetic manner, the former music teacher from Inverness moved discreetly among them, listening to their woes, offering advice and occasionally intervening with his superiors on their behalf. *Peace Patrol* reads like an international *Who's Who*. As well as the Hohenzollerns, its pages are crowded with the names of military and political celebrities, European royalty and the British aristocracy – all of whom, it seems, were on intimate terms with the ubiquitous colonel.

In the summer of 1919 Stewart Roddie had visited Princess Margaret of Prussia, youngest sister of the former Kaiser and granddaughter of Queen Victoria. Although she and her husband, Prince Frederick Charles of Hesse, still lived near Frankfurt in the vast Schloss Friedrichshof at Kronberg (inherited from her mother, Empress Frederick), they did so in grief and poverty. Not only had they lost two sons in the war, but their lands had also been confiscated. They received nothing from the state, and their own resources had been wiped

out by inflation. Stewart Roddie describes how he stood in
the hall as the Princess slowly descended the broad stairway
to greet him. 'In her long, severe black dress with little collar
and cuffs of white lawn she made a picture of infinite sadness,'
he wrote.[27] Several years later, Joan Fry and a party of Quakers
also visited Friedrichshof:

> We took our courage in both hands and went to the
> Schloss. We were only kept waiting a short time before
> we were ushered into a fine drawing room which looked on
> to a beautiful lawn. After a minute or two the Grand Duke
> and Duchess, or, as we ought to say, the ex-royalties, came
> in from an adjoining room and talked to us in a quite sim-
> ple and friendly way. We all stood for it seemed that they
> did not wish us to stay long. Marion said that she saw the
> lunch table ready in the room from which they came ...[28]

Princess Margaret's correspondence makes plain just how short
of cash they were: 'Many, many thanks for the letters, also for
the hairnets,' she wrote to Lady Corkran* in 1924. '£2 does
indeed seem too little for the tables so perhaps we had better
wait for a better opportunity. Would you send me a cheque
for the white one? I am so grateful to you for getting as much
as you did for it although more would have been welcome.'[29]
Despite Princess Margaret's troubles, her letters reveal that she
had not entirely lost interest in the contemporary world. An
advertisement pinned to one reads: 'Wave your hair yourself
in ten minutes. No heat, no electric current required. Just slip

---

* Lady (Hilda) Corkran was lady-in-waiting to Princess Beatrice,
Queen Victoria's youngest daughter.

the hair into a West Electric Hair Curler.' On this, the Kaiser's sister has scribbled, 'Do you think all this is true? Would you advise trying the curlers? No doubt it is all exaggerated.'[30]

When Stewart Roddie visited Friedrichshof, he had been outraged 'to find the place over-run by black troops'. Indeed, France's deployment of colonial soldiers provoked a chorus of criticism – and not just from Germans. In those unasham-edly racist times, many British observers saw it as a conscious attempt by France to heap yet further humiliation on Germany. Joan Fry noted the rising resentment among the Germans who had to provide extra homes for 'the many unwanted brown babies, who cannot be put in such homes as are provided for white children'.[31] An American Quaker, Dorothy Detzer, was shockingly outspoken:

I arrived at Mainz about four in the afternoon, on September 3rd. When we climbed off the train to the platform I suddenly went sick at the sight which greeted our eyes all along the platform. One had heard so much of the French occupation, and I was expecting to see troops like our southern darkies. Instead we found savages. I lived for over a year in the Philippine Islands and my first reac-tion was that here was Moco-land again – only that the natives were in uniforms instead of g-strings as would be their native 'costume.' And I think that pity for them was stronger than anything else. I can't quite see why we should expect more from this race than we should from uniformed monkeys. They do not – from their faces – seem much more developed.

She was equally horrified by a huge torchlight parade in Wiesbaden composed of African soldiers carrying posters depicting caricatures of 'Hun heads'. A French bystander informed her that such parades were held frequently, their purpose being to remind the Germans who had won the war. 'I shall never forget', wrote Detzer, 'the looks on the faces of those silent Germans who stood watching that parade.'[32]

Crossing a road in Düsseldorf, one particularly cold winter's day in 1923, Jacques Benoist-Méchin, a young officer serving with the French occupying force, was also struck by the incongruity of meeting a platoon of *Tirailleurs marocains* [Moroccan sharpshooters], 'their faces bronzed by African sun'. Like Dorothy Detzer, he confessed to feeling sick at the sight of them. 'What were they doing here in this filth and fog?' he asked.[33] His account of life in the occupied Ruhr suggests that, if it was miserable for Germans, it was not much better for the French. When he first reported for duty, his senior officer explained that they were more or less in a state of war. The wires had been cut and they were completely isolated. He would be ill advised to walk anywhere alone. The German workforce, backed by the government, had chosen to defy the French in the only way open to them – passive resistance. Not that their protests were always that passive. On 1 February Benoist-Méchin recorded 1,083 acts of sabotage. He captures the bleakness of conditions in the occupied zone with his description of the Krupp factory at Essen to which he escorted twenty French engineers: 'It is snowing again. Cranes, pylons and gigantic chimneys dominate the landscape. Four enormous furnaces, their massive profiles carved against an apocalyptic sky, are dead. Their carcasses have been abandoned.'[34]

It was difficult for travellers (at least the Anglophones), whatever their personal interpretation of events, not to be touched by the plight of the people they encountered in the immediate post-war years. Germans from all walks of life told them repeatedly how betrayed they felt – by the Kaiser, their politicians and generals and especially by President Wilson and the Treaty of Versailles. Through no fault of their own, they had lost their colonies, their coal, their health and prosperity and – most distressing of all – their self-respect. The currency was worthless while the absurdly high reparations could never be met since the Allies were intent on depriving them of their raw materials. Nor could they understand why England constantly gave way to a revengeful France whose brutal black soldiers, so they contended, freely raped and murdered.[35] And how were they to explain all this to the next generation, to their undernourished, rickety children who, thanks to the so-called peace treaty, now faced a future under the heel of Bolshevists and Jews? Although foreign travellers were aware that in parts of the countryside life was slowly returning to normal, and that the native thrift, industry and self-discipline remained unimpaired, most returned home with an overriding sense of the country's suffering. Too many Germans, in their experience, were hungry, cold and without hope.

It was against this background that, on 15 November 1922, Captain Truman Smith arrived in Munich – a city still festering with civil unrest and political intrigue. Smith, now assistant military attaché at the American Embassy in Berlin, had gone there to report on the National Socialists. This political party was not thought to be of much importance but the American ambassador wanted more information. Smith was therefore asked to make enquiries among Hitler's entourage and if possible to meet Hitler himself to assess his abilities and potential. Three days later, Smith pencilled into his notebook: 'Great excitement. I am invited to go with Alfred Rosenberg to see the Hundertschaften [companies of 100 men] pass in review before Hitler on the Cornelius Street.' Afterwards he wrote:

> A remarkable sight indeed. Twelve hundred of the tough-est roughnecks I have ever seen in my life passed in review before Hitler at the goosestep under the old Reichflag, wearing red armbands with Hakenkreuze ... Hitler shouted 'Death to the Jews' etc. and etc. There was frantic cheering. I never saw such a sight in my life.[36]

Several days later Smith was introduced to Hitler, who agreed to meet him the following Monday. The interview took place on 20 November at 4 p.m. in the third-floor room of Georgen Strasse 42. The American remembered the room as being like 'a back bedroom in a decaying New York tenement, drab and dreary beyond belief'.[37] Looking back in later years, Smith wished that, rather than just record Hitler's political views, he had concentrated more on his personality and idiosyncrasies.

Some months later, Jacques Benoist-Méchin's command-ing officer came into his office to ask if he knew anything about a political party recently founded in Munich by a cer-tain Aloysius Hitler? The request had come directly from the French war ministry, whose notice had been drawn to the fact that this Hitler was giving speeches to roomfuls of fanatics in which he denounced everything and everyone – including France. Benoist-Méchin had never heard of Hitler or his party but suggested that they consult the British.

Two days later back came the response. According to the British source, there was nothing to be alarmed about. The National Socialist Party was just a fire in the straw that would vanish as quickly as it had materialised. The men involved were Bavarian separatists of no significance and with no possibility of influencing events outside Bavaria. In fact, Hitler might even be worth encouraging since he wanted to claim independence for Bavaria, which might lead to the reinstatement of the Wittelsbach monarchy and possibly even the break-up of the German Reich. 'And by the way,' the message continued, 'Hitler's first name is Adolf – not Aloysius.'[38] On 10 November 1923, almost exactly a year after Smith's interview with Hitler, Lady D'Abernon recorded in her diary that her husband had been woken in the middle of the night by a senior German diplomat, anxious for advice on how to deal with an uprising in Munich. The chief agitator, she noted, was 'a man of low origin' called Adolf Hitler.[39]

3

Sex and Sun

I n the months leading up to Hitler's November putsch, the
Weimar Republic's prospects could scarcely have looked
bleaker. Passive resistance to the French occupation of
the Ruhr may have eased German humiliation but because the
government had to print money to pay the strikers, it also
fuelled hyperinflation. Horace Finlayson, financial adviser to
the British Embassy, kept a daily record of the exchange rate.
His first entry, on 15 August 1923, records 12,369,000 marks
to the pound, then on 9 November (the day of Hitler's failed
putsch) 2.8 billion and five weeks later a dizzying 18 billion.[1]
Numa Tétaz – a Swiss studying engineering in Munich – lived
through the crisis:

> Almost everyone is into dealing. What is bought today for
> a million can be sold tomorrow for a billion. The key is
> always to find someone who thinks more slowly than the
> seller. Everyone knows it can't go on like this but no one
> has any idea what to do. You swim in a dirty and deceptive
> stream. Everyone lives in dread but somehow carries on.
> We don't talk much politics in our group. I only realised
> the next day that the putsch had happened.[2]

The putsch took place in Munich on 8–9 November 1923. Hitler, General Ludendorff and other leading Nazis, together with about two thousand supporters, marched to the city centre intending first to seize control of Bavaria before toppling the national government. The putsch failed when they were confronted by armed police who killed sixteen of them. Two days later Hitler was arrested and charged with treason. Although the putsch had failed, Hitler's subsequent trial attracted huge publicity, providing him with a perfect opportunity to present his views to the nation. He was sentenced to five years but in fact served only nine months in prison, where he was comfortably lodged, allowed visitors – and provided with plenty of paper to write his book *Mein Kampf*.

If hyperinflation and Hitler's putsch were not challenging enough, the government – itself riven with dissent – had also to deal with separatists in the Rhineland, communist insurrection in Saxony, and an army on whose loyalty it could not depend. Many observers believed that Germany might simply fall apart. Yet for some foreign visitors it was precisely this sense of overwhelming crisis that made it such an absorbing destination. Many were sympathetic but others, like seventeen-year-old Californian Dorothy Bogen, were not:

> Saw gobs of British soldiers – very cheering sight!! Three cheers!! Lots of French at Bonn, first time ate liqueur chocolates. Took train from Cologne to Berlin – long trip but good food. Saw the only German soldier in Germany – he looked lonesome but not shabby or poor – oh no! Got to Berlin. Nice hotel but dumbbell waiters – all hopeless cases. Never again for Berlin. Have sworn off Germany, Germans and Berlin. Jamais, jamais encore!! They gimme the pip![3]

However, by the time Joan Fry and Stewart Roddie left Germany in 1926 the situation had been transformed. Indeed businessman Joel Hotham Cadbury, writing to the Quaker magazine, *The Friend*, wondered why the Quakers were still sending aid to Germans when he had just seen them drinking vast quantities of champagne in Arosa and buying expensive motor cars, lingerie and furniture in Paris? Nor was this affluence apparent only abroad. Cadbury noted how Hamburg was humming with new investment – ship canals, electric power plants and inland harbours.[4]

The man credited more than any other with Germany's recovery was Weimar's greatest statesman, Gustav Stresemann. Although chancellor for only three months (August–November 1923), he was foreign minister in successive administrations until his death in 1929. The historian John Wheeler-Bennett, who lived in Weimar Germany for several years and knew everyone worth knowing, described Stresemann as 'one of the most unlovely-looking men' he had ever seen. 'Porcine of feature, his little eyes set close together, his hair cropped close over a nearly bald pink skull and the inevitable roll of flesh behind the neck.'[5] His wife, on the other hand, so Lady D'Abernon noted, was one of the best-looking women she had met in Germany, though, she added, 'it is not forgotten in Berlin that Frau Stresemann is of Hebrew origin'.[6]

Despite his appearance,* Stresemann had just the qualities needed to steer his country out of crisis. Lord D'Abernon likened him to Winston Churchill: 'Both brilliant, daring and bold.'[7] Convinced that the only way forward for Germany was

---

* A portrait of Stresemann by Augustus John hangs in the Knox-Albright Gallery at Buffalo, New York.

a coalition of the political middle ground, Stresemann struggled to contain extremists on both left and right. Recognising
that passive resistance was inflicting more harm on Germany
than on France, he ended the strike in September 1923,
thereby taking the first step in stabilising the mark. Then, with
his introduction of a new currency, the Rentenmark, solidly
backed by land and industrial plant, the inflation that had
so devastated the country was finally brought under control.
Soon one Rentenmark was worth a trillion of its predecessor. Stresemann was also the prime mover in persuading his
government to accept another major landmark in Germany's
revival – the Dawes Plan (1924). Essentially, Germany was to
regain control of the Ruhr while reparations – although still
hefty – were to be repaid on a sliding scale. It was a short-
term fix but one described by Stresemann as a 'gleam of light
on the otherwise dark horizon'.[8] With the mark stabilised and
the Dawes Plan in place, the much-needed foreign loans
and investment – particularly from America – began to flow
into Germany.

The Treaty of Locarno, signed in London on 1 December
1925, set the seal of international approval on Germany's reha-
bilitation and ushered in a period of détente that was to last
until Stresemann's death. The diplomat and publisher, Count
Harry Kessler, noted in his diary that the town of Locarno
(on Lake Maggiore) 'is wholly under the spell of Stresemann.
There are photos of him everywhere. He is immensely popular, behaves with utmost friendliness to everyone and goes
four times a day to Frau Scherurer's *pâtisserie*; she raves about
him.'[9] After the treaty and Germany's entry into the League of
Nations in 1926, the recovery gathered pace with such speed
that only ten years after the Armistice Germany could claim
to be the world's second-greatest industrial power.

Despite this turnaround, Lord D'Abernon's successor, Sir Ronald Lindsay, was not looking forward to his new post. 'I find the Treaty of Versailles dull reading and tracts are *à debout dormir* [so boring as to make one sleep on one's feet]. As far as I can make out, work at Berlin is that of persistently sweeping water uphill with a very inefficient broom.'[10] But other foreigners who visited or lived in Germany during the heady years between Locarno and the Wall Street Crash took a different view. Suddenly, Germany (especially Berlin) was modern, innovative, sexy and exciting. Even the chronic political instability gave life there an edge – particularly appealing to those keen to escape the staid conventionality of Britain.

For Christopher Isherwood and, as the title of his book puts it, *His Kind*, Berlin 'meant boys',[11] but there was also a certain defiance in their choice of the nation that had so recently killed their fathers and older brothers. The sense of having cast off class and country was liberating – even intoxicating – and could be relished not just in the boy bars and nightclubs of Berlin, but also in quite ordinary experiences. Eddy Sackville-West (later Lord Sackville and cousin of Vita Sackville-West) wrote of his pleasure at walking in the 'Scotch mist' near Dresden where in 1927 he lived for some months immersing himself in the German language and music. 'Driving back in the bus, I had the same experience as before of independence, and delight in every shop front as it passed, and in saying "Hauptbahnhof".'[12]

Yet only three years earlier Sackville-West had travelled to Germany not to seek boys but to be cured of them. In 1924 he spent several months at Dr Karl Marten's clinic in Freiburg where, in the company of other homosexuals, he was subjected to charlatan therapies and bogus psychoanalysis. Marten explained to Eddy that his indigestion was due to a maternity complex and, in order to cure his homosexuality, pumped him full of a substance that 'at the end of dinner', so the unfortunate Sackville-West recorded in his diary,

> had a sudden effect on the seminal glands and I spent 3½ hours of intolerable agony. Martin [sic] said my subconscious mind was prepared for pain just there. God! What agony it was! I thought the pain flowed in and out like a lamp in the wind swaying to and fro in gusts of agony.[13]

In March, Sackville-West and a fellow patient, Eddie Gathorne-Hardy,* engineered a brief escape:

> Started at 5.30 a.m. for Berlin. Lovely day. Felt like going home for the holidays from my private school. Dawn over Berlin country too lovely. Masses of pine trees and silver birches and hoar-encrusted earth. A white sun. *Ariadne auf Naxos* at the opera – too exquisite for words. Small town Berlin. So featureless and like a provincial Paris. None of the charm of Vienna. Not *one* street except Unter den Linden.

A few days later the two Eddys set off for Danzig only to discover that they did not have the right documents. 'Passports wrong! Shot out on to the Steppe at Lauenburg, a foul little town on the Polish frontier. We were heroic! Vile expensive hotel. Walked in the snow and fell into water. Oh what misery!

---

* E. Gathorne-Hardy was the third son of the Earl of Cranbrook and a member of the Bright Young People set. A respected antiquarian, he worked at one time for the British Council.

The hideous houses and ugly, *unreal* people; the hollow voices and empty air!' Danzig, however, when they finally reached it, was a success. 'What a place! Houses like English Elizabethan with yellow and dark red bricks. Huge black and white warehouses on the frozen Mottlau. The Kran Tor quite divine, the Cathedral indescribable.' Nevertheless three days were quite enough and it was a relief to be back in Berlin. 'How comfortable the Adlon is! Had a delicious little supper in pyjamas and Eddy's fur coat.'[14]

Christopher Isherwood's first experience of Germany was equally remote from the cabaret Berlin with which his name is so closely linked. In 1928 he spent the summer in Bremen with his cousin, Basil Fry, the British vice-consul. A ridiculous figure, Fry embodied all that Isherwood, W. H. Auden, Stephen Spender and so many others of their generation were intent on rejecting. A verse from one of Fry's published poems, 'England', says it all:

> Go thou to England, rest awhile thy brow
> Upon her breathing bosom, cool and free,
> And she shall lay her arms around thee now
> Within the arms of her protecting sea.[15]

Isherwood's first sight of Germany was Blumenthal on the Weser estuary where his ship docked early one summer's morning. A consular official met him some thirty miles up the river at Bremen. 'We drove through the vine-grown suburbs. Dense lilac. The clean houses with fronts of embossed stucco. Gay trams. Boulevards past a Laocoon fountain, the vomiting python pleasantly drenching the shoulders of the statue under hot sunlight.' As might be expected, 'boys' featured prominently in his first impressions: 'Germany is utterly the boys' country. In their absurd ingle's* coloured lace-up shirts, socks and braided yachting forage caps. All on bicycles.'[16]

Despite the odd flirtation, Isherwood did not enjoy staying with his despised cousin. But his first visit to Berlin less than a year later was an altogether different experience, and one which, although lasting little more than a week, he later regarded as among the most decisive events of his life.[17] His old friend W. H. Auden, who had already been in the city some months, introduced him to a world so deliciously unlike stuffy post-war England that by Christmas 1929 he had returned to Berlin for an indefinite stay. As he wrote in his memoir, when asked at the border the purpose of his journey, he could have truthfully replied, 'I'm looking for my homeland and I've come to find out if this is it.'[18]

By then Auden had returned to England leaving Isherwood with only one English acquaintance in Berlin – the chaotic, alcoholic archaeologist, Francis Turville-Petre. At the time, Francis was receiving treatment for syphilis at the Institut für Sexualwissenschaft [Institute for Sexual Research] – one of the most striking manifestations of Berlin's newfound modernity. Set up in 1919 by Dr Magnus Hirschfeld, this was no hole-in-the-wall operation but a serious attempt to address scientifically a vast range of sexual behaviour. A major part of Hirschfeld's mission was to persuade the world that homosexuality was neither a disease nor a crime but a perfectly normal part of the human condition. As well as being a clinic and research centre (it had an impressive archive and a library of some 30,000 volumes), the Institute sought to educate the wider public with numerous lectures on every aspect of sex. Several

---

* A word invented by Isherwood and his friend Edward Upward.

thousand visitors came each year from all over Europe. Many were treated for specific problems but others wanted simply to explore their own sexuality. Some, no doubt, went only to be titillated by the contents of the Institute's museum, referred to by Auden as 'pornography for science. A eunuch's pleasure.'[19]

> Here were whips and chains and torture instruments designed for the practitioners of pleasure-pain; high-heeled, intricately decorated boots for the fetishists; lacy female undies which had been worn by ferociously masculine Prussian officers beneath their uniforms. Here were the lower halves of trouser-legs with elastic bands to hold them in position between knee and ankle. In these and nothing else but an overcoat and a pair of shoes, you could walk the streets and seem fully clothed, giving a camera-quick exposure whenever a suitable viewer appeared.[20]

Such exhibits made a startling contrast to the fine furniture that stood in the Institute's formal rooms – a reminder that the building had once belonged to Brahms's great friend, the violinist Joseph Joachim. Turville-Petre rented rooms next to the Institute (situated on the north-west corner of the Tiergarten) and it was here, in a small, dark room overlooking an inner courtyard, that Isherwood also installed himself. Every evening the two young men would head for the boy bars, a favourite being the Cosy Corner on Zossener Strasse in a working-class district of the city. Isherwood later wrote that he used to think of the two of them as traders

> who had entered a jungle. The natives of the jungle [working-class German boys] surrounded them – childlike, curious, mistrustful, sly, easily and unpredictably moved

to friendship or hostility. The two traders had what the natives wanted, money. How much of it they would get and what they would have to do to get it was the subject of their bargaining. The natives enjoyed bargaining for bargaining's sake; this Francis understood profoundly. He was never in a hurry.[21]

Despite their promiscuity, Auden, Isherwood and Spender (who at first based himself in Hamburg) longed for more permanent relationships. Spender explained to Isaiah Berlin how he set about this quest:

> I am making a heroic effort to discover a very suitable boy, in order that I may stick to him and this involves accosting nearly every boy that I meet. It is perfectly easy to do that in Germany. I see a boy, I then ask him for a match to light my cigarette. Then I make up some absolutely absurd question. He looks rather puzzled, so then I tell him that I am English and can't explain myself properly. Then I offer him a cigarette and the machinery has begun. Then I make an appointment with him. Unfortunately here there is a snag because when he goes home and tells his parents how he has met an Englishman they forbid him ever to meet me again. That's most of my non-working life.[22]

Bars like the Cosy Corner or Westens (where Rupert Brooke wrote *Grantchester*) were a far cry from the glamorous nightclubs depicted in the 1972 film *Cabaret*. 'Nothing could have looked less decadent than the Cosy Corner,' Isherwood wrote. 'It was plain, homely and unpretentious.'[23]

There was no question that Berlin offered its visitors – especially the Anglo-Saxons – sexual and intellectual adventures

unobtainable in their own countries. In 1927 Sackville-West
spent Christmas in Berlin with Harold Nicolson. He reported
on the 'strange, wild nightlife', which he confessed to a friend
he preferred 'rather squalid and furtive'. He explained how it
all took place 'around an enormous, prim, gothic church, built
in the nineties when the quarter was a sort of Cromwell Road.
Now it looks rather sad and ghostly surrounded by electric
signs and disreputability of all sorts – like somebody at a party
pretending not to be shocked.' To E. M. Forster he related how
he had been 'dragged from one homosexual bar to another.
The behaviour is perfectly open ... And some of the people
one sees – huge men with breasts like women & faces like
Ottoline [Morrell], dressed as female Spanish dancers – are
really quite unintelligible ... They just moon about like great
question marks ...' He spent that night with a Lithuanian peasant covered in mother of pearl buttons, afterwards reporting
that he had not been in the least frightened when this 'beautiful creature' had insisted on taking a loaded revolver to bed,
adding, 'he was very friendly and charming'.[24] The artist Francis
Bacon was also briefly in Berlin in 1927. Only seventeen, he
was taken there by one of his father's friends who had been
instructed to make a man of him. Talking about the experience
some forty years later, Bacon recalled: 'Perhaps Berlin was violent to me because I had come from Ireland which was violent
in the military sense but not in the emotional sense in the way
Berlin was.' It was not, however, the 'very, very exciting nightlife' that left the deepest impression on the teenage Bacon, but
the Adlon Hotel breakfast – 'wheeled in on wonderful trolleys
with enormous swans' necks coming out of the four corners'.[25]

But for all the sexual freedom and thrill of Berlin's avant-
garde, many of this 'bright young' generation were equally
struck by the ugliness of the city and of Germans in general.

Disparaging comments on the latter's physical appearance are commonplace, the caricature of the Boche with bulging neck and bulging eyes being, according to many foreigners, all too close to the truth. One traveller having just returned from the Rhineland complained: 'The Germans eat too much meat and during the afternoon consume large teas with rich cakes. The national health would improve greatly if a crusade advocating two meals a day and no nibbles in-between were embarked upon.'[26] Even the pro-German Lord D'Abernon was overheard in an undiplomatic moment at a party asking, 'Why do Germans have three double chins at the back of their necks?'[27] And after writing at length in her journal of how much she loved the German people, Emily Pollard, whose uncle was the Governor of Virginia, John Garland Pollard, could not help adding – 'But don't they have size!'[28] This perceived unloveliness of the Germans contributed to Spender's neurosis, brought on, so he confessed to Isaiah Berlin, by long train journeys:

> I get so angry with my fellow passengers that I feel sick, gastric, sweaty, dirty, mad throughout every minute of a journey and leave the train always in a state of nervous exhaustion with wild pictures running through my brain of the fat babyish, shaved heads of middle-class Germans, and of great bumming, gay smiling German girls, gross rays of self-conscious sunshine, who excite all my repressed sadistic dislike of ugly women and deceitful Woman in general.[29]

The sometime poet and critic – more often drunk and embittered – Brian Howard made his feelings quite clear when he wrote to a friend from the Hospiz der Berliner in October 1927:

I am very depressed and very lonely. I hate Berlin so much
that I am coming home almost immediately. It is unbearably ugly, and quite quite awful ... I don't know where
anything is, I have no money and this hotel is appalling ...
When I arrived they were singing hymns. No one speaks
and my smoking is considered an outrage ... The Unter
den Linden is awful. Everything is noisy, vulgar, overcrowded and commercialised. The buses go at 50 mph
and are veritable death traps ... The homosexual life of
Berlin is fantastic from a psychologist's point of view but
very dreary from the point of view of a human being. God
how alone I feel.[30]

A couple of years later the American composer Paul Bowles
(whose surname Isherwood purloined for Sally Bowles in
Goodbye to Berlin) wrote: 'I have come to the decision that
Berlin is the least amusing place I have ever seen. It is the
synonym for stupidity. I should be quite happy if I never see
the city again after today ... It is difficult to get away from the
heavy arm that hangs above like a threatening pressure. Berlin
is not a beautiful city.'[31]

Nor was it just the ugliness of the capital that aroused
foreign censure. Eddy Sackville-West lived in Dresden with
a middle-class family in their comfortable middle-class villa
– 'large and wastefully built and hideous, hideous'. He acknowledged that the family was extremely kind to him and that he
was even beginning to be 'quietly happy', but he was irritated
by the son who 'has a way of clapping his hands on entering
the room, which is absolutely maddening. And then, he is so
ugly and spotty.'

Although Englishmen like Sackville-West believed that by
escaping to Germany they had abandoned their upper-class

background, in reality (excepting Isherwood and Auden) they were incapable of shedding their deep sense of cultural superiority. Tom Mitford, Lord and Lady Redesdale's only son, and an enthusiastic Germanophile, wrote from Austria to his cousin Randolph Churchill on the advantages of mixing with 'one's own kind' when abroad, 'for I know how ghastly it can be at times to live at close quarters with a thoroughly middle-class family – however nice they are'.[32] As Eddy put it, 'How much less I like *any* foreigners than an English person *really*!'[33] There is more than a whiff of all this in a lecture Harold Nicolson (at the time serving in the British Embassy) gave at Berlin University, described by the wife of the British ambassador, Lady Rumbold:

> He gave a most entertaining lecture in the University yesterday in English, in which he compared the very different character of the English and German. It was half serious and half jesting, and I think left the students high and dry and not quite knowing how to take it. To all of us it was delightful. His description of the English character with its curious shyness, which you meet in no other nationality, was so true. The Englishman instinctively protects this sensitiveness by growing a sort of shell in the form of a particular kind of manner, and code of 'good form', sometimes also a superior air vis-à-vis foreigners, which is all calculated to camouflage his shyness. Harold says the English and Germans will *never* understand each other.[34]

Nevertheless, it is clear that after entertaining the Nicolsons and Woolfs to tea at his house in Berlin, Harry Kessler had understood his English guests perfectly: 'Leonard Woolf, clever and imaginative, is a bundle of nerves who trembles as he speaks … Virginia Woolf is very typically upper-middle class, of the best kind, don's daughter, while Mrs Nicolson [Vita Sackville-West] is just as typically aristocratic, the great lady, of slender build and great elegance, with ease of manner and style in every movement, a person who has never experienced a moment's embarrassment or a feeling of social barriers.'[35] Of Harold Nicolson himself, Kessler wrote, 'He is an entertaining personality, but somehow I do not like him, without quite being able to make out why.'[36] Neither of Kessler's female guests took to Berlin. Vita, who according to Lady Rumbold had 'enormous feet and hands, quite remarkably so', spent as little time there as possible during her husband's posting to the British Embassy, while Virginia declared the city to be a 'horror' and one she would never visit again.[37]

In his book *The Dark Valley*, Piers Brendon sums up what it was about Berlin that so offended the intelligentsia: 'Berlin, with its muster of straight grey streets named after national heroes and its drab uniform squares filled with the statues of forgotten generals, seemed more a monument to the Prussian spirit than the site of a new Babylon.'[38] And it was true that, while at night the capital may have earned its reputation as a modern Sodom, its appearance by day had more in common with a traditional German *Hausfrau*.

Foreigners may have poured scorn on the stolid appearance of the older generation but they were also impressed by Germany's modernity, of which nudity – by no means confined to nightclubs – was an exciting expression. The healthy vigour of the scantily clad youths they met out hiking in the countryside or sunbathing by swimming pools had no parallel back home. The sight of two young couples playing a ball game in the woods near Berlin delighted the British novelist and women's rights campaigner Cicely Hamilton, who

spent several summers travelling all over Germany in the late
Weimar years:

> The two young men of the party were clothed in noth-
> ing but attenuated trunks. Of the girls one wore shorts,
> or loose bathing-drawers, and the garment known as a
> brassière – a considerable expanse of the diaphragm being
> visible between the two. While the other, an agile slip of a
> lass, contented herself with bathing-drawers only and was
> naked from the hips upward. As girls and men alike, they
> were entirely unembarrassed by the passing spectator.[39]

This passion for stripping off was no mere minority fad but one
shared by Germans of all social classes. Foreigners were struck
by the sight of railroad construction gangs and farm workers
their tanned bodies bare to the waist. And, as one traveller
pointed out, 'you would never see in Germany a gardener
mowing the lawn wearing a thick waistcoat, heavy trousers,
and a bowler hat, as I did on my second day back in England
during the hot weather'.[40]

Auden, Isherwood and Spender liked to holiday (in the
company of various boys) on Rügen – an island in the Baltic
Sea. Here, on the long sandy beaches, naked bathers lay in
their hundreds. Spender described how the boys 'who had
turned the deepest mahogany walked amongst those people
with paler skins, like kings among their courtiers', adding, 'the
sun healed their bodies of the years of war, and made them
conscious of the quivering, fluttering life of blood and muscles
covering their exhausted spirits like the pelt of an animal'.[41]
Even Aristide Maillol, who as a Frenchman and a sculptor must
have been well accustomed to naked bodies, was astonished
by the display of nudity that confronted him at a Frankfurt

open-air swimming pool. His host, Harry Kessler, explained this was all part of a new outlook on life since the war. 'People want really to *live* in the sense of enjoying light, the sun, happiness, and the health of their bodies. It is ... a mass movement which has stirred all of German youth.'

This longing for sun and light was reflected in contemporary architecture. Maillol was especially impressed by Römerstadt, Frankfurt's social housing experiment, '*C'est la première fois que je vois de l'architecture moderne qui est parfaite. Oui, c'est parfait, il n'y a pas une tache* [It is the first time that I have seen modern architecture that is perfect. Yes, there is not one blemish].'[42] In tune with the needs and aspirations of the new generation, the architect Ernst May built his Römerstadt houses on egalitarian principles, ensuring that all the occupants enjoyed the same access to sunlight and fresh air. Equally stirred by Germany's modern buildings, Cicely Hamilton marvelled at the glass walls of Walter Gropius's Dessau Bauhaus that brought the cult of sunlight right into the workplace. Tourists arriving in Hamburg, she noted, were now more likely to be directed to the Chilehaus – a thrilling ten-storey example of 'Brick Expressionism' – than to the city's picturesque medieval quarter.[43]

Geoffrey Cox, a young New Zealander on his way up to Oxford University as a Rhodes scholar, was similarly invigorated by this unstuffy approach. Having just visited the Berlin exhibition 'Sun, Air and a Home for Everyone', he wrote to his mother from Heidelberg: 'The great thing in Germany today is the emergence of the new type of person. One sees them everywhere – sunburnt, wearing sensible clothes and of splendid physique. There are innumerable physical culture clubs and bathing societies etc. and every attempt is made to get people out into the open.' He went on to praise the way people dressed:

More sensibly even than in New Zealand. The men
wear soft shirts often without ties – even shorts are not
unknown. Many of the girls wear no stockings, only socks.
You may be dressed in the height of fashion in Berlin in
a soft shirt open at the neck and grey flannels. Moreover
they wear bright colours – even the men wear yellow and
blue shirts – I am wearing one now comfortable and smart
looking. Price 4/6![44]

Nor was this new-found freedom confined only to men.
According to the journalist Lilian Mowrer, wife of Edgar
Mowrer, the *Chicago Daily News* correspondent in Berlin, a
woman could do what she liked in Weimar Germany. With
thirty-six women in the Reichstag, Germany could boast more
women parliamentarians than any other country and, in theory
at least, women could enter any profession they chose. Mowrer
cited them working as electrical engineers, machine construc-
tionists and even slaughterers – 'Margarethe Cohn could strike
down a steer with a single blow of the mallet.'[45]

But for all those foreigners lured to Germany by sex, sun
and the promise of a brave new world, there were plenty of
others who travelled there in search of quaint houses, cobbled
streets, brass bands and beer. There is no mention in Emily
Pollard's diary of such avant-garde delights as cross-dressing,
jazz or Josephine Baker's banana dance, and it is quite likely
that she had never heard of Max Reinhardt, Bertolt Brecht or
the Bauhaus. Her travel account is a reminder that much of
Weimar Germany remained untouched by the liberal modernism that has come to symbolise its fifteen-year existence. In
Hildesheim the locals stared at Emily and her friend, Marge,
with open curiosity so unused were they to American tourists.
Emily describes the women there wearing dirndls, clogs and

dark blue aprons and records how she and Marge fell in love
with the narrow streets and the city's 'seven hundred medieval
buildings'. 'Many times I felt I simply couldn't take another
step but a sight of a group of those medieval homes made me
forget how weary I was.'

Emily and Marge also stayed at Goslar in the Harz
Mountains where they met a large group of young *Wandervögel*
[hikers]:

> School children, with their packs on their backs and canes
> in hand, as well as older pupils seem to adore this outdoor
> activity. They haven't been spoiled by the auto. The canes
> are covered with silver insignia. Each little town has its
> own and the children add one to their stick as they visit a
> new one. You could tell by the number which were the old
> timers and which were out for the first time.[46]

For any foreigner travelling through the countryside in late
Weimar Germany, an encounter with the eager young par-
ticipants of the *Jugendbewegung* [Youth Movement] was
inevitable. Foreigners were impressed. What better way to
instil patriotism, team spirit and a healthy love of nature in
the rising generation? The cheap hostels in which the hikers
lodged overnight were models of orderliness, cleanliness and
simplicity – qualities so central to the national perception of
what it meant to be a 'good' German.

However, on closer inspection these youthful cartels were
not quite as innocent as they seemed. Cicely Hamilton sounded
a note of caution. 'There is danger in the Youth Movement,' she
wrote, 'which may be summed up in the one word – Politics.'
She had been quick to notice that the majority of these groups
were junior branches of existing church societies or political

parties intent on indoctrinating the young with their own particular brand of sectarianism. 'Some of these young people', Hamilton noted, 'are taking to their politics early and taking to them vigorously.' On her weekend rambles she would often meet 'parties of imps – little creatures who, as yet, should know nothing of politics – trudging out into the woods, in crocodile formation, with the Red Flag marching at their head.' Nor was it only young communists who made her uneasy. 'The Brown Shirts are the most striking example of youth trained to partisan thinking,' she observed, adding, 'They are not an unfavourable example. Their doctrines may be dangerous and their methods provocative but the lads themselves – so far as I have seen them – are of clean, upstanding type.' She went on to inform her readers that 'the young Brown Shirts were a branch of the National-Socialist-German-Workers-Party', a title, as she points out, that is much too long for everyday use so 'has mercifully been shortened to – Nazi'.[47]

4

'The Seething Brew'

Emily Pollard liked the Germans. She appreciated their good manners and their diligence; she enjoyed the food and even learned to like feather quilts ('they don't seem to know about blankets, perhaps they didn't have them in the middle ages'). And although she visited more shops than Expressionist art exhibitions, she was not immune to the new mood, noting that 'Germany is very ahead of us in its adoption of the modern', a view confirmed by a visit to Berlin's Tempelhof Airport. Formerly a Prussian parade ground, by 1930 it had become the largest airport in the world, with some fifty aeroplanes landing each day from all parts of Europe. The airport ranked high on Berlin's list of tourist attractions, where, for a small entry fee, any member of the public could enter and stay as long as they liked. 'Great crowds gather out there to sit at small tables and eat and drink to the tune of the motors,'[1] Emily observed. Cicely Hamilton was also smitten. 'There is always something happening, or about to happen; a new and lovely monster rushing out to meet the wind, an arrival swooping down from heaven knows where!'[2]

Two years earlier, Tempelhof had been the scene of some excitement when John Henry Mears and Charles Collyer landed their single-engine monoplane at the airfield during their successful bid to break the record for the fastest circum-navigation of the world. Before reaching Berlin they had been lost over the great expanse of flat farmland to the west of the city and so had decided that their only option was to land and ask for directions:

> Suddenly we heard shouting and a ruddy-faced farmer run-ning toward us, waving his arms. Behind him were three little boys, blond and fat all shouting. And then two lit-tle girls, their aprons flying, their yellow pig-tails flapping behind them, their shrill, childish voices raised in excite-ment. A whole flock of geese waddled with self-important haste from the barnyard adding their raucous cries to this Teutonic bedlam.[3]

Racing against the clock, the men stayed only a few hours in Berlin but long enough for Mears to comment on the wide boulevards 'as clean as the kitchens of a German housewife', and the policemen 'as smart and dignified as army officers'. Refreshed by breakfast of ham and eggs at the Adlon Hotel, and great fat seidels [mugs] of dark, foaming beer, icy cold, they took off from Tempelhof twelve hours behind schedule, dipped their wings in salute, and headed off for Russia. They reached New York on 22 July 1928 having broken the record with a journey lasting 23 days, 15 hours, 21 minutes and 3 seconds.[4]

Tempelhof Airport, so symbolic of the new Weimar spirit, was often the first port of entry for the scores of visitors who flocked each year to the British Embassy. And after Sir Horace and Lady Rumbold's arrival in Berlin in September 1928, they came in

ever-increasing numbers. This was not surprising. It was a thoroughly comfortable billet from which to explore the city or to
plan further travels in Germany. Ethel Rumbold was impressed
with her new residence, 'its five drawing-rooms, the ball-room
and her "perfectly colossal" bedroom'. But not the 'truly ghastly
staircase lit by tall brass lamps with white *glass globes* all the way
up'. To her surprise she found the Germans pleasantly quiet and
unassuming with 'none of their former arrogance'; in fact, 'an
agreeable contrast to the French, Belge [sic] and Spaniards'.[5]

Sir Horace's tenure was to last five years and, as the political scene grew darker, he was to be for many visitors a
reassuring reminder of what it meant to be British. One guest
described him as having a 'round, red, baby-face, a joke eye-
glass and an intensely stupid expression behind which he hid,
with true British perfidy, a needle-sharp brain'.[6] After meeting the family at the railway station, Harold Nicolson wrote
to his wife, 'Rumbie, Mrs Rumbie, Miss Rumbie, & Master
Rumbie ... all got out of the train in a row, & each one clasp-
ing a novel by John Galsworthy. I never saw anything look so
English, & solid & decent.'[7] Lady Rumbold, the daughter of
a diplomat and a niece of Lord Lonsdale, was born to be an
ambassador's wife. Warm and funny, she charmed everyone.
When they arrived in Berlin, with their twenty-two-year-old
daughter, Constantia, their son Anthony (also destined for the
Foreign Office) was about to go up to Oxford.

The Rumbolds' first social event was 'a quiet little dinner
of 30' in honour of the leader of the Labour Party, Ramsay
MacDonald. The servants wore black and silver state livery ('less showy than the red and yellow') while the table
was sumptuously adorned with gold plate and pink carna-
tions. The guest list included Albert Einstein and the Oswald
Mosleys ('she looking lovely and beautifully turned out, not

at all *Labour*!*). 'Dashing' Lady Drogheda was also there and
Lord Curzon. But it was the chancellor, Hermann Müller,[†]
who really took Lady Rumbold's fancy. 'He is quite the most
German thing you ever saw', she told her mother, 'large, fat,
heavy, with massive square head, roll of fat at the back of his
neck, in fact *typical*! But to talk to, charming, simple unaffected
and natural.'[8]

Two days earlier Ramsay MacDonald ('a most attractive
individual, so good-looking and *distingué*') had addressed a
packed Reichstag – the first foreigner ever to do so. 'He was
introduced by the Speaker as the man who had stood for
British neutrality at the beginning of the War, which made
me *hot*,' Lady Rumbold reported indignantly, 'but otherwise
all was serene, and he talked more of the future. It was *odd* to
be there with a party of Bolsheviks sitting just behind us, and
I, incidentally, in official mourning for the Russian Empress!'[9]

Some guests overstayed their welcome: 'We *still* have
our M.P. with us,' Lady Rumbold complained a few months
later. 'He came for a couple of nights and will have been here
8 when he leaves! He is good company but *still* it is rather
indiscreet to stay so long.'[10] The MP in question was the thirty-
two-year-old Conservative Member for Chippenham, Victor
Cazalet, who, blissfully unaware of his 'charming' hostess's
irritation, noted that he had seldom spent a more enjoyable
week. Immediately before arriving in Berlin on 5 January 1929,
he had been a guest of the Bismarcks:

---

* She was formerly Lady Cynthia Curzon, the first Lord Curzon's
second daughter. She died of peritonitis in 1933.
[†] Hermann Müller (1876–1931) was twice chancellor, 1920, 1928–
1930. He was one of the German signatories of the Treaty of Versailles.

Very comfy house (ugly), plenty of hot water. It is almost twenty miles from Hamburg and in the midst of great woods. Party of 18. Austrian, German and Sweden. How charming are the Swedes. Full of fun and simplicity. I loved them all ... Everyone talks English. We ate off the place. Cold carp, hare etc. Not very appetising. Most of the estate is forest which pays pretty well in Germany. On Thursday we have our hare and pheasant shoot.

The next day they hunted deer and boar:

We all had our bags examined after lunch by a typically Prussian inspection. After dinner all the animals are laid out in front of the house and lit by flares. Then we all go out to look at them and the buglers play various tunes – very cold work. The beating is all regulated by bugler. The head forester is a very great swell, a sort of head agent. He wore two pairs of glasses [binoculars] and saluted with great courtesy as he placed us each drive.

A mandatory tour of the museum and the Iron Chancellor's private quarters did not impress Cazalet: 'Very, *very* ugly – incredibly so and very unforgettable.' For an irrepressible enthusiast like the young MP, a Prussian shooting party was an intriguing experience, but it was nevertheless with relief that he left on the 1.33 train for Berlin, and the comforts of the Embassy. Once in the capital, he was immediately struck with the friendliness shown to the British by the Germans. 'No one seems to feel antagonistic. Nearly everyone delighted to see you and talk about the war.'[11]

Certainly the Duke of York (later King George VI) did not encounter any hostility when in March 1929 he became the first British prince to visit Berlin since the war. He and the Duchess stayed briefly at the Embassy on their way to Crown Prince Olaf's wedding in Norway. 'We quite lost our hearts to the little Duchess,' wrote Lady Rumbold, 'she is a pearl of great value. So pretty, so soft, such a lovely smile, no frills and yet much dignity.'[12] The visit was unexpectedly prolonged when a train delay resulted in the royal couple staying a night and an extra day. Lady Rumbold was quite unperturbed. 'They had no wish to sightsee or to go to church, so after a peaceful morning, we took them to the golf-club at Wannsee with Harold Nicolson. Luckily the Crown Prince was *not* lunching there,'[13] she noted to a friend, knowing that an accidental meeting between the German ex-royal and his British royal cousins would have been a cause of considerable diplomatic embarrassment. The previous day the Duke and Duchess had been given a tour of the Schloss, the Kaiser's former residence:

> Even his tiny bedroom which is never shown, and which looked rather tragic lumbered up with things, and wall paper very dilapidated. It was quite small and dark looking on to a courtyard, with a tiny dressing-room next to it. In his study is the famous table on which he signed the order for the mobilisation of the Army on 1st August 1914. This writing table is made out of wood from *The Victory*, and the huge inkstand is a model of it, with the famous Nelson signal 'England expects etc.' in coloured flags. Curious isn't it?[14]

Reflecting on the transient nature of empire, the Duke was depressed by what he saw. 'He thought it dreadfully sad,' remarked Lady Rumbold, 'and kept on referring to the fact that in such a short space of time all was completely changed and nobody seemed to care. And it is true. It does seem very cold-blooded. The Hohenzollerns are now just history!'[15]

⁓

Nevertheless, the fate of the Hohenzollerns continued to fascinate foreigners despite their obsession with Berlin's modernity. As Cazalet noted in his diary, 'Berlin is an interesting city. Excellent pictures – good deal of life. V. expensive. Interesting people. Three subsidised operas every night – all packed. Plays excellent, cinemas v. good. I saw 2 Bolshevik films, 1st class photography, poor propaganda – what a time to live in!'[16]

Like so many visitors, he was astonished by the quality and diversity of the arts in Weimar Germany. In 1927 Eddy Sackville-West had chosen to live in Dresden because he knew he could go to 'a marvellous' concert' or opera every single evening. Five of Richard Strauss's operas were premiered at the Dresden opera – then the best in Europe. On 12 April 1929 it cancelled its advertised programme to make way for a performance by the twelve-year-old Yehudi Menuhin. That night he played the Bach, Beethoven and Brahms violin concertos to an ecstatic audience. 'The big sold-out building reverberated the joyous enthusiasm,' wrote the *Volkstaat*. The week before, Yehudi had played in Berlin with the Philharmonic under Bruno Walter to an equally rapturous response: 'There steps a fat little blond boy on the podium,' wrote one critic, 'and wins at once all hearts as in an irresistibly ludicrous way, like a penguin, he alternately places down one foot then the other. But wait, you will stop laughing when he puts his bow to the violin to play Bach's violin concert E-major no. 2.'[17] Henry Goldman, the New York banker who had given Menuhin his violin (the Prince Khevenhüller Stradivarius), had come from New York especially to attend the concert.

The *Berliner Morgenpost* reported that the audience 'amongst them Einstein, Max Reinhardt, and all the poets and musicians of Berlin, overwhelmed the grace-gifted Yehudi with a hurricane of applause'. Afterwards, Einstein, allegedly with tears in his eyes, met the American prodigy backstage: 'My dear little boy, it is many years since I have had the privilege of receiving a lesson such as you have taught me tonight.'[18] But this outpouring of joy at a Jewish boy's genius only briefly masked the persistent drumbeat of anti-Semitism. Although still a peripheral figure in the late 1920s, Hitler now regularly denounced Jewish musicians. For Bruno Walter, conducting the young Yehudi that night, the clock was already ticking.

Opera and concert tickets were not cheap but Lilian Mowrer thought theatre seats so 'monstrously' expensive that she became drama critic for a London magazine in order that she might see as many plays as she wanted. She soon concluded that not only were the Germans the greatest theatre-goers in Europe but also the most educated – even if they did look bourgeois compared with the smart audiences in London or Paris. Mowrer counted over 100 towns with their own theatre company and thirty with a permanent opera house, a happy legacy of pre-unification days when 'Germany' consisted of thirty-eight sovereign states and four free cities. Mowrer was much taken with German stagecraft. 'The sheer mechanics of scene-shifting were prodigious; whole sets dropped out of sight, or dissolved in darkness while new scenes, with actors in them, rose on elevators, or descended from above.'[19] For the intellectually adventurous, plays by the likes of Hauptmann, Wedekind, Bronnen and (the 'degenerate looking'[20]) Brecht were on offer, as well as the latest works by Schoenberg, Hindemith or Richard Strauss. Bauhaus architecture, Expressionism, Dada and the searing caricatures of

George Grosz disturbed and stimulated. As Mowrer put it, 'You felt so intensely alive in Germany.'[21]

Contemporary German cinema was equally thrilling and foreign visitors were eager to visit the Universum Film AG (UFA studios, where in 1929 *Der blaue Engel* was in production). In a break from their normal round of diplomatic duties, Sir Horace and Lady Rumbold spent a day on the set where they were photographed with Marlene Dietrich. They also watched the filming of a Russian spectacular in which 100 or so mounted Cossacks 'rode to Petrograd'. 'The crowds were all *real* Russians to get the correct types,' Lady Rumbold informed her mother, 'and a real Russian General led the troops, earning 25 marks a day for which he was thankful.' However, she added, as the snow was made of salt, and everything on the set was sham and shoddy, 'it did rather take away all one's illusions'.[22]

Brenda Dean Paul, one of London's 'bright young things', was among the many aspiring actors hoping to find fame and fortune with UFA. Her acting career was to prove a disaster but she did leave a vivid account of the few weeks she spent in Berlin while pursuing it. A young attaché at the British Embassy introduced Brenda to the nightlife. Within a few days she had met Prince Lexy Hochberg of Pless, Max Reinhardt and Conrad Veidt – the most popular actor in Berlin. She recounted her 'average day':

> Getting up about one, lunch would generally be very late (which is the German fashion), and I would go ... to Robert's in the Kurfürstendamm, generally after a visit to Figaro, the famous hairdresser in the same street. At Robert's you can get anything from a mint julep to some complicated oyster dish. You sit up at the long bar and are sure to see any number of stage and film celebrities. Lunch finished by three or

four o'clock, there would be dancing at the Eden or Adlon
Hotels. Imagine dancing in any London hotel at tea-time?
What a dreary odd spectacle it would represent. But in
Berlin it is part of the average day and the chic thing to do.
Then cocktails at the Jockey Club until seven or eight, when
Berlin goes home to rest before dinner which is generally at
about ten o'clock. Horscher was a restaurant which I would
frequently go to, being very greedy. It was the gourmet's paradise. An old and once sumptuous private house, Horscher
still maintains that atmosphere of Edwardian *grand luxe*,
with its deep crimson walls and tables arranged in horse-box
fashion around the walls of the former library ... any loud
talk or laughter is met with stony glances. Hardly a place
for a social meal but more of a religious rite ... When not
dining at Horscher I would go to the Neva, a famous Russian
restaurant ... Then about eleven or twelve one would think
about dancing, about really beginning the evening.[23]

The serious part of the evening took place after midnight in
expensive nightclubs – very different in style from those fre-
quented by Auden, Isherwood and Spender. Loelia Ponsonby
(later Duchess of Westminster) 'goggled' at the 'ravishing dim-
pled blond' sitting at the next table in the Eldorado 'who in
reality was a sergeant in the Uhlans' (Polish light cavalry).
And, after visiting a club that advertised itself as 'Dancing for
Gentlemen only', she commented that the 'middle-aged men
in sporting attire solemnly dancing the tango together, cheek
to cheek, looked so like caricatures of nice old German fathers
that one couldn't really take them seriously'.[24] Her friend,
twenty-five-year-old Constantia Rumbold, wrote up the Berlin
nightlife, citing a string of fashionable venues including the
Beguine – the first of the city's burgeoning black bars:

It was a dim arcade lit with red lamps and smelling like the subway. At the end a half open door. Beyond the door, the muffled thumping of a drum, the jumbled cacophony of a saxophone. A thin haze of blue smoke and tables tightly packed. Here lounged students, millionaires, businessmen, and artists cheek by jowl with artists' models and ladies of the town. With eyes half closed, drugged by the music, they swayed rhythmically and speechlessly on the dance floor. There was one Negress who sang, a fat one, in low cut satin dress ... The dim lights would be dimmed still further and she would start to croon, beating time with her feet. She crooned faster and faster, louder and louder, more and more shrilly ... while her fat body twisted and turned in spasms of agony and she threw out her arms in a frenzy, screaming 'everybody noo wot was trubblin' her, crying for de Carolinas.' There was always thunderous applause. She would sing again and again, her rich, fruity voice rolling out through the room in plaintive wail, her body never still.

But the evening was still not over. The final treat for 'jaded bummellers' was chicken soup and hot sausages at the Künstler [Artist's Corner], hidden away in a quiet street. The heavy outer door was opened only a crack in answer to the bell. On entering, the visitor crossed a silent courtyard before descending a flight of stone steps to a small underground room furnished simply with tables and benches. In one corner a blind man softly played the piano. 'The soup was hot and delicious, the beer golden and ruddy, and here one might see or hear artists or painters, writers and pseudo intellectuals clustered round the deal tables.'[25]

Then on 24 October 1929 – Black Thursday – the Wall Street stock market crashed and with it Germany's hopes of sustained prosperity. In fact, even before the financial meltdown there had been signs that the gilt on Weimar's 'golden' years was wearing thin. Stephen Spender recalled how oppressed he had felt by the poverty he had seen in Hamburg the previous summer, adding: 'I now have little desire to indulge my usual transports … as owing to the common distress of this country where formerly the hordes of prostitutes could be regarded as merchandise, now I cannot think of them except as carrion: and it is no pleasure to imagine myself playing the part of the foreign vulture.'[26]

Lilian Mowrer claimed to have seen the crisis coming. As well as reviewing plays, she wrote more general pieces and, along with other journalists, was regularly invited by the German state railway to visit less well-known parts of the country. She had been shocked by the 'orgy' of public spending she saw everywhere:

> When I was shown these splendid new constructions …
> these spacious tenement houses grouped round tree-lined
> courtyards, or the charming one-family houses of the new
> residential quarters, I would compare them with what I saw
> in other countries. The reconstructed areas in France looked
> very cheap and mean beside all this German opulence.[27]

But, as Mowrer realised, the fatal flaw in this 'carnival of public spending' was its dependence on short-term American loans so that, when the bubble burst and the debts were called in, the consequences for Germany were catastrophic.

A year after the crash Sir Horace noted that government ministers were no longer hosting or attending big dinners:

'They are really not able to afford to return the hospitality shown to them by foreigners but, besides this, they are no doubt rather afraid of the reaction which a photograph of a big banquet might have on officials whose salaries they are cutting ... the plenturous [sic] feasts offered by Jewish bankers, which have hitherto been a feature of the Berlin season, will not be given this year. All this will be of immense benefit to one's digestion.'[28]

The general hardship soon intensified. Spender, for instance, noted that it had become impossible to enter a shop in Berlin without being bothered by beggars. Many French visitors, however, were sceptical, believing the Germans were yet again using an economic crisis as an excuse to avoid paying reparations. 'Frenchmen returning from Berlin are full of the incredible extravagance and manifest luxury which exist there,' the writer André Gide told Harry Kessler.[29] And Emily Pollard, dining at Goslar in the summer of 1930, was able to enjoy 'a regular feast for the gods' that included among its six courses green turtle soup and dressed crab.[30]

Nevertheless, Christopher Isherwood, who a year after the crash was lodging in a tenement slum with his current boyfriend's family, was closer to the truth when he later wrote: 'Here was the seething brew of history in the making – a brew which would test the truth of all the political theories, just as actual cooking tests the cookery books. The Berlin brew seethed with unemployment, malnutrition, stock market panic, hatred of the Versailles treaty and other potent ingredients.'[31] In other words, exactly the conditions required by the National Socialists to convince voters that Hitler's own brew of dictatorship, hatred and perverted patriotism offered their only hope of national renewal.

When on 26 February 1924 Hitler had stood in a Munich court facing charges of treason after his failed putsch, few doubted that his political career was over. Yet two days later the *Manchester Guardian* reported, 'Hitler is the hero of the hour. His defence which takes up columns in this morning's newspapers has made a great impression.' With a 'torrent of histrionic emotionalism, full of froth', the thirty-four-year-old Hitler had caught the attention of the entire nation. His impassioned condemnation of the Weimar government, Jews and the Versailles treaty resonated with many Germans – not least the judge who gave him an absurdly light sentence of nine months. But as the *Manchester Guardian* journalist watched the trial unfold, he was puzzled by Hitler's apparent lack of motive. 'He is not filled with the consciousness that he is fighting for the downtrodden and oppressed,' he wrote. 'He plotted and risked his life and the lives of others for no intelligible motive.' Nor, he added, was there any sign of self-interest or personal ambition to explain why he had undertaken such enormous risks. Nevertheless, Hitler's public relations triumph at his trial was undisputed, even though the National Socialists continued to remain on the fringe of German politics in the years immediately following his release. It was, however, during this relatively quiet period that Hitler became the unchallenged leader of his party. From now on he was always 'Der Führer'.

Then, on 14 September 1930, the political scene changed dramatically when the Nazis won 107 seats at the federal election. The long period of waiting was over. What is more, Hitler, having learned the lesson from his failed putsch, had achieved his success legally. The press baron Lord Rothermere, in Munich at the time, was delighted, believing that Hitler had opened up a new era for Germany. He urged his fellow countrymen to recognise the advantages German fascism could

offer Europe – especially in the fight against communism.[32]
Rumbold was more sceptical. He reported to King George V
a month later, on 13 October, after the Reichstag had met for
the first time since the poll:

> I was in the Reichstag when these German fascists made
> their entry in their forbidden uniforms, which consist of a
> khaki shirt, breeches and puttees, with the 'Hakenkreuz'
> on the arm. One of the leaders was in plus-fours, in which
> he did not look particularly well. They arrived at the House
> with overcoats on so as to conceal their uniforms and their
> entrance might have been staged by a music-hall Mussolini.
> But whilst their proceedings are often very undignified and
> childish, they certainly have succeeded in arousing a new
> spirit in the country which expresses itself in a wish to 'get
> a move on'.[33]

To Sir Horace it seemed that the new Nazi deputies were
merely play-acting and their fascist salute was still a novelty –
even to them. 'They soon came up against the Communists,'
he wrote to his mother, 'the two parties shouting insults at one
another across the floor of the house. The temporary Speaker
– a venerable and magnificent "beaver" of eighty-three – was
impotent to stop the proceedings, which were both childish
and undignified.'[34]

Later that day violence erupted on to the streets. Deeply
shocked, Rumbold described to his son how groups of young
Nazis had smashed the windows of Jewish shops, among them
the famous department stores Wertheim and Tietz. Sir Horace
clearly saw no contradiction between his very real distress at
such conduct and the casual anti-Semitism in which he, like
so many of his class and generation, regularly indulged. 'I am

appalled by the number of Jews in this place,' he had written
to his predecessor, Sir Ronald Lindsay, shortly after arriving
in Berlin. 'One cannot get away from them. I am thinking of
having a ham-bone amulet made "to keep off the evil nose",
but I am afraid that even that would not be a deterrent.'[35]
And in referring to 'a sort of Sionist congress' at which he was
invited 'to meet a lot of Hebrews at a dinner',[36] his disdain
is unmistakable. Neither was his good-hearted wife immune:
'Really we mix with the oddest people. Yesterday we had tea
with the Afghans. Today we are tea-ing first with some Jews
called Israel (which you can't camouflage), and then with the
Turks. Tomorrow we adorn the Persians' drawing room. Does
Lucy have such people in Oslo?'[37]

Even the economist John Maynard Keynes, author of *The
Economic Consequences of the Peace* (1919), who readily sang
the praises of Jewish friends like Einstein and the banker Carl
Melchior, wrote after a visit to Berlin, 'Yet if I lived there, I felt
I might turn anti-Semitic for the poor Prussian is too slow and
heavy on his legs for the other kind of Jews, the ones who are
not imps but serving devils, with small horns, pitch forks and
oily tails.' He added how unpleasant it was to see a civilisation
'so under the ugly thumbs of its impure Jew who has all the
money and the power and the brain'.[38]

Cicely Hamilton, a thoughtful traveller and certainly not a
Nazi supporter, reflected the views of many of her fellow countrymen when she attempted to justify German anti-Semitism.
She identified envy as the prime cause of *Judenhetze* [hatred
of Jews]:

A people that has suffered and is bitterly poor sees a race
that climbs and flourishes upon the ruin of its own fortunes. Small wonder if envy does stir in its heart and it

snarls accusations of profiteering against all who belong to the race. Is it not because he has fattened on the miseries of others that Israel today dwells lordly in the Kurfüstendamm which was once the aristocratic quarter, the Mayfair of imperial Berlin?[39]

Addressing the 'Jewish question' in his book *Hitler*, Wyndham Lewis, writer, artist, co-founder of the Vorticist movement, or – as Auden described him – that 'lonely old volcano of the right',[40] went a step further by dismissing the whole subject as a 'racial red herring':

To the Anglo-Saxon I would say: Do not allow these difficult matters to sway you too much (though decidedly warning this crude Teuton to be civil, when in your company). But still allow a little *Blutsfühl* [blood ties] to have its way ... in favour of this brave and very unhappy impoverished kinsman. Do not allow a mere bagatelle of a *Judenfrage* [Jewish question] to stand in the way of that![41]

Hitler, which had a swastika emblazoned on its cover, was the first full-length analysis of the Führer and published only four months after a brief trip Lewis made to Berlin in November 1930. The violence, he told his readers, was entirely instigated by the communists, who also abetted the police in shooting innocent Nazis.

Lewis was present at 'a monster meeting' in the Sportpalast where Hermann Göring, newly elected to the Reichstag, and propaganda genius, Joseph Goebbels, addressed a crowd of twenty thousand. 'There was something like the physical pressure of one immense indignant thought,' he observed.[42] Lilian and Edgar Mowrer attended a similar gathering: 'Long before

we reached the Potsdamerstrasse, our taxi was halted by out-
posts of brown-shirted stalwarts, who allowed us to pass only
after examining our invitation card,' Lilian recorded. Finally
they were allowed into the hall, its walls painted in brilliant
futuristic colours. Not only was every one of the twenty
thousand seats taken, she noted, but the corridors between
the seats were also crammed with spectators. Yet more were
massed at the back 'like a great choir'. Lines of uniformed
men, with leather boots and peaked caps, kept order. 'They
stood to attention in the stiffest manner, but were ready to
dart into action at the slightest attempt at heckling. Their attitude was challenging, defiant, warlike; their expression most
aggressive. The atmosphere of the whole place was as highly
charged as a powder factory.'[43] Yet even after witnessing such
an event, Wyndham Lewis was still able to write, 'It is essential
to understand that Adolf Hitler is not a sabre-rattler.'[44] And to
underline the point, he headed one of his chapters 'Adolf
Hitler: A Man of Peace'.

In the wake of their first major electoral success, the Nazis
lost no time in demonstrating arrogance and brutality. Yet, to
many foreign observers, it seemed that they had also injected
a new dynamism into the country. It was not easy, even for a
seasoned diplomat like Sir Horace Rumbold, to read the political tealeaves. Nevertheless, he was convinced, as he reported
to the foreign secretary, Arthur Henderson, that whatever
happened to the National Socialists, their determination to
improve Germany's position both nationally and internationally 'was here to stay and would act as a spur to this or any
other German Government of the future'.[45]

5

The Noose Tightens

By the spring of 1931, as Rumbold made clear to the Foreign Office, living conditions in Germany had gone from bad to worse:

> No one has any money, the price of bread does not fall, unemployment remains high ... People do not see how they are going to come through the winter. They seem to themselves to have nothing to lose and nothing to hope for ... it is the lack of any hope which makes the situation seem to them so depressing and makes it difficult for Brüning [the chancellor]* to keep them in hand.[1]

Tourism was badly hit, with holiday resorts recording a 30 per cent drop in visitors during the summer of 1930. The Depression caused similar problems across Europe but Germans felt particularly aggrieved since they bore the additional burden of reparations. Furthermore, the increase in private motor travel meant that in places where once visitors

---

* Heinrich Brüning (1885–1970) was chancellor, 1930–1932.

had spent a week they now stayed only a few hours. But the biggest threat to traditional travel was the sudden growth of organised tourism. For although the new charabancs (early motor coaches) enabled many more people to visit Germany, the groups they transported spent substantially less per head than did the individual traveller. Southern Germany, with its many tourist attractions, among them Bayreuth (home of Wagner's Festspielhaus) and Oberammergau with its world-famous Passion Play, was less affected than the north. In Bavaria, so the *Observer* reported, 'excellent fare, and friendly treatment in the gaily painted houses are offered at moderate prices', unlike the 'so-called weekend resorts around Berlin which have never recovered from the unpleasant effects of the new-rich in the inflation period'.[2] But if the stream of foreign tourists slowed markedly during the early 1930s, German innovation, skills and culture continued to attract businessmen, scientists, intellectuals – and eccentrics. 'At 4 o'clock Eric Gill* arrived,' Kessler recorded in his diary, 'at once drawing attention to himself at the station on account of his extraordinary garb: knee-length stockings, a kind of short black cowl, and a stridently colourful scarf'.[3]

Certainly there was no shortage of visitors flowing through the British Embassy. Most were warmly welcomed – others less so. 'Here we flourish,' wrote Lady Rumbold,

> and are greatly pleased with the ball last night, which went with great pep. We must have been well over 600 so it was a *marvellous* feeling to have done off such a crowd!

---

* Eric Gill (1882–1940) was a British sculptor and printmaker, closely associated with the Arts and Crafts movement.

It was rather 'historic', as it was the first time that Naval and Military officers had come since 1914 ... Edgar Wallace was one of the personages who came, a horribly common man, with a most unpleasing face. Still it rather thrilled people to meet him.[4]

But if the creator of *King Kong* failed to please Lady Rumbold (Wallace's publishers claimed that, at the time, a quarter of all books read in England were written by him), she was entranced with Amy Johnson, the twenty-seven-year-old aviator who only the previous year had made history by flying solo to Australia in her Gipsy Moth, *Jason*. Greeted in Sydney as 'the little woman of whom the Empire is so proud', she was now a reluctant world celebrity. Longing to escape the pressures of public life, she arrived in Berlin from Cologne one night in early January 1931, en route to Warsaw, Moscow and, she hoped, ultimately Peking. Despite it being the depths of winter, she planned to fly along the trans-Siberian railway some 4,000 miles all the way to China. To the Rumbolds it seemed nothing short of suicide. 'She started off into the blue not having made any arrangements of any kind,' noted an incredulous Sir Horace. 'She knows no language but her own, is carrying English pound notes and had not got detailed scale maps.'[5] The utter folly of Amy's mission aroused his wife's maternal instincts:

Such a dear little thing; looks anything but strong, has a soft gentle voice and manner. She was dreadfully tired and cold on arrival having lost her way and flown for 1½ hours in the dark. One had such a feeling of wanting to protect her from herself, she seemed so young and rather pathetic, not a *bit* an upstanding strong-minded wench. She looked

so neat in her green leather flying costume, and out of a
tiny suitcase she produced a charming dark blue afternoon
frock, her one change.

Amy set off for Warsaw the next morning with only a thermos
of hot tea and a packet of sandwiches but she was at least
equipped with a Russian fur-lined helmet – given her by the
Embassy chaplain. 'I do hope she will come back,' commented
Lady Rumbold.*

A few weeks later, on 9 March 1931, Charlie Chaplin
arrived in Berlin to promote his last and most successful silent
movie – *City Lights*. 'Your mother wouldn't rest until she got
hold of him,' Rumbold wrote to Constantia, 'and he is coming to dine and do a play with us tonight. We shall attract a
lot of attention.'[6] He was right. The Pathé News clip reporting Chaplin's arrival in Berlin bore the caption: 'Kings might
almost envy reception delirious crowds gave famous screen
comedian.' Thousands of people lined the streets all the way
from Friedrichstrasse station to the Adlon Hotel, where he
stayed in the royal suite as a guest of honour. However, not
all those greeting him were friendly. In the mistaken belief
that Chaplin was Jewish, Nazis gathered outside the Adlon
to yell abuse at him, while a group of communists threatened to smash the Adlon's windows if he didn't receive their

* Lady Rumbold to her mother, 7 January 1931. After becoming lost
on her way to Warsaw, Amy Johnson made a forced landing in fog.
She then travelled to Moscow by train where she was a great success.
She never reached Peking but in July 1931 she and her co-pilot Jack
Humphreys became the first pilots to fly from London to Moscow in
one day. Flying across Siberia, they then set the record for the fastest
flight from Britain to Japan.

delegation.[7] The Nazi rhetoric was echoed in the National
Socialist newspaper, *Der Angriff*, edited by Goebbels, which
called him the 'Jew Chaplin' whose 'typically Jewish screen
figure was leading German youth away from the heroic
ideal of the manly German Siegfried', thus 'undermining the
future of the German race'.[8] Such was the virulence of the
Nazi campaign that Chaplin left Berlin early, missing the premiere of his film.

If the British and Americans were relatively popular in
Germany during the Weimar years, the French were emphatically not. Indeed, when it came to apportioning blame for
their misfortunes, many Germans believed that France lagged
not far behind the Jews or the government. It was fortunate,
therefore, that André François-Poncet, the French ambassador,
was a man of cheerful disposition. He arrived in Berlin on
21 September 1931, just one week before his prime minister, Pierre Laval, and foreign minister, Aristide Briand, who
were making the first official visit to Berlin of any leading
French statesman since the time of Napoleon. Everyone, Lady
Rumbold remarked, was nervous. For it was clear that, despite
the best efforts of politicians on both sides, relations between
France and Germany remained as strained as ever and that
neither public nor press had any appetite for détente. After a
banquet at the French Embassy, 'a muffled noise rose from the
street', recorded François-Poncet. 'Going out onto the balcony
we saw a small group of people milling about in the square.
Suddenly a cry rose, uttered in French. We thought we understood – "*Sauvez-nous!* Save us!" But Briand, whose ear was still
keen and whose mind was still shrewd, set us right. "No," he
explained. "That voice said "*Sauvez-vous!* Get out of here!""[9]

Lady Rumbold did not much approve of the French either:

> I was a bit tired dining out last night at the French Embassy, a tiny dinner to sample various champagnes. The French Ambassador is a tremendous talker and not endowed with much tact. Horace was not very happy with some of his remarks considering there were 2 Germans there. There is something I don't quite like about the French. I think they have too good an opinion of themselves, rather like cheeky little boys.[10]

Two months earlier Ramsay MacDonald – by now prime minister – and the foreign secretary, Arthur Henderson, had also made their way to Berlin but to a very different welcome. 'The Prime Minister was heartily cheered,' Rumbold recorded with satisfaction. 'I noticed a number of Nazis in the crowd, who gave him the Fascist salute. When I came along, a man in the crowd shouted: "*Es lebe der Englische Botschafter. Hoch!* [Long live the British Ambassador]" whereupon the big crowd cheered heartily. I must say I never expected to be cheered by a German crowd.'[11]

The British and French ministers visited Germany at a time of acute economic distress. The failure of an Austrian bank in May 1931 had triggered a financial collapse across Europe, intensifying the already severe depression. Misery and fear multiplied, adding yet more grist to the fascist mill. '*What* unpleasing times these are,' wrote Lady Rumbold. 'And when I think of the heavy monthly account to be paid on October 1st with the £ down yesterday to 13/6d, I feel distinctly gloomy.'[12] As usual, she blamed the French.

At the mercy of fluctuating currencies, travellers now frequently found themselves stranded without enough money to get home. Even affluent young men like Tony Rumbold's Oxford friends would turn up unexpectedly at the Embassy unable to afford a hotel. Tom Mitford was studying German law at Berlin University. That November in a letter to his cousin, Randolph Churchill, he wrote: 'People are feeling the desperate situation at last and very little money is wasted on unnecessary pleasures.' He added, 'You might, if you feel inclined, send me the £10 you owe me, as I am finding life expensive with the very adverse exchange.'[13]

Cash, however, was not a problem for Lady (Nancy) Astor MP and George Bernard Shaw. Despite their differing political views, the two were close friends and, as with so many visitors to Berlin, had chosen to spend a couple of days there en route to their real destination – Moscow. Lady Rumbold thought GBS 'not Irish for nothing with his strangely attractive manner, twinkling blue eyes, and a soft burry voice!' and she later read with amusement of the enthusiastic reception he received in Russia from his 'Bolo' friends. Despite diminishing funds, the Rumbolds continued to entertain such visitors in style; however, outside the Embassy everything, Lady Rumbold observed, was paralysed. 'People can't travel or buy anything, and there is great fear of food shortage. Of course they are very nervous remembering the days of the inflation. It all appears quite quiet, but people look sad and worried, and the skies are grey and depressing.'[14]

In March 1932 a presidential election was held. This was an event of real importance because, in reaction to the Weimar government's growing instability, Hindenburg's powers had been significantly increased. He was now able to legislate by decree and dismiss or appoint governments at will. A few weeks before the vote the Rumbolds attended a dinner hosted by the field-marshal who had by then been president for seven years. 'I was glad to have been armed into dinner by the great Hindenburg,' wrote Lady Rumbold. 'It might very well be his last official dinner, as he may not be re-elected as President.' Pitted against the old gentleman were Adolf Hitler and the communist leader Ernst Thälmann. In the end Hindenburg was comfortably re-elected but for those who, like Stephen Spender, hated the 'continual parade of political parties, police and army on the streets', Hitler was an alarmingly strong runner-up. Thanks to the lasting political chaos and public discontent, it was now plain that the Weimar Republic's days were numbered. As Spender later wrote, they had entered the '*Weimardämmerung* [twilight in Weimar]'. 'Tugged by forces within and without, by foreign powers and foreign money-lenders, industrialist plotters, embittered generals, impoverished landed gentry, potential dictators, refugees from Eastern Europe, the government reeled from crisis to crisis, within a permanent crisis.'[15]

The political turmoil (there were twenty-nine different parties in the Reichstag) resulted in five elections that year. After lecturing at Hamburg and Berlin in January, the Conservative MP Bob Boothby told Winston Churchill that the Germans 'are in a hopeless mess. They have no flair for politics; and their parties are a mad jumble of conflicting forces and theories, based on institutions like the Trade Unions and the Catholic Church, which ought to be outside the business altogether.' But he thought the people still 'tremendously formidable', adding, 'I don't blame the French for being frightened.' Unconvinced by Hitler, with whom he had a lengthy interview, Boothby summed up his views on the Germans: 'The two things that impressed me most were their workers' houses which are magnificent; and their orderly desperation.'[16]

Twenty-two-year-old Geoffrey Cox happened to be in Berlin for the July 1932 federal election. Although this gave the Nazis great gains (230 seats) and made their party the largest in the Reichstag, they still did not have a majority. Cox described the lead-up to the election in a letter to his mother:

> Public meetings were banned so there were no big crowds, just many people in the streets buying newspapers and waiting for results. There were plenty of armed police about, and sentries at Hindenburg's door. Occasionally a police car would dash by with a group of police in it holding rifles and bayonets and a bugler blaring furiously for the traffic to clear aside. Afterwards came a whole horde of cars, cycles and motorcycles, all eager to see the fun. I think they rather like all this, though the position is undoubtedly desperate. I give Germany six months more before she either goes communist or [in her determination to expand East] has a war with Poland. The great danger I feel is that the Dictator party will make war as soon as they have got the German army up to strength in order to counter the forces of Communism. It is a hell of a shame as the Germans are such splendid people. Amongst the younger people there is a sort of eager desperation, as they realise that they are going to be the cannon fodder. As one German student said to me 'what are we to do? The only thing is to go to the barricades and fight!'[17]

Cox spent the rest of that summer learning German in the university town of Heidelberg. Set against a backdrop of pine-covered hills, it reminded him of Dunedin in his native New Zealand. He admired the red sandstone ruined castle, the arched bridge over the River Neckar and the old university buildings. 'Even the students appear picturesque. Most of them wear the uniform caps of the various duelling clubs, and a surprisingly large number have sabre scars on their cheeks.' Seen as a mark of class and distinction, fencing scars, particularly among students, had been regarded as a badge of honour since the early nineteenth century. The profusion of music was an additional pleasure:

> The voices of housemaids singing in the morning as they spread mattresses to air over wooden balconies; gramophones in canoes on the river, bands of hikers, mandolins strumming, marching towards the hills; the jazz band in the café in the castle gardens in the evening; strollers singing in deep German voices far into the night. Upstream, where the village of Heilbronn stood red-roofed and white walled on a green hilltop, approached by a white dusty road alongside which the hay was neatly scythed under the apple trees, a little orchestra in the village café played a tune from the stage hit of the day.[18]

It was not just the surrounding landscape that made Cox feel so at home. He was also struck by the informality of the professors he saw walking around the town in their shirtsleeves, carrying their swimming costumes and eating ice cream. 'There is no stand-offishness about these people – none of the master–pupil attitude.' In that last Weimar summer, Cox, together with congenial fellow students and his landlady's granddaughter, swam each morning in the river, picnicked, canoed and played tennis. Only the distant factory chimneys of Mannheim reminded them of the outside world where 'Fascism and Bolshevism and wars and revolutions and crises exist'.[19]

But even in idyllic Heidelberg, Germany's social tensions were plain to see. Cox's landlady, dressed always in black, had lost her husband and all three of her sons in the war. In common with her neighbours, she was crippled financially by taxes and all the usual post-war difficulties. Furthermore, Cox's professor was strongly pro-Nazi. 'When Hitler comes all will be well,' was his regular refrain. Tony Rumbold was also studying German that summer – in Munich. He too was lodged with an impoverished middle-class family but his teacher was no National Socialist. 'Tony's poor little professor spent three weeks in a Nazi prison,'* Lady Rumbold informed her mother. 'He had castor-oil poured down his throat just because he was a Socialist. He is so broke he begged Tony to pay him ten lessons in advance as he has to support his mother.'[20]

Of all the foreigners studying at Heidelberg University in 1932, none was more conspicuous than Milton S. J. Wright, for the simple reason that he was an African-American. He was, as he himself admitted, 'somewhat of a curiosity'. The public was familiar enough with black boxers, jazz-band players and minstrel men but few people in Heidelberg had actually met a black person. And, as Wright pointed out, the concept of 'Negroes as cultural ladies and gentlemen' was to most people completely novel. He remembered how passers-by would often stop to gaze at him, expecting him at any moment to break into a dance. Sometimes he was asked if he was an African prince. In fact, Wright, a Columbia graduate, was at Heidelberg University studying for a PhD in economics. Ten years later, just after Pearl Harbor, he gave an interview to the

---

* It is unclear what exactly Lady Rumbold meant by 'Nazi prison' as she wrote this before the Nazis came to power.

Pittsburgh Courier in which he recounted the extraordinary tale of how he had met Hitler.

Each summer Heidelberg put on a spectacular *son et lumière*. The castle, set high above the River Neckar, was bathed in red 'flames', in memory of its destruction by the French in the seventeenth century. Then, as the lights on the castle faded, the sky was set ablaze with fireworks. In 1932 Milton Wright, together with fellow members of his fraternity, watched the show from the river in a boat decked out with lanterns. When it was over, the crowd sang '*Deutschland über Alles*' before listening to Hitler give one of his customary hate-filled speeches. Afterwards, Wright and his companions adjourned to the Europäischer Hotel where Hitler was staying, and where they had planned to have dinner. But Wright had been spotted. As they entered the dining room, he was accosted by two of Hitler's SS guards, who informed him that the Führer wished to see him. Before entering the room where he was to meet Hitler, Wright gave his passport to one of his friends with instructions to inform the American Consul if he did not re-emerge. He need not have worried. 'The time with Hitler was spent almost entirely by his asking me questions about Negroes in the United States,' Wright recalled. 'Of course I had little opportunity to answer because he would no sooner ask a question than he would immediately proceed to give his own answer.' Despite this, Wright found Hitler unexpectedly courteous. 'It was a bit surprising to me', Wright told the reporter, 'that he seemed to know so much about Negroes in America' – though the only ones he mentioned with any respect were Booker T. Washington and Paul Robeson. Hitler told Wright that he considered 'Negroes' third-class people, destined forever to be slaves of one kind or another, because, Hitler argued, if they had any backbone they would not have allowed the whites to lynch, beat and segregate them without rising up against them. He asked Wright why he wanted 'a white man's education' when he knew that he would never be able to use it like a white man. He suggested that Wright's Heidelberg experience would only make him more miserable once he returned to America. Initially Wright was flattered when Hitler praised his German, telling him that he spoke it better than any American or Englishman he had ever met. However, Hitler then remarked that he had always heard that 'Negroes' were natural born imitators, clearly the reason why Wright had gained such mastery of the 'Master language'.

The American summed up the encounter by recalling how calm Hitler had appeared and how intensely interested he had been in everything Wright had told him. 'Although he spoke loudly, deliberately and with finality, he never lost his poise and composure.' Before dismissing him from his presence, Hitler instructed a bodyguard to give Wright a signed photograph of himself and suggested they meet again in Munich. There is a coda to this odd tale. Wright's PhD was on 'The Economic Development and Native Policy of the Former German Colonies, 1884–1918'. After he returned to America it was translated from the original German into French and English and sent back to Germany. It was then widely circulated throughout Europe by the Nazis as part of their campaign to regain Germany's lost African colonies. One wonders how many of them were aware that its author was black.[21]

In September 1932 Sir Horace's waistline, always a matter of concern, led the senior Rumbolds to spend their last Weimar summer at the Bohemian spa of Marienbad, whose hundred or more natural springs were thought to cure digestive disorders and alleviate rheumatism. 'Horace's cure is going on very well,' Lady Rumbold told her mother, 'he has taken off 12 lbs already.' The spa, dominated by grandiose hotels built in the latter part of the nineteenth century, had long since attracted the rich and famous – Goethe, King Edward VII, Chopin, Wagner and the Emperor Franz Joseph among them. Its popularity had survived the war so that the Rumbolds found themselves taking the waters along with a handful of the English aristocracy, King Alfonso of Spain and Count von Metternich. Presiding over their cure was the 'great doctor', Porges:

> Last night Porges gave a dinner party – a splendid event. We were invited and there were sundry of his patients sitting at his smart and laden table. He made a little speech first, and said that a 'truce' was called and that they could eat and drink and make merry. It is an amusing idea, this happens always in the middle of the cure, for very special patients! He has a rich and rather nice Hebraic wife, and it is very well done.[22]

One patient conspicuously absent from Dr Porges's chosen few was Margaret Sanger, the American birth-control pioneer. She too was at Marienbad that summer, suffering from severe fatigue and a general weakness. 'Here I am,' she wrote to a friend, 'sleeping in Goethe's own room, with his very own stove and clock before me and his portrait and that of his last love's hanging high above me.'[23] Dr Porges injected her ovaries with various substances and gave her a mud-pack to hold against her liver. Like everyone else at the spa, she was expected to drink vast quantities of the horrid-tasting water. Sanger did not hold a high opinion of her fellow patients:

It's amusing to see crowds of grown up fat men & women
walking around to music with green or blue or red glasses
in their hands sucking water out of glass tubes like babies
on their bottles. They are all so ugly looking & so hideous
in shape, I wonder God can make such monstrosities.[24]

One day Lady Rumbold drove over to the nearby spa of
Karlsbad to visit 'some *sad* Spaniards and some equally *sad*
Germans. So strange that both "our" countries should have
fallen on such evil days! [Sir Horace had been ambassador in
Madrid before Berlin.] Some formerly *very* rich Spaniards were
living in a poky and dirty little hotel. We sat in the horrid little
dining-room. The Germans were all right financially but very
bitter and miserable. They both, husband *and* wife, had been in
politics, and he was a popular and well-known man.'[25] However,
there was no sign of economic hardship at the luncheon party
Lady Rumbold hosted for King Alfonso a few days later:

> The lunch was a huge success. King Alfonso in the best of
> moods and full of most amusing anecdotes of King Edward
> and others. Everyone was entranced. Besides, the most deli-
> cious lunch, of *truites au bleu*, partridges, cold ham, peach
> compôte and cheese. The table had red and yellow dahl-
> ias (the Spanish colours) which the King noticed at once,
> and added that the green stood for 'Verde' which Spanish
> Royalists say means 'Viva el Rey de Espana!' So all that was
> good. We then went over to play golf.[26]

While King Alfonso took the waters at Marienbad, Thelma
Cazalet was visiting empty factories and youth unemployment camps in the Rhineland. The latter aimed to provide
short-term, low paid work for those aged between eighteen

and twenty-five. Thelma, like her brother Victor, a Tory MP, was in Germany on a fact-finding tour with a group of fellow parliamentarians. In a few pencil-scribbled lines, she summed up her impressions:

> Germans loathe the Poles – mainly because they are Asiatic. They take for granted we are on their side against the French and feel we could and should take a firmer stand with them. They have no idea about conditions in England. They imagine we have hardly suffered and have forgotten the war. *Very* insensitive as a nation. No doubt Hitler's party has saved Germany from a Socialist/ Communist government by splitting the people up. Nearly all the young are Hitlerites. Germans all assume we shall be on their side in the next war.[27]

Meanwhile, as the Weimar Republic entered its last months, André Gide had not entirely given up hope of a Franco–German reconciliation. In everything that mattered most, he believed Germany was thirty years ahead of France. His fellow country-man, Roger Martin du Gard,* visiting Berlin for the first time in November 1932, was even more enthusiastic. Having made a conscious study of Berlin street-life, he believed that 'the new man, the man of the future, is being created in Germany ... the type of man will arise who will embody the synthesis between past and future, individualism and socialism'.[28]

However, Lady Rumbold's account of the streets that autumn presents a rather different picture: 'Berlin has been

---

* Roger Martin du Gard was awarded the Nobel Prize in Literature in 1937, ten years before his close friend André Gide.

exciting these last days, bristling with police,' she wrote to her mother. 'One would think we were on the verge of a revolution. Two days ago they made a fine to-do up and down the Leipziger Strasse. Not a pane of glass of that huge shop Wertheim is left, and they smashed the windows of most of the shops with Jew names.' It was 'the "Nazis" who do the mischief – a kind of Fascist', she added, in case her mother was not yet familiar with the term. Walking by herself one Sunday from the Embassy to the Schloss, Lady Rumbold rounded a corner to see a 'whole band of Nazis rushing after one miserable Communist, whom they proceeded to batter. There are lorries full of police who go tearing up and down the Linden. So far no shooting, and people seem to be enjoying it. It certainly adds to the amusement of walking out.'[29] But with the appointment of Hitler as chancellor, any 'amusement' turned quickly to horror.

When, even after his July election success, Hitler had still not been offered the chancellorship, Hindenburg famously remarked, 'That man for Chancellor? I'll make him a postmaster and he can lick the stamps with my head on them.'[30] But after six months of political twists and turns, Hindenburg, against his better instincts, was persuaded to change his mind. Shortly after noon on 30 January 1933, the new Reich chancellor, Adolf Hitler, and his cabinet assembled in the president's rooms. Standing before Hindenburg, Hitler swore to uphold the Constitution, to respect the rights of the president and to maintain parliamentary rule. In fact, exactly fifty-two days later, on 23 March, the Enabling Act was passed marking the end of the Weimar Republic. The Act gave Hitler the right to rule without the Reichstag, thus in effect handing him complete power. If his elevation to chancellor did not technically bring an end to the Weimar Republic, the oath he uttered that day was to prove its death rattle.

6

Monster or Marvel?

Writing to Stephen Spender a couple of weeks before Hitler became chancellor, Christopher Isherwood complained how dull German politics had become – 'there is no longer that slightly exhilarating awareness of crisis in the gestures of beggars and tram-conductors'.[1] But whatever else it may have been, the spectacular torchlight procession that followed Hitler's inauguration on 30 January 1933 was not dull. A Nazi extravaganza on the grandest scale, it brought to a climax the day that would change the world for ever.

Constantia Rumbold watched from her bedroom window:

The column of light started like a glittering serpent through the avenues, beneath the Brandenburg Gate, across the Pariser Platz and in to the Wilhelmstrasse. All the youth of Germany was on the march that night. Six abreast they came in their brown shirts, each man carrying a flaming torch and there was no break in the procession for five long hours. The torches cast a weird, pink dancing light over the usually austere grey street and huge distorted shadows played on the walls of houses. Blood red banners splashed

by crooked swastikas fluttered in their hundreds, from vast
ones carried shoulder high by standard bearers to the small-
est paper flags waving in the hands of children.[2]

Venturing outside, she managed to work her way through the
crowds until she stood before the Chancellery where at a window she could see the vast frame of President Hindenburg half
hidden by a curtain. A few hundred yards further on, Hitler
stood rigidly to attention on a balcony – his arm outstretched.
Although he was silhouetted against brilliant light, Constantia
could make out his 'tense face looking as white as his over-large
collar'. Lilian Mowrer remembered the bitter cold; how sparks
from the torches crackled in the frosty air and how during the
endless procession she shifted from one foot to another in a
vain effort to keep warm. Nor would anyone present that night
ever forget the tramping boots and beating drums; the Nazi
marching songs and raucous shouts of '*Deutschland erwache;
Kommen die Juden* [Germany awake; the Jews are coming]'
or the 'triumph rampant on every face'. 'Pressed up against
the houses, jostling each other on the pavements,' Constantia
wrote, 'the women of Germany, the mothers, wives and sisters
of those marching men took up the cries, waving handkerchiefs
and scarves, laughing a little hysterically as they clung to door-
steps and perched on window-sills.'[3]

For the level-headed daughter of a British diplomat, or
for liberal Americans like the Mowrers, it was a disturbing
experience. Aware that this was not a night for a foreigner
to be on the streets, Constantia returned to the Embassy to
find her father sitting alone in a back room, trying to ignore
the clamour outside. As they went upstairs to bed, Sir Horace
wondered where it would all lead. It was a rhetorical question,
for it was clear to Constantia that 'no-one who had witnessed

the soul of Germany marching that night could be in any doubt'.[4] However, it was to be several months before Hitler could enforce his dictatorship. In order to pass the Enabling Act that would give him complete power, he needed a more convincing mandate. A federal election was called for 5 March.

A couple of weeks after Hitler's inauguration, Owen Tweedy and Jim Turcan were driving along a small country road to Bonn in a second-hand Morris bought for £10. They had been friends since Cambridge University, where Tweedy had read modern languages. Both men, now in their mid-forties, had been wounded in the war. Tweedy had subsequently spent many years in the Middle East but was currently earning his living as a freelance journalist based in London. It was in the hope that the new Germany would provide enough copy to interest newspapers such as the *Daily Telegraph* that he had set out on his present mission. The amiable if chaotic Jim had taken leave from his engineering job to keep him company. The two men were in high spirits. It was 'a lovely day, keen, frosty and sunny' and 'as we got near the Rhine', Tweedy wrote in his diary, 'it became very jolly, the villages were homely and pretty and there were good fields, no hedges and lots of trees.' The only jarring note was the election propaganda confronting them at every turn. Tweedy thought the swastika less offensive than the huge ugly lettering used by the communists, sometimes stretching thirty or forty yards along a wall.[5]

But despite the aggressive slogans they were relieved to discover that 'Bonn was still Bonn – clean healthy and somehow buoyant'. The lovely old town of Weilburg, seventy miles to the east, with its narrow twisting streets running up the hillside and timbered houses – their roofs white with snow – was another reassuring reminder of the old Germany, familiar to Tweedy since his schooldays. In Kassel, they found an old inn – 'like the Feathers in Ludlow' – where there was a great fat innkeeper with a great fat wife, jolly servants, cheap rooms, good food and friendly people full of advice on which route they should take.

By the time they reached Kassel they had been in Germany a week but as yet had seen nothing of the terror tactics, the physical violence and intimidation, used by the National Socialists during the election campaign. Indeed, Nazi brutality so effectively silenced all opposition that one British resident, forced to remain anonymous for fear of reprisal, reported in *The Nineteenth Century and After* that it had been left to foreign journalists, mostly American and English, to offer any protest.* 'Hostile criticism from a German', he wrote, 'was suicide – more often economic, sometimes physical.'[6] Yet even those most obviously at risk were totally unprepared for the Nazi onslaught. Abraham Plotkin, an American left-wing activist of Russian-Jewish origins, was astonished by the complacency of his German colleagues. After meeting a number of wealthy Jews in Berlin on 6 February, he wrote in his diary, 'Strange as it may seem and it seemed strange to me, they were not concerned very much now that Hitler has come to the front. Their attitude is that it was bound to come ... and that it is best perhaps that the Hitler fire run its course.'[7]

The following weekend Plotkin and a Dutch trade unionist walked for hours through the woods near Berlin with the president of the German Clothing Workers Union trying hard to convince him of the danger facing the trade unions:

---

* This was the first time in the journal's long history that a contributor had been allowed to remain anonymous.

> I asked a dozen alternative questions – what would happen
> if Hitler did this or did that – to all of which he smiled and
> said that every one of the questions I raised had been fully
> discussed and the possibilities weighed ... Hindenburg
> would not tolerate any dictatorship that was established
> either through sheer terror or through unconstitutional
> means ... Nothing we could and did say disturbed his
> placid calm.[8]

Hitler threw himself into the election campaign, flying all over
the country in his private aeroplane *Richthofen* – then the fastest in Germany. On 23 February, Gareth Jones, along with
Denis Sefton Delmer of the *Daily Express*, stood in the snow
at Tempelhof Airport awaiting the arrival of the new chancellor. The two young men had been invited to accompany Hitler
to a political rally in Frankfurt. While Delmer recorded the
scene with his cine camera, Jones, a bold investigative journalist just back from Russia, jotted down notes: 'Then a cry: "The
Leader is coming." A car drives through the snow. Out steps
a very ordinary looking man. Looks like middle-class grocer.'
Observing Hitler's boyish delight at Goebbels' new car, Jones
was surprised by his relaxed manner: 'Not a poseur, natural,
no tragic gestures.' Half an hour later Jones and Delmer were
6,000 feet above Berlin – the only non-Nazis on the flight. 'If
aeroplane should crash,' Jones scribbled in his notebook, 'the
whole history of Germany would change.' As the Elbe curved
beneath them, he recorded how Hitler – his ears plugged with
cotton wool – studied the map. Goebbels, seated just behind
him, was constantly laughing. Small, dark and with 'remarkably lively eyes', he reminded Jones of a South Wales collier.
'He is to be one of the great figures in Germany. Looks a
"brain," smart.' Meanwhile Hitler's bodyguards, in their black

uniforms embellished with silver skull and cross-bones, were particularly chatty. One of them – 'a tall well-built young man; row of white teeth; like a smart bus driver' – told Jones how only a couple of nights earlier he had picked up a communist protester and 'crashed his skull apart' on a piano. Despite this, Jones noted that he had seen nothing cold about his fellow passengers, 'they could not be more friendly and polite, even if I were a red-hot Nazi myself'.[9]

Four days later, at five past nine on the evening of 27 February, Denis Sefton Delmer, now back in Berlin, received a telephone call from a garage attendant with the startling news that the Reichstag was on fire. Running the mile and a half from his office, he was one of the first to arrive at the burning building, where flames were funnelling up through the great glass dome in a pillar of fire and smoke. 'Every minute fresh trains of fire engines were arriving, their bells clanging as they raced through the streets.' Lady Rumbold and Constantia were driving home after a Beethoven concert conducted by Wilhelm Furtwängler. Seeing the commotion they parked and joined the watching crowds. Delmer, ducking under ropes, managed to reach one of the Reichstag entrances just as Hitler leapt from his car and, followed by Goebbels and his bodyguard, 'dashed up the steps two at a time, the tails of his trench coat flying, his floppy black artist's hat pulled down over his head'. Inside they found Göring – more massive than ever in a camel-hair coat, his legs astride 'like some Frederician guardsman in a UFA film'. He informed Hitler that communists had started the fire and that an arrest had already been made. Delmer followed Hitler and his party into the building: 'Across pools of water, charred debris, and through clouds of evil smelling smoke we made our way through rooms and corridors. Someone opened a yellow, varnished door, and for a moment we peeped into the blazing furnace of the debating chamber. It was like opening the door of an oven.' Hitler then turned to him and said, 'God grant that this be the work of the communists. You are now witnessing the beginning of a great new epoch in German history, Herr Delmer. This fire is the beginning.'[10]

'Heavens! What a place this is for alarms and excursions,' wrote Lady Rumbold a few hours later.[11] Summing up popular reaction to the catastrophe, she reported to her mother that, although it was unlikely anyone would ever get to the bottom of it, most people, even Hitler's supporters, assumed the fire had been started by the Nazis themselves in order to discredit the communists before the election.*

The day before the Reichstag went up in flames, Tweedy and Turcan found themselves at a 'terribly smart *thé dansant* [tea dance]' in Lübeck's best hotel – the Stadt Hamburg. They had arrived there looking like 'a pair of soiled Rip Van Winkles' after visiting one of the much-lauded labour camps for the unemployed, deep in the frozen countryside. The camp – a long low building like an overturned boat – reminded Tweedy of Peggotty's house in *David Copperfield*. After seeing all over it and inspecting one of its neat clean dormitories, 'looking rather like a left-luggage office', they had been invited to lunch. At a blast from the leader's whistle, everyone stood up and sang a medieval marching song – 'Never Say Die'. Unappetising

---

* Fritz Tobias convincingly argues in his book, *The Reichstag Fire: Legend and Truth* (1963), that the Nazis were not in fact responsible for burning the Reichstag and that Marinus van der Lubbe, the Dutchman who was executed for the crime, committed it single-handedly on his own initiative.

soup of cocoa and sago was followed by hefty helpings of
potatoes and gravy, a little meat and half a pickled cucum-
ber. The plight of the young men depressed Tweedy. 'It seems
terribly hard that those boys for whom life should be just
beginning are actually in a dead end.' However, the drive to
Lübeck soon restored his spirits. The unmade road took them
through charming villages whose mellow red brick houses cast
long shadows across the snow in the fading light. Lübeck, with
its ravishing fourteenth-century streets, spires and gables, was
a treat – 'the best medieval town I have ever visited', noted
Tweedy.

The following day they set off on the 180-mile journey to
Berlin. Bored by the 'deadly dull' north German landscape and
the road stretching to infinity, they decided to spend the night
at the small town of Ludwigslust. Next morning as they were
leaving, the landlady appeared in a state of great excitement
having just heard news of the Reichstag fire – '*Alles ist veloren
in Berlin* [All is lost in Berlin],' she cried, wringing her hands.
'*Es brennt uberall!* [It is burning everywhere!]' 'Would we be
held up?' Tweedy wondered. 'Was this the beginning of more
things?' Forty miles from Berlin they lunched in a small village
where gossip was rife. Hitler was on the warpath; communists
had started the fire; their leaders were all under lock and key;
Berlin was under martial law. 'Good luck to you. Because you
are English you might get through. But if you don't, come
back here. Our beds are good, our food excellent.' They drove
cautiously to Spandau, about ten miles west of the city centre.
All was calm. Then on to Charlottenburg, the Tiergarten and
finally the Brandenburg Gate where they found nothing more
threatening than heavy traffic.

On 2 March, three days before the election, Tweedy was
introduced to the Taverne – a small restaurant well known

as the favourite haunt of Berlin's foreign correspondents. The low, smoky rooms, filled with wooden benches and long tables, reeked of wine, beer and coffee. A roar of conversation drowned out the orchestra.[12] Each night the journalists gathered there to pool news of the latest atrocities. Robert Bernays, a recently elected Liberal MP, at first thought the conspiratorial atmosphere of the Taverne faintly absurd until he realised that the correspondents really were in danger, not least from trumped-up charges of espionage. They did not, however, impress Tweedy – 'a rather grumpy, messy lot reminding me of Bloomsbury at its worst'. More fun was the party he attended at the Egyptian Embassy where, among the Bolivians, Swiss, Swedes and Americans, was a Finnish lady 'looking exactly like a pat of butter'. At another party they met 'Hitler's principal ADC – a dashing and ornamental fellow, rather like a top-heavy Michaelmas daisy in Naval uniform'.*

Their first encounter with the dark side of the new Germany took place on the eve of the election when they saw a boy beaten and kicked by a troop of Nazis. 'We were scared stiff and fled at full speed,' Tweedy recorded. 'We were thankful when the doors of the hotel closed safely behind us.' As another British visitor in Berlin during the election campaign put it, 'Fear made cowards of us all.'[13]

Hitler's success at the poll on 5 March came as no surprise. Tweedy listened to the results on the wireless in the crowded lobby of the hotel. 'There was no real excitement and no applause. Hitler won all along and that was that.' A

---

* Identified as Ernst 'Putzi' Hanfstaengl. Half American, he had been educated at Harvard and was a close friend of Hitler. In 1933 he was head of the Foreign Press Bureau.

week later Tweedy was expressing astonishment at the breath-taking change in so short a time. 'The election has completely altered Germany both outwardly and inwardly so much that it is hard to realise that we are in the same country that we entered a month ago. The Nazis are out-fascismising Fascismo.' Two days later they left Berlin, thankful to escape the post-election turmoil.

By now Tweedy, like many other foreigners, was thoroughly confused. There was much to dislike about this uncouth new society yet was he being too critical? After all, Hitler was 'not a bad man'. True, he had a streak of 'hysterical madness', but hadn't every great movement been the inspiration of an eccentric? In the preceding weeks, Tweedy had conducted countless interviews with people from every conceivable background. Many were hostile to Hitler but many more were seduced by the new 'faith'. It was 'buoyant, exciting and alive. It was not patronising. It broke down social barriers, provided pageantry and stimulus.' It was, in a nutshell, a new gospel. Furthermore, wrote Tweedy, 'the police are quite charming'.

Because the Reichstag lay in ruins, the opening of Parliament took place in the Garrison Church at Potsdam on 21 March before the tomb of Frederick the Great. The diplomatic corps was there in force. 'We were beautifully placed in a gallery facing the President's chair,' recorded Lady Rumbold, 'so we saw and heard marvellously. I must say the organisation was *perfect*, not a hitch anywhere and everything up to time.' Behind the emperor's empty chair sat the crown prince, while the gallery above was filled with old generals and admirals – 'an *impressive* sight in their field-grey uniforms and decorations'. In the body of the church was a great mass of SA [storm trooper] brown shirts. Lady Rumbold described how 'Hitler, looking more than ever like Charlie Chaplin [*The Great Dictator* was not screened until 1940], sat on the edge of his chair, rather small and pathetic in his little black frock coat.'[14] That evening another colossal torchlight parade almost prevented the Rumbolds from reaching the State Opera House where Nazis were gathering *en masse* for a gala performance of Wagner's *Die Meistersinger*.

By then, Tweedy and Turcan had reached Jena – 'a charming old-world town'. They were staying in an inn ('very like the Red Lion in Cambridge') that was crowded with Nazi supporters celebrating the opening of the Reichstag:

> Our fellow roisterers were great fun. The Weal Shooting Club literally pouring beer down their necks, old ladies with far away looks thinking of the good old days which now might return, students, whole families and one girl in a sort of Nazi uniform. It was terribly noisy but good fun and very good-tempered.

Two days later, on 24 March, Hindenburg signed the Enabling Act handing Hitler all the powers he had so persistently sought. With the Reichstag now redundant, the last flicker of democracy had been snuffed out.

After the election the weather turned unusually mild – 'Hitler's weather,' remarked the porter's wife at Isherwood's lodging-house on Nollendorfstrasse, which, like all the other streets in Berlin, was now swamped with swastikas. It was unwise not to display them, Isherwood noted. It was also unwise not to step aside for uniformed Nazis, or to refuse them donations when they entered restaurants and cinemas rattling their collection boxes. It was impossible to escape the loudspeakers blaring out speeches by Göring and Goebbels – '*Deutschland erwacht* [Germany awake]'.

Soon the boy bars began to disappear. The more intelligent boys went to ground while 'the silly ones fluttered around town exclaiming how sexy the storm troopers looked in their uniforms'.[15] As it was common knowledge that the SA leader, Ernst Röhm, was homosexual, the more optimistic in the gay community must have felt that their time had come. But within weeks hundreds were murdered or incarcerated – 'for their own protection' – in the newly opened concentration camp at Dachau.

The persecution of homosexuals was, however, a sideshow compared with that of the Jews. On the morning of 1 April, storm troopers all over Germany took up positions in front of Jewish shops, blocking their entrances. They held placards exclaiming '*Deutschland erwache: die Juden sind unser Unglück* [Germans awake: the Jews are our disaster]'. The previous day, while filling his Morris with petrol near Leipzig, Tweedy had noticed a lorry crammed with household goods at the adjacent pump. Talking to the owner, he discovered that he and his wife were 'Jews on the flit'. After months of intimidation they had decided to cut their losses, shut up shop and head for Switzerland. Their story, soon to become so commonplace, struck Tweedy at the time as 'odd but eloquent'. By now he had experienced quite enough of Nazi Germany to realise that 'the Jews are for it'. After listening to a broadcast detailing the meticulously planned boycott, he wrote, 'This is one of the few occasions when I have sympathy with Jewry.' Less than a month since the election, Tweedy had learned enough about Hitler's Germany to make sure that before submitting his luggage to examination by the border police he had obliterated the names of all the people recorded in his diary.

Thankful now to be leaving Germany, Tweedy did not stay to see the full effect of the boycott. Lady Rumbold did. 'It was utterly cruel and Hunnish,' she wrote to her mother.[16] In Berlin, all along Kurfürstendamm, the city's most famous shopping street, the windows were plastered with bright yellow posters bearing a similar message, many embellished with a caricature of a Jewish nose. A number of foreigners defiantly turned out to shop in the empty Jewish stores. Lilian Mowrer went on a spree in the Kaufhaus des Westens, while Isherwood chose to shop in Israel's. At the entrance he recognised a boy from the Cosy Corner, now a brown-shirted storm trooper. It soon became clear to foreigners that many of their German acquaintances, whatever their former political views, were signing up with the Nazis, simply to survive. In May, just before he left Berlin for good, Isherwood wrote of his landlady:

> Already she is adapting herself, as she will adapt herself to every new regime. This morning I even heard her talking reverently about 'Der Führer' to the porter's wife. If anybody were to remind her that, at the elections last November, she voted communist, she would probably deny it hotly, and in perfect good faith. She is merely acclimatizing herself, in accordance with a natural law, like an animal which changes its coat for the winter.[17]

James Grover McDonald, chairman of the Foreign Policy Association and soon to become the League of Nations Commissioner for Refugees Coming from Germany, arrived in Berlin from America a couple of days after the boycott. Tall and fair, McDonald recorded in his diary how the Nazis regarded him as an ideal specimen of Nordic superiority. Why, then, they repeatedly asked, did he not share their racial

beliefs? 'But surely you, a perfect Aryan, could not be unsym-
pathetic to our views?' remarked one economist. Germany, it
was explained, was 'fighting the battle of the white race' and
doing so without any help from the decadent French, who
were 'becoming Negroid', or from the Americans whose own
need of purification was so obvious. McDonald was urged to
attend a Nazi funeral so that he might see for himself the
new morality in action. No one any longer took notice of
the 'drooling' priest but when the Nazi official snapped
to attention, saluted and spoke, a thrill went through the
crowd. 'That is spiritual leadership.'[18] On 7 April Hitler told
McDonald in a private interview, 'I will do the thing that the
rest of the world would like to do. It doesn't know how to get
rid of the Jews. I will show them.'[19]

But, as McDonald soon discovered, anti-Semitism was not
confined to National Socialists. Travelling by train from Berlin
to Basle, he talked with a fellow passenger he took to be a
salesman. Although not a Nazi, the latter's views were clear:
'The Jew is the bacillus corrupting the German blood and
race. Once a Jew always a Jew, he cannot pass from one kind
of animal to another. The Jews are but 1% of the German
population but they have dominated our culture. That cannot
be tolerated,' he said, adding rather curiously, 'They are not so
serious in their effect on the Latin races as on the Germans.'[20]

For all the foreigners, mainly journalists, who tried in the first
months of the Third Reich to expose the true nature of the
Nazi revolution, there were plenty of others ready to praise
it. To them, Hitler was a visionary; an inspired leader who, at
a time when so many other nations languished, was putting
his people back to work, creating exciting new infrastructure

and, most evident of all, restoring his country's pride. Prior to Hitler's takeover, the number of foreign visitors to Germany had been dropping. But now, those with professional interest began to return, eager to see for themselves the nascent Third Reich and to make up their own minds about the mixed messages coming out of it. Was it a modern Utopia that other countries should be striving to emulate; or was it, as so many newspapers would have them believe, a horror-show of brutality, repression and anti-Semitism?

A British academic, Philip Conwell-Evans, was among the regime's earliest apologists, although, as Karina Urbach points out in her book *Go-Betweens for Hitler*, it is even now not clear whether Conwell-Evans was a genuine Nazi supporter or working for British intelligence.[21] At the beginning of 1933 he was teaching diplomatic history at Königsberg University, where the philosopher Kant had spent most of his life. Given Königsberg's position as capital of East Prussia and its proximity to Poland and the Baltic States, it was hardly surprising that his students took a keen interest in foreign affairs. 'They sit round a table in the corridor at four o'clock every day and we have vigorous discussions on current events,' recorded Conwell-Evans. He never denied Nazi violence, but, like so many other pro-German commentators, was convinced that the press grossly exaggerated it. By emphasising the street brawls and beatings, newspapers gave their readers the false impression that such behaviour was integral to National Socialism when in fact, Conwell-Evans wrote, 'only a very small minority of roughs bring the movement into disgrace in these ways. The vast majority are animated by idealism and a desire for sacrifice and service on behalf of the community.'[22] Like many on the right, Conwell-Evans felt deep kinship with the Germans. It was commendable to support the Nazis not just because Hitler was reversing the injustices of the Versailles treaty, but because of shared blood. Instead of squabbling over such minor issues as 'the Jewish question' or a few disaffected radicals, Britons and Americans should be standing shoulder to shoulder with their Anglo-Saxon German brothers, ready to fight the common enemy – communism.

Unlike Conwell-Evans, Robert Bernays was a fierce critic of National Socialism. Nevertheless he too was impressed by the steely focus of the Nazi students whom he made a point of meeting while on a short, exploratory visit to Germany. One young man invited him to his room at Berlin University. The room, Bernays remarked, was itself an encapsulation of the movement. Although bare and crude, each article in it had special significance – especially the enormous map of Germany on the wall and a list of the confiscated colonies marked in red. The sole photograph in the room was of Hitler, and the only furniture a deal table and two hard-backed chairs. In one corner stood climbing equipment, in another a duelling outfit. The only other items in the room were a wireless set and a row of beer mugs – trophies of student drinking bouts. As Bernays observed, a film producer trying to illustrate the rise of the Nazis could not have invented a more convincing stage set.[23]

Evelyn Wrench, chairman of *The Spectator* and another early visitor to Hitler's Germany, travelled there determined 'to understand the other fellow's point of view'. Although condemning unreservedly the regime's treatment of Jews, he tried to put it in context. On returning to England in April, he reported that many of his German friends were convinced that their government's anti-Semitism would soon pass. They had been keen to remind Wrench that Germany had just undergone an almost bloodless revolution and, naturally at such times, 'as you English know from history', regrettable things happened. Reflecting on the Black and Tans' conduct in Ireland in 1920, Wrench – ever the pourer of oil on troubled waters – readily acknowledged that it was not just in Germany that such unpleasantness occurred. The anti-Jewish campaign, he concluded, was caused by a widespread (and, by inference, a not unreasonable) sense that, at a time of high unemployment and economic hardship, 'the Jew has got a disproportionate share of the "plums"'. Despite having heard in Berlin youths cry out '*Juden verrecke* [death to the Jews]', Wrench returned to England convinced that the German government was on the brink of dropping its anti-Semitic crusade. 'The best service we can do the Jews in Germany', he argued, 'is to try and maintain an impartial attitude towards Germany and show that we are really desirous of understanding German aspirations.'[24]

Others recently returned from observing the Third Reich's first weeks agreed, just as they also recognised Conwell-Evans's glowing account. Memories of generous hospitality, neat clean houses, intense land cultivation, colourful window-boxes, mugs of foaming beer and, above all, Germany's reinvigorated youth, far outweighed the odd encounter with brown-shirted aggression. 'Spring is in the air,' wrote American playwright Martin Flavin in March 1933:

> The buds are cracking out. It is wholly and completely lovely. There is no superficial aspect of distress of any kind. Beautiful and quiet countryside – in the cities you could hear a pin drop. Frankfurt (where this is written) is possibly the loveliest small city in the world. Perhaps I have a weakness for Germany and Germans. Cleanliness, efficiency, capacity, order, I like these things. And *youth* and *strength* I like, and the fine fact or illusion of *going somewhere* – of having *an objective* – and the tragic nature of their plight

appeals to me – this pitiful too lateness and pathetic struggle to catch up; – and (gorgeous irony) to catch up with
something which may be quite possibly already done and
waiting only for that thick black cloud which hovers in
the Eastern sky.[25]

However, Goebbels' next propaganda stunt must have given
even enthusiasts pause for thought. The ceremonial burning of
books in Germany's thirty-odd university towns laid bare Nazi
intentions, recalling Heinrich Heine's famous words: '*Dort, wo
man Bücher verbrennt, verbrennt man am Ende auch Menschen*
[Where they burn books, they will end by burning people].'

Sixteen-year-old Dymphna Lodewyckx had recently
arrived in Munich from Australia to spend a year studying at
one of the city's high schools. She soon became used to heiling Hitler before and after each lesson, and writing essays on
such topics as, 'How can German girls serve our nation?' On
10 May she was with her mother in the crowd watching the
'lovely torchlight procession of gorgeously arrayed students
parading through the floodlit city'. When the students reached
the Königsplatz they lit a great bonfire. Around it, thousands
of books – condemned as degenerate or 'un-German' – lay
waiting to be flung on the flames. For Dymphna, too young
perhaps to grasp the full significance of the event, 'the flickering torches, blazing books, glaring flares and decorative
students' were 'awe-inspiring'.[26] But it is hard to understand
how an academic like Conwell-Evans (who held a doctorate
from Oxford University) could have viewed such barbarism
with equanimity. 'I was an interested witness of the burning of
the books by the [Königsberg] university,' he wrote, as if commenting on a football match. By noting that burning books in
Germany was a tradition started by Luther, and that 'it was of

course more symbolic than comprehensive',[27] he sought to give a shocking act some semblance of respectability – a tactic often deployed in the coming years by Hitler's foreign defenders.

Meanwhile in Berlin the incineration was carried out on a massive scale. A crowd of forty thousand gathered in the square between the university and the opera house to watch the spectacle. Along five miles of streets students, their torches held aloft, escorted the trucks and cars that had been requisitioned to transport the condemned books. Frederick Birchall of the *New York Times* described the scene:

> All the student corps were represented – red caps and green caps, purple and blue, with a chosen band of officers of the duelling corps in plush tam o'shanters, white breeches, blue tunics and high boots – with spurs. Bearing banners and singing Nazi songs and college melodies, they arrive. It was towards midnight when they reached the great square. There, on a granite block of pavement protected by a thick covering of sand, had been built up a funeral pyre of crossed logs some twelve feet square and five feet high.

Naturally, Lady Rumbold and Constantia were there, on this occasion escorted by three stalwart young diplomats. Constantia described how the students threw their flaming torches on to the pyre as they filed past. Soon it was a roaring blaze with huge tongues of flame shooting up into the sky. Lady Rumbold, who thought the students quite demented and 'wanting in a sense of humour', wondered why, as they were destroying Jewish literature so enthusiastically, they did not burn the Bible as well – 'it would be logical'.[28] They listened to the students' president, in full

Nazi regalia, urging his fellow students to protect the purity of German literature. As their books were committed to the flames, the guilty authors were named: 'Sigmund Freud – for falsifying our history and degrading its great figures', Erich Maria Remarque (author of *All Quiet on the Western Front*) – 'for degrading the German language and the highest patriotic idea'; the list seemed endless. In addition to Jewish writers, figures such as Thomas Mann (winner of the Nobel Prize in Literature in 1929), Helen Keller and Jack London were among the damned. Papers and books ransacked from Dr Magnus Hirschfeld's Institute of Sexual Science were pitched on to the fire with particular fervour. Then came the climax when at midnight Goebbels mounted a rostrum and declared, 'Jewish intellectualism is dead ... the German soul can again express itself.'

As bonfires burned all over the country, Birchall finished his piece for the *New York Times*: 'There is going up in smoke more than college boy prejudice and enthusiasm,' he wrote. 'A lot of the old German liberalism – if any was left – was burned tonight.'[29] Hitler had been in power exactly one hundred days.

7

Summer Holidays

By the summer of 1933 the confusion surrounding the Nazi revolution had deepened. While those travellers with entrenched political views – right or left – found ample proof to support their respective agendas, many others returned home not knowing what to believe. Was the implementation of socialist principles inspired by idealism or dictatorship? Were voluntary labour camps genuine philanthropy or a front for something more sinister? Were the endless marching bands, swastikas and uniforms joyful expression of restored national pride or harbinger of renewed aggression? Even the politically sophisticated found Hitler's Germany ambiguous. As for reports of people taken from their homes in the middle of the night, of torture and intimidation, many foreigners simply looked the other way, hoping that if they focused on the positive in National Socialism, the nastier aspects might soon disappear. It was much harder to ignore the persecution of Jews. But then many foreign visitors to Germany in 1933 were themselves anti-Semitic, if only casually. To them, the discomfiture of a few Jews seemed a small price for the restoration of a great nation – a nation, moreover, that was Europe's chief bulwark against communism.

However, French left-wing journalist Daniel Guérin had no doubts about the true nature of Nazi Germany. In May he set out to bicycle from Cologne to Leipzig via Hamburg and Berlin. Only the year before he had been on a long walking tour through what was then the Weimar Republic, so was well qualified to chart the changes that had taken place in the short time since Hitler had assumed power. He found them devastating:

> For a socialist Germany beyond the Rhine was like exploring a city in ruins after an earthquake. Here only a short time ago was the headquarters of a political party, a trade union, a newspaper, over there was a workers' bookstore. Today enormous swastika banners hang from these buildings. This used to be a Red street; they knew how to fight here. Today one meets only silent men, their gazes sad and worried, while the children shatter your eardrums with their 'Heil Hitlers!'[1]

Only one year before, the Essen youth hostel had been full of peaceful backpackers. Now it overflowed with young Nazis in boots and belts – 'the tie of the Hitler Youth lying across their khaki shirts like a black stain'. On his previous visit Guérin had listened to Bohemian songs sung softly to guitars. This time 'The Storm Troopers are on the March' and 'Hitler's Flag Calls Us to Battle' were bellowed out in a suffocating room that reeked of sweat and leather. But, as Guérin noted, 'When you sing in chorus you don't feel hunger; you aren't tempted to seek out the *how* and *why* of things. You must be right since there are fifty of you side by side, crying out the same refrain.' When he did challenge one Hitler Youth, the young man's only response was: 'Look, haven't we saved the planet from Bolshevism?'[2]

It was a claim, endlessly repeated by the Nazis, that resonated with many foreigners, especially the likes of Lieutenant
Colonel Sir Thomas Moore MP, who had served two years in
Russia immediately after the Revolution. He travelled regularly to Germany in the 1930s and after meeting Hitler for
the first time, in September 1933, wrote, 'If I may judge from
my personal knowledge of Herr Hitler, peace and justice are
the keywords of his policy.'[3] Moore's hatred of communism
was extreme, but the political views of Sir Maurice Hankey,
cabinet secretary to the British government since 1916, were
a model of measured judgement. Yet even he assumed that the
astonishing renewal of confidence he and his wife observed
everywhere, as they drove through Germany that August (singing Bach chorales), was a result of Hitler having delivered the
country from Bolshevism.

It was a theory bluntly rejected by Sir Eric Phipps,
Rumbold's successor as British ambassador. He maintained
that Hitler had vastly overplayed the communist card but had
done so to great effect. The Nazis knew perfectly well that
the threat had in fact been minimal, but by harping on it ad
nauseam had succeeded not only in brainwashing the German
public but convincing many foreigners that the Führer had
single-handedly prevented the 'red tide' from sweeping across
Germany and the West.[4]

Although Hankey insisted that his only motive in going to
Germany was to have a holiday, feedback from his trip was naturally taken very seriously in Whitehall. He soon realised that,
despite the intense campaign to ensure that every German
citizen, high school, university, government office and institution devoutly embrace Nazi doctrine, enthusiasm for it differed
noticeably from one *Land* [region] to another. The citizens
of Baden-Württemberg, for instance, still clung to a liberal

tradition that in some respects had more in common with France than Prussia. In towns like Darmstadt, Heidelberg and Karlsruhe the Hankeys spotted many fewer swastikas on the houses and cars. Dresden, with its stubbornly 'Red' reputation, was another city where support for Hitler was far from universal. As for the Rhineland, Hankey thought it a particularly prosperous and cheerful region – a view shared by Nora Waln, the best-selling American writer who lived in Bonn during the mid-1930s. National Socialism had arrived relatively late in the Rhineland and even then was tempered by Catholicism and by fear that any overt display of militarism might provoke another French invasion. 'These Rhinelanders have wine in their veins, not blood,' a Berlin friend told Waln shortly after her arrival. 'They care more about carnival than politics.' He made clear that as soon as Germany reoccupied the Rhineland this attitude would have to change, adding ominously, 'Their life and vigour must be harnessed more practically to the service of the State.'[5]

But despite such regional variation, there was in the summer of 1933 no escaping the overwhelming Nazi presence throughout Germany. 'Looking back,' Hankey concluded a few weeks later, 'the impression I have is that of a non-stop pageant; incessant marching and counter-marching by the Nazis; brass bands; singing, not musical, but of a jerky, staccato kind; patrols; Fascist salutes; khaki uniforms everywhere.' The whole country, he reported, was in a state of extraordinary exaltation. 'Hitler has put us on the up-grade again' was a phrase constantly repeated to him by everyone from prominent lawyers to garage attendants.

The willingness of the middle class to accept the extra burdens imposed on them by the Nazis surprised him. Women too seemed happy to give up the freedoms that they had so recently won under the Weimar government. Not only were they now discouraged from working, but they were also heavily censured if they smoked in public or wore make-up. Nevertheless, in general, everyone seemed remarkably prepared to make any sacrifice demanded of them provided, Hankey noted, it was in the interests of the German people. And it was by no means all sacrifice. He reported the shops full of goods, the trams spick and span, hot water flowing in hotel bedrooms, and everywhere well-dressed people consuming vast quantities of beer and wine. It was, he remarked, 'as if the whole of Germany was on holiday'.[6]

No foreign traveller in Germany in 1933, however unobservant, could fail to notice the extraordinary extent to which the young were caught up in the Nazi movement, whether signed up with the SA, SS, Hitler Youth or voluntary labour. After closely observing them for three weeks, Hankey felt he better understood French paranoia since it seemed impossible that these ardent, disciplined youths would not demand weapons at the first sign of trouble. And, given the speed with which this could be accomplished, there was no doubt in his mind that 'Hitler had sown the dragon's teeth'.[7]

The parades, ceremonies, bands and saluting used so effectively to prime young Aryans, no longer took place only on the great Nazi festivals like the National Day of Labour (with which Hitler had replaced May Day), but were re-enacted every Sunday in every city, every town and every village. This weekly 'collective madness', as Guérin described it, began at 7 a.m. with loudspeakers blaring out the Nazi anthem, the 'Horst Wessel' song, and continued until the inevitable torchlight parade, close to midnight. On one such summer Sunday, Guérin found himself among a delegation of veterans. They were wearing their old uniforms and spiked helmets and had come from miles around to take part in the festivities. As they stood listening to the Forty-Second Storm Trooper platoon's concert, Guérin noticed the ecstasy with which the girls around him reacted to the first faint sounds of tramping boots signalling the approach of further SA troops – a reminder of the disturbing eroticism underlying Nazism. 'Without boots, without the aroma of leather, without the rigid and severe stride of a warrior,' he wrote, 'it's impossible today to conquer these Brunhildes.'[8]

Nothing could have been more in contrast to the colour and cacophony of that occasion than the dark, dank tunnel under the Elbe in Hamburg, which Guérin visited with his communist comrades several weeks later. Guérin also went to the slums where the men lived in 'worm-eaten wooden houses' and where on the walls could be seen defiant graffiti – 'Death to Hitler' and 'Long Live the Revolution'.[9] There were apparently still some places left in Germany where even the Nazis did not venture.

Hankey was struck by Germany's isolation. Not only were people unable to travel abroad but their heavily censored newspapers offered few clues regarding what was happening in the rest of the world. Nevertheless, the Germans he met were intensely curious about Great Britain. The GB sticker on his car proved a passport to success with officials, Nazis and the general public alike. He was perplexed as to why his modest Morris Eight should arouse such interest until he realised that it was simply because it was British. It was very pleasant, Hankey recorded, to find England held in such high esteem and to realise how anxious ordinary Germans were to be well thought of in return.

The Hankeys, their holiday over, crossed the border back into Belgium. They did so with relief. For all the kindness and hospitality received during their three-week holiday and for all the beautiful scenery, good food and comfortable hotels, it had, in the end, been an unsettling experience:

> On arriving in the quietness of Spa in Belgium my wife and I both had an astonishing sense of having come back to civilization. All the shouting and noise and singing of the Nazis; all the excitement and stimulation had vanished. We felt we were among normal people in a country living under normal conditions and never have I felt so much the steady solidity of England as since my return from Germany.[10]

Hankey and Guérin were both trained observers keen to get a grip on the political situation, but other foreigners, like the American artist Marsden Hartley, found it possible to live an entirely blinkered existence in Nazi Germany. Just as Guérin was setting off on his long bicycle ride, Hartley arrived in Hamburg for an indefinite stay. For one who was not himself a fascist or an anti-Semite; who spoke good German, knew the country well and was an enthusiastic advocate of the contemporary art so detested by the Nazis, the letters he wrote that summer are surprisingly naive. While admitting that the treatment of the Jews 'is pretty terrible', Hartley believed that 'Hitler as a person does represent a fresh feeling in idealism and national piety'.[11] In another letter, he wrote:

> I hardly know I am in Germany ... I seldom speak to anyone because I never meet anyone ... I suppose one should be more human and care that hundreds are suffering from hunger ... But one doesn't see them ... because they don't come out of their houses – they can't beg because they

will be put into prison for it. So all I see are the well to do
eating buckets of whipped cream and tons of food because
they can have it ... well it's too complex to go into and
besides, I don't feel I dare talk to these people on the street
because I am a foreigner ... So I go about my business,
which is minding my own.[12]

Hartley was already a convinced Germanophile when he
arrived in Hamburg but by the summer of 1933, just six
months after Hitler had assumed power, ordinary tourists had
become wary of Germany. Accounts of 'Jew baiting', book
burning, sterilisation laws, concentration camps and the ruthless liquidation of all opposition did not make good copy
abroad, particularly in the countries Hitler most wanted to
seduce – England and America. Newspaper articles like that
comparing Nazis with the Ku Klux Klan (published in the
Manchester Guardian shortly after the book burning[13]) were
hardly an inducement.

Although the Nazis hated internationalism, they well
understood the importance of tourism as a propaganda tool.
It was essential that their negative image abroad be coun-
tered – and not just by Germans. Foreign tourists must be
given such a memorable experience in the Third Reich that
once back home they would spontaneously sing its praises.
Luring them to Germany was therefore a high priority for the
Reich Committee for Tourism, founded in June 1933. This
powerful bureau rose splendidly to the challenge. Potential
visitors were reassured that – whatever they may read in their
'Jewish' newspapers – life in the Third Reich was entirely
normal. Germany was 'a peace-loving, trustworthy and progressive nation, a joyful country of festival-goers, hearty eaters,
smiling peasants and music lovers'.[14] Travel brochures showing

picturesque villages, colourful costumes and friendly policemen were sent abroad stripped of anti-Jewish virulence – now
reserved only for the domestic market. 'See for yourself', one
pamphlet boasted, 'how Germany is going ahead: no unemployment, production at peak levels, social security, gigantic
projects for industrial development, economic planning,
organised efficiency, a dynamic will of pulling together – a
happy energetic people who gladly share their achievements
with you.'[15]

Ultimately, the campaign worked. Over the next few years
many once hesitant holidaymakers succumbed to Germany's
charms and found the country so delightful that they returned
again and again. In the summer of 1933, however, the Reich
Committee for Tourism's propaganda had yet to bear fruit.
Foreign tourists were still so thin on the ground that fifteen-
year-old Bradford Wasserman and his fellow Boy Scouts – on
their way to the fourth World Scout Jamboree, in Hungary –
must have caused something of a stir. Bradford, a Jewish boy
from Richmond, Virginia, may not have known much about
politics but his views on Hitler are clear: 'We have to wear blue
neckerchiefs through Germany because that big sissy Hitler
doesn't allow red to be worn. He is "utsna [nuts in pig Latin]".'
Bradford's brief diary entries – mixing tourist banalities with
glimpses of the Nazi nightmare – have particular pathos:

> We went to Munich by train. It was a very tiresome
> trip. We arrived at Munich at 10 o'clock. I washed and
> went to sleep. A Nazi came to our train when we were
> in Munich and going out I saw a boy 7 or 9 years old –
> wore a Nazi uniform. We saw several old forts and we saw
> the Black Forest. The weather is rainy. This Nazi was on
> Hitler's staff.

Bradford's diary entry for Dresden, where opposition to Hitler was still rife, reads: 'I bought some of us ice cream. There were between 200 and 150 killed in Dresden before we came. Tomorrow we are going sightseeing. We went round to the different hotels getting labels. I saw some of Hitler's men.' Bradford, a keen shopper, was disappointed to find it imposs-ible to bargain in Berlin. 'I went shopping. Money seems to fly. I see many Nazi flags and shops where Nazi uniforms, knives etc. are. It is very hard to jew people down and when trying to jew someone down they showed me a sign saying fixed prices.'* A visit to Potsdam, however, was a success. 'Coming up the river was beautiful. I got a small piece of wood from the floor of the Kaiser Palace. You see a lot of Hitler's gang and children in that uniform. I took a picture of the Orangery because it was so beautiful. A band of Nazis just went by singing.'

For a teenager abroad for the first time, the trip must have been unforgettable. Yet, despite the brevity of his journal, one senses Bradford had absorbed quite enough of the new Germany to be thankful that he was returning to America even if the ship was 'not so hot'. Once at sea, he noticed 'there is [sic] a lot of Jews and Germans on board. I imagine these are glad to be out of Germany. I see a man with a Yarmulke on now. I am getting sleepy.'[16]

Clara Louise Schiefer, from Rochester, New York, spent a month in Germany that summer, with a school party. They hiked, sang barbershop and ate large quantities of ice cream.

---

* The term 'to jew down', now taboo, was once widely used. There was an outcry in 2013 when a Republican politician from Oklahoma was heard to say 'jew me down on a price' during a public debate.

As Clara's diary makes clear, food was a high priority. 'In Goslar we had a *grand* feast, tomatoes and everything,' and in Wuppertal she notes, 'a very good tea with many different kinds of cake and one especially gorgeous cherry pie'.[17] The teenagers stayed in *Jugendherbergen* [youth hostels], including the first to be established anywhere in the world, at Altena, sixty miles north-east of Cologne. Opened in 1912 by a local schoolmaster, Richard Schirrmann, it was embedded in a twelfth-century castle perched on a hill overlooking the town.

After the war, Schirrmann's initiative had quickly caught on, so, with youth hostels mushrooming across Europe, he had given up school mastering to run the movement. An idealist, he hoped that with his founding of the International Youth Hostel Federation in 1932, young people from differing backgrounds would come to understand one another better and promote world peace. His timing could hardly have been worse. Such spineless sentiments had little to do with shaping young Germans into a compassionless, disciplined Master Race. Inevitably Schirrmann lost his job, and the youth hostel where Clara and her schoolmates had so recently sung with their new German friends soon echoed to the marching songs of the Hitler Youth. Clara makes no mention in her diary of the Nazis, Hitler or the 'Jewish question'. Her Germany is a benign, cheerful country, full of sunshine and singing. Political comment is equally absent in the diary kept by Louise Worthington, a schoolteacher from Kentucky. Although that August she spent three weeks travelling all over Germany, the only time she mentions the Jews is when describing their quarter in Nuremberg: 'Then came the Jewish streets, Hof and Gassen – narrow crooked and dirty.'[18]

Mary Goodland wanted to improve her German before going up to Oxford University in the autumn of 1933, so arranged to spend a few weeks staying with a family in Düsseldorf. She recalled, with perfect clarity at the age of 100, how unaware she had been then of the momentous changes taking place in Germany. But so indeed were her hosts. It was only when the elegant art nouveau windows of Tietz, the local Jewish department store, were shattered (at 4 a.m. on 1 April) that Frau and Herr Troost, after much earnest discussion, decided that they had better follow their neighbours' example and put up some Nazi posters. By the same token, Herr Troost thought it might be politic to take part in the next SA torchlight parade. Not an energetic man, he went by taxi. When he returned, also by taxi, it was not Germany's resurgence, the iniquities of Versailles or hatred of the Jews that he wished to discuss, but the enormous mosquito bites on his ankles acquired during the march.[19]

~

Shortly before the Rumbolds left Berlin for good in the summer of 1933, Constantia had received a curious invitation. Lexie, a young woman of her own age whom she knew slightly, asked her if she would like to meet some of Hitler's personal bodyguard – the Schutzstaffel, better known as the SS. These men, Lexie explained, were all Bavarians who had supported Hitler right from the start and been with him during the Munich putsch.

The next evening Constantia found herself in Lexie's expensive car heading east towards Berlin's canal quarter. They stopped outside a large, gloomy house, which, she was informed, belonged to Captain Ernst Röhm. When Lexie knocked three times the front door 'swung dramatically open'. No one was there. But at the top of a steep staircase stood a storm trooper ready to usher them into 'a blaze of light'. Twelve men greeted Constantia with a click of the heels and a stiff nod. Their black and silver uniforms embellished with skull and crossbones, their high black boots, heavy belts and prominent revolvers, struck her as oddly out of place in the *gemütliche* [cosy] Berlin drawing room with its heavy mahogany furniture, china stove and candle-lit table. Then she noticed something rather odd about the room – a number of spring beds were let into the walls. 'Why so many beds?' she asked innocently. After an awkward pause it was explained that Captain Röhm had many visitors from distant parts of the Reich so that it was necessary to have beds for them in case they should wish to spend the night. Röhm, she was told, was very sorry not to be there but sent his personal greetings. He hoped that she would enjoy the typical Bavarian feast that had been prepared in her honour. Once seated, Constantia recalled, 'I had to pinch myself from time to time to make sure I really was sitting at the end of that long wooden table with Lexie opposite and between us, in the flickering candle-light, twelve of the toughest men I have ever seen.' Then the propaganda began in earnest. Convinced that whatever they said to her would go straight to the British government via her father, the young men did not hold back:

> They worked very hard all through the sausage course, each in turn saying his piece in the manner of a gramo-phone record. It was impossible to interrupt. When at first I ventured to argue a point or bring my own views into the conversation, I found that it threw them out of gear completely. They looked at me with complete uncompre-hending stares. There would be a pause followed by a bout of toasting in beer then the gramophone record would start again. I gave it up.[20]

Towards the end of the meal, the door suddenly opened and in walked Rudolf Hess. Constantia noticed how his dark hair stood up in a shock above his forehead and that under his remarkably bushy eyebrows his eyes were bright and grey. Interest in the British ambassador's daughter vanished instantly as Hitler's disciples clustered round their Deputy Führer, eager to hear the latest Party news.

Unlike Röhm and Hess, Joachim von Ribbentrop was relatively unknown in the summer of 1933. Because his wife was a member of the Henkell champagne family and he spoke good English, he was regarded as socially superior to most of Hitler's inner circle – even if his 'von' was a fake. Ribbentrop became a familiar figure on the diplomatic circuit, although few foreigners at the time were aware of his Nazi links. After first meeting him at the French Embassy, Constantia often went to his house in Dahlem to play tennis. 'The Ribbentrop villa was white and modern and stood in a small garden. It was attractively furnished and full of contemporary French pictures. There was a tennis court and a swimming pool. It had a sham look of the South of France,' she recalled. After a strenuous game (he was a good player), she and Ribbentrop would sip lemonade and talk politics. 'You in England don't seem to realise that Germany is the bulwark between Bolshevism and the rest of Europe,' he would say, constantly repeating the all-too-familiar mantra. His wife, Annelise, Constantia observed, 'wore a permanently fretful expression' thanks to endless headaches and a large brood of boisterous children. Years later 'a prominent German' told her that Ribbentrop had become a Nazi only because of wounded pride. Scorned by the Grafs and Junkers as an upstart wine salesman with no quarterings, his application to join Germany's most prestigious club had been rejected. It was at this point that he had turned to the Nazis.[21]

After weeks of exhausting farewell parties, the Rumbolds finally left Germany on 1 July 1933. That same afternoon, Arthur Duncan-Jones, Dean of Chichester, flew into Tempelhof Airport having, 'except for the noise', thoroughly enjoyed the flight. The Dean was on a mission. The Church of England's recently formed Council on Foreign Relations, chaired by the Bishop of Gloucester, had asked him to report on the state of the Evangelical Church. Although the contrast between Trollopian Chichester and Nazi Berlin was by any measure striking, the Dean plunged into his task with enthusiasm, clearly revelling in its cloak and dagger flavour. 'I cannot possibly describe the last 24 crowded hours,' he wrote to his wife, 'even if it was wise to do so, which it is not. I have a feeling that my arrival is already known.' He attended a crowded service at the Karl Friedrich Gedächtniskirche to hear the Nazi bishop, Joachim Hossenfelder, preach. 'Nun Danket, Ein Feste Burg, Hallelujah Chorus, and all that,' he reported to his wife. 'Lots of Nazis. Well, Well! Am now enjoying a cigar and a glass of Mosel. Shall fly back on Tuesday. I feel as though I have been in an Anthony Hope, Phillips Oppenheim, Edgar Wallace story.' Signing off, he added, 'Oh how German are the Germans, & Luther the worst of all!'[22]

An introduction by a society fascist whom the Dean had met on the aeroplane led to an unexpected audience with the Führer himself. 'I gathered that there had been considerable difficulty in obtaining this interview,' the Dean reported to the Council on Foreign Relations, 'and when I went in to see him I felt that the atmosphere was somewhat strained.' However, he came away convinced that on balance Hitler was speaking the truth when he had told him that, as a Catholic, he had no wish to be mixed up in Protestant affairs or to interfere with the Church's freedom.

Although his trip was so short, the Dean felt that he had grasped the situation well enough to be able to report with confidence to the Council. He had learned that even those suffering under the new regime continued to support Hitler because they regarded the Nazis as the only alternative to Bolshevism. Christ had now become more important as a leader in the fight against communism than as the saviour from sin. 'They really believe, many of them,' the Dean wrote, 'that Hitler is sent by God, and that the success of his movement after such small beginnings and after ten years of struggle, is plain evidence that God has worked a miracle.' The big question was what, if anything, should the Church of England be doing? Having interviewed many clergy on the front line, it was a point on which the Dean was quite clear – any expression of sympathy with the persecuted by the Church of England would be regarded as 'absolutely disastrous'.[23]

Other foreigners interested in the welfare of the Church soon began to realise that the 'religion' favoured by many Nazis had little to do with traditional Christianity. Philip Gibbs, a journalist-cum-author, recorded a compelling analysis of the Nazi faith given him by a French businessman whom he met in Germany in 1934. It was, the Frenchman told him, quite simply a hark back to paganism – tribal and racial. The new religion emphatically rejected constitutional government, Parliament and free discussion. Chieftains would govern the people under one supreme chief whose word would be law. And, in the manner of the old deities, he would be half god and half warrior. National boundaries would no longer exist because, in this system, blood called to blood. The ultimate goal was a loose confederation of Germanic tribes whose roots lay deep in the primeval forest. Scandinavian groups in Poland, Hungary and Russia would be allowed to join as they too sprang from the German forest. The old gods were not dead. They were only sleeping. They had been dispossessed by the Christian myth, which, hostile to instinct and nature, had weakened the German spirit, devitalising and dehumanising it. Now strength, courage and vitality would again stand as the true virtues of manhood, casting aside introspection, intellectualism and morbid consciousness. The pagan gods, the pagan spirit, would stride back into life.[24]

How much of all this the Dean of Chichester was able to absorb on his brief trip to Berlin (the Bishop of Gloucester assured the Bishop of Chichester that £25 of the Dean's costs would be reimbursed) is hard to say. But in a letter written several years later the Dean maintained that many Germans had now abandoned the Christian creed, preferring instead to recite, 'I believe in the German mother who bore me. I believe in the German peasant who breaks the clod. I believe in the German workman who makes things for the people. I believe in the dead who gave their lives for their people. For my God is my people. I believe in Germany.'[25] Curiously, the chief prophet of this pan-German vision was an Englishman, Houston Stewart Chamberlain, while its Mecca was a small town lying – not deep in the German forest – but among the gently rolling hills of north Bavaria, halfway between Berlin and Munich, called Bayreuth.

8

Festivals and Fanfares

The son of a British admiral, Houston Stewart Chamberlain had in his youth developed an obsessive attachment to Germany, balanced by an equally obsessive dislike of his native country. In 1882 he was baptised into the Wagnerian faith by attending six consecutive performances of *Parsifal* at Bayreuth. Overwhelmed by Wagner's fusion of music, drama, religion and philosophy, not to mention Aryan heroes and primeval forest, Chamberlain had met a world that chimed perfectly with his own. In 1899, at the age of forty-five, he published *The Foundations of the Nineteenth Century*, an uncompromisingly anti-Semitic work. Its central message was simple: 'Physically and mentally, the Aryans are pre-eminent among all peoples; for that reason they are by right … the lords of the world.'[1] The book quickly became a bestseller – and not just in Germany. Chamberlain presented his repugnant thesis so cogently that it won acclaim in France, America and especially in Russia. In Britain, George Bernard Shaw called it a historical masterpiece. Before the First World War, 100,000 copies were sold and by 1938, 250,000. The Kaiser was so enraptured that he exclaimed to Chamberlain: 'God has sent the German people your book.'[2] For Hitler, the work was to become a sacred text and its author, who in 1908 married one of Wagner's daughters, his favourite prophet.

It is a curiosity that two of Hitler's earliest and most ardent acolytes should have been British. Related by their respective marriages and living next door to one another in Bayreuth, Houston Chamberlain and Winifred Wagner (née Williams) became so implacably German that they did not even speak English to each other. Both had experienced unhappy childhoods, Winifred particularly so. Orphaned very young, she was eventually adopted by an elderly German couple who introduced her into the Wagner circle. In 1915, aged eighteen, she married Wagner's forty-five-year-old son, Siegfried. The following year Chamberlain became a German citizen.

With the outbreak of the Great War, a prolonged twilight had descended on Wagner's music dramas. Still on stage of the Festspielhaus in 1919, under thick layers of dust, were the sets for *The Flying Dutchman*, ready for a performance on 2 August 1914 that had never taken place. The previous day, just before the third act of *Parsifal*, Germany had declared war on Russia. By the time Harry Franck visited Bayreuth five years later, the festival's future was looking grim. The 'gala performance' he attended at the Festspielhaus was hardly encouraging. He noticed the orchestra pit filled with broken chairs and music stands, while the orchestra itself seemed scarcely alive. 'A single light, somewhat more powerful than a candle, burned high up under the dome of the house and cast faint, weird flickers over its dusty regal splendour.' Although outside it was a warm summer's evening, inside the hall was so cold that the thinly spread audience 'shivered audibly in their scanty *ersatz* garments'.[3]

But in the summer of 1923, despite inflation and the

general gloom, preparations were already underway for the reopening of the festival the following year. Auditioning for the roles of Sigmund and Parsifal was the great Danish tenor, Lauritz Melchior. Then unknown, he arrived in Bayreuth with his patron, the highly successful and, more to the point, wealthy British writer Hugh Walpole. The latter had become infatuated with Melchior (who he called David) after hearing him sing at a promenade concert in London. Although on this occasion Walpole remained in Bayreuth only ten days, it was long enough for romantic entanglements to develop worthy of a *Twelfth Night*. Melchior, a serial womaniser, was adored by Walpole, who in turn was adored by Winifred, whose husband, Siegfried, was homosexual. Despite the complications, Walpole became close to Winifred, whom he described as a 'simple sweet woman'.[4] He admired her pluck in confronting her 'insuperable difficulties' and was touched when she personally escorted him to pay homage to the Master's grave at the far end of the garden. Only a few weeks later, on 1 October 1923, Winifred accompanied another man to Wagner's grave, one with whom she was to become even more besotted. It was the day that marked the beginning of her notorious friendship with Adolf Hitler and his equally notorious association with the Bayreuth Festival.

Hitler could not be present for the reopening of the festival in 1924 for the simple reason that he was still in prison after his failed putsch. But he was there the following year, on 23 July, seated – with Hugh Walpole – in the Wagner family box for a performance of *Parsifal*. 'A day of drama,' noted Walpole. 'Thunder everywhere inside and out.'[5] He made no mention of Hitler on that occasion but fifteen years later, in an article for a London literary magazine, recalled his impressions: 'I thought him fearfully ill educated and quite tenth-rate,' he wrote. 'When Winnie Wagner said he would be the saviour of the world, I just laughed ... I thought him silly, brave and shabby.'[6] Both men were deeply moved by the performance. The Englishman because of his unrequited love for Melchior, singing the title role: 'He gave a superb performance – everyone ecstatic.'[7] And Hitler, who, with 'tears streaming down his face',[8] must surely have seen in Parsifal a reflection of himself – the simple innocent summoned by fate to heal Germany's hitherto incurable wound.

Naturally Hitler's presence at the 1925 festival added greatly to its National Socialist flavour, already strongly apparent the year before. Then, Winifred had been sharply rebuked for speaking English to Walpole at the Festspielhaus, while, to the horror of foreign and native Wagnerians alike, Hitlerites in the audience had risen spontaneously at the end of *Die Meistersinger* to sing '*Deutschland über Alles*'. But if blatant jingoism was now an inseparable part of the festival, Walpole still felt able to tell his publisher: 'They are all kindness itself to me and indeed I must say that the musical Germans, when you get them away from politics, are most warm hearted,' though, he went on, 'The inside intrigues are amazing.'[9] By early August, he had had enough, 'I shall not be at all sorry to leave this place. The weather is so atrocious and there are so many things that get on one's nerves.'[10] He departed Bayreuth on 8 August, never to return.

The most dazzling foreigner ever to be associated with the festival was Arturo Toscanini. While Wagnerian xenophobia prevented him from conducting at Bayreuth in the 1920s, his own political instincts should have warned him to stay away in the 1930s. But the maestro's love of Wagner proved even stronger than his hatred of fascism. So, ignoring Bayreuth's deteriorating atmosphere and warnings from Jewish friends like Francesco von Mendelssohn, he accepted Siegfried's invitation to conduct at the 1930 festival with such enthusiasm that he even refused payment. His appearance caused a sensation – and not just musically. For conservative Wagnerians, any foreigner, conducting in the holy of holies, let alone an Italian, was utter blasphemy. Yet Toscanini's *Tristan* and *Tannhäuser* were so overwhelming that even the most fanatical were converted. As *Time* magazine put it:

> *Tannhäuser* soared sonorously sublimely to its final great choral of pity and pardon. When it was ended critics outdid one another in hailing the performance as the most brilliant Bayreuth opening in years. Before him no South European had held the conductor's wand at the Festspielhaus. After each act the great audience cheered tempestuously, threw hats, stamped, applauded, called for conductor and cast. But they called vainly. There are no curtain calls at Bayreuth.[11]

The Italian's success, however, presented the traditionalists with a problem. As it was impossible, Wagnerian Paul Pretzsch asserted, 'for such an ideal performance of German music to be within the capabilities of a pure Latin', there had to be some explanation. Pretzsch found it: 'The great intermixing of Nordic blood in northern Italy', he wrote in a local newspaper, 'has often been stressed even in our own day by race researchers.'[12] So, to everyone's relief, Parma-born Toscanini was an Aryan after all. Not that he behaved like one. According to Winifred Wagner's secretary, he was so infuriated with the second violins during his first rehearsal that he smashed his baton in two, threw the pieces over his shoulder and stamped his foot.[13]

Musically, Toscanini's appearance at Bayreuth the following year was a further triumph but behind the scenes it was
a different matter. A string of incidents led him to leave the
festival, declaring that he would never again conduct there. He
had come to Bayreuth, he famously wrote to Winifred, as if it
were a temple but had instead found himself in an ordinary
theatre.[14] However, as Toscanini made plain in a New York
interview, it was not just management and artistic differences
that had caused the rift. In the spring of 1931 he had formally rejected Mussolini's Italy only to arrive in Bayreuth a
few weeks later to find Wagner's daughter-in-law actively promoting National Socialism. He was not, he declared, prepared
'to make Wagner's genius amenable to Hitler propaganda'.[15]
Nevertheless, after intense pleading from the Wagner family,
he agreed to conduct at the 1933 festival. But Hitler's rise to
power that January changed everything. Acutely conscious of
the persecution of Jewish musicians like Bruno Walter and
Otto Klemperer, Toscanini was the top signatory of a protest
message cabled to Hitler from America. Winifred was convinced that a personal letter to the Italian from the Führer was
all that was needed to smooth things over. She was wrong. In
May 1933 Toscanini sent her the following message: 'The sor-
rowful events that have wounded my feelings as a man and as
an artist have not yet undergone any change, contrary to my
every hope. It is therefore my duty … to inform you … it is
better not to think any longer about my coming to Bayreuth.'[16]
For such a devoted admirer of Wagner, it was a painful decision, causing him many years later to lament, 'Bayreuth! The
deepest sorrow of my life.'[17]

The wisdom of Toscanini's decision to boycott the festival was emphasised by a *Manchester Guardian* article
headed, 'BAYREUTH FESTIVAL 1933 "FEATURING" HERR

HITLER'.[18] In it, the paper's music critic, Walter Legge,* complained that casual visitors could be forgiven for thinking they
had arrived at a Hitler rather than a Wagner festival. In previous years, he wrote, dozens of ceramic Wagners used to gaze
into space from the windows of china shops and booksell-
ers prominently displayed the Master's autobiography. 'Now
the china shops are full of Hitler plaques, and *Mein Kampf*
has displaced *Mein Leben*.' Following Toscanini's withdrawal,
hundreds of foreigners had returned their tickets – promptly
redistributed to loyal Nazis. Legge described how, after waiting many hours outside the Festspielhaus for the Führer, the
audience would rush to their seats to gaze admiringly, 'almost
reverently', at his box until the lights were lowered. 'At the
end of each act the centre of attraction changed immediately
from the stage to the Chancellor.'

Friedelind Wagner, Winifred's rebellious elder daughter,
fiercely opposed to the Nazis, recorded one striking example
of Hitler mania at Bayreuth. The wife of the Austrian bass
baritone Josef von Manowarda wore a huge gold swastika on
her right hand held in place by chains fastened to a bracelet
and to rings on her thumb and little finger. When questioned
about this curious ornament, she replied that it covered the
spot where the Führer had kissed her.[19] Legge summed up
the 1933 festival with perfect understatement: 'It would be
idle to pretend that the outward display of national politics
has increased the pleasure of the international music-lover.'[20]

~

---

* Legge later married Elisabeth Schwarzkopf.

The Bayreuth Festival was far from being the only Nazi extravaganza to take place annually. Keenly aware of the power of spectacle to bind people to their regime, the Nazis made sure that festivals and rallies of one kind or another took place regularly throughout the year. In October, it was the turn of the peasants.

On the Bückeberg, a small hill close to the Pied Piper's town of Hamelin, a harvest festival like no other took place each year from 1933 to 1937. When American novelist Nora Waln mentioned to a group of liberal German friends how much she wanted to go, she was puzzled by their awkward silence. She realised she had put her foot in it but why? What could be more innocent than a harvest festival in the picturesque Harz Mountains attended by thousands of farmers in traditional dress? Her young friends, Rüdiger and Otto – devoted members of the Hitler Youth – were kind, sensitive boys who had described it all to her with intense enthusiasm. How peasant families dressed in purple and orange, green, blue and crimson travelled by bus or train to Hamelin from every corner of the Reich. Then, forming a stream of brilliant colour, their elaborate headdresses bobbing up and down, they walked the five miles to the Bückeberg – itself ablaze with autumn leaves. Those who arrived early were able to find a place among the grey boulders of the summit from where they could enjoy a panoramic view. To the casual observer, it was a touching scene with biblical overtones, but one, as Nora Waln's German host made clear, that was in reality made hideous by the Nazis. Perhaps she was unaware, he added, that it was to such a granite summit in the Harz that Mephistopheles had led Faust – a point that would have no doubt been lost on Rüdiger and Otto.[21]

Waln never did get to the harvest festival but, at 10 o'clock on the morning of 1 October 1933, a *Times* reporter stood on the

Bückeberg in 'broiling sun' waiting with thousands of peasants for the great moment, six hours later, when Hitler and his entourage would arrive. The whole event was a brilliantly orchestrated sop to the farmers on whose 'pure blood, simple strength, and freedom from debt' the Nazis promised, they intended to build the new Germany.[22] Konrad Warner, a Swiss journalist who was present at the 1935 festival, was struck by the extraordinary tension in the air, the palpable expectancy of this immense crowd as it surged over the hill, everyone looking for somewhere to stand or squat until the sacred moment when their Führer would come among them. At long last his motorcade could be seen in the distance on the plain below. 'As it drew closer,' Warner wrote, 'the uninterrupted "Heil" of thousands and thousands of voices rolled like a hurricane from the hillside down towards the man who had cast his spell on the German people.'[23]

The British, French and American ambassadors regularly turned down invitations for the harvest festival but in 1934 the Belgian minister Comte de Kerchove decided to accept, determined to prove, in Sir Eric Phipps's words, that he did not always 'follow in the wake of the Great Powers'.[24] He and his wife watched the cavalry perform complex manoeuvres in the shape of a swastika, listened to interminable speeches and enjoyed the autumn scenery. But the 'bouquet' of the proceedings, so the Comtesse reported to Lady Phipps, was a mock battle centred on a specially constructed village in the valley below. Perched on the hill like exotic birds, the peasants had a grandstand view. They loved it. Warner reported how a great 'Aaah' went up at the speed of the tanks, the raging fires and exploding shells, and especially when shark-like planes flew low over the 'captured' village and bombed it to pieces. 'The drone of the engines', wrote Warner, 'blended with the cheers of the crowd.'[25]

This heady mix of folk tradition, modern warfare, fire-works, food and, of course, the Führer himself, added up to the perfect family day out. But, as the *Times* correspondent reported, the Nazis' hitherto immaculate organisation unrav-elled the moment everyone started for home. For miles around the roads became so jammed that thousands of people were forced to sleep in the open. 'Never', he concluded, 'had the town of Hamelin seen such a concourse since the days of the Pied Piper.'[26]

If it is unlikely that many foreign tourists attended the Bückeberg Festival, they went in droves to Oberammergau's Passion Play. On 1 August 1934, Thomas Cook & Son placed an advertisement in *The Times*:

> **GERMANY IS NEWS...**
> Everyone is talking about Germany today – speculating, wondering and in many cases exaggerating. Too many people confuse political upheavals with interference to the normal life of the community, and would doubtless be pleasantly surprised to find that life in Berlin is as peaceful and pleasant as it is in London.[27]

Thomas Cook had good reason to play down any bad news coming out of Germany that summer for it marked the ter-centenary of the Oberammergau Passion Play. When last performed, in 1930, the play had attracted some 100,000 for-eigners, mostly British and American, so expectations were high for this, the anniversary year. Cook, a keen temperance man, had always regarded his travel business primarily as a religious and social enterprise. Fortunately piety and Mammon happily combined when it came to dispatching groups of tourists to Oberammergau – a feat that Cook's Tours had accomplished with great skill since 1890. It was the perfect package holiday. A world-class event set in a medieval village, performed by peasants against the stunning backdrop of the Bavarian Alps. Reassuringly safe for young women travelling on their own, the tour offered all comers a satisfying combination of pleasure and purpose. Little wonder that Cook's Tours was anxious not to let politics get in the way.

The origins of the Oberammergau Passion Play go back to 1633 when the villagers, devastated by bubonic plague, vowed to enact Christ's Passion once every ten years if God spared those still surviving. Convinced that the Almighty had honoured his side of the bargain they kept to theirs by performing the play for the first time the following year. After forty years they switched to the turn of every decade. It should therefore have taken place in 1920 but that proved impossible so soon after the war. Two years later, however, despite continuing economic hardship, the villagers were ready, even though food was so scarce that foreign visitors were instructed to bring their own. Ignoring such logistical difficulties, Cook's was quick to realise that the 1922 Passion Play offered a golden opportunity to reintroduce British tourists to Germany. Its monthly magazine billed the production as 'a Feast of Reconciliation', at the same time underlining the fact that thanks to inflation the trip cost less than it had in 1900. True, the horrors of the war were still painfully fresh in the public mind, but who could fail to be tempted?

With its long street of neat wooden cottages, and low-spired church, its scattered little homesteads among their opulent orchards, its crystal-clear torrent of the Ammer

racing beneath the wooden bridges, its enclosure of flowery
meadows encircled by pine-clad slopes rising to the rocky
heights of the Bavarian Alps, with the towering peak of
the Kofel carrying its massive marble cross, Oberammergau
is a community of simple peasant craftsmen, woodcarvers
and potters who produce this Passion Play ... with rev-
erent devotion and enthusiastic skill, in fulfilment of an
ancient vow.[28]

By 1930 thousands of people across the world had come to
regard Oberammergau's villagers and their play as a unique
relic from a simpler, more spiritual past – now irretrievably
lost. As one British journalist put it, 'The whole affair seemed
to belong to the childhood of the modern world.'[29] This time-
warp fantasy was enhanced by the charm of Oberammergau's
painted houses, the unspoiled mountain scenery and the fact
that those villagers taking part in the play (around a thousand) grew their hair and beards to biblical length. The women
meanwhile continued to wear their traditional long red, blue
or black skirts and aprons. Many foreign visitors like American
writer and suffragist, Ida Tarbell, believed that the intensity
of the villagers' involvement with the Passion Play set them
apart from ordinary mortals: 'Whatever they do seems to be
simple, direct, honest, coming from within, and still untouched
by imitation, greed or trickery.'[30] Another commentator staying in the pension owned by Alois Lang, who played Christ
in 1930 and 1934 and was a committed Nazi, noticed how
his American guests would ask him to bless their children.[31]
In a society weary of war and economic depression, such a
tableau – real or imagined – was bound to inspire a flood of
sentiment. 'Oberammergau,' Raymond Tifft Fuller wrote in
1934, addressing his readers directly,

lies sixty miles south of the great city of Munich, and
1,050 feet nearer the stars. Much nearer Heaven too, as you
will come to know! A few hours later it is sunset; you have
gathered unto yourself something more than first fleeting
impressions. You have, perchance, known a new meaning
to the words permanence, faithfulness, sincerity.[32]

Not everyone was seduced. Sydney Larkin (father of the poet
Philip Larkin), who saw the play in 1934, thought the village
'the most commercialised piece of religion conceivable'. He
had heard of the famous Anton Lang who had played Jesus
in 1900, 1910 and 1922, and had pictured him at his bench in
a 'humble little shop' carving wooden figures. In reality, Larkin
wrote in his diary, the shop was 'a huge establishment which
would not disgrace the West End of London. It has many
windows and many departments ... it is many years, I should
say, since he did any woodwork.' He conceded that the play
was finely produced but was sceptical that it was entirely the
work of 'so called' peasants. 'The structure of the theatre',
he observed, 'indicates a large amount of capital and is as far
removed from one's conception of village life as anything could
be.' In fact, he went on, 'The thing taken together is a huge
fraud and the embodiment of humbug.'[33]

It is noticeable how enthusiasts like Tifft Fuller conspicuously failed to mention Oberammergau's bad fairy
– anti-Semitism. From the start, the Passion Play had por-
trayed the 'murderers of Christ' with a virulence that made
it a propaganda gift to the Nazis. Here was a centuries-old
peasant drama depicting, in Hitler's words, 'the whole mire
and muck of Jewry'.[34] Included among the 50,000 Americans
who attended the 1930 production was the anti-Semitic Henry
Ford. 'Mr Ford,' reported the *New York Times*, 'expressing

his emotion and delight, today presented an automobile to Anton Lang,* leaving Herr Lang to select the car he fancied at Munich.'[35] But Ford was only one of dozens of international celebrities at Oberammergau that year. Rabindranath Tagore was so inspired by the experience that he immediately composed his only major poem written directly in English – 'The Child'. Ramsay MacDonald was an old hand. In 1900, he and his wife had spent a week walking to Oberammergau 'as pilgrims'. But this, his fourth visit, was particularly significant as he was the first British prime minister to visit Germany since the war.

Hitler was a keen advocate of the Passion Play, believing that it should be performed all over Germany. What better way to demonstrate the threat posed by the Jews to Aryan blood? Such views provoked fears in the foreign press that the 1934 production might be transformed into a Nazi extravaganza complete with Nordic Christ and Teutonic scenery. But although a number of villagers were seen in Nazi uniform, 'looking very ill with their long hair',[36] to the relief of foreign enthusiasts the play's text remained 'pure'.

In its coverage of the British visitors attending the Passion Play that summer, *The Times Court Circular* failed to mention two schoolmistresses – Miss Lucy Fairbank and Miss Clarice Mountain from Linthwaite, West Yorkshire. Thrilled by their first visit to Oberammergau in 1930, they had returned for the tercentenary but this time armed with a cine camera. After learning how to use one with the Huddersfield Screen Players,

---

* Anton Lang's portrayal of Christ in 1900, 1920 and 1922 made him an international celebrity. He spoke the prologue in the 1930 and 1934 plays.

Lucy had dashingly bought a cine camera for herself. So rare at the time was such an object in the hands of a middle-aged woman that it was only after 'enquiries at their Munich hotel and from a policeman in the street' that they decided '*after all* it would not be too dangerous to be seen carrying a camera'.[37] Their arrival at Oberammergau entirely lived up to expectations:

> One steps from the train and is transported into a different world – a world which seems dream-like and fantastic. Long haired men with white shirts and embroidered braces and strong brown limbs showing beneath their short leather breeches, heave suitcases on to their broad backs as if they are light as matchwood. Up the main street with its high gabled houses, across the little bridge which spans the River Ammer – the human mass comes from the station. One arrives at the village square with its quaint old Post Inn on one side and the Wittelsbach Hotel on the other. Balconies with cascades of flowers, deep eaves sheltering busy swallows, painted walls and sun umbrellas everywhere.[38]

On 13 August 1934, Lucy and Clarice stood outside the Wittelsbach hotel waiting for Hitler to appear. Although jostled by an excited crowd, Lucy was able to capture moving images of the Führer as he was driven off to the play in his open car. Once inside the theatre, it is unlikely that Hitler noticed, sitting just a few rows in front of him, 'but not so directly in front that we could not, without bad manners, turn sometimes to look at him', were Mr and Mrs Geoffrey Russell of Hampstead, London. They observed with interest the shabbiness of his mackintosh and the fact that he was accompanied by only one guard. As they watched the meeting of the Sanhedrin on stage, and the rousing of the crowd against Jesus, the couple had the 'inescapable feeling' that they were in the play scene of *Hamlet*. Covert glances in Hitler's direction revealed him reading his text and looking through opera glasses 'just like anybody else'. At the end of the play he left without fuss. 'But the fact of his presence', Russell wrote, 'so persistently assailed and vexed the mind that in order to give to the Passion Play the attention it deserved it was necessary to go again.'[39]

Among those at the Passion Play that year were a number of Baptists who had travelled to Germany for the fifth Baptist Congress. This huge event – attracting some 900 delegates from all over the world – took place in Berlin at the Sportpalast between 4 and 10 August 1934. Although (in a hall festooned with swastikas and crosses) the congress roundly condemned racism and anti-Semitism, the American contingent saw much to admire in Hitler. 'Surely a leader who does not smoke or drink, who wants women to be modest and who is against pornography cannot be all bad.'[40] In fact, as another delegate recorded, 'it was a great relief to be in a country where salacious sex literature cannot be sold, where putrid motion pictures and gangster films cannot be shown'. In this light even the famous book burning of the previous year met with the American Baptists' approval since 'The New Germany has burned great masses of corrupting books and magazines along with its bonfires of Jewish Communistic libraries.'[41] The German press was quick to note the unsegregated presence of thirty African-American ministers at the Congress. One of them, Michael King Sr, was so inspired by his visit to Germany – and in particular by the reforming example of Martin Luther – that on returning to Atlanta he changed both his and his son's name to Martin Luther King.

On 2 August, two days before the Baptists began their delib-
erations, President von Hindenburg died. Lucy and Clarice,
on their way to Oberammergau, had become aware of this
momentous event when they heard the tolling of the cathedral bells as their train pulled into Cologne station – 'all was
very solemn and doleful'. The president's funeral took place
on 7 August at the grim, fortress-like Tannenberg Memorial in
East Prussia, 300 miles north of Oberammergau.* For the *Daily
Telegraph* reporter, twenty-three-year-old Hugh C. Greene
(future director general of the BBC and younger brother of
Graham Greene), 'the day at Tannenberg was hell'. After a
sleepless night on the train, he sat with his fellow journalists for four hours on an 'extremely hard' seat waiting for
the show to begin. 'My memento of that is a small boil on the
appropriate spot.' Afterwards, sitting in blazing heat in
the middle of a field, he wrote up his story. 'The black of the
Nazi guards, the grey of the Reichswehr, the green of
the Göring police, the steel blue of the "air sportsmen", the
olive green of the Labour Corps and the brown of the Storm
Troops', he recorded, 'united with exotic uniforms of aged
generals and foreign military attachés to form a picture of
uniformed strength.'[42] Sir Eric Phipps, present along with the
rest of the diplomatic corps, reported that Hitler's last words
at the funeral were to consign the great man to Valhalla or as
Phipps put it, 'that abode of false and dreary Wagnerian gods
where no civilised being would wish to spend a weekend'.[43]

* Tannenberg was the site in East Prussia where Hindenburg defeated
the advancing Russians between 26 and 30 August 1914.

With Hindenburg gone, there was nothing to stop Hitler combining the offices of chancellor and president. In a plebiscite held twelve days later, the country gave him an overwhelming mandate making his dictatorship even more unassailable. In pious, picturesque Oberammergau, 92 per cent of the villagers voted for Hitler, prompting a Berlin newspaper to demand 'Did Judas Vote No?'[44] According to the *New York Times*, when news of Hitler's massive majority reached the village, a victory bonfire was lit on a nearby hillside. 'About a thousand visitors, many of them from overseas, watched the inhabitants, who are almost all members of the Passion Play cast, gather about the fire to celebrate the Leader's success.'[45]

Apart from its overt anti-Semitism, the Passion Play's message held little appeal for any hard-core Nazi. But the neo-pagan celebrations surrounding the summer solstice were a different matter. On Midsummer Eve, as thousands of bonfires were lit across Germany, Nazi orators roused German youth to a patriotic frenzy. Hesselberg, a hill 125 miles north of Oberammergau and the highest point in Franconia, was designated the Nazis' Holy Mountain. Here, the *Gauleiter* [political leader] of Franconia, Julius Streicher, orchestrated an annual Teutonic festival of fire dancing, prayers to the sun and Führer worship. A speech delivered by Göring from the Hesselberg summit was a direct challenge to Christianity:

> No church has been built so beautiful, so great, so mighty and so strong in faith as the dome of God over this mountain. If others say we have cast aside our faith then we ask them, when has there been in Germany a deeper or more passionate faith than today? When has there been stronger faith than the present faith in our Führer?[46]

It was, however, made clear that non-Germans were not automatically to be excluded: 'If foreigners with good Nordic blood ascend this mountain,' Streicher told the gathered thousands, 'they will all descend it again purified and capable of understanding Germany. They will feel the power which has welded Germany into a community.'[47] Although few ordinary foreign travellers appear to have taken up Streicher's offer, one very un-ordinary young Englishwoman did. On 23 June 1935, twenty-year-old Unity Mitford stood on the podium next to Streicher, thrust out her gauntleted arm in a Hitler salute and addressed the crowd of 200,000. Two and a half months later, she was to be present as an honoured guest of Hitler at one of the most dramatic spectacles ever devised by the Nazi regime: the annual Nuremberg rally.

9

Heiling Hitler

On 1 September 1933 the American Consul in Frankfurt, Robert Heingartner, switched on his wireless to listen to what the German newspapers were describing as the biggest meeting ever held in the world – the fifth National Socialist Party Congress in Nuremberg. He soon turned it off. As he noted in his diary, 'Hitler was speaking about the evils of Marxism, his usual line of talk. When I tuned in half an hour later he was still on the subject, a little hoarser but still going strong.'[1] Heingartner was a sceptic but hundreds of other foreigners who attended the Nuremberg rallies between 1933 and 1938 were overwhelmed. Many of them, at least those who were not committed fascists, must have looked back in later years with astonishment at their gullibility. Few, though, were as honest as Michael Burn in confessing it publicly. In a memoir published in 2003, Burn reproduced a letter written to his mother from Nuremberg in 1935, when he was a young journalist working for the *Gloucester Citizen*:

> The Party Rally finished this morning. I cannot really think coherently after this week. It has been wonderful to see what Hitler has brought this country back to and taught to look forward to. I heard him make a speech yesterday

at the end of it all which I don't think I shall ever forget
and am going to have translated. Please send me a Bible.[2]

It was for anyone, even an outsider, impossible to react objec-
tively to the Nuremberg rallies. The spectator was either, like
Burn, swept up in an orgy of emotion or, as in the case of the
writer Robert Byron, utterly repelled. 'There can be no compromise with these people,' Byron wrote from Berlin after
attending the 1938 rally. 'There is no room in the world for
them and me, and one has got to go.'[3] Whether thrilled or
appalled, no visitor from overseas could fail to be bowled over
by the sheer scale of the pageantry. The incessant marching and
beating of drums, the sweeping searchlights, flaming torches,
and thousands upon thousands of gigantic red and black
swastikas flapping in the breeze, were all skilfully deployed to
pay homage to the one supreme chieftain, the demi-god pre-
ordained to lead his tribe out of darkness to its rightful place
in the sun. For hours, foreign visitors, many of them personal
guests of the Führer himself, would watch wave after wave of
young Aryans goose-step past in perfect synchronisation – a
whole generation programmed to believe in its right to rule
the world. And which foreigner, just a tiny speck in the vast
sea of adoring disciples, could be certain at that moment that
such a thing would never happen? With the roar of a million
'Heils' ringing in their ears, all non-Germans must have felt a
shiver run down the spine – whether of fear or exhilaration.

The *Manchester Guardian* reported that the 1934 rally
was like Russia's 1 May, America's Independence Day, France's
Bastille Day and Empire Day in Great Britain all rolled into
one and lasting a week.[4] It was a compelling image but one that
does little to convey the true power of Hitler's grotesque *son
et lumière*. No one did that better than Leni Riefenstahl, whose

film of the 1934 rally, *Triumph of the Will*, is arguably the most famous documentary ever made. Rhodes scholar Geoffrey Cox, back in Germany after a two-year absence, watched her at work – 'A striking figure, in this most masculine of settings, in a cream coloured suit and a close fitting hat, standing with her camera crews at the side of the saluting stand.'[5]

Rather less well known is *Victory of Faith*, the film Riefenstahl made of the 1933 rally, which although attended by half a million people was a relatively modest affair compared with its five successors. Hitler's megalomaniac architectural schemes, intended to rival those of the classical world, had yet to be realised (many never were), while fewer prominent foreigners were present than at the later rallies. On 3 December 1933, the *Observer*'s correspondent in Berlin was invited to the gala premiere of *Victory of Faith*. In an article headed 'Hail Caesar', he described it as 'one long apotheosis of the Caesar spirit in which Herr Hitler plays the role of Caesar and the troops play Roman slaves'. He recommended that the film be shown abroad as widely as possible so that 'the intoxicating spirit moving Germany these days' might be better understood.[6] As it turned out, the reporter was one of the few foreigners ever to see the documentary because a few months later Hitler ordered all copies destroyed. The reason was the key role played in the film by Ernst Röhm, head of the SA and at the time Hitler's closest colleague. But only ten months after the rally Röhm was dead, victim of an internal power struggle that reached its climax on 30 June 1934 – the Night of the Long Knives – when scores of Nazis accused of plotting to overthrow Hitler were murdered. It was not until the 1990s that a copy of *Victory of Faith* was discovered in Britain.

There can have been few foreigners who 'Heiled Hitler' with more enthusiasm than Unity Valkyrie Mitford. Ever since she first became infatuated with the Führer at the 1933 Nuremberg Rally, her arm would shoot out on every possible occasion. Even Sir Eric and Lady Phipps, all too familiar with distressed upper-class parents whose daughters had fallen in love with 'dreadful SS types', were taken aback by Unity's brisk 'Heil Hitler' as she entered their Berlin drawing room. Sir Eric, who was a good head shorter than the strikingly built Unity, responded by standing on tiptoe and shaking her out-stretched hand.[7] Some months later, Jessica Mitford shared a cabin with her sister on a Mediterranean cruise. She described how Unity would lie on her bunk at night and after saying her prayers to Hitler would solemnly raise her arm in the Nazi salute before falling asleep.[8] The story of Unity – the fifth of Lord and Lady Redesdale's famous brood of seven – is that of an unhappy, not particularly bright young woman find-ing glamour and purpose in a cult religion. She might have become prey to any number of eccentric beliefs or deities but unfortunately for her, and those around her, she fell for the Führer.

An unsophisticated groupie, Unity was a famous special case but countless other young people of similar background travelled and studied in Germany between the wars, giving rise to the question – why were they there? That the British estab-lishment should have seen fit to prepare its offspring for adult life by sending them to such a vile totalitarian regime is puz-zling, to say the least. Even those in sympathy with Hitler's aims of defeating communism and restoring his country to greatness would hardly have welcomed a Brown Shirt as a son-in-law. Yet, despite the Great War and growing awareness of Nazi iconoclasm, Germany's traditional grip on British intellectual imagination remained as strong as ever. Here, in the midst of Nazi barbarity and boorishness, these gilded youths were expected to deepen their education and broaden their outlook. What better way for a young man to prepare for Oxford or the Foreign Office than to immerse himself in Goethe, Kant, Beethoven and German irregular verbs? Moreover he could do so very cheaply by lodging with one of the many impoverished *Baroninnen* [Baronesses] offering rooms in university towns such as Munich, Freiburg or Heidelberg.

One of the first decisions any traveller had to make when crossing the border in the mid-1930s was whether or not to 'Heil Hitler'. By 1934, when Unity first moved to Munich, the Nazi salute was so pervasive that it had become imposs-ible to duck the issue. In the early years of the Third Reich it was still just defensible to salute in a spirit of goodwill and without feeling politically compromised. After all, many of the Nazis' 'achievements' appeared, on the surface at least, highly commendable, leading optimists to assume that the brutal-ity and anti-Semitism, so harped on by Hitler's critics, would abate as conditions continued to improve. John Heygate, in his late twenties, had no hesitation in giving the frontier guards a Nazi salute as he drove his sports car into Germany one sunny March day in 1934. For some months he had been employed at the UFA studios in Berlin directing and writing English scripts but on this occasion he was bound for Prague. Feeling conspicuous in his open Magna MG, he played safe by heiling everyone in sight:

> I enjoyed it. It was a game. And the youths and children in the villages enjoyed it. They stood by the roads and in the fields with right arms solemnly stretched towards the enemy's motor car and laughed when the enemy appeared

a friend … My right arm grew stiff with replying. I prayed
for a device like a direction indicator, which would flap
aloft a metal hand while I got on with the job of driving.[9]

Heygate, an old Etonian, had a few years earlier caused a scandal by absconding with Evelyn Waugh's wife, whom he later
married. As with many in his social circle, his political sympathies were well to the right. Consequently, although there was
much to make fun of in the new uncouth Germany he also
found much to admire. The flags fascinated him. Driving along
village streets 'roofed with swastikas', he passed 'like a modern
knight beneath crusades of ruddy banners'. It occurred to him
that it might be 'fun' to fly his own Hakenkreuz so he had one
fitted to his car by a delighted garage attendant. But the fun
faded when, as he watched the tiny swastika beat 'proudly' in
the wind, he experienced a 'sudden awe'. For a moment the
flag seemed to him 'much more than something to be waved
and draped from windows. It was a fighting banner which went
before and men followed after.'[10]

When he reached the Austrian Tyrol, he wrote to his friend
Henry Williamson, author of *Tarka the Otter* (1927). Except
for Germany, he told him, all the European countries were
in a desperate state. And given the strength and purpose of
German youth, he was not in the least surprised that they
were terrified. He went on to describe how Austria was now
organised into secret lodges. Runners from Germany were sent
across the mountains every day to pass on Nazi propaganda
to Austrian villages. Vast swastikas would suddenly flare all
over the Tyrol or be visible on a mountainside carved out of
the snow. Heygate admitted that even he was carrying copies
of the forbidden Nazi paper (given him by the exiled head of
the Austrian Nazi party in Munich), which he was distributing

clandestinely. The underground fight for Nazism in Austria, he told his friend, was a fascinating story.[11]

Heygate's contemporary, Robert Byron, moved in similar circles (they both knew the Mitfords) but reacted very differently. 'I hardly know how to contain myself', he wrote to his mother from Danzig, 'when they say Heil Hitler to one another down the telephone. And that salute, when a couple of friends happen to part in a crowded bus, also has an hysterical effect, but I suppose I will get used to it.'[12]

In fact failure to salute, even for a foreign tourist, became increasingly risky. 'I had a curious experience the other night,' Geoffrey Cox informed his brother in New Zealand. 'A Brown Shirt hit me because I didn't salute a Nazi flag.' It had been close to midnight when, on a dark Berlin street, the young New Zealander had met a column of SA troops marching to a railway station on their way to the Nuremberg rally. 'He hit me from the side, unseen, while I was arguing with two others,' recounted Cox, adding that because he had not felt frightened he even remembered the incident with some pleasure. He had, he explained to his brother, experienced 'a kind of elation standing there in the middle of a hostile crowd and not feeling scared. Of course I could have been braver – I should have hit them back, even if it meant I was properly beaten up. But that'll come next time.'[13]

Given Cox's robust views, it was as well that he did not visit the Feldherrnhalle [Field Marshals' Hall] in Munich – the Nazis' most sacred monument. Here, at the site of Hitler's abortive putsch, two temples of white stone had been erected to house the massive lead-coloured coffins of the sixteen 'martyrs' who had died that November night in 1923 when the police had opened fire on Hitler and his followers. 'All day and in all weathers there are pilgrims to this place,' wrote British writer and journalist, J. A. Cole. They may come as laughing coach-loads of tourists, or happy family parties out on a trip, but as they draw near their demeanour changes, they mount the steps slowly and quietly, look for a minute or more at the coffins below, give the Nazi salute and then slowly make their way to the other shrine.'[14] Everyone who passed the Feldherrnhalle – whether on wheels or on foot – was required to salute the monument. Eighteen-year-old Tim Marten, who had just left Winchester College and was studying for the Foreign Office, thought it hilarious when he spotted a fat man falling off his bicycle while trying to heil and steer at the same time.[15]

When, on a visit to Munich, Derek Hill's mother told him how much she would like to catch a glimpse of Hitler, he took her to the Carlton tearooms – one of the Führer's regular haunts. Just as they were about to give up, Hitler arrived with Goebbels and Hess. Derek immediately telephoned his friend Unity to let her know that Hitler was there. A few minutes later she appeared in a taxi – trembling with emotion at the prospect of seeing her idol at close quarters for the first time. 'This is the kindest thing that's ever been done for me in my life,' she told Derek. 'I'll never forget it.' Arguably Unity was mentally unstable but the apolitical Mrs Hill, a Scot, was emphatically not. Yet even she was so caught up in the moment that, to the astonishment of her son, she gave a Nazi salute as they left.[16]

Eighteen-year-old Joan Tonge was made of sterner stuff. Wearing her 'fetching stripy ocelot fur coat and Cossack hat', she attended an SA rally escorted by a smart Prussian officer. All had been well, she recalled, until the 'Heil Hitlers' started. Then, 'like an offensive bit of rhubarb', she had stood – arms rigidly at her side – refusing to salute. Within seconds 'several squat and ugly Brown Shirts came galloping up, shouting ferociously and windmilling their arms' until 'Helmut stamped over with his ankle-length overcoat swirling, shouting even louder at them that I was an Engländer'.[17]

Kenneth Sinclair-Loutit and 'Matthew' (his real name was probably Robert Dummett[18]) were already undergraduates at Trinity College, Cambridge, when they decided to spend the summer of 1934 bicycling from Hamburg to Salzburg. On disembarking from the SS *Kooperatzia* (a Soviet ship was the cheapest way of travelling to Hamburg), they walked into town, bought bicycles for £3 each and set off. Despite having agreed to join forces, they hardly knew one another and soon discovered how little they had in common. Thanks to an affair with the wife of his former Heidelberg professor, the right-wing Dummett spoke excellent German. Sinclair-Loutit did not. Furthermore, since witnessing a recent hunger march in Cambridge, his politics had moved decisively to the left. Locked in this uneasy partnership, the two young men headed south. Dummett was immediately impressed by German discipline ('so lacking in England'), by the autobahns and labour camps, and by the high standard of cleanliness everywhere. Sinclair-Loutit, on the other hand, found the trappings of National Socialism increasingly repellent. 'The two of us managed well enough until we got close to the newer Germany,' he recalled. 'I can still feel the surprise that shook me in Lüneburg when Matthew gave the Nazi salute at an improvised shrine containing a bust of the recently deceased Hindenburg.'[19] It was, his companion suggested, a simple act of politeness like taking off one's hat when going into a church. But to Sinclair-Loutit the salute was nothing less than public endorsement of a thoroughly unpleasant regime.

The incessant cry of 'Heil Hitler' eventually got on the nerves of even the most tolerant traveller. Edward Wall was a

young schoolmaster who, with his friend Tom Iremonger, spent
April 1935 touring Germany in a Baby Austin. He recorded
how in Helmstedt their excellent lunch

> was rather spoilt by the insistent way everybody, would
> on entering or going out, give the Heil Hitler greeting and
> then salute everybody else *in turn*. Sitting near the door,
> we had more than our fair share of these salutations. One
> must perhaps expect that the inhabitants, of what the AA
> route described as 'a level countryside with many industrial
> centres', should show their Nazi enthusiasm rather more
> aggressively.[20]

However, the fact that not every German was a dedicated Nazi
became clear a few days later in Bayreuth (described by Wall
as a 'German Cirencester') when an elderly couple entered the
café where the young men were eating. 'He flapped his hand
loosely from the wrist up to face level,' noted Wall, 'and let his
forearm bend feebly from the elbow, saying at the same time,
as modestly as could be, and as if he were saying "sleep well"
to a child, "Heil Hitler".'

Wall and Iremonger were not particularly political but
through the Schlauch family, whom Wall knew from an earlier holiday, they discovered how hard life could be for those
on the wrong side of the regime. Herr Schlauch, a Lutheran
pastor, had recently served a short term in prison for having
preached against the worship of Teutonic pagan deities. A Nazi
minder in the congregation – there was one now present to
vet every sermon in every church – had denounced him. Since
his release, the blacklisted Schlauch had been unable to find a
job. This experience, so commonplace by the mid-1930s, did
not, as might be expected, automatically lead to a sense of

solidarity with fellow victims. Wall noted that Frau Schlauch, despite her husband's predicament, was full of praise for the Nazis for having banned Jewish novelists – 'thereby cutting much unhealthy sexual literature out of circulation'.[21]

Wall's account of their holiday is full of vivid images: the white sandy road winding through a dark, mysterious pine forest, the group of factory workers delighted by King George V's birthday greetings to Hitler and the cigarette cards depicting French military police brutalising German civilians in the Ruhr. *Der Triumph des Willens* [*Triumph of the Will*], watched in a smoky cinema 'chock full and terribly over-heated', was as unpleasant as the stuffy opera where old ladies hissed at a fidgeting Iremonger to have more '*Rücksicht* [consideration]' for others. They warmed to the burly Bavarian policemen in their 'blue blue tunics' and shiny black helmets adorned with pointed silver knobs, but feared for a recklessly outspoken anti-Nazi bookseller in Aachen. One impression stood out from all the others – the extraordinary profusion of signs proclaiming a single message: '*Juden sind nicht erwünscht* [Jews not wanted]'.[22]

The two young Englishmen spent a particularly pleasant day on the shores of the Ammersee. 'The clouds had rolled back and a stiff breeze made the huge expanse of lake look more like some inlet of the sea,' Wall wrote on 28 April 1935, as they sat enjoying *Kaffee und Kuchen* [coffee and cake] looking out across the water. Some way to the north-east of the lake, Sinclair-Loutit and Dummett had a few months earlier been nearing Munich when fifteen miles short of the city Dummett suddenly insisted that they pedal a long stretch without pause. Only afterwards did he give his reasons. On examining the map, he had noticed how close they were to Dachau, the concentration camp that had opened shortly after Hitler became chancellor. Dummett was anxious lest their presence in the area arouse suspicion. Sinclair-Loutit had never heard of Dachau so Dummett had to explain that the camp was the Nazis' method of dealing with 'wasters, idlers, social undesirables, Jewish profiteers and riffraff' by re-educating them through work.[23] Hugh Greene, who was in Munich at the time trying to establish himself as a journalist, picked up a cautionary verse from the family he lodged with: '*Lieber Gott, mach mich stumm, Dass ich nicht nach Dachau komm!* [Dear God make me dumb, so I won't to Dachau come!].'[24] A few months later the infamous sign '*Arbeit macht frei* [Work Sets You Free]' was erected over Dachau's entrance.

Dummett need not have worried. The German authorities, initially at least, proved so willing to show off their concentration camp to foreigners that by the mid-1930s Dachau had become something of a tourist attraction for American and British visitors, particularly politicians and journalists. Relieved not to have detected any undue misery or discomfort, Victor Cazalet MP thought the camp 'not very interesting though quite well run'. In his diary he noted, 'adjutant says most prisoners Communist. If that is the case, then they can stay there for all I care.' Nevertheless, he thought the Nazis 'fools' for not freeing the majority of prisoners since it was obvious that any opposition to the regime was now utterly impotent in the face of 'Hitler's complete and overwhelming power'.[25] Cazalet's fellow Member of Parliament, Sir Arnold Wilson, was more ambivalent. Wilson travelled extensively in Germany between 1934 and 1936 seeking to understand the new Germany through countless in-depth conversations with the widest possible range of people. The many articles he produced as a result were published in *Walks and Talks Abroad* (1939). In July 1934 he addressed a large audience at Königsberg when he spoke of National Socialism in glowing terms:

During the past three months I have watched Young
Germany at work and at play in every part of the country.
I admire the intense energy evoked by the National Socialist
Movement. I respect the patriotic ardour of German youth.
I recognize, I almost envy, the depth and earnestness of the
search for national unity which inspires your schools and
colleges: because it is wholly unselfish, it is wholly good.[26]

Yet he did not let his enthusiasm for the Nazis cloud his impressions of Dachau. Having observed that the men seemed as well housed and fed as in any of the voluntary labour camps, he wrote that 'there was in the atmosphere of the camp something against which my soul revolted'.[27] James Grover McDonald (American High Commissioner for Refugees Coming from Germany) agreed. As the prisoners snapped to attention before him, he had looked into their eyes. 'What I read there, I shall not forget,' he wrote that evening in his diary. 'Fear, haunting fear, a sense of utter subjugation to an arbitrary ruthless will.' But his guide, when pressed on why the need for such a camp, was keen to point out that Germany was still in the throes of a revolution, and that whereas in most revolutions political prisoners were shot, at Dachau 'we try to reform them'. After the tour, McDonald was thankful to find the Munich art gallery still open, 'thus enabling me to get the taste of terror of the camp out of my mouth'.[28]

Decades after the war, commando, writer and poet Michael Burn unearthed his account of a visit to Dachau in 1935. He was appalled to discover how indifferent he had been to the more brutal aspects of the camp.* The commandant's account

* The commandant who Burns met was Heinrich Deubel. A few months later Himmler sacked him for being too lenient.

of the horrific punishments meted out had at the time caused him merely to comment: 'Those who may shudder will remember that the cat-of-nine-tails is even in England not yet obsolete.'[29] Why, he wondered years later, had he not, as a reporter for the *Gloucester Citizen*, demanded to know what kind of trial or defence the prisoners had been allowed; or how the Nazis could morally justify incarcerating an individual simply for criticising the government? Equally shocking to the older, wiser Burn was his hypocrisy in subsequently convincing himself (and the wider world) how traumatised he had been by Dachau. But he was not the only foreign visitor at the time to shrug off the camp's hideous implications. Anti-Semitism was rife among the English upper classes, as it was in France and large sections of America. By the same token, the fate of the communists, gypsies, homosexuals and 'lunatics', who ended in Dachau alongside the Jews, was by no means a burning issue for everyone. Certainly eighteen-year-old Derek Hill, swept up in the thrill of studying stage design in Munich, did not dwell on the intrinsic evil of the place. He spent a day at the camp in 1934 observing it for the near blind *Morning Post* journalist, Peter Matthews. They lunched in the same room as the prisoners but were seated at 'high table' with Commandant Theodor Eicke – an arrangement that reminded Hill of dining in an Oxford or Cambridge college.[30]

⌒

Throughout the 1930s a steady stream of 'nice English girls' arrived in Munich to be 'finished'. A number of them attended Baroness Laroche's school where Unity also lodged for a while. Their days, spent in gentle study of art, music and German, were punctuated with picnics, cultural expeditions and tea-dancing. 'We met a great many young army officers,' recalled

Joan Tonge. 'They were madly elegant, arrogant and conceited, and had tremendous presence. Their uniforms were immaculate and their self-esteem Perspex strong.' [31] Ariel Tennant, another teenager in Munich at the time, studying art, was struck by how many people in England refused to believe her accounts of Nazi aggression. When, on a brief visit home, she described some of her more alarming experiences, she was dismissed as being too young to understand.[32] Like her cousin, Derek Hill, she was also a friend of Unity's and remembered walking with her in the Englischer Garten when Unity seized her arm and demanded that she admit to liking Hitler – 'If you don't I shall give your arm another twist.'[33]

A couple of evenings a week the girls would go to the opera – only a few miles from Dachau. For Sarah Norton (later briefly married to Viscount Astor), Wagner's *Ring* cycle was torture,[34] but after hearing *Tristan* for the first time, Lady Margaret Boyle, daughter of the Earl of Glasgow, wrote fourteen ecstatic pages home. 'So glad you enjoyed the opera darling,' her mother replied.[35] Sarah Norton was acutely conscious of the 'atmosphere of fear' haunting the city. Hating the Nazis, she would go with like-minded friends to the Carlton tearooms where they would sit as close as possible to Hitler's table and pull faces at him. 'It was a pretty senseless occupation,' she later recalled, 'because I do not think they noticed us but it gave us vicarious pleasure.'[36] Hitler's table always had a card placed on it saying 'RESERVIERT FÜR DEN FÜHRER'. On one occasion, a young English art student pinched it and stuck it on his girlfriend's coat. She was lucky to get back to her Baronin's establishment without being arrested.[37] Sarah Norton was eventually caught vandalising a publicly displayed copy of Julius Streicher's virulent anti-Jewish newspaper *Der Stürmer* and sent home by the Foreign Office. Her mother's reaction was better than expected: 'Well done, despite your nuisance value. I hope you learned the language.'[38] She had in fact learned it well enough to be employed at Bletchley Park during the war.

Although Hugh Greene was implacably opposed to the Nazis from the moment he set foot in Germany, it was important that as an aspiring young journalist he observe them as closely as possible. On 11 January 1934 he wrote to his mother,

> Things are becoming considerably more interesting here with the New Year. I have taken to going to a café where Hitler often is in the hope of seeing him. Last week I went in one evening and there he was in his corner. Later Goebbels came in as well. Goebbels is a little man with a limp but most attractive looking with a charming smile.[39]

The 'café' in question was the Osteria Bavaria – the Führer's favourite restaurant. It was here that Unity famously stalked Hitler for months until finally, one Saturday in February 1935, she was invited to join him at his table. They discussed his favourite film, *Cavalcade*, and how the Jews must never again be allowed to start a war between two Nordic races. Later that day, in a letter to her father, Unity announced that she was so happy she wouldn't mind dying.[40]

A few months after Unity's first meeting with Hitler, a large group of Chinese students turned up in Berlin. They went there not to immerse themselves in Goethe or to study National Socialism but because it was cheaper than spending the long summer vacation in Paris where they were based. For them, the concept of a summer holiday was entirely alien but in Paris they had discovered that 'even beggars pick up their sticks or their violins and go off to the country to beg for a couple days' worth of food to show that they are on their summer holidays'. On reaching Berlin, their immediate problem was to find somewhere to stay. Rooms were rented out on the first day of the month but they had arrived on the fifteenth. 'We walked all day with no success, our legs so tired we could walk no further and ended up in the house of a Jew,' wrote Shi Min, author of their collective memoir.[41] Delighted by the size and comfort of their rooms, they soon settled in. Shi Min particularly admired the flushing lavatory. 'Sitting on it', he recalled with delight, 'was more comfortable than the Dragon Throne in the Qing palace. Smoking a cigarette, reading a copy of *Space Wind*, words cannot describe the marvel.' There was much else to wonder at:

> The streets of Berlin are broad and clean with neat rows of
> trees of identical height on either side. You never see horse
> dung in the middle of the road and there is no waste paper
> on the pavements, something that the inhabitants of Paris
> could not imagine … pots of flowers are placed on every
> sill surrounded by a small iron railing so that seen from a
> distance it is as if innumerable small gardens have been
> attached to the heavens and the precipices of the walls.

But there was nothing naïve about these young Chinese who had been in the West quite long enough to absorb European prejudices. 'Opening the window, we yellow-faces leaned out to enjoy the cool breeze,' wrote Shi Min. 'We know that "third grade inferior" peoples and nationalities cannot aspire to the fortunes of superior ones. This is the unfairness of god; he should not have made people's skins in a variety of different colours.'

The students were fascinated by the contrast between

French and German women. In France, noted Shi Min, 'they wore clothes of a hundred colours and different types of shoes – you would never find two dressed identically'. But German women wore 'flat shoes on their big feet and clump along the street like camels'. Their clothes looked as if 'they had been borrowed from an aunt'. There was another striking difference. At the countless sports facilities in and around Berlin, women were as active as the men. 'Wearing shorts and singlets with bare legs and spiked shoes they did sports like boys, forgetting that they were young ladies. If there is a war, they could all participate unlike in France or China.' Keenly observant, Shi Min perfectly understood the Jewish situation:

> They have no influence in any government organisa-
> tion. They don't have power to defend themselves, yet
> they are rich. The police gentlemen frequently deal with
> them impudently. Fill in a form today, fill in a receipt
> tomorrow; they cannot move freely. All they can do is
> obediently follow the 'Regulations for Jews', and live like
> a daughter-in-law.

It was impossible, he concluded, to know how much people really believed in Hitlerism but he found the constant heiling sickening. As for Nazis in general, he observed that 'they have a high opinion of themselves walking along the street, body upright, nose (German noses are short and small) cockily in the air, they really do look like the world's superior people'. The police often stopped the students to ask if they were Japanese. Shi Min recounts how they would blush with embarrassment as they nervously admitted to being Chinese. 'They dislike the Japanese but respect them,' he wrote. 'They are sympathetic to Chinese but look down on them.' Sensitive to the current deplorable conditions in his own country, he added, 'no need to go into the reasons, nor to blame them'.

If a tour of Dachau was de rigueur for any serious traveller during the early years of the Third Reich, so too was a visit to a labour camp. Geoffrey Cox made up his mind to go one better. On 7 August 1934 he wrote to his brother, 'I'm on my way to work in a work camp. I start this afternoon. I've had a stay in Germany which is just incomparable. I'll write it all to you later. But if ever I have got under way in my life, it's been in the last fortnight.'[42] Cox's three weeks in a labour camp near Hanover were not unpleasant. Naturally there was a great deal of 'heiling Hitler' and marching about in drab grey uniforms – spades sloped on shoulders like rifles. But for a tough young New Zealander the work was not arduous. Cox found himself digging ditches across swampy moorland and cutting down undergrowth to bind into faggots. When their section leader was not watching, he and his fellow workers, mostly from Hanover and the Ruhr, would 'take a spell in the sun or hunt adders in the heather'. He became very fit.

> Starting work at 7 a.m. in countryside like East Anglia, we marched across fields with woods on the horizon still hazed with mist, or where at midday great cloud masses moved across the wide blue North German sky. Working, scrubbing out the barrack room, playing football, stealing out at night to secure a supply of pears from a nearby peasant orchard, I quickly merged into the easy camaraderie of the young.[43]

There was no weapon training as such, although Cox excelled at a game in which 'you sprinted a hundred yards, crawled another ten, and then threw long-handled dummy grenades towards a bull's eye traced in the dust'. When he suggested that this was military training, his fellow workers were pained. Did he not know that it was merely a schoolboy sport played in every German school? Although his camp comrades enjoyed the militaristic side of their camp life – many preferred to drill than to play football in the afternoons – none were ardent Nazis. Cox summed up his camp experience in an article in *The Spectator*. He did not on the whole think that the Labour Service in Germany could be accused of advocating war, but it was certainly making sure that if war came 'the youth of Germany would be ready both in body and mind to face the field of battle'.[44]

Cox possessed all the initiative and drive needed to extract the most out of his travels in the Reich, but for an insecure young man, like Antony Toynbee, eldest son of the historian Arnold J. Toynbee, Nazi Germany was to prove the worst possible environment. During most of his time at Bonn University – studying Russian and Serbian, as well as fencing – he was both depressed and confused. One moment he was at a rally protesting against the Treaty of Versailles, singing the 'Horst Wessel' song and heiling Hitler ('there is a lot to be said for the Hitler salute, by the way, as a means of developing the muscles of the sword arm'[45]), the next he was toying with communism, 'I must get M to tell me about communism because I don't really know much about it. If I like the idea of it I may become a proper serious one. It would be exciting and something against the beastly Nazis.'[46]

A few months later he had made up his mind – at least for the time being. On 11 May 1934 he recorded in his diary how he had joined an embryonic communist cell that planned to operate under the guise of a bridge club. 'In view of this,'

Toynbee noted, 'it is thought that all the members should know how to play bridge. I don't, so yesterday M taught me.' The young men's immediate ambition was to take part in an uprising being planned in Saarbrücken should the plebiscite on 13 January 1935 result in the return of the Saar region to Germany. 'The rifles and machine-guns would probably be of the French model,' Toynbee duly noted after one of their 'bridge' sessions. 'I said that Thomson machine-guns might be used as well, because they would be very useful for street fighting. M mentioned the possibility, in the event of the revolt succeeding, of some of us being given nominal ranks in the Red Army.' It was, of course, pure *Boy's Own* fantasy, its futility underlined by Toynbee detailing their plans in his diary. Such naïveté might be endearing were it not for the danger to which he exposed them all – particularly as he lived with a pro-Nazi family. In any case, Toynbee himself never really believed in either communism or the uprising: 'This all sounds very far-fetched and unlikely,' he admitted in his diary, 'but it is exciting to speculate about it, and, if nothing happens at all, it will still be amusing to read all this later on.'

With his career as a revolutionary finished before it had begun, Toynbee continued to spend his time in Bonn looking for the right girl, rowing on the Rhine ('rowed to Linz 46 K on fixed seats') and drinking. 'The last part of the evening we spent in a very disreputable but interesting *Lokal* in a rather low part of town. There were crowds of Jewesses there, that profession being one of the few that are still open to non-Aryans in Germany.' Just occasionally he saw something to lift his spirits:

Two bright memories on this gloomy November day: one was a view we had across the Rhine valley with the hills behind, from the heights above Oberkassel, just as it was gathering dark and the lights were coming out. The other was the graveyard, with all the graves lit up by candles because it was All Souls. It looked most lovely and it gave me an extraordinary feeling of the people not really being dead.[47]

In her memoir, Biddy Barlow, who herself came from an intellectual family and was married to Erasmus Barlow, one of Charles Darwin's grandsons, reflected on the oddity of her parents sending her to Germany at such a time:

It was a paradox of the thirties that parents with liberal left wing views almost invariably sent their children to Nazi Germany when they wanted their minds broadened by a spell abroad. My sister had studied art in Stuttgart, my brother attended Tübingen University and Erasmus stayed near the Black Forest with a schoolmaster's family after he left school.[48]

Did the parents of these fresh-faced young people not read newspapers? Or was it that they simply thought of Nazi violence and philistinism as an irrelevant sideshow compared with the joys of Schiller and Bach? In Biddy Barlow's case it seems that it was largely a matter of pragmatism. Her family hated Hitler, dreaded him beginning another world war and despised the idea of a master race, 'but the exchange rate was good'.[49] Whatever the wider explanation, it is clear that for many British people there existed a baffling disconnect between their traditional regard for German culture and the realities of National Socialism. The result was that, despite the deteriorating political scene, young people continued to explore Nazi Germany right up until the eve of the Second World War.

10

Old Soldiers

In September 1935 the Embassy's first secretary, Ivone Kirkpatrick,* had just returned from a 600-mile motoring trip through Mecklenburg and Pomerania having seen 'a lot of people'. Although Kirkpatrick encountered plenty of poverty and discontent, he concluded that the Führer's grip on the population was so complete that 'it is difficult to see what political or economic event can shake Hitler off his perch'. He thought 'the new citizenship law' (the notorious 'Nuremberg laws' that stripped Jews of their nationality) a particularly clever stroke. 'Every German will be obliged to toe the line in order to get his citizenship certificate and when he has got it, he will have to continue to be a fervid supporter of the Government for fear of losing it.'[1]

---

* Kirkpatrick was wounded in the First World War but turned down a place at Balliol College to return to the fighting. He interviewed Rudolf Hess following the latter's flight to Scotland in 1940 and was appointed High Commissioner for Germany in 1950. He ended his career as permanent under secretary at the Foreign Office.

Truman Smith, who thirteen years earlier had been the first American official to interview Hitler, was now military attaché at the US Embassy. He believed that 'Germany is still not of one mind', but agreed with Kirkpatrick that popular criticism was directed against the Party – not the Führer. Hitler's biggest problem, in his view, was the wretchedly poor quality of the Nazi leaders who had emerged out of the 'desperadoes and riffraff' flung to the surface after the Great War. Although these semi-thugs, now parading as *Gauleiters* [heads of regional branches of the Nazi Party] and government ministers, were deeply unpopular, curiously, as Smith observed, people's resentment rarely seemed to spill over to affect the Führer himself. 'Germans, irrespective of class,' he wrote, 'adore and revere this strange man and the qualities they attribute to him of selflessness, lack of ostentation and participation in the joys and sorrows of the German people.'[2]

It is significant that Kirkpatrick, who had not lived in Germany before the Nazis took over, emphasised the privation he saw whereas Arthur Yencken, an Australian diplomat who had served in the British Embassy during the Depression and also happened to be travelling in Germany in September 1935, had a very different perspective:

Anyone revisiting Germany after two or three years' absence must be struck by the great improvement in the appearance of the people. The horde of monstrosities from Eastern Europe has, of course, largely vanished from the streets and cafes, but that is not all. The whole population seems to have been spruced up. Everywhere trousers have been neatly and firmly creased; there seems to have been a national ironing and a national hair cut, though once again, alas, the nippers have not known where to stop. Young men

no longer slouch about apeing the disgruntled proletariat.
They have taken a pull at themselves, and apparently a
willing pull. They have recovered their self-respect.[3]

One odd thing Yencken noticed was how much blonder the
nation had become since he was last there. According to official statistics over 10 million packets of hair dye were sold in
1934 while 'lipstick so beloved of Jewesses' had been deemed
un-German and relegated to the dustbin.[4] When Truman
Smith's eleven-year-old daughter drew a picture in class of
her American grandmother with bright red lips, her teacher
responded with horror, 'Oh Kätchen, grandmothers don't use
lipstick!'[5] Yencken also recorded more serious matters such
as the extensive food shortages, the fact that so many people
were only working part time and that the material of which
the 'neatly creased trousers' were made was not going to keep
its wearers warm in winter. One former SA trooper told him
that, as he and his friends could not afford winter clothing,
they were 'daily anointing themselves to encourage growth
of body hair'.[6]

Yencken, who had won an MC in the war, was not unsym-
pathetic to the familiar arguments justifying the mistreatment
of Jews. After four years as a diplomat in the Weimar Republic,
he shared the opinion – by no means confined to Nazi sympathisers – that Jewish domination of German affairs had
been detrimental. He cited the bookstores which 'throughout
Germany were littered with morbidly revolting publications',
as well as the theatres and cinemas, which, he argued, exhib-
ited 'the same pornographic tendency' and were entirely under
Jewish control. 'The country definitely needed cleaning up,'
he wrote in his report to the Foreign Office.[7] And to a good
many of the military men who visited Germany in the Third

Reich, it appeared that the Nazis were making an excellent job of doing precisely that.

~

'Commandant' Mary Allen was not, of course, an 'old soldier' but she always behaved as if she were. Indeed, it is hard to imagine any individual further removed from the Nazi ideal of German womanhood than Mary. Not only did she have no interest in *Kinder, Küche, Kirche* [children, kitchen, church], but her immaculate uniform, jackboots, cropped hair and enormous ego were a blatant challenge to male authority. Yet despite this, late one night in March 1934, Mary walked from her Berlin hotel, across the snow-covered Wilhelmplatz, to the Reich Chancellery for a private meeting with Hitler – pipping Unity Mitford to the post by nearly a year.

It was not Mary's first visit to Germany. In 1923, when the British Army still occupied the Rhineland, she had been asked by the War Office to send six women from her Women's Auxiliary Service to Cologne to assist the German police in controlling prostitution. The request was a personal triumph since only two years earlier Mary had herself been prosecuted for wearing a uniform resembling that of the Metropolitan police and fined ten shillings. At last, or so it must have seemed at the time, Mary had won official approval for the permanent women's police force that she was so determined to establish. But it was a false dawn. Despite the success of her Cologne mission, the Metropolitan police had their own plans for introducing women into their ranks and these did not include the self-styled 'Commandant' Allen. Undeterred, Mary travelled widely during the mid-1920s (a photograph shows her in uniform on a camel in front of the pyramids[8]), preaching the need for women police to anyone who would listen.

In 1934 she was back in Germany. Her mission was to persuade the authorities to set up a women's police force founded
on Nazi doctrine. In her memoir, published two years later, she
records how she sat 'absolutely entranced' at a mass meeting
'beside the Chancellor's charming sister, listening to the great
Dictator'.[9] She describes the waves of emotion that swept
through the hall and 'rotund German Generals in frayed and
faded wartime uniforms, their bald heads pink with excitement'.[10] Mary was such a convincing self-promoter, at least
outside her own country, that the Nazis must have assumed
that she was an important member of the British establishment despite being only a woman and a freakish one at that.
Or perhaps they simply regarded her as an honorary man.
At any rate, even though it was midnight and Hitler had just
finished a two-and-a-half-hour speech, he agreed to see her. 'A
few moments in the lift,' Mary recalled, 'a short walk through
ante-rooms piled high with flowers', and she was in the presence of 'one of Europe's most remarkable men'.[11] In private
she found the Führer – as did so many other foreign visitors
– a charming man, 'courteous, quiet, patient'. Indeed, Sir Eric
Phipps constantly struggled to convince British visitors that
this 'charming' individual they had just met would regularly
rant and rave at him during their private meetings.[12] In a letter to the Foreign Office, Phipps noted how after one such
fraught interview he had been informed that the Führer had
sought to calm his nerves by drinking tumblers of cold water
and eating large amounts of boiled cabbage. 'I also was rather
tired,' remarked Phipps, 'but did not seek recovery by the same
means.'[13]

Naturally Mary Allen was deeply gratified when Hitler
assured her that Göring had it in mind to recruit 100 policewomen for Berlin. Mesmerised by her encounter, Mary was

convinced that Hitler was 'an enduring friend of England and a blood brother of the ordinary decent people of Europe, whatever their nationalities, who want peace for their trade and safety for their children'.* Her meeting with Göring a few days later was similarly satisfactory, especially as he agreed that it was essential for any future Nazi policewomen to wear uniform. Their shared obsession with uniforms found rather different expression. While Mary wore the same austere police uniform day in and day out (sometimes with a monocle), Göring delighted in sporting one gorgeous outfit after another. His Reichsmarschall uniform, the most dazzling of them all, included a jewel-encrusted baton. He liked to change his costume to suit his mood, often, as Sir Eric Phipps recorded in one dispatch, several times during the same function.

Although Phipps (described by the American correspondent William Shirer as looking 'like a Hungarian dandy with a perfect poker face'[14]) detested every aspect of National Socialism, occasionally something would happen to amuse him while at the same time offering a telling insight into the more absurd aspects of Nazi behaviour. One such occasion took place early in June 1934 when he was invited, along with forty or so of his diplomatic colleagues, to Göring's shooting estate in the Schorfheide – an hour's drive north-east of Berlin. 'Our host as usual was late,' Phipps reported, 'but eventually arrived in a fast racing car driven by himself. He was clad in aviator's

---

* Allen, p. 151. This passionate endorsement of Hitler was to cause her difficulty later. On 6 November 1940 she came before a committee whose task it was to decide whether she was dangerous enough to be interned. 'What is your opinion of [Hitler] now?' she was asked. 'I have not any,' she replied. (NA, Mary Allen papers, HO 144/1933).

garments of India rubber with top boots and a large hunting knife stuck in his belt.'[15] The main purpose of the day was to show off a new bison enclosure. To open the proceedings, Göring made a speech celebrating the beauties of the primeval German forest (he had recently been appointed 'Master of the German Forests') in which had roamed primeval German beasts. His intention, he told the diplomats, was to recreate an ancient *Wald* [forest], thereby ensuring that modern Germans would be able to see primitive German animals in an authentic German setting. When he finished speaking,

> three or four cow bison were driven towards a large box containing a bull bison. A host of cinematograph operators and photographers aimed their machines at this box preparatory to the exit of the bull. Those, who like myself, have seen the mad charge of the Spanish bull out of his *torril* [holding pen] looked forward to a similar sight on this occasion, but we were gravely disappointed for the bison emerged from his box with the utmost reluctance, and, after eyeing the cows somewhat sadly, tried to return to it. This part of the programme, therefore, did not fulfil our expectations.[16]

Later the diplomats were driven across the forest in horse-drawn carriages to Carinhall, Göring's shooting lodge overlooking a lake, where their host, clutching a large harpoon, greeted them in 'white tennis shoes, white duck trousers, white flannel shirt and a green leather jacket with the large hunting knife still stuck into his belt'. After another speech, in which Göring extolled the beauty of Carinhall, built of the finest German materials, the diplomats were invited inside. To their surprise, they found a tree growing in the living room, waiting, Phipps surmised, for Wagner's Wotan to plunge into its trunk the mystic Sword destined to remain embedded until released by a true German hero like Siegfried – 'or General Göring'.[17] No one could poke fun at the Nazis more adroitly than Sir Eric, but the day's absurdities also gave rise to serious concerns. Göring, Phipps wrote in his dispatch, had shown off his toys that day like a 'fat spoilt child', but he went on to warn that Hitler's minister for aviation 'also possessed other toys, less innocent ones with wings which might some day be launched on their murderous mission in the same childlike spirit and with the same childlike glee'.[18]

Of the constant stream of visitors passing through the British Embassy during the 1930s, a great many of the men had of course fought in the Great War. As it turned out, a number of the bravest and most decorated former soldiers to sign the Embassy visitors' book were also enthusiastic supporters of the Nazi regime. Lieutenant Colonel Graham Seton Hutchison had won the DSO and MC and been mentioned in dispatches four times. After the war he served in Germany on the Inter-Allied Commission, was a founder member of the British Legion and became a successful writer of adventure fiction. More surprising, by the time Hitler came to power, he was on the Nazi payroll as a publicist and had founded an extreme anti-Semitic fascist party, the National Workers' Movement. A few days after Göring's bison party, Hutchison wrote to the right-wing American poet, Ezra Pound: 'I've made a close study of Germany for 12 years and now some of the leaders. There is a crudeness which the best intelligence recognises, but you will see it shape all right.' Not one for false modesty, he continued, 'Among Englishmen, probably none is

listened to with greater respect in Germany than myself, especially in Bavaria. Germany isn't militarist today, I am certain of
it.'[19] As an extremist, Hutchison was representative of only an
eccentric minority, but he nevertheless expressed a widespread
view among veterans when he wrote, 'We who survived the
Great War are more concerned than any others that peace shall
be preserved. On medical grounds it can be properly assumed
that since we were physically fit to do battle in the last war,
our children will be among the first to be called to national
service to fight the next.'[20]

That men who had fought in the trenches should do everything possible to prevent such a war happening again is easy
to understand but does not entirely explain why a number
of them became so obsessed with fascism. Captain George
Henry Lane-Fox Pitt-Rivers, grandson of Augustus Lane-Fox
Pitt-Rivers whose anthropological collection forms the basis of
the Museum in Oxford bearing his name, had fought bravely
and been wounded in the war. Like his grandfather, he was
a distinguished anthropologist, but he was also a eugenicist.
On 28 November 1934, the *Königsberger Allgemeine* newspaper reported on a lecture he had given at the university:
'Pitt-Rivers sees race as a biological group characterised by
a common ownership of a firmly defined number of character traits, which distinguish this group from others.'[21] An
innocent enough sentence, but the viciously anti-Semitic
Pitt-Rivers was soon having regular meetings with the likes
of Professor Karl Astel, chairman of the Hereditary Health
Supreme Court – the court in Weimar that decided who was
to be forcibly sterilised. 'Our mission', Astel wrote to Himmler,
'is ceaselessly to promote a nobler, sounder, healthier life in
conformity with the species.' He went on to say that he had
a number of experiments in mind, including an investigation

into homosexuality. 'For this work I need from you at least a hundred classified homosexuals from Thuringia and I would ask you to send them in the near future.'[22] This was the man with whom Pitt-Rivers (related to Clementine Churchill and the Mitford family) developed a warm friendship.* 'I send you all good wishes for the new year,' Astel wrote to him on New Year's Eve 1935, 'and above all for the continued progress of the science of Race-hygiene in your country'.[23]

⁓

On 15 July 1935 a convoy of motorcars slowly made its way through a vast crowd of Berliners. A photograph shows many of them cheering with arms outstretched, but others look on more sceptically. All, however, seem curious to catch a glimpse of the passengers. In an open car at the head of the procession, sits Major Francis Fetherston-Godley smiling broadly, his own arm aloft in an uneasy compromise between friendly wave and fascist salute.[24] The major was leading a delegation of five members of the British Legion on a goodwill mission in the hope that the natural comradeship of old soldiers might make a real contribution to world peace.

The motives of the delegation were entirely honourable, and the personal integrity of each member beyond reproach, yet controversy surrounded the enterprise from the start. The fact that the Prince of Wales had given it his blessing – in remarks that were later broadcast throughout Germany – was enough to ensure that it received worldwide publicity. The Nazis seized

---

* After the war Pitt-Rivers' elder son, Michael, was tried for 'buggery'. The trial turned out to be one of the catalysts for the reform of homosexual law.

on the future king's words as signalling an encouraging shift by the British government to a more pro-German policy. This appeared to be confirmed by the signing of the Anglo-German Naval Agreement in June 1935. Hitler, believing the treaty to be the first major step towards a formal alliance with Britain, described the day it was signed as the happiest of his life.[25] The arrival therefore of the British Legion delegation just one month later was a propaganda dream come true. When Fetherston-Godley laid a wreath at the war memorial in Unter den Linden, he did so watched by thousands, under the full glare of the Nazi media.

Some weeks later, the *Regimental Chronicle of the Prince of Wales Volunteers (South Lancashire)* published an account of the British Legion tour. 'In view of the prominence given to our visit,' wrote Lieutenant Colonel Crosfield, DSO, 'it was only natural that we should meet some of the heads of the Government, including that wonderful personality, Hitler himself.'[26] Crosfield, whose response to losing a leg in the First World War had been promptly to join the RAF, came from an old Quaker family and was no fascist. Indeed, by his own admission he went to Germany deeply prejudiced against Hitler. But then he met him:

> Hitler stands in a category quite by himself. No one comes near him either in intensity of purpose nor in the marvellous devotion which he has inspired. We were privileged to spend an hour and a half with him, a great portion of which time was taken up with discussing war experiences and in comparing notes about the various battle fronts … We came away deeply impressed with his simplicity, sincerity, fanatical devotion to his country, and feeling convinced that he was genuinely anxious to avoid another world war.[27]

Despite his enthusiasm for the Führer, Crosfield was under no illusion that National Socialism would work in Britain. He disliked the obsession with uniformity, the stifling of all criticism, and the assumption that those who had been in the party longest should by right have 'the best plums'. Nor was Crosfield convinced by the argument that anti-Semitic policies were directed only against 'the low type of Jew' who had invaded Germany since the war. But, given the immense warmth of the delegation's welcome and the lavish hospitality bestowed on them, it would have seemed churlish, if not downright rude, to harp on such awkward issues. There was one problem, however, that could not be ducked. As part of the Munich itinerary, the organisers had cunningly arranged for Fetherston-Godley to lay a wreath on the Nazi 'martyrs' memorial at the Feldherrnhalle. This was taking goodwill too far and the major saw to it that that programme was hastily revised.

Having attended a reception at Hitler's mountain retreat in Berchtesgaden and lunched with the Görings at their nearby villa, the group was taken on the mandatory tour of Dachau. What they could not have known was that the 'degenerate criminals' paraded before them were in fact camp guards in disguise, and that numerous other foreigners had been similarly duped. The delegation ended its tour in Cologne where they received the most spectacular welcome of all. 'The whole of Cologne was floodlit in our honour,' Crosfield wrote. 'The quayside was lined 10 rows deep by the inhabitants, and from the quayside to our hotel we drove the whole way through dense ranks of the citizens shouting "*Heil den Engländern* [hail the British]", a magnificent tribute to the splendid behaviour of our troops during the occupation.'[28] Was this really the reason? Or was it just another example of the Nazis' brilliant stage management? On their way back to England, Fetherston-Godley and his colleagues no doubt clung to the illusion that their efforts had been worthwhile, although in reality the idea that their delegation, however well-meaning, could have made the slightest difference to Hitler's ambitions was sadly misplaced.

A couple of weeks later, another British delegation set out for Germany with equally good intentions but a much lower profile. This one consisted of churchmen and educationalists who, although they went to Berlin as 'Christian' rather than 'old' soldiers, were motivated by much the same incentives. They were to attend an academic conference with the idea of exploring Nazi thinking on philosophy, economics and education. It was a learned group. Among the theologians were Bishop Neville Talbot, the Dean of Exeter, Spencer Carpenter, and the Reverend Eric Fenn (assistant director of the Student Christian Movement). The educationalists included John Christie, headmaster of Westminster School, and an economics professor from Leeds University. Two women were also in the party – Elizabeth Pakenham (later Lady Longford) and Amy Buller, the instigator and organiser of the conference. Eric Fenn remembered 'the stupefaction of the Nazis at the spectacle of Mrs Pakenham – a good-looking mother of two children and yet an Oxford graduate, a Labour councillor and an author who knew a good deal about economics'.[29] In other words, a woman light years away from the *Kinder, Küche, Kirche* version so beloved by the regime.

Amy Buller, a formidable woman in her mid-forties and currently warden of a women's hall of residence in Liverpool, knew Germany well. At first, like many other foreigners, she had been impressed by the Nazis but on recent visits had become increasingly disturbed by all that she saw and heard.[30]

It was, she now felt, a matter of urgency to arrange a proper dialogue between the theologians and academics of each country. So, with the backing of the Archbishop of York, William Temple, she energetically set about organising a conference.

It took place in the Kaiserhof – the hotel at which Hitler had established his headquarters before he became chancellor. Dean Carpenter recalled Amy warning them that the room where they gathered each day had a 'listening-in-machine' concealed up the chimney, and that they should take great care not to mention any German by name. The professors they encountered 'were personally most friendly', remarked Carpenter, 'but they said some surprising things'.[31] One speaker defined for them the various types of socialism. 'There is Marxian Socialism. That is an abomination. There is Christian Socialism, which means giving relief to the poor man. There is no harm in that. But the real thing is National Socialism.'[32] Most worrying of all was the statement (made during a lecture entitled 'Humanism') that all philosophy was founded on race. 'And that from a professor of philosophy,' noted an astonished Carpenter. One evening a clandestine meeting was held in what Fenn described as 'a basement café of dubious reputation'. It had a very low ceiling, so that Bishop Talbot, who was six feet seven inches tall, had to bend double to enter. A girl at one of the tables, Fenn recalled, 'gazed in astonishment at Talbot's aproned and gaitered figure and asked her companion, "*Was für ein wunderbares Tier ist das?* [What is that amazing creature?]"'[33] It was a rare moment of humour in what was in every other respect a dispiriting week. Although one of their number suggested that there might be something in dictatorship if the right sort of dictator could be found,[34] the group returned home their good intentions in tatters, full of foreboding for the future.

On 4 August 1935, a few days after the British Legion delegation arrived home, Lady Domvile woke her husband at 4 a.m. at their house in Putney. Within an hour Vice-Admiral Sir Barry Domvile, KBE, CB, CMG, was on his way to Croydon airport and by noon had landed at Tempelhof Airport in Berlin. His host was Walter de Sager – a pro-Nazi Swiss-German businessman based in London who had invited Domvile to Germany on a fact-finding tour. The vice-admiral, recently retired president of the Royal Naval College at Greenwich, and former head of British Naval Intelligence, was exactly the sort of prominent foreigner that the Nazis wanted to target. Domvile's first impressions during the short ride to the Adlon Hotel were pleasing. Relieved to have left behind 'gloomy' Croydon, he found Berlin, with its street cafés and colourful window boxes, refreshingly cheerful. Even better, there was no speed limit, no 'early closing' and motorists could park where they liked. So much 'for this *verboten* [forbidden] country and England the land of the free', he commented in his diary.[35] But he was puzzled to be staying in a hotel and not at the de Sagers' apartment. Who, he wondered, were his real hosts?

The next day he was collected from the hotel by Theodor Eicke, Chief Inspector of Concentration Camps but formerly Commandant of Dachau where only a few months earlier he had played host to James McDonald and Derek Hill. Escorted by an official car, they drove out to the suburbs, heading for the headquarters of the Adolf Hitler Regiment. This elite regiment, commanded by Hitler's erstwhile chauffeur, Josef Dietrich, consisted of hand-picked men from the SS – 'enormous fellows', noted Domvile, 'brought up on high moral principles and sworn to Hitler's allegiance'. Greeted with a barrage of

'Heil Hitlers', Domvile soon, in his own words, 'became quite adept' at the Nazi salute. This was just as well because, after watching the drum tattoo, the admiral was invited to inspect the guard and take the salute as it marched past in immaculate goose step. By now it had become clear that his real host was none other than the head of the SS himself – Heinrich Himmler. 'What a funny world it is!' Domvile observed.[36]

At the reception held in his honour after the parade, Domvile noticed that some of the officers wore a ring embossed with a skull. The Death's Head ring, he learned, was a personal gift from Himmler to any SS man who had shown exceptional courage. Examining one of them, Domvile saw inscribed on its inner surface 30.6.34. This was the date of the Night of the Long Knives, when Himmler had finally seen off his rival, Ernst Röhm. Domvile was unaware that Eicke, with whom he had just been chatting so pleasantly, had volunteered to execute Röhm in his prison cell after the latter refused to commit suicide. Dietrich, who Domvile judged 'rather a rough mannered man, but a good leader', had also emerged from Hitler's famous purge with flying colours. One moment he had been the Führer's driver, the next a general in the SS.

After leaving the barracks, Domvile called on Sir Eric Phipps. The record does not reveal what account of his eventful morning he gave the ambassador but he would no doubt have conveyed his conviction that an Anglo-German entente was a high Nazi priority.[37] With Domvile, at least, the SS had hit upon a worthy target, as the vice-admiral was unmistakably an establishment figure who had genuinely worked in positions of influence. But in general, the Nazis' crude efforts to understand the British did little to bring closer the longed-for alliance. The leadership's ignorance of British history is neatly summed up in an anecdote recounted by the Embassy's first secretary, Ivone Kirkpatrick. Julius Streicher, seeking to illustrate to a Berlin audience how hopeless the British were at grasping the Jewish threat, told them that the 'Jewish politician Disraeli had been ennobled by Queen Victoria under the title of "Lord Gladstone"'.[38]

The next morning Mr and Mrs de Sager collected Domvile in their Mercedes and drove south. Somewhere south of Leipzig they stopped for lunch where their waiter told them how he had recently paid five marks to see a man beheaded. After watching many decapitations in China, he had wanted to compare techniques. 'He said the Germans were very skilful with the axe,' Domvile recorded, before returning to a favourite theme – the loveliness of German window boxes.

The importance attached by the Germans to Domvile's visit became crystal clear when several days later the admiral found himself lunching with Heinrich Himmler at the latter's villa at Tegernsee, forty miles south of Munich. That afternoon they set off for the mountains where, up in the wild Bavarian forest, they would hunt and bond like true Aryan brothers. 'We drove', wrote Domvile, 'through lovely woodland – on an appalling road with sheer drops – to HH's hunting box, 1,100 metres.' The fastidious Domvile, already unhappy at having to share a room with de Sager, discovered that there was only cold water and 'the bog' consisted of nothing but a deep hole. The fat cook slept on a shelf in the kitchen. 'A primitive spot,' he noted. It was a long way from Putney.

Next morning, Himmler woke Domvile at 3.20 a.m. singing 'God Save the King'. Domvile responded with 'Heil Hitler'. Willy Sachs – Nazi owner of the engineering firm Fichtel & Sachs, who also owned large tracts of Bavaria – was in charge of the proceedings. It was he who led Domvile up the mountain in the breaking dawn in search of something to shoot.

Sachs's 'feudal' relationship with his retainers particularly impressed the admiral, reminding him of the 'desert Arabs and their slaves'. Just as they were about to give up and return to the hut, a chamois obligingly appeared offering the admiral his chance of glory. To everyone's relief, he hit it. 'Sachs' joy was ludicrous,' wrote Domvile. 'He embraced me and kept on saying how happy he was. He insisted on my calling him Bill so I christened him "Bill of Bavaria". I finished up as the finest hunter in the Bavarian Alps.' The beast was then ceremoniously transported back to the hunting box, where 'Bill did the goosestep on the veranda'.

It emerged that Göring – Master of the German Forest – had personally granted a special hunting permit to Domvile. That night there was more bonding.

We had a regular Bavarian evening – accordion player and 3 dancers, 2 male. The local dances are very extraordinary – much leaping, crying and smacking of bums, soles of feet, thighs etc. and a pretence of lifting the girls' skirts, reminiscent of highland reels. Bill got very excited – sang, danced with the fat cook. Everyone did a turn, Walter de Sager, Wolff,* Himmler – only I sat out. So the fun went on, waxing hotter with relays of food and drinks. I retired at midnight … they went on till after 3 a.m. when every drop of the considerable amount of drink brought up was finished. HH very charming.

* Karl Wolff was Himmler's Chief of Personal Staff and SS liaison officer to Hitler.

By the time they returned to Tegernsee, the party had swollen to include a husband and wife broadcasting team from Chicago, Mr Finsterwald (an American diplomat) and his wife, as well as Hitler's staunch defender in the House of Commons, Lieutenant Colonel Sir Thomas Moore MP. On 12 August they all set out to spend the day at Dachau. It was hot and Domvile's nerves were beginning to fray. 'I had to give up my seat in the front of the car to that bitch of a woman Mrs Finsterwald who has an epidermis like a rhinoceros and who should never have been allowed to come.' They spent several hours with the inmates – 'No definite type, all sorts,' wrote Domvile, who of course had no idea that the 'prisoners' were actually prison guards in disguise. 'A lot of crimes against small girls, a murderer or two ... went into one room full of buggers.' Both men praised the comfort and good order of the camp, agreeing how splendid it was of the Nazis to give these 'dregs of humanity' a fresh start. The group left Dachau (with souvenir wooden beer mugs made by the real prisoners) much impressed by all they had seen. 'The English press have been disgraceful lately with their lies about Germany,' Domvile wrote that night in his diary.

But a couple of days later his mood had begun to sour. The de Sagers were increasingly irritating, the weather had turned wet and cold, 'Moore kept hammering away at the Jews' and travel arrangements were in 'a first class muddle'. Domvile commented: 'The Nazis are quarrelling too much amongst themselves, there are three foreign departments – von Ribbentrop's, the Nazi FO and the ordinary one – all in competition.' Domvile's trip to Germany confirmed a deep belief, shared by so many men who had fought in the Great War, that without a strong alliance between England and Germany there could be no world peace. While the new

Germany was all very well, it was nevertheless with considerable relief that two weeks after he had first arrived in Berlin, Domvile boarded an aeroplane for home.[39]

Three weeks after Admiral Domvile had returned safely to Putney, an unusually exotic visitor arrived in Berlin. With his fleets of cars, wives and children (there were at least 88 of the latter), Sir Bhupinder Singh, Maharaja of Patiala, was everything a maharaja should be. Extravagant, bejewelled and a first-class cricketer, he was also an honorary Lieutenant Colonel in the British army. After attending King George V's jubilee celebrations earlier in the year, he had retreated to a health spa in France. From there, on 9 August, he wrote to Colonel Neal at the India Office with instructions for his forthcoming travels. Apart from visiting the King and Queen of Belgium and the Queen of Holland (whom he had not yet had 'the pleasure of visiting in her own country'), he particularly wanted to meet 'that rising dictator, Herr Hitler'. It would, he told the Colonel, 'afford me so much pleasure to see him and thus allow me to judge him on his merits or otherwise'.[40]

Despite some initial reluctance, Berlin responded positively. Not only did the maharaja employ a number of Germans in Patiala but he had also filled his hospital with German equipment and invited German interior designers to decorate his palaces. The commercial potential was clear but the Nazis must have also realised that his visit gave them a perfect opportunity to tweak British sensitivities over India. So, despite the fact that the maharaja's chief medical officer was Jewish, it was agreed to push out the boat – even to the extent of granting Sir Bhupinder an audience with the Führer. The interview did not begin well. The maharaja opened their conversation by complaining of how on his last visit to Berlin a German doctor had charged him the astonishing sum of £15,000 for a single consultation. This did not please the Führer and it was only when the maharaja began to express his enthusiasm for the new Germany that the mood lightened.

Sir Bhupinder warmly welcomed Germany's growing influence in India and recommended that the Consulate General be moved from Calcutta to Delhi or Simla – 'closer to the target'. He argued that, although Germany could not compete with Japan in 'bazaar goods', when it came to the big technical installations it could certainly give England a run for its money. As part of this skilful wedge-driving exercise, the maharaja no doubt understood exactly what he was doing when he asked the young diplomat Baron Dietrich von Mirbach for the name of a good German lawyer capable of writing a new constitution for Patiala.* It was a request that, in the light of the British government's continued reluctance to deal more closely with Hitler, would have been keenly noted by von Mirbach's superiors.

A great many former Allied soldiers travelled to the Third Reich during the 1930s and naturally their responses to the Nazis differed widely. While all were united in their determination to prevent any repeat of the trenches, a few, like Captain Pitt-Rivers, became so seduced by Hitler's dictatorship that

---

* The Government of India Act had been passed in London only a couple of weeks before the maharaja's visit to Germany. For a full account of the maharaja's visit see von Mirbach's report, Auswärtiges Amt Poitisches Archiv, Berlin, R77444.

they appeared to lose all sense of right and wrong. Many more, of whom Lieutenant Colonel Crosfield is a good example, allowed their normal critical acumen to become dulled by Nazi propaganda. The question that thoroughly decent men like Crosfield should have been asking after a visit to Hitler's Germany is why, if government by brutal suppression, corrupt law and the merciless persecution of all opposition was unacceptable in Britain, should it have been any less so in the Third Reich? The tragedy is that, by turning a blind eye to such searing issues, these gallant soldiers only succeeded in bringing closer the very conflict that they so desperately sought to avert.

11

Literary 'Tourists'

reedom of expression is so fundamental to a writer that it comes as a shock to discover how many celebrated literary figures of the twentieth century were drawn to fascism. The very notion that writers of the stature of Ezra Pound, Wyndham Lewis or Norwegian Nobel Prize-winner, Knut Hamsun, could openly condone a regime that publicly burned books, or tortured and killed people simply for expressing a view, is deeply perplexing. Yet T. S. Eliot is among those who have been charged with fascist leanings, while W. B. Yeats was a supporter of the Irish Blueshirts.* And even if such accusations are unfounded or exaggerated, the question remains – how was it possible for any foreign writer of conscience not to be actively *condemning* a dictatorship whose hallmarks were brutality, censorship and suppression?

Such matters seem to have been of little concern to Henry Williamson, whose book *Tarka the Otter* won the Hawthornden Prize in 1928. He saw in Hitler's Germany

---

* The Blueshirts was the name given to a pro-fascist organisation operating in Ireland during the 1930s.

only what he wanted to see. As an infantryman in the trenches he had taken part in the famous Christmas truce of 1914, an intense experience that had convinced him – contrary to all the propaganda – that he was essentially at one with his enemy. Then, fifteen years after the war, his own country still mired in depression, he saw Hitler leading the Germans to a bright new future while at the same time rekindling their hunger for national tradition. The Nazi cry of '*Blut und Boden*' was the longed-for summons to a simpler era when peasants worked their land in harmony with nature, and tribe and territory were one. For Williamson, immersed in the natural world, this mystical past had profound romantic appeal. In Hitler, he saw a leader in perfect sympathy with such views and, moreover, one whose Hitler Youth movement was inspiring the young.

Early in August 1935, Williamson, then living in Devonshire, received a letter from his old friend and fellow writer, John Heygate, inviting him to attend the Nuremberg Reichsparteitag [Reich Party Day] and offering to pay his fare.[1] After Heygate's adventures in the Tyrol distributing Nazi propaganda, he had returned to his job at the UFA studios in Berlin. He explained to Williamson that the invitation came from the *Reichsschrifttumskammer* [Office for the Direction of German Writers], clearly the real source of funds. Unperturbed by the fact that such a sinister-sounding government department should even exist, Williamson eagerly accepted. The Nazis had made a wise investment. From the moment he set foot in the country, the naturalist and novelist became an ardent advocate for the regime, soaking up its propaganda, never questioning its claims. He was particularly attracted by the Führer's vision ('an improved version of Lenin's'), 'based on every man owning, in a trustee-to-nation

sense, his own bit of land and fulfilling himself in living a natural life'.[2]

Recording his visit a year later, Williamson described how
they had left Berlin for Nuremberg early on 7 September
in Heygate's MG. 'We rushed into the faint mists of sunrise,
smoothly at 82 mph,' he wrote. 'It was thrilling to pass field-
grey troops on the march, long boots and lumber wheels faintly
dusty, each soldier wearing a flower in helmet or tunic.' As they
neared Nuremberg, fireworks lit up the horizon making it 'glow
and dilate as though with gunfire'. On arrival, Williamson was
astonished to see so many foreigners, most of them billeted in
railway carriages shunted into sidings. He noted the 'lines and
lines of Mitropa coaches filled with military attachés, secretaries, embassy underlings, Oxford Groupists, Boy Scout bosses,
journalists, social lecturers, industrial millionaires, dozens,
scores, hundreds of foreigners including unclassified outsiders
like ourselves'.

By 8 a.m. the next day, the two men were already seated
in the vast Luitpoldarena [Nazi Party rally grounds]. 'We had
a good place at the end of a gangway,' Williamson recalled.
'I sat on the edge, sleeves rolled up sunbathing.' But within
minutes his day was ruined. Not by the terrifying display of
totalitarianism unfolding before him, but because, 'A bulky
rump thrust itself against my lean one, and I was squeezed
up out of my end seat. I turned and looked at this fleshy
cuckoo ... I saw he had, in his pale podgy hands, a large
envelope, the address of which was Oxford University.' A
name then came into view revealing that Williamson's unwelcome neighbour was none other than the Reverend Frank
Buchman, American founder of the Oxford Group.[3]

The Oxford Group, later known as Moral Re-Armament,
had a catchphrase – 'God Control'. Buchman's big idea was

that world peace would come only through 'God-controlled nations' created by 'God-controlled personalities'. And as he witnessed the true extent of the Führer's power that day, magnified by the adoring millions, he must have dreamed of what a 'God-controlled' Hitler could achieve for his movement. Here was a leader, a genuine *Übermensch*, who had already proved himself by defeating the Anti-Christ in the guise of communism. 'This far-seeing seer may show us the way out,'[4] Buchman subsequently wrote. But neither he, a man of God, nor the sensitive nature-loving Williamson appear to have shown the least concern for the Jews who, so it was announced at that very same rally, were within days to be legally stripped of their citizenship.

Buchman often travelled in Germany during the mid-1930s, at a time when the Oxford Group enjoyed considerable success throughout Europe. His penchant for royalty and comfortable hotels did not go unnoticed, although he liked to present himself as a simple man ('an extra travel bag was a sin'), who toiled 'from country to country, from home to home, from heart to heart'. He wanted to bridge 'the gulf between Haves and Have-nots, between class and class, between nation and nation'. The only time he paused on these 'arduous' journeys was 'to let the still small voice give him the direction for his future course'.[5] A couple of weeks after Nuremberg, Buchman's divine guide led him to Geneva, where, with memories of Führer, flags and pounding boots still fresh in his mind, he made a speech: 'There are those who feel that internationalism is not enough,' he told his audience. 'Nationalism can make a nation. Super-nationalism can make a world. God-controlled nationalism seems to be the only sure foundation for world peace.'[6]

Williamson was just one of a number of English guests officially invited by the Nazi Party to Nuremberg that year.

Unity Mitford, her sister Diana Guinness (by then, Sir Oswald Mosley's mistress) and their brother Tom (shortly to join the British Union of Fascists) also numbered among the honoured guests. Some of these, so the British military attaché Major Hotblack reported back to London, were heard to express 'very anti-British views'. He marked out Williamson as being a 'particularly talkative critic', noting that he also went round falsely claiming to be a special correspondent of *The Times*.[7] Although Williamson's enthusiasm for National Socialism remained at high pitch, he began to weary physically. 'The masses and movement had exhausted my eye nerves, accustomed to grass, trees and sameness of valley life,' he wrote. After spending a further week on a Nazi-organised tour for foreign journalists, Williamson's German excursion ended ingloriously in Berlin at the Adlon Hotel:

> My Reichs checks gave out; I had no money; the others went back to England; I sat alone wondering how I could get a few marks to tip the bedroom valet, and pay my fare back to Bremerhaven and Southampton. I didn't like to borrow from John [Heygate]; nor go to the Berlin publisher of my sole translation, *Tarka* – which anyway had earned only about 11 marks in the past year. At last I confided in our host from the Propaganda Ministry, who came into the lounge. He went to the hotel office, and returned, ordered coffee. While we drank, he covertly slid a bundle of notes across the table, murmuring, with eyes averted, 'This will fix it for you.' 150 marks.[8]

It would be easier to feel more sympathy for Williamson if, after the war, he had admitted that he had been wrong. But in 1969 when interviewed by Roy Plomley on *Desert Island*

Discs, he said merely that he had not then been wise enough to know that 'a man of tremendous artistic feeling should never be in charge of a nation'. The nearest he came to acknowledging Nazi crime was when he remarked that Hitler had been a perfectionist 'and once you begin to force perfectionism on other people you become the devil'.[9]

~

Norway's most famous novelist, Knut Hamsun, was in terms both of literary achievement and devotion to Nazi Germany in a different league. His books, with their focus on the individual ego and their spontaneous style, had a profound impact on European writing. When Hamsun won the Nobel Prize in 1920 for *Growth of the Soil*, Thomas Mann commented that it had never been awarded to a worthier recipient. Hemingway recommended Hamsun's novels to Scott Fitzgerald; André Gide compared him to Dostoyevsky. Anticipating the likes of Kafka, Joyce and Sartre, the Norwegian was regarded by many leading writers as the progenitor of modern literature.[10] But if the emotional and psychological thrust of his novels inspired the literary avant-garde, paradoxically Hamsun also struck a deep chord with the Nazis. Indeed, he achieved the remarkable feat of being cited as a favourite writer by both Hermann Hesse and Joseph Goebbels.

The Nazis despised any hint of modernism but Hamsun, who was born into a peasant family and grew up in the harsh beauty of the Arctic Circle, won their admiration for his Nordic reverence for Nature and the *Blut und Boden* themes that emerge particularly in his later novels. Even more important from the Nazi point of view was the fact that this world-renowned writer was so utterly and so publicly dedicated to their cause. An added bonus was that his profound love of all things German was matched by an equally deep hatred of all things English. Hamsun bitterly denounced the British as arrogant hypocrites bent on world domination through treachery and murder. Hitler, on the other hand, was a crusader, a reformer ready to forge a 'great Germanic world community' in which Norway would play a key role. Despite his empathy for Germany – 'I am ... a Norwegian and a German,' he once telegraphed to the Nordic Society[11] – he spent surprisingly little time in the country. When, after an absence of thirty-five years, he returned there in January 1931 at the age of seventy-two, he was greeted by newspaper headlines reading '*Willkommen Knut Hamsun*'. Indeed, so intense was the public excitement that he felt unable to leave his Berlin hotel room. Two days later he departed with his wife and son by train for Italy.

Although Hamsun never himself stayed long in Germany he made sure that his children did, believing that it was only among the 'decent and supremely capable German people' that they would receive a proper education. 'I send my children one after the other to Germany,' he wrote to a friend. 'For years they have found a home there, are in good care there and return as mature human beings.'[12] This statement was not entirely borne out by the facts. A few weeks after he wrote those words, his youngest daughter Cecilia, aged sixteen, was sending home distressing accounts of life in Berlin. Hamsun was having none of it:

> Cecilia you are living in a great and wonderful country. You mustn't go writing to the maid about this or that person committing suicide, they will think it is awful in Germany. Write about the things Hitler and his government are achieving, despite the whole world's hatred and hostility.

You and I and everybody will thank and bless Germany. It
is the country of the future.[13]

For all his enthusiasm, however, he was not overjoyed when
his son Tore joined the SS, commenting, 'It is both a good
thing and a bad thing.'[14] He certainly did not welcome the
extra cost involved. 'You wrote in a previous letter that you
would not need more than DM 250. I added DM 50 and yet
now you want more for an SS coat! Remember that you are
in a penniless country ... if I were in your shoes, I would act
as modestly as possible and hide the fact that your name is
Hamsun rather than court favouritism because of it. Think
about it, Tore!'[15]

⁓

The travels of American novelist Thomas Wolfe offer a more
nuanced perspective. Wolfe's deep love of Germany was no
doubt heightened by the fact that his books sold particularly
well there – even the Nazis adored him. When he arrived
on his fifth visit, in May 1935, his recently published book,
Of Time and the River, was already causing a stir. Lionised in
Berlin, he was swept up in a 'wild, fantastic, incredible whirl of
parties, teas, dinners, all night drinking bouts, newspaper interviews, radio proposals, photographers and dozens of people
chief among them Martha and the Dodds'.[16] William E. Dodd
(described by Truman Smith's wife Kay as 'small with wrin-
kled, dried up, colorless skin and hair; his soul was the same'[17]),
was the American ambassador and Martha his unconventional
daughter. In her book *My Years in Germany*, Martha wrote, 'To
the desolateness of the intellectual life of Germany, Thomas
Wolfe was like a symbol of the past when great writers were
great men.'[18]

On his way to Berlin Wolfe had passed through Hanover, where he had lunched at Knickermeyer's. 'Huge oaken Germanic, Bürgerbräu place with heavy Wotans – food to match – great ships' models hanging from ceiling – young aviators, special table and waiters' obsequious haste to serve them.' Less appetising was a pub entered by chance: 'I opened a door and was immediately greeted by such a slough of filth and fetid odors, and stupid and corrupted faces that my heart recoiled. An old man all hair and eyes and yellowed whiskers … was sitting at one of the tables, slobbing up some mess out of a plate on to his whiskers.'[19] But this unlovely scene was for Wolfe an aberration that bore little relation to the real Germany. That Germany was a land of romantic beauty where 'the green is the greenest green on earth and which gives to all [its] foliage a kind of forest darkness, a legendary sense of magic and of time'.[20] Wolfe is equally persuasive when describing the urban scene:

> A tram, cream-yellow, spotless, shining as a perfect toy, slid past, with a kind of hissing sound upon the rails and at the contacts of the trolley. Except for this the tram made no noise. Like everything they made, the tram was perfect in its function. Even the little cobblestones that paved the tramway were spotless as if each of them had just been gone over thoroughly with a whisk-broom, and the strips of grass on either side were as green and velvety as Oxford sward.[21]

Although friends like Martha Dodd did their best to open Wolfe's eyes, he was as reluctant to let go his German idyll as he was to be influenced by the views of others. But, although on that occasion he returned to America his illusions largely intact, seeds of doubt had begun to take root.

A year later he was back in Germany. Prohibited by currency restrictions from taking his substantial royalties out of the country, he decided to spend them there on a long holiday. When it was over, Wolfe left Berlin by the Paris train on the first leg of his journey home. At the frontier town of Aachen there was a scheduled stop of fifteen minutes and it was here that he experienced his Damascene moment. Having become friendly with his fellow passengers, he strolled with them along the platform while waiting to re-board the train. But as they returned to their compartment it was clear some terrible crisis had occurred. Wolfe instantly recognised the signs: 'You do not know, of course, the precise circumstance, but what you sense immediately is the final stage of tragedy ... Even before one arrives one knows from this silent eloquence of shoulders, backs, and heads that something ruinous and horrible has happened.' It quickly emerged that this particular drama centred on another of Wolfe's fellow travellers, a nervous little man with whom he had conversed all morning and had nicknamed Fuss-And-Fidget. It was only now that Wolfe discovered that his new friend was Jewish and had been caught trying to leave Germany with a large sum of money. The official who arrested him, the American noted, had 'high blunt cheekbones, a florid face and tawny mustaches ... his head was shaven, and there were thick creases at the base of the skull and across his fleshy neck'. Wolfe did not particularly like Jews but he found himself

trembling with murderous and incomprehensible anger. I wanted to smash that fat neck with the creases in it, I wanted to pound that inflamed and blunted face into a jelly. I wanted to kick square and hard, bury my foot, dead center in the obscene fleshiness of those clumsy buttocks. And I knew that I was helpless, that all of us were ... I felt impotent, shackled, unable to stir against the walls of an obscene but unshakable authority.[22]

There was, however, one weapon Wolfe did have in his power to deploy – his pen. But, as he well knew, publication of the story would come at great personal cost. His books would be banned in Germany and he would never again be able to visit the country that he adored. 'I Have a Thing to Tell You' was published in the *New Republic* a few months after he returned to America. It is a powerful piece that concludes with a touching goodbye. 'To that old German land with all the measure of its truth, its glory, beauty, magic and its ruin,' Wolfe wrote, 'to that dark land, to that old ancient earth that I have loved so long – I said farewell.'[23]

In October 1935 the Swiss literary and cultural philosopher Denis de Rougemont took up a post at Frankfurt University teaching literature. His academic friends in Paris were astonished but, as he explained, he believed that it was important to study Hitler in his own setting through the eyes of both his followers and his victims. Possessing a cooler head than Thomas Wolfe, de Rougemont set about dissecting Hitler's Germany with admirable objectivity. The result is a forensic examination of how the regime affected ordinary people in their daily lives, meticulously catalogued in *Journal d'Allemagne*. Wanting to be sure that his observations would stand the test of time, de Rougemont waited two years before publishing his journal in 1938.

Although he arrived in Germany convinced that 'Hitlerism' was a right-wing movement, the more he talked to people from different backgrounds, the more confused he

became. After a few weeks in Frankfurt, he found himself wondering, *'le régime est-il de gauche ou de droite?* [Is the regime
on the left or the right?]'[24] What unsettled him was the fact
that those who stood most naturally on the right – lawyers,
doctors, industrialists and so on – were the very ones who
most bitterly denounced National Socialism. Far from being
a bulwark against communism, they complained, it was itself
communism in disguise. They pointed out that only workers
and peasants benefited from Nazi reforms, while their own
values were being systematically destroyed by devious methods. They were taxed disproportionately, their family life had
been irreparably harmed, parental authority sapped, religion
stripped and education eliminated.

De Rougemont, a federalist who had little time for totalitarianism of any colour, was unimpressed by these cries of woe.
He blamed the middle classes for not having faced up to social
problems during the Weimar period. Now they were equally
supine in the face of Hitler's excesses. 'If I ask them how they
are going to resist,' wrote de Rougemont, 'they duck the question. I make them admit that brown bolshevism, although
identical in their view, is less awful than red. There have been
no massacres and everything takes place in a progressive well-
organised manner.'[25]

The academically inclined Amy Buller would have argued
that de Rougemont's criticism was unfair. Her links to the
higher echelons of the Church of England, and involvement
with the Student Christian Movement, took her regularly to
Germany between the wars, where she interviewed dozens of
middle-class professionals. In her book *Darkness over Germany*
(1943) she vividly records the torment so many experienced
in trying to decide how best to resist the Nazis. The truth was
that Hitler's brutal suppression of all opposition had been so

swift and so total that anyone wanting to set their face against the Party was left with the stark choice of exile or martyrdom. Otherwise they were doomed to an agonising compromise. One young schoolmaster told Buller that many of his colleagues would have preferred concentration camp to the daily torture of teaching Nazi doctrine were it not for the fact that their dependents would also be made to suffer.[26]

De Rougemont was not alone in questioning the distinction between National Socialism and communism. Many foreigners wondered how it was possible that two such violently opposed political movements could share so much common ground. Kay Smith, who prided herself on calling a spade a spade, listened intently to a lengthy exposition on National Socialist theory before asking, 'But Rochus, what then is the difference between National Socialism and Communism? The German threw up his hands in horror, *"Psst Katie, das darf man nicht sagen* [Hush, one must not say that]."'[27] Seventeen-year-old Joan Wakefield (whose family motto was 'Be Just and Fear Not') was even bolder. Fresh out of an English boarding school, she was studying German at Berlin University. Sitting one afternoon in a crowded hall listening to a lengthy Nazi harangue, she rose to her feet and with her very English accent asked the speaker if he would be so good as to explain to her the difference between National Socialism and communism. There was a shocked silence. When, with some pride, Joan later recounted this episode to her landlady, the Baronin turned white, terrified that her young lodger's faux pas might rebound on her.[28] In a letter to her sister Debo several years later, Nancy Mitford wrote, 'Actually I have always said that there wasn't a pin to put between Bolshies & Nazis except that the latter, being better organised, are probably more dangerous.'[29]

This, then, was a question often raised by foreigners but, as de Rougemont discovered, one that rarely received a satisfactory response. A former militant communist offered him partial insight when he explained why, at the age of fifty, he had decided to swap sides:

> We want work and our cup of café au lait in the morning ... that is enough. Politics don't interest the workers when they have food and work. Hitler? Now that he has won, he has only to implement his programme. It was almost the same as ours! But he has been more cunning, he reassured the bourgeois by not immediately attacking religion ... I will tell you one thing: if they abandon him, all these fat pigs who are around him ... I will go and fight for him! He at least is a sincere man; he is the only one.[30]

As for where exactly National Socialism stood on the political spectrum, de Rougemont concluded that, although the regime was a good deal further to the left than had been appreciated in France, it was much less so than the German bourgeoisie tried to make out.

When it came to the 'Jewish question', de Rougemont, like so many other foreigners travelling or living in the Third Reich, liked to emphasise the difference between the 'liberal European' type and the 'vulgar, arrogant' Jew who, by implication, always emanated from Eastern Europe. In making this distinction, such people displayed their own latent (and often unconscious) anti-Semitism. One Jew of the 'right' kind, a friend of de Rougemont's, told him how he had worked tirelessly for Franco–German reconciliation. 'He cannot really conceive Hitlerism in all its absurdity,' the Swiss remarked. 'It is not the anti-Semitism that seems to him so extraordinary

– far from it! Many Jews share it – rather it is the idea of a world founded on force where there is no place for rational thought.' As for the 'wrong' kind, like those de Rougemont saw each day gathered at a café on the Opernplatz, it was these Jews who, in his view, were the real source of the problem. 'Paunchy and ringed, a cigar in the middle of the mouth', they justified the worst of Hitler's propaganda. 'No need to resort to openly false documents like *The Protocols of the Elders of Zion*,' he commented. 'It is enough to finger these bellies or to recall the parent humiliated by their children who are never first in a class in which there are Jews present.'

Given that Leonard Woolf was Jewish, it is curious that he and Virginia should have chosen to drive through Germany in May 1935 on their way to Rome. Harold Nicolson (with whom they had stayed in Berlin seven years earlier) suggested they would be wise to consult the Foreign Office first. Woolf thought it quite absurd that 'any Englishman, whether Jew or Gentile, should hesitate to enter a European country'.[31] Nevertheless he took with him protection in the form of a letter signed by Prince Bismarck, then a diplomat at the German Embassy in London.

Once in Germany, the Woolfs set off up the Rhine but, unlike most other foreign tourists, were not enthusiastic. Leonard thought it 'one of the few really ugly rivers in the world',[32] while Virginia described the country as 'pretentious', the scenery 'operatic', the hills 'high but insignificant', and the famous Rhineland towers and ruins 'correct'. The river 'runs with coal barges like Oxford Street', she added.[33] In Heidelberg she noticed, 'the dons and their daughters tripping out to each other's houses with pale blue Beethoven quartets under their arms'.[34] The Woolfs' initial obsequiousness to Nazi authority soon turned to anger as they were forced to drive at a snail's pace along a road lined with euphoric crowds awaiting a Göring motorcade. As it turned out, their short stay in Germany was transformed – not by Bismarck's impressive letter – but by their pet marmoset, Mitzi. Perched on Leonard's shoulder, she was an instant celebrity wherever they went, melting the hardest Nazi heart. 'Pig-tailed school-children, yellow-haired Aryan Fräuleins, blonde blowsy Fraus, grim storm troopers', Leonard wrote, 'went into ecstasies' over the little furry creature. For it was quite obvious to everyone that no one possessing such 'a dear little thing' could possibly be a Jew.[35]

Communist Maria Leitner had neither cuddly animal nor princely letter to protect her on the illicit journeys she made through the Third Reich between 1936 and 1939 – only courage. Born to a Jewish German-speaking family in what is now Croatia, she grew up in Budapest. By the time she went undercover in Germany, she had worked all over Europe as well as spending five years travelling the American continent where she had supplemented her writing income with menial cleaning jobs. Her novel *Hotel Amerika* (1930) is an exposé, as she saw it, of the American dream. In another of her books, *Elisabeth, Ein Hitlermädchen* (1937), she laid bare the extent to which the Nazis had kidnapped German youth – a theme endlessly reiterated by despairing parents to de Rougemont. 'Every evening my two children are taken over by the Party,' the wife of a lawyer complained to him:

> My daughter is 18 and the leader of a group of young girls who she has to manage twice a week for gymnastics and political culture. She also has to make sure they do relief

work for the poor and visit them when they are sick –
another means of control as everything is reported back
to the Party. With all that we hardly ever see her anymore
so how can parents maintain their authority? The Party
comes before everything. We are only civilians to our children. They feel that they are soldiers … Naturally they are
delighted. They feel free because liberty for a teenager is
when you don't have to be with your family.[36]

Maria Leitner was in her forties when, in a series of articles
published by foreign left-wing newspapers,* she set about
relentlessly exposing the dark underbelly of Nazi rule. On her
travels through rural Germany, she came across plenty of the
Blut und Boden that had so inspired Hamsun and Williamson,
but the blood and soil she encountered was far removed from
the 'romantic' image of peasant life exploited by the Nazis.
These peasants were too grindingly poor to be inclined to celebrate any heroic union with their land.

A village schoolteacher told Leitner how in winter they
were completely cut off. Paths were impassable and, despite
the farmers' desperate need, no roads had been built. 'They
are contracted to provide eight cart journeys to the school,' he
explained, 'but they are often reluctant to fetch me, as their
horses can't make it.' The air in his classroom was stuffy. The
farmers, responsible for the heating fuel, could not bear to see
the window open, even for a minute. Fifty-two children of
mixed ages sat in one room. Stuck up on the board between
pictures of Man, tooth care and insects, were images of Aryans

* For example, *The Paris Daily*, *The Word* (Moscow) and *The New
World Stage*.

and Jews. 'Which of you has a toothbrush?' Leitner asks. 'The children laugh.' She tries another question: 'Tell me what you had for lunch yesterday?' 'Potato soup,' they all chorus – except for one little boy. 'We had roast duck.' 'Was it a family celebration?' 'No, our duck suffocated.'

As Leitner points out, villages like this played an important role in the Nazis' rise to power. Before Hitler, the farmers had been largely apolitical but in the early days of National Socialism they had sat in their pubs (the one in this village, she noted, had shining glaciers and gentians painted on its stained black walls) listening to and believing everything the Nazis promised them. A few years later they did not even have milk for their own families. Because the children had to work so hard in the fields, they had little time or energy for learning. Yet although they could barely read or write, there were subjects in which they excelled. Racism, of course, but they also knew everything about air defence. 'Why do we need air defence?' the local Nazi group leader asked them. 'Our air minister Göring says every German town and village is reachable by bombers so air defence is a question of survival for our people,' intoned one child. 'How far can a modern bomber fly?' '500 km.' 'What is the bomb load of such a bomber?' '1,500 kg....'[37]

Leitner's most chilling reports, however, centre not on rural poverty but on Germany's preparations for war. It is a mystery how this distinctly Jewish woman was able to extract so much about secret Nazi projects without attracting suspicion. It is one, however, unlikely to be resolved as Leitner was to perish in uncertain circumstances in 1942 in Marseilles while trying to obtain a visa for America. Of all the disturbing pieces that she wrote from Nazi Germany, arguably the most striking is *Die Stummen von Höchst* [*The Dumb Ones of Höchst*]. Leitner visited Höchst, a Frankfurt suburb named after its dye factory, one summer in the mid-1930s when the lime trees were in full bloom. But their customary sweet scent was overwhelmed by an all-pervading stench. 'The houses near the factory are tight shut. People dare not let the air in. Once this fearful stink takes control, it can't be got rid of. It mixes itself like a horrible unwished for spice into food; it appears in dreams like some terrible portent.' One old man sitting on a bench by the factory told her that there had never before been such a smell in Höchst, and he was now seventy-two. He went on in a whisper: 'No one may talk about what they are brewing up, but they must have discovered a most deadly poison.' All the workers, he told Leitner, were forced to swear an oath in writing that they would never disclose anything they learned inside the factory. 'They may make us keep our mouths shut,' he went on, 'but the dumb ones have given away their secret.' 'Who are they?' Leitner asked. 'The fish,' he replied. A substantial fish farm operated close to the factory and it turned out that a tiny amount of poison had found its way through a factory drain into the nearby River Main. Suddenly, literally from one hour to the next, the carp and tench had started to die in a way that no one had ever seen before. Then they began to rot, spreading a sickening stink. Tens of thousands of dead fish were thrown on to the riverbank. The workers drafted in to clear the putrefying corpses, Leitner later learned, were to suffer nausea and stomach cramps for weeks. Naturally the fishery authorities wanted to claim against the factory but were told that any publicity would be regarded as treason. They remained silent.

It so happened that, on the first Sunday after the leak, there was a nationwide angling competition. For four hours, hundreds of fishermen sat on the banks of the Main but not one caught a single fish. 'They went sadly home,' wrote Leitner:

Were they thinking of the fish they had failed to hook or had they caught a terrifying glimpse into the future of Mankind? The poison is intended for human beings like them, not harmless fish. Only a drop had reached the Main but what about the vast quantity being brewed up in the Höchst dye factory? If humans are the target will life on our planet cease suddenly overnight, as in the waters of the Main?[38]

Maria Leitner was nothing if not bold but it took a particular kind of courage to walk into Düsseldorf's public library and ask, in front of a roomful of silent employees, to see the Heinrich Heine room. 'They all stare at me as though I were some sort of mythical animal,' she wrote. The library also housed a museum commemorating Albert Schlageter, the Nazi super-hero who had been executed for sabotage during the French occupation of the Ruhr. Until Schlageter, Heine had been Düsseldorf's favourite son. But Heine was Jewish and the room in the library that contained his books, his bust – even his stuffed parrot – had for many years been locked and forgotten. Leitner's request to see it was greeted with utter bewilderment. Eventually a 'gaunt' man led her down a long passage and unlocked the tainted room. Inside everything was covered in dust. For a few precious minutes she was allowed to commune with the poet's books in their frayed bindings. 'Then we are out. The key rasps again.'[39]

Samuel Beckett's experience of Nazi bureaucracy was more prosaic: the irritation of negotiating access to censored art during the six months he spent in Nazi Germany became depressingly routine. Having recently turned his back on academe, and with the idea of a possible career in the museum world,* he embarked on an intense study of Germany's art collections. But by the time he reached Hamburg in September 1936, a great many paintings, as well as art historians, condemned by the Nazis as decadent or impure, had already been removed from the public arena. Then, a few weeks after his arrival, an explicit order was sent out to art galleries and museums to strip their walls of 'degenerate' modern pictures. Across the country thousands of masterpieces by the likes of Klee, Nolde and Munch were cast into darkness. Sometimes Beckett was permitted to view them in the cellars, where many ended up, but as often his requests met with blank refusal. Nevertheless, he managed to see a surprising amount of modern art while he was in Germany and meet many leading contemporary artists. In Hamburg he encountered most of the well-known circle of painters living there and became all too familiar with the miserable conditions under which they were forced to work. Despite his natural sympathy for their plight – forbidden to exhibit, harassed by Nazi inspections, their libraries seized – he grew weary of the grim stories recounted by these 'great proud angry poor putupons in their fastnesses', finding himself unable 'to say yessir and nosir any more'.[40]

Much of Beckett's travel record is devoted to meticulous analyses of the hundreds of paintings he saw. But it is also full of the minutiae of daily life, particularly meals – how much they cost, what exactly he ate – 'breakfast in a restaurant, honey and tiny testicular rolls'.[41] Not that he enjoyed much

---

* In 1933 Beckett had applied for an assistant curator job at the National Gallery, London.

of it. 'German food is really terrible. What *can* one eat?'[42] It was the inconsequential details of human experience that most absorbed him – the 'straws, flotsam, etc., names, dates, births and deaths' because, he argued, this was all that he could really *know*.[43] Any attempt to make sense of human chaos, whether on an individual or historical scale, was futile. As his biographer James Knowlson puts it, 'Beckett liked chronologies, loved tiny, verifiable details of individual human lives and had no time for broad sweeping analyses of motives or movements.'[44]

This perhaps explains why the diaries contain so little overt condemnation of the Nazis, although no one who has read them could be in any doubt about how much Beckett – who was to join the French Resistance in the war – loathed the regime. But rather than impose his own commentary, Beckett chose instead to chart the Nazis with studied objectivity. A bookseller with whom Beckett had become friendly wrote of Beckett to a mutual acquaintance: 'He only measures everything according to intellectual standards and will never be able to understand our distress here in Germany however much effort he may invest in exploring appearances and people.'[45] Whether or not that was true, Beckett was quick to pick up on the absurd, such as the story he heard involving a servant and a milkman. In order to prevent *Rassenschande* [racial impurity], no Aryan servant under forty-five was allowed to work in a Jewish household. When a puzzled milkman asked a Herr Levi's Gentile housekeeper how come she worked for him, she replied that she was partly Jewish. When subsequently her even more perplexed employer asked her why she had lied to the milkman, she replied that she could not possibly admit to being forty-five.[46]

In Dresden, Beckett found a kindred spirit – Will Grohmann, an influential Jewish art critic who had been dismissed from his post as director of the Zwinger Gallery as early as 1933. The two had long discussions about the predicament of the intellectual under the Nazis. Grohmann was philosophical, explaining to Beckett that even were it possible to leave he would not, because he believed that it was more interesting to stay. 'They can't control *thoughts*.'[47]

Before arriving in Hamburg, Beckett had written in his diary, 'But what will Germany be, for 6? months, but walking around, mainly?'[48] And walk he certainly did, often lonely, depressed and in acute discomfort. He suffered constant ill health during his time in the Third Reich – herpes on his lip, a sore nose, an agonising lump on his scrotum, a festering finger. Then there was the freezing weather, lack of money, rain and leaking shoes. It is the stuff of Schubert's *Winterreise*:

Walk blindly in the icy cold by Brühl, without seeing Wagner's birthplace or Kätchen Schonhopf's in Goethestr, without seeing Gellert's lodging in Grimmaischstr, without seeing Lessing's student lodging; by Thomas kirche without getting the slightest whiff of Johann Sebastian; more and more frozen in Neumarkt where I see Goethe's student lodging but no Clara Schumann's birth house. Collapse finally into Auerbach's Keller where I look again at Seffner's pleasant Goethe statue ... and I creep along blindly shivering and eat curried mutton in beer department. Then crawl further till I can't stand any more and collapse into Felsche, which is too full. So I leave a little warmer and get as far as Café Fürst Rechschezler, where the coffee is execrable and the newspapers abundant. My spirits are so low that I read The Times. Then rapidly back to Hotel Nord where the new room is no warmer or pleasanter than the old, but perhaps quieter.[49]

But the gloom occasionally lifted to reveal poetic moments such as that experienced by Beckett in Berlin on New Year's Eve, 1936.

> A walk through the Tiergarten ... lovely mild radiant day ... see the most wonderful bunch of balloons ... rainbow cypress gently swaying ... ducks in dusk taking wing from the water with the sound of consternation and settling again with a long liquid vale, flying fiercely in pairs down the axes of the water so different in the air than afloat. How I ADORE solitude.[50]

By the time Beckett reached Munich in March 1937 he had grown tired of travel, a fact that probably influenced his downbeat view of the city. 'The Isar is a poor kind of a piddle after the lyrical Main in Würzburg and the heroic Danube in Regensburg,' he wrote to a friend.[51] Right from the outset of his trip, Beckett had recognised that 'Germany *must* fight soon (or burst)'.[52] As he boarded the aeroplane for England on 1 April 1937, he was convinced that he would never return.[53]

Of course, literary figures of all sorts travelled in Germany during the Third Reich, ranging from Albert Camus to Karen Blixen, Max Frisch to Sven Hedin. Inspector Maigret's creator Georges Simenon bumped into Hitler in a hotel lift,[54] while Graham Greene, according to his brother Hugh, 'was so won over by the charm of Berlin ... he would almost like to live here'.[55] Jean Genet might have stayed longer in Germany had his attempts to live as an existentialist criminal among the Nazis not been so frustrated. 'It's a race of thieves,' he wrote. 'If I steal here, I perform no singular deed that might fulfil me.

I obey the customary order ... I am not upsetting anything. The outrageous is impossible. I'm stealing in the void.'[56] Jean-Paul Sartre spent nine months on a scholarship in Berlin but both his diaries covering the period and his correspondence with Simone de Beauvoir (who visited him several times) are lost. Somerset Maugham, despite having had his books burned by the Nazis, travelled regularly to Munich for *Fasching* [carnival], with his lover Alan Searle.[57]

But the writers discussed here, apart from Hamsun who was to have a dramatic confrontation with Hitler in 1943, not only spent a substantial amount of time in Nazi Germany but also recorded their experiences immediately or soon afterwards. As a result, their impressions have suffered no literary reshaping in the light of post-war hindsight. Furthermore, they represent both ends of the political spectrum and, in de Rougemont's case, the middle ground. Of this small but telling sample, only Thomas Wolfe's views underwent dramatic change as a result of personal experience. By the mid-1930s it was difficult for anyone interested in politics not to have an opinion about Hitler. You were either for him or against. Intuitively we tend to think of writers as being liberal and more open-minded than the average individual, but when it came to Nazi Germany it seems that many of them, like more ordinary mortals, had already made up their minds even before they arrived there.

Beckett was travelling in Germany just after the Olympics at a time when the Third Reich had reached its zenith. But, as is clear in the next chapter, unlike him, the thousands of foreigners who flocked to see Hitler's Games were for the most part willing prey to the Nazis' persistent and persuasive propaganda.

12

Snow and Swastikas

The notion that sport and politics can be kept separate has never looked more absurd than in 1936 when Germany hosted both the winter and summer Olympic Games. The Nazi political machine permeated every aspect, from the elaborate opening ceremonies to each team's breakfast menu. The unprecedented invasion of foreign visitors gave the Nazis the perfect opportunity to make their case to the world. Their unremitting propaganda set out to persuade each foreigner that the new Germany was not only a formidably efficient and powerful nation, but a tolerant, fun-loving one too. And in this, by clever use of smoke and mirrors, it largely succeeded.

If, as the French ambassador, André François-Poncet, suggested, the summer Olympics marked 'the apotheosis of Hitler and his Third Reich',[1] they were brilliantly heralded six months earlier by their winter counterpart. Although conducted on a much smaller scale, the fourth Winter Games, held at the twin villages of Garmisch-Partenkirchen ('separated by a stream and a hyphen'[2]) encapsulated many of the elements that were shortly to make the Berlin Olympics so notorious yet so fascinating.

They opened on 6 February. Arnold Lunn, the pioneering British skier through whose efforts the slalom and downhill races were to be included in the Olympics for the first time, sat shivering in the stand as he waited for the ceremony to begin. His son Peter, captain of the British team, was so anti-Nazi that he had refused to take part in the parade. 'Suddenly,' Lunn wrote, 'through the driving snow a procession appears, headed by the Greek team. Their standard dips in salute to one who would have been more at home in Sparta than in Athens … From the brazier a flame burns up in a flurry of snow, and the Olympic beacons on the hills repeat the Olympic fire. Fire, driving snow and wind.' When, in a radio interview a few days later, Lunn was asked how he thought the Games were going, he could only say: 'Germans, may I tell you a little secret. There are still people who ski for fun.'[3]

Rather to his surprise, the journalist William Shirer found himself enjoying it all. 'This has been a more pleasant inter-lude than I expected,' he wrote. 'The scenery of the Bavarian Alps, particularly at sunrise and sunset, superb, the mountain air exhilarating, the rosy-cheeked girls in their skiing outfits generally attractive, the games exciting, especially the bone-breaking ski-jumping, the bob-races … the hockey matches, and Sonja Henie.'[4] His enthusiasm for the Norwegian skating star* might have been more restrained had he seen the fervent salute with which she had greeted Hitler in Berlin only a few days earlier. The Norwegian newspapers were not impressed. Headlines appeared the next day, 'Is Sonja a Nazi?' Given how much she enjoyed mixing with Nazi top brass, it was not an

---

* Henie won gold medals in three successive Olympics. She later became a Hollywood film star.

American teenager Dorothy Bogen (back row, third from the right), in a tourist bus on her way to Potsdam to visit Sanssouci, Frederick the Great's summer palace, 17 September 1922.

Charlie Chaplin contemplating the famous Greek altar in the Pergamon Museum on 13 March 1931. As a result of the Nazis' virulent campaign against him, he cut short his visit to Berlin.

Published only a few months after the end of the First World War, this brochure was an attempt on the part of twenty leading hotels to encourage American tourists to return to Germany.

Thomas Cook & Son made the most of such celebrated events as the Oberammergau Passion Play and Wagner's Bayreuth Festival to promote Germany to the British public. This advertisement appeared on 4 April 1934 in the weekly magazine *Punch*.

Thomas Cook brochures from 1937, 1938 and 1939, giving little hint of the political crisis engulfing Europe. They continue to present Germany as a happy, benign country whose kind-hearted people want only to give their foreign visitors the best possible experience.

Constantia Rumbold (right) and her cousin Edith Lowther. Like her mother (Lady Rumbold), Constantia observed Weimar Germany with wit and perception.

Lady Rumbold flanked by her children, Constantia and Anthony. Sir Horace is seated. The Rumbold family presented a quintessentially British image to the hundreds of visitors who passed through Berlin during the five years that Sir Horace served there as ambassador.

Hitler's propaganda machine produced many such posters during the Olympics. This example demonstrates Germany's strength and power. Others were designed to convince foreigners of Nazi 'benevolence'.

GERMANY
BERLIN·1936
16· AUGUST

OLYMPIC GAMES
INFORMATION AND HANDBOOKS FROM ALL TOURIST AND TRAVEL AGENCIES

A lone runner bearing the Olympic torch makes his way through the massive but perfectly disciplined crowd, to the stadium where the Olympic flame was ignited before some 100,000 spectators.

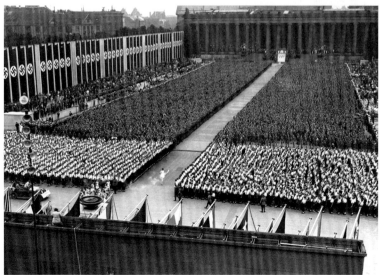

Above: Members of the Matthews family (and friends) with Hitler at Berchtesgaden, 1935. The family were on holiday and had met the Führer by chance while walking near his house. Their father, a Bournemouth GP, kept this photograph on the mantelpiece in his surgery until a patient reported it to a local policeman who suggested that it might be prudent to put it away until after the war.

Opposite, top: A British tourist considers his cooking pots while on vacation in Germany sometime during the 1930s.

Opposite, bottom: Former British soldiers at the Neue Wache war memorial, 1938. There were many exchanges between British and German First World War veteran organisations in the late 1930s in the vain hope that such meetings would contribute to world peace.

Front covers of the *AGR* from June and September 1938. The *AGR* continued to publish 'good news' stories about Nazi Germany right up until its last issue in August 1939.

Hundreds of ardent members of the Hitler Youth salute as they listen to a speech given by Adolf Hitler at the 1937 Nuremberg rally.

unreasonable question. Shortly after the Games she accepted an invitation from Hitler to visit Berchtesgaden.

Unlike Shirer, Westbrook Pegler, whose 'Fair Enough' column was syndicated all over America, was not resident in Germany and he therefore felt able to take a tougher line. His hostility to the Nazis was clear from the moment he arrived 'somewhat apprehensively' in Munich:

> The station was full of the blond type of men and women, most of them tramping along in ski boots, tearing for jerk-water trains for the mountains and steel cleats screeched on concrete platforms. They were ostentatiously healthy and rugged, and the long-legged girls in ski pants carried their rucksacks and skis asking no favour from the men.[5]

Pegler described the Games as a 'great politico-military demonstration conducted by the Nazi State under the nominal auspices of the International Olympic Committee (IOC)'.[6] He was right, of course, but, as Shirer pointed out, the hundreds of foreign visitors to Garmisch saw only the 'lavish' and 'smooth' way in which the Nazis had organised everything. Moreover, contrary to expectations, 'they were greatly impressed with their kind manners'. When Shirer organised a lunch party for the American Embassy's commercial attaché to brief visiting businessmen on the true state of affairs, the diplomat's words fell on deaf ears.[7] His audience believed the propaganda because they wanted to. Like so many others watching Hitler's progress from afar, they preferred to assume that the journalists and diplomats had got it wrong. True, the Nazis were a little over-zealous at times, but when you saw them close up, they were really not so bad.

When Californian Mary Tresidder stepped off the train at Garmisch together with 'a mad rush of people, skis and luggage', it was not the rights or wrongs of National Socialism that preoccupied her, but how to get up on to the ski slopes as quickly as possible. 'Bundled ourselves into the first bus in front of the Bahnhof,' she recorded in her diary on 8 February, 'and so the *Torlauf für Damen* [women's alpine skiing] where Christl Cranz* was, in a blaze of glory and enthusiasm, making the fastest time in each of the two runs with a sereneness [sic] and rhythm beautiful to see … G-P very picturesque.'[8] Christl Cranz may have been the star of the show but it was a Canadian skier, Diana Gordon Lennox, intrepid daughter of an admiral, who won the crowd's heart. Her squad of four, hastily put together at the last minute, was not in good shape. She herself had broken several fingers while training, one of her teammates had a bandaged foot and another was recovering from flu. As they waited at the top of the mountain for their turn, the bottom seemed a terrifyingly long way away. 'I think I became another person in another world before the start of the big downhill ski race,' their captain wrote shortly afterwards. Diana, her arm in a cast, carrying a single pole, 'black hair flying in the wind', crossed the finishing line last, but – to the delight of some 30,000 spectators – with her glass monocle still firmly in place.[9]

The US women skiers, known as the 'Red Stockings', may have been faster than the Canadians but they were no match for the German team with whom they shared accommodation. For the Americans this was not an unqualified success. Allotted the second sitting at mealtimes, they found themselves eating

---

* Cranz (1914–2004) dominated skiing championships in the 1930s. In 1936 she won the gold medal for the newly established combined alpine race.

the Germans' leftovers, and, by the time they were allowed into the bathroom, there was no hot water. 'I shall never forget how our hearts sank when those husky German Fräuleins marched into the dining room and tucked into their sausages and sauerkraut,' recalled their captain, Alice Kiaer. 'When we saw the German girls on the course our hearts sank even further. They are superwomen.' Kiaer was invited to inspect the downhill course with a German official. Part of the way down they came to a large pine tree lying across the trail. 'Dr Votsch pulled a little whistle out of his pocket and blew one blast.' Two minutes later ten Nazi soldiers emerged from the forest skiing in single file and singing in close harmony. At a word of command they removed the tree and disappeared back into the forest – still singing.[10]

Tresidder's diary is devoid of any political comment even though she and her husband, who was later president of Stanford University, were taken to see the Brown House (Nazi headquarters) in Munich and the Feldherrnhalle – the sacred Nazi tomb. But then, in the midst of so much festivity ('got in on the Fasching ball, a carnival affair, very gay'[11]), why spoil the fun? Nor does Ivan Brown, the American bobsled gold medallist, once mention the Nazis in his letters home. In common with many of the American athletes who took part in both winter and summer Olympics, there was little in Brown's modest rural background to prepare him for his European adventure let alone a studied appraisal of German politics. Addressing his wife as 'Dear Girl', his letters are a mixture of excitement, homesickness and frustration:

> Well here we are and what a time. Everybody is lovely to us and its lonesome but I think I can make it all right ...
> These mountains rear up above us like towers. We went

to the bob run this morning and what a run, it is so much
better than ours and not so steep but lots of curves and
looks good to me.[12]

'Hitler is a fine looking fellow – much bigger than his picture
shows,' he wrote to her after the opening ceremony. 'I hope
you heard it as your boy was marching as proud as a peacock
and all for you.'[13]

For fifteen-year-old Lady Mairi Vane-Tempest-Stewart,
youngest daughter of the seventh Marquess of Londonderry
and his wife Edith, 'a marvellous lunch' was the chief memory of her first day at the winter Olympics – 'oysters on top of
caviar'.[14] Her father firmly believed that the best way to secure
peace in Europe was to engage with Hitler rather than spurn
him. Consequently, although he no longer held office (he had
been secretary of state for air in Ramsay MacDonald's cabinet), he was viewed by the Nazis as such a key figure in their
attempt to build bridges with Britain that no effort was spared
in making the visit a success. It began in Berlin. Naturally a day
at Carinhall, Göring's hunting lodge, was a must. 'Mother shot
a fallow [buck],' Mairi recorded in her five-year diary, 'Father
a red deer and I a fallow.'[15] Mairi was not only a good shot
but had piloted her first aeroplane at the age of twelve so was
likely to have been more absorbed than most teenage girls by
a visit to the Junker factory at Dessau. 'It was very interesting
and we saw all the aeroplanes and engines being made. We
had lunch there and I was given a Junker model. Had dinner
with Hitler.'[16] Such quaint juxtapositions turn up regularly
in her brief diary entries: 'We had lunch with the Duke of
Saxe-Coburg then we went to a labour camp.'

It is unlikely that the Londonderrys, despite their connections, were aware of the existence of Haus Hirth five miles west of Garmisch. As the pages of its guest books reveal, this modest chalet had been a Mecca for literati, mainly British and American, since the early 1920s. Siegfried Sassoon, Rex Whistler, the American actress Katharine Cornell, art historian John Pope-Hennessy, writer Edith Olivier as well as public figures like Lord Esher and George Vincent (president of the Rockefeller Foundation) are among the distinguished names that regularly appear down the years. It was at Haus Hirth that William Walton composed the last movement of his Viola Concerto and it was there that Stephen Tennant – then brightest of Bright Young Things – conducted his affair with Sassoon while recovering from tuberculosis. A more surprising figure to emerge from the guest book is Chiang Kai-shek's adopted son, Chiang Wei-kuo, who was in Germany to train with the Wehrmacht's elite alpine troops. The warm conviviality of Haus Hirth must have made a striking contrast to his normal routine of climbing steep mountains off piste with a thirty-pound rucksack on his back.

Johanna and Walther Hirth, the owners, were themselves impeccably connected. Johanna's father had been Chief Justice of the Grand Duchy of Hesse while her brother, Emil Preetorius, is generally regarded as the Bayreuth Festival's most brilliant scene designer. But after the war inflation destroyed the family's wealth, forcing Johanna and Walther to retreat to his mother's chalet at Untergrainau. Here, under the Zugspitze, the highest mountain in Germany, and surrounded by dachshunds, hens and hazel bushes, they earned a living by charging their hand-picked guests £1 a day. The foreigners adored the 'tall queenly' Johanna for her dirndls, her immaculate English, her dexterity with a vacuum cleaner and above all for her ability 'to cope with everything from a broken leg to a broken heart'.[17] The thickset Walther, from whose lederhosen enormous knees protruded, was less sophisticated but endeared himself to his guests with his eccentric English, such as 'God bless your income' and 'I am in all ways a Communalist'.[18]

John Christie, founder of Glyndebourne Opera, tried to analyse why so many intellectuals were drawn to Haus Hirth:

> Everyone always seemed to enjoy themselves ... and yet there was precious little that we did except talk, and perhaps a little walk. None of us were climbers or skiers, there was no cricket or rugby football and yet we all seemed to go back year after year ... Now one comes to think of it, it was something of an achievement to establish this place of assembly based only on the views you could see by looking up ... It had no Opera Festival, no cricket week, nor any of the focal points of an English entertainment, and yet it worked.[19]

When intellectual conversation became too demanding, the guests could turn to traditional Bavarian pursuits such as the woodcutters' dance held annually in the village, although it was not until 1935 that outsiders were allowed to attend. The woodcutters, reported one American visitor, looked resplendent in their green hats, jackets and trousers, their strong chiselled features and long beards reminding her of images of the Apostles. At the feast, which began after church on Sunday and continued until 6 a.m. the following day, large quantities of pork fat were served, washed down with – in the foreigners' view – a particularly foul-tasting beer. An ear-splitting blast signalled the beginning and end of each dance.

But in the winter of 1936, foreigners were in Garmisch for one thing only – the Olympics. And if many of them in retrospect appear to have been politically naïve, there were others who simply chose not to question matters too deeply. No one, however, could ignore the uniforms. They were everywhere, leading Pegler to comment that the village 'looked like a little town behind the Western Front during an important troop movement'. He was particularly incensed by the military camouflage-painted vehicles that went 'tearing through the streets off to the mountains splashing melted slush on to the narrow footway'. Exactly why it was necessary to maintain such a strong military presence in a small mountain resort where sportsmen were drawn together in friendship was a question that even the dauntless Pegler ducked for fear of being accused of spying. But he had to admit that all traces of anti-Semitism had disappeared. The familiar signs forbidding Jews to enter this or that had been systematically removed. Despite Nazi thoroughness, Pegler noted that copies of *Der Stürmer* (Julius Streicher's anti-Semitic tabloid) were occasionally smuggled into Garmisch and shown to incredulous foreigners.

Several days into the Games, 'with 10,000 swastikas stirring faintly in the light winter wind', Hitler made another appearance. 'This was the Dictator's day,' Pegler wrote. 'The Olympics were of secondary importance, if any.' He remarked how strange it was that, although the Führer's presence produced a great turnout of military power, jammed up traffic and 'completely obscured the peaceful ideal to which the Games were dedicated', Hitler sat in his low box at the hockey rink, quite unprotected and apparently delighted to greet the endless stream of strangers who approached him. 'He gave his autograph', observed Pegler, 'as willingly as Babe Ruth and in astonishing contrast to the ill-tempered refusals of Colonel Lindbergh and Greta Garbo.'

The Winter Games came to an end on 16 February. 'Big Bag,' wrote Lady Mairi, 'end of ice hockey, England won. Gala night. Danced with lots and lots of people.'[20] Pegler described the closing ceremony:

> The fireworks up on the mountain at the closing exercises were a beautiful display of color and the military search-lights washed the snowy hills in artificial moonlight as the batteries of 3 inch guns banged away in a concealed position halfway up the slope, reminding us all that the beautiful Olympic flame, which was now dying slowly on the tower, was only a light after all and didn't mean a thing.[21]

Yet again, it had fallen to a journalist to spell out the truth, although, as preparations for the Berlin Olympics gathered pace, too few of Pegler's readers were prepared to accept it. If Lord and Lady Londonderry read his column, they would have dismissed it as yet another example of irresponsible journal-ism; just one more unwarranted slur on a great country, which, under its inspired leader, was doing its best to come to grips with an uncertain future.

On returning home Lord and Lady Londonderry wrote fulsome thanks to their German hosts. While the Marquess, writing to Ribbentrop, did at least touch on more awkward issues such as Hitler's policy in Europe and anti-Semitism, his wife's letter to Hitler is one of unbridled admiration. 'To say that I was deeply impressed is not adequate,' she wrote. 'I am amazed. You and Germany remind me of the Book of Genesis in the Bible. Nothing else describes the position accurately. The beauty of the buildings is something that I shall not forget.

Their strength and simplicity are I feel symbolic of their creator.'[22] Clearly the trip – the first of six that Lord Londonderry
was to make to Germany over the next two years – had been
a success. But it also aroused wide suspicion. Shirer wrote in
his diary ten days after the Games were over, 'Learn that Lord
Londonderry was here around the first of the month ... He is
an all-out pro-Nazi. Fear he has not been up to any good.'[23]

On 7 March 1936, three weeks after the closing ceremony
of the Winter Olympics, and in flagrant breach of the Treaty of
Versailles, German troops reoccupied the Rhineland, which
had since the war remained a demilitarised zone. For days Kay
Smith had sensed something was about to happen – 'one felt
it in the air'. Then, on 6 March, at a reception in their Berlin
apartment, she had overheard a conversation:

> It was a warm day. The doors to the balcony were open.
> I was standing nearby when I saw Remondeau [French
> military attaché] take von Pappenheim [a senior officer
> on the German General Staff] by the arm and draw him
> out on the balcony. I edged nearer, my back to the bal-
> cony and them. I heard Remondeau ask: 'Are you going to
> reoccupy the Rhineland?'... Pappenheim was taken by sur-
> prise. He turned red and began to stammer ... 'No surely
> not.' 'Do you swear on your honour?' 'Ich schwöre.' ... I
> could scarcely wait to tell Truman that the reoccupation
> was certain![24]

That same evening Denis de Rougemont was crossing the
Opernplatz in Frankfurt when he saw newspaper headlines
announcing that the Reichstag had been summoned to a

special meeting the following day. Next morning he could hear the Führer's furious ranting on his neighbour's radio, although not clearly enough to make out what he was actually saying. But he knew that it must be important because his fellow tenants had double-locked their doors and were leaving their bells unanswered.[25] In Berlin, 340 miles to the north-east, Kay was also listening on her wireless. She recalled how Hitler, after his usual tirade, dropped his voice to a more normal pitch before announcing that German troops were at that very moment crossing the Rhine Bridge. 'Then we heard the bells of Cologne cathedral ring out.'[26]

As Hitler's speech drew to a close, de Rougemont could hear doors banging all over the apartment block and hurried footsteps on the staircase. 'The landlord's son comes out of the cellar gesticulating, a bottle in his hand,' he wrote in his diary. 'He runs up the stairs two at a time, whistling the Horst Wessel Lied. Neighbours are talking animatedly. I catch the word "Frankreich [France]" shouted out ... Flags are already appearing on the balconies.' He went out to buy a newspaper. 'Is it war?' the vendor asked. 'War, good God!' replied de Rougemont, 'just because you are putting a few soldiers on your borders. The French aren't that crazy.'[27]

Truman Smith thought otherwise. The moment he reached home, he asked his wife how long she needed to pack up their flat. She told him three days. 'Three days! Thirty minutes is all you will have if the French react as they must ... the bombers will be here in half an hour.' She packed two suitcases, filled the car with petrol and stood by ready to flee with their young daughter at the first faint throb of an aeroplane engine.[28] But, although the windows of the French Embassy were ablaze all night, no bombers appeared. Nor did they the next day, nor in the weeks to follow. Hitler's great gamble had paid off.

One month later, undeterred by the dramatic events in the Rhineland, the Charterhouse hockey team boarded the boat train at Victoria Station and set off for Cologne. It was the first time the school had ever sent a team abroad. A big crowd watched their opening match, played on a scrubby uneven field, though it was soon clear that the spectators were far more interested in the players than the score. 'We had evidence of a fact, the truth of which we were to find subsequently wherever we went,' a member of the team wrote in the school magazine, 'that certain aspects of the "English boys" were highly diverting to the natives.' The boys' 'various and original styles of coiffure', their strange clothes and particularly their eccentric headgear, were in startling contrast to the standard Nazi dress of uniform, cropped hair and jackboots. The outstanding memory of the tour, which included Leipzig and Dresden, was the 'marvellous friendliness' of everyone they met. Summing up, the author wrote: 'From the moment when, as the German papers put it, "the English boys began to thaw", we felt ourselves true ambassadors of peace and goodwill. We felt that if international relations depended on Charterhouse hockey teams wars and rumours of wars would cease forever.'[29] On 8 July 1941, one of the hockey ambassadors, Charles Petley, would be killed when his aeroplane was shot down over the Netherlands on its way to bomb Osnabrück. He was twenty-three.

It was as well there had been no need for Kay to leave Berlin because four months after the Rhineland crisis the Smiths found themselves playing host to Colonel Charles Lindbergh – arguably the most celebrated celebrity of his time. As military attaché, Truman Smith had for some while been struggling to give Washington an accurate assessment of German air power. Who better to help him than the world's most famous aviator? Lindbergh and his family were living in England where they had taken refuge from the overwhelming publicity following the kidnapping and murder of their baby son in 1932. Smith wrote to him there outlining his problem and inviting him to come over to Germany. To his great delight, Lindbergh accepted.

On 22 July, Lindbergh's wife, Anne, noted in her diary:

> Leave for Germany. Up early ... Drive off to airport at Penshurst. So strange, quiet, and English. The hanger big and empty except for our little gray low wing monoplane. No sound except lots of birds twittering in the eaves. The long feathery grass heavy with dew ... the oast-house at the end of the field, the sheep.

After refuelling in Cologne they flew over the Harz Mountains, then 'Potsdam and the lakes and tiny sails. The palace. Berlin ahead, lots of green and lots of water. The field: Junkers planes all out in lines.'[30] They landed at Tempelhof where the Smiths, along with numerous high-ranking Nazis, were waiting to greet them. Kay was excited, although a little apprehensive 'as Lindbergh was reputed to be so "difficult"'.[31] She need not have worried. A little later, sitting on the balcony of their apartment, getting to know each other in the warm summer twilight, the four embarked on a friendship that was to last many years.

The Lindberghs' visit was a gift to the Nazis – especially coming as it did one week before the opening of the Berlin Olympics. The next few days were packed with tours of airfields, factories and far too many social events for Charles Lindbergh's liking. The major speech he delivered at a lunch in the Berlin Air Club received international coverage, although none of the

German newspapers dared to comment editorially. This was not surprising since Lindbergh made the point that, thanks to modern aviation, it was now possible to obliterate everything the civilised world most valued. 'It is our responsibility', he concluded, 'to make sure that ... we do not destroy the very things which we wish to protect.'[32] This was not a sentiment likely to find favour with the Führer. At that same luncheon, Mrs Lindbergh caught a telling moment in conversation with General Milch, chief architect of the post-war Luftwaffe. She remarked to him that the English had always felt very close to the Germans in character, race and temperament:

> 'You think so?' His eyes sharpened for a second as he looked quickly at me. It was one of those glances that are like a crack of light, letting one see through to a vista beyond. He showed in that glance, pleasure, eagerness, hope, vulnerability, held under check behind that quick taken-by-surprise 'You think so?' He can't make conversation about it. They are so eager for it. That sense of vulnerability...[33]

The social climax of the Lindberghs' nine days in Berlin was lunch with Hermann Göring, to which the Smiths were also invited. 'A large black open Mercedes came to take us to the Air Marshall's residence,' Kay recalled, 'motorcycle outriders and all ... On entering the hall we found all the air heroes of Germany drawn up in a circle facing the entrance with Göring in the center in a white uniform with Frau Göring beside him.' After lunch, when the guests were gathered in the library,

> The doors were flung open and in bounded a young lion ... He was much startled by seeing so many people and not too happy. Göring placed himself in a large armchair. 'I

want you to see how nice my Augie is. Come here Augie.'
The lion bounded across the room and sprang into his lap.
He put his paws on Göring's shoulders and began licking
his face. I stood behind, a large table between us at a safe
distance. Suddenly an aide laughed. The startled lion let
loose a flood of yellow urine all over the snow white uniform! A wave of red flowed up Göring's neck. He tossed
the lion from him with a wave of his arm and sprang to
his feet. The lion bounced off the opposite wall. Göring
wheeled to face us, his face red with anger, his blue eyes
blazing. 'Who did that?' he demanded. Frau Göring rushed
forward, putting her arms around him she cried 'Hermann,
Hermann, it is like a little baby.' This mollified him. The
lion was led away. 'Yes it is like a little baby,' he said. Then
we all laughed pleasantly.[34]

Truman Smith had reason to be well pleased with his initiative. As he had predicted, so eager were the Nazis to impress
Lindbergh that they had given him access to aeroplanes and
information they would never have granted a mere attaché.
The Germans were equally delighted since it was clear they
had succeeded in convincing Lindbergh that the Luftwaffe was
more powerful than it really was. And of one thing they could
be certain. Any intelligence transmitted to Washington and
London by Colonel Lindbergh could not fail to impress. The
Lindberghs, although initially adamant that they would not
attend the Olympic Games, were spotted on 1 August by the
New York Times correspondent seated – surrounded by Nazi
uniforms – among the sprinkling of privileged foreign guests
invited to watch the opening ceremony from Hitler's box. The
next day they left Germany in their own aeroplane. But they
would soon be back.

13

Hitler's Games

On 1 August 1936, hundreds of thousands crowded the streets of Berlin hoping to catch a glimpse of the Führer as he was driven to the Olympic stadium. 'At last he came,' wrote Thomas Wolfe, who attended the Games with Martha Dodd. 'Something like a wind across a field of grass was shaken through that crowd, and from afar the tide rolled up with him, and in it was the voice, the hope, the prayer of the land.' Wolfe noted how Hitler stood in his car erect, motionless and unsmiling, 'with his hand upraised, palm outward, not in Nazi-wise salute, but straight up, in a gesture of blessing such as the Buddha or Messiahs use'.[1] As the Führer descended the Marathon steps into the stadium, escorted by top Nazis and members of the IOC, the spectators rose as one, noted Birchall in the *New York Times*, 'their arms outstretched and voices raised in frantic greeting'.[2] At that moment the orchestra and military bands burst into Wagner's *March of Homage*. Then, as Hitler took his seat, the crowds roared out *'Deutschland über Alles'* followed by the inevitable 'Horst Wessel' song.

The splendour of the occasion was 'immensely enhanced', reported the *Manchester Guardian*, 'by the nobility of the great

Stadium in which it was carried out'.[3] Kay Smith agreed. Along with many other foreign commentators, she admired the stadium's austere simplicity. Built of cement and seating more than a 100,000 spectators, it was half sunk below ground level so that walking into it from outside visitors found themselves already half-way up the tiers of seats looking down on the green grass and the red running tracks far below. On top of the towers flanking the great Marathon Gate, wrote one journalist, could be seen steel-helmeted military bands, 'the gestures of the conductor clear and tiny against the western sky'.[4] Richard Strauss was also there, conducting the Berlin Philharmonic and a 1,000-strong choir dressed in white.

'No nation since ancient Greece has captured the true Olympic spirit as has Germany.'[5] Surprisingly, it was not Propaganda Minister Joseph Goebbels who spoke these words, but the president of the American Olympic Committee, Avery Brundage. Having fought off various attempts to boycott 'Hitler's Games', Brundage must have felt profound relief as the opening ceremony – captured so brilliantly on film by Leni Riefenstahl – unfolded before him. The organisation was impeccable, the atmosphere warm and festive, but beyond that the Germans had shown themselves sensitive to the more spiritual side of the Games by bringing to Berlin the sixty-three-year-old Greek peasant who had won the first modern marathon at the 1896 Olympics. As for anti-Semitism, look as he might, Brundage could see no trace of it anywhere.

At 4.15 the Olympic bell began to toll. How many of the thousands who heard it that day knew in their hearts that its benign inscription – *I Call the Youth of the World* – was in fact a summons to war? With the tolling of the bell, the Greeks, in line with tradition, led the athletes into the stadium: As the *Olympia-Zeitung* relates,

Spiridon Louis [dressed in national costume] separates
himself from his comrades. In his hand is the simple olive
twig from the grove at Olympia. Forty years ago he won
the first Marathon race. Today he brings the patron of the
XI Games greetings from his homeland ... The Führer
rises ... The Greek Marathon victor stands eye to eye with
Adolf Hitler. A few words of greeting. The noble bow of
a peasant, the pride on the countenance of Adolf Hitler.
The most beautiful moment in the opening celebration
is over.[6]

It was perhaps fortunate that Spiridon did not live to see
Hitler invade his country four and a half years later. As each
nation marched past the Führer, the crowd's cheers rose or fell
depending on whether or not its athletes acknowledged him
with a Nazi salute. The latter was so similar to the Olympic
salute that there was much confusion among both teams
and spectators as to exactly who was doing what. The New
Zealanders, according to the *New York Times*, solved the problem neatly by doffing their hats to a German athlete, having
mistaken him for Hitler.[7] Their manager, Sir Arthur (later
Lord) Porritt, who was also a member of the IOC, kept a
diary. Set against all the hype of the day, his entry for 1 August
is refreshingly succinct:

Official service at Cathedral, top hats and tails. To unknown
soldier's tomb. March past of Army, Navy and Air – full
goose step! To Lustgarten for youth display (49,000!)
and arrival of Olympic torch. Met Göring, Goebbels.
Lunch with Hitler at his house. Procession to stadium
(Hindenburg airship overhead). Opening ceremony. March
past of teams, lighting flame, pigeons etc.[8]

Freed from their cages, the pigeons, mentioned by Porritt, immediately did what birds do. 'We had these straw hats on, Buster Keaton hats,' recalled American track athlete Zamperini, 'they were nice looking. We were all out there on the field when all these pigeons were released. They circled right overhead and dropped on us, and you could hear on these straw hats, splat, splat. Everybody tried to stand at attention, but it was pretty hard.'[9]

The story that emerges from interviews given by the American athletes decades later is a stirring one. Many came from poor backgrounds and, before being chosen to represent their country in Berlin, had never travelled further than their local town. Crossing the Atlantic was in itself a huge adventure. Their outstanding shared memory of life on board the SS *Manhattan* was 'food, endless food'.[10] For marathon runner Tarzan Brown, a Narragansett Indian from Maine, this unaccustomed largesse was to prove fatal. He put on so much weight during the voyage that when it came to the day of the marathon several weeks later, he had to give up after the first mile.

When the SS *Manhattan* reached Germany, she made her way slowly up the Elbe towards Hamburg in the gathering dusk. As the ship steamed past countless brightly lit beer gardens, thousands of Germans, singing, dancing and cheering, crowded on to the riverbank to watch it pass. For the young Americans, it was an uplifting experience. 'These people were serenading the whole team all the way along this gorgeous river,' water-polo player Herbert Wildman recalled. 'It was probably the most beautiful sight I have ever seen. I'll remember it as long as I live.'[11] In Berlin, enthusiasm for the Americans reached fever pitch. Everywhere, they were surrounded by hundreds of curious people, a reminder of just how isolated Germany had become under the Nazis. 'A crowd would gather following us around to see what we were looking at,' remembered Wildman. 'Few of them spoke any English but when we laughed they would all laugh too.'[12]

The Olympic village (about fifteen miles from central Berlin) was a further excitement. Zamperini, son of an Italian immigrant coal miner, remembered 'wild animals' running around, a sauna built especially for the Finns and grass so manicured it was fit for a golf course. Each country had its own menus – 'you could get anything you wanted from corned beef to T-bone to filet mignon – it was just wonderful'.[13] If someone dropped a banana skin, a young German attendant would materialise instantly to scoop it up. Many foreigners commented on the extraordinary cleanliness of Berlin during the Games – 'there wasn't a vacant lot that had a weed in it'.[14] But the few who ventured beyond the Olympic bubble encountered a different story. The American water polo team went to the northern outskirts of Berlin to play a friendly match at Plötzensee – site of the notorious Nazi prison where some 3,000 people were to be executed. They were surprised to find that the 'swimming pool' was just a roped off section of a seedy canal. 'It's a little tough practicing when you're trying to dodge the sewage floating by,' Wildman recollected. The sight of children aged three or four splashing around in the filthy freezing water astonished him, as did the ability of the German team – 'I couldn't believe how good they were.'

There were more surprises in store. Herman Goldberg, a Jewish baseball player from Brooklyn, wanted to know what lay beyond a certain door in his Olympic village quarters. He opened it to find another door and behind that a chain. Unloosing the chain he went down to the basement where he found himself in a huge cavernous area built of reinforced concrete, fifteen inches thick. 'I didn't know what it was for but I sure found out … Panzer tanks.' Then a caretaker appeared shouting, 'Raus raus raus, get out of there, get out of there.'[15] Wildman, equally inquisitive, wanted to know more about the gliders he saw everywhere. 'From what we understood, they'd just have to yank the front nosepiece off, hook a motor on it and turn it into a fighter plane.' The same went for the buses that ferried them between the Olympic village and Berlin. Wildman noticed brackets round the top of the bus. After persistently asking the bus driver what they were for, he eventually got the answer – 'Well that's where the machine guns go.' It was a shock to realise that an ordinary-looking bus could within minutes be transformed into an armoured vehicle.[16]

Such sinister discoveries, coupled with the fact that, when the Americans travelled to and from Berlin, they would often see young men crawling on their bellies through the woods with rifles and full packs, gave gymnast Kenneth Griffin 'a sort of eerie feeling that Germany really was preparing for war'.[17] This came as a complete surprise because Griffin, like most of his fellow athletes, had known almost nothing about the Nazis before arriving in Germany. Nor indeed had they received any formal briefing other than being told that they must behave themselves.[18] African-American John Woodruff, winner of the 800 metres, confirmed this general state of ignorance. 'When we went to the Olympics, we weren't interested in politics. We were only interested in going to Germany, participating in our events, and trying to win as many medals as we could win and come home.'[19] In contrast, twenty-year-old Halet Çambel, a member of the Turkish fencing team, was deeply political. As a daughter of the new Turkish republic (founded only thirteen years earlier), and as the first female Muslim to take part in the

Olympics, she was astonished by her fellow athletes' apathy to National Socialism. She loathed the Nazis and would have preferred not to be in Berlin at all. When asked if she would like to meet Hitler, she famously said, 'No.'[20]

Although American journalists did their best to unearth stories of discrimination against black and Jewish members of the US team, they received little cooperation from either group. Hitler may have refused to shake hands with Jesse Owens, winner of four gold medals, but the German people took the great black athlete to their hearts, chanting 'Oh-vens! Oh-vens' whenever he appeared. Others behaved less well. After one of Owens' triumphs, an Italian diplomat remarked sarcastically to Truman Smith, 'Let me congratulate you on this splendid American victory.' Smith responded, 'Never mind, Mancinelli, next year with your Ethiopians you too may have a fine victory.'[21]

Frederick Birchall, covering the Olympics for the *New York Times*, thought the Nazi attitude to the African-American athletes strange, since a runner like Woodruff not only met Aryan ideals by obtaining an objective with the utmost possible speed but when seen in profile 'is a perfect reproduction of the sacred swastika'.[22] Woodruff himself had only good memories of the Germans. He suffered no racial prejudice when sightseeing in Berlin. On the contrary, people crowded round him asking for his autograph. 'I didn't notice anything negative at all the whole time that I participated in those 1936 Olympic Games,'[23] he remarked years later. Archie Williams, the African-American 400 metres gold-medallist, made plain the underlying point in an interview with the *San Francisco Chronicle*. 'When I came home, somebody asked me "How did those dirty Nazis treat you?" I replied that I didn't see any dirty Nazis, just a lot of nice German people. And I didn't have to ride in the back of the bus.'[24]

His Jewish colleague Marty Glickman who, with his fellow Jew Sam Stoller, was suddenly dropped from the relay event for no apparent reason, made a similar observation. Asked if he was aware of any anti-Semitism while he was in Berlin, he replied: 'I heard nothing and I saw nothing which was anti-Semitic in any way except for the day that I was supposed to run the trial heats of the 400 metre relay. And that was the first and only anti-Semitism that I experienced. And I experienced it from American coaches, not from Germans.'[25]

These athletes may not have seen any obvious discrimination against Jewish and black competitors during the Olympics, but their female teammates were unquestionably treated as inferior beings – at least in terms of living standards. No luxury quarters or fillet steaks for them but rock-hard beds and boiled beef and cabbage. Johanna von Wangenheim was in charge of the women's dormitory – a brick building close to the stadium. Eager, in an interview with the *Sydney Morning Herald*, to demonstrate her modernity, Freifrau von Wangenheim claimed that she was entirely in favour of the young women receiving male friends in the house. 'I cannot conceive of a hearty handshake with a masculine comrade in sport as being less proper than such a greeting between feminine athletes.' Furthermore, to help the young women in her charge feel at home, a 'supervising stewardess' was always at hand to give advice in three languages on 'just where a girl must look in the House if her bobbed hair is out of order, or a silk stocking needs attention, or a rain-soaked skirt requires ironing out'.[26] Swimmer Iris Cummings remained unconvinced, describing the Freifrau as 'a domineering cranky old gal'.[27]

One foreign visitor the regime was particularly keen to court was Sir Robert (later Lord) Vansittart, head of the Foreign Office. Well known for his robust anti-Nazi views, he had intended to turn down his invitation to the Olympics. But an 'intangible whispering campaign', directed by the extreme pro-German lobby in Britain against his brother-in-law Eric Phipps (who was to leave Berlin the following year to become ambassador in Paris), persuaded him to change his mind. Fully aware of his bête-noire status in Germany, Vansittart was relieved to find that 'this embarrassment' soon thawed and was followed by 'a general rush of interest that turned to geniality'.[28] With an Olympic truce, as he put it, lying 'thick above the city', the Nazis were so anxious to avoid 'rough passages and disputable corners' that Vansittart's formal meetings were relatively anodyne.

In 'A Busman's Holiday', written shortly after his return to London, Vansittart penned portraits of the key players. Having met the Führer formally, and dined with him in the Reich Chancellery, he described Hitler as 'amiably simple, rather shy, rotundly ascetic, bourgeois with the fine hair and thin skin that accompany extreme sensitiveness ... not humorous, not alarming, not magnetic' but 'with great natural dignity or anyhow a dignity which is now natural'.[29] This benign reading did not, however, mean that Vansittart was blind to the violence and hatred consuming Hitler; nor to the state of extreme nervous tension in which he kept everyone both in Germany and abroad. Indeed, since arriving in Berlin the diplomat had several times heard the Olympic stadium likened to a volcanic crater.[30] As for Ribbentrop, Vansittart could find nothing good to say. He was not alone. Everyone despised him, even his own colleagues – even Unity Mitford. Describing him as shallow and self-seeking, Vansittart added,

'No one who has studied his mouth will be reassured.'[31] Ribbentrop's reaction to Britain's top diplomat was equally negative – 'never was a conversation so barren'.[32] Of Göring, Vansittart observed, he 'enjoys everything, particularly his own parties, with the gusto of Smith minor suddenly possessed of unlimited tuck in the school stores'. Although he could not take Göring entirely seriously, he was charmed by Frau Göring, as indeed were many foreigners. 'His really nice wife', he wrote, 'is a young lady of Riga, likely to keep her seat as well as the smile on the face of the tiger.'[33] The only leading Nazi with whom Vansittart felt a genuine rapport was Goebbels. 'I found much charm in him – a limping slip of a Jacobin, as quick as a whip and often, I doubt not, as cutting … he is a calculator and therefore a man with whom one might do business.'[34] The feeling was reciprocated. 'He can doubtless be won over for us,' Goebbels recorded in his diary. 'I work on him for an hour. I expound the Bolshevik problem and explain our domestic political operations. He gains a new understanding … He leaves deeply impressed. I have turned on a light for him.'[35]

Vansittart was a busy man. Between attending Olympic events and meeting the Nazi hierarchy, he fitted in a Greek tragedy ('perfectly staged and execrably acted'[36]), and two long talks with King Boris of Bulgaria. The king, 'who had arrived in Berlin to increase the prospects of an heir through an operation on the Queen', first suggested that they rendezvous in a wood. In the end they met at his hotel but as the king was convinced that his room had been bugged, their discussion was 'somewhat cramped'.[37]

King Boris (who, according to Goebbels, secured an arms deal while in Berlin[38]) was by no means the only royal in town. Among his fellow guests at the lunch hosted by Hitler on

the opening day of the Games were Crown Prince Umberto
of Italy and his sister Princess Maria of Savoy, the Crown
Prince of Greece, Prince and Princess Philipp of Hesse, Prince
and Princess Christoph of Hesse and Prince Gustaf Adolf of
Sweden. That same day, the King of Denmark's niece, Princess
Alexandrine-Louise, first met the handsome German count to
whom within a couple of weeks she was to become engaged.*
But although, as the *New York Times* put it, 'in all its history
Berlin has never had so many polyglot visitors',[39] the total
number of foreigners fell some ten thousand short of expectations. The disappointing deficit of British and Americans was
partly offset by a large influx of Scandinavians, among them
the famously pro-Nazi explorer Sven Hedin. 'I am convinced',
he said in a newspaper interview, 'that the Olympic Games
have much greater significance for the future than the League
of Nations.'[40]

Always on the lookout for such controversial comments, or
stories of derring do, the hundreds of journalists covering the
Games must have been delighted when, just before the finish
of the men's 1,500 metre freestyle event, 'a plump woman
conspicuous in a red hat … broke through the cordon … and
kissed Hitler. The crowd of thirty thousand rocked with laughter.'[41] When later asked what prompted her to do such a thing,
Mrs Carla George de Vries of Norwalk, California, said, 'Why
I simply embraced him because he appeared so friendly and
gracious … I am a woman of impulses I guess.'[42]

During the second week of the Olympics, the Vansittarts,
along with the rich and glamorous from all over Europe
and America, attended one extravagant entertainment after

* Luitpold zu Castell-Castell; he was killed in Bulgaria in 1941.

another. 'Orchids have been sold out in Berlin for two days,' proclaimed the *Chicago Tribune*, 'and new flowers are being rushed up to the capital from outlying cities because women attending the official parties given by the German government in honour of the Olympic Games have bought every flower available.'[43] As the French ambassador pointed out, Hitler was always keen that high-ranking foreigners should attend such events. He wanted them of course to be dazzled by Nazi style and panache, but he also wanted his public to know that they were being dazzled. 'The German people, like their master,' wrote François-Poncet, 'combined an inferiority complex with a sense of pride.'[44]

Göring set the ball rolling on 6 August by hosting a state banquet at the opera house where scores of footmen in pink eighteenth-century livery lined the stairs holding torches in glass containers and ballerinas flitted delightfully between tables. Rather less 'dazzling' was a reception for 1,000 guests held at the British Embassy, dismissed by American-born Sir Henry 'Chips' Channon MP as 'boring, crowded and inelegant'.[45]

On the morning of 11 August, Ribbentrop's appointment as ambassador to London was announced. That evening he and his wife gave a party in the garden of their house at Dahlem. Prominent among the many British peers present were press barons Rothermere, Beaverbrook and Camrose. Because the Vansittarts danced enthusiastically and stayed late, Ribbentrop hoped that perhaps after all Sir Robert had not found Berlin so repulsive.[46] 'I enjoyed myself quite wildly,' wrote Channon. 'The lovely evening, the fantastic collection of notabilities, the strangeness of the situation, the excellence of the Ambassador's (or more correctly Frau von Ribbentrop's) champagne, all went somewhat to my head.'

Splendid though it was, the Ribbentrop party was to be eclipsed only two days later. Not content with having already hosted one magnificent occasion, Göring held another on the lawns of his brand new Air Ministry – then the largest office building in Europe. The far end of the garden, shrouded in darkness, was suddenly illuminated to reveal an eighteenth-century village complete with *schuhplattling* [traditional folk dancing] peasants, inn, post office, bakery, donkeys and merry-go-round. Göring himself, reported the French ambassador, rode the carousel until he was breathless.[47] Vast women distributed pretzels and beer among the revellers. 'There has never been anything like this since the days of Louis Quatorze,' a fellow guest remarked to Channon. 'Not since Nero,' retorted Channon, adding that both Goebbels and Ribbentrop were 'in despair with jealousy'.[48] The Goebbels' party took place the night before the final day of the Games on an island in the River Havel. All the Olympic teams were invited. Iris Cummings, delighted by the green lawns, vast white tablecloths and delicious food, recalled that a number of athletes got drunk on the copious quantities of 'Rhine champagne' on offer. The evening ended with a barrage of fireworks. When at last they ceased, 'the skies were still light for some time,' wrote Channon, 'before darkness dared to defy Goebbels and steal back again.'[49] These Nazi extravaganzas even impressed the worldly Vansittart, who commented, 'the taste of their entertainments is remarkable'. But the stupendous cost of it all led him to be thankful that Britain had relinquished its claim to the next Olympiad. 'The Japanese can have it and welcome.'[50]

After the closing ceremony on 16 August most of the athletes packed their bags and headed for home. So too did Frank Buchman, the ubiquitous leader of the Oxford Group who had been much in evidence during the Games. Ten days after returning to America, Buchman gave an interview to the *New York World Telegram*. It caused a sensation. 'I thank Heaven for a man like Adolf Hitler,' he said, 'who built a front line of defense against the anti-Christ of Communism.' Of course, he did not condone everything the Nazis did. 'Anti-Semitism? Bad, naturally.' But, he continued, 'think what it would mean to the world if Hitler surrendered to the control of God. Or Mussolini. Or any dictator? Through such a man God could control a nation overnight and solve every last bewildering problem.'[51]

Vansittart, on returning home, came to rather different conclusions. He had undoubtedly enjoyed himself – 'I left Berlin with many warm personal likings and with gratitude for generous and universal hospitality.' There was, however, 'a reverse side to the medal, a thin, almost transparent profile, with a high forehead and frightened eyes' whose name was 'Israel'. One evening a Jew had visited Vansittart at the British Embassy, entering secretly through a back door. He murmured – 'he never raised his voice above a murmur' – that were the visit known about, it would be the end of him. Vansittart recorded how often he had been tempted to bring the plight of the Jews into his discussions with the Nazis but had been warned by Phipps that any intervention would do far more harm than good to the victims. Summing up his impressions of the Germans three weeks later, Vansittart wrote: 'These people are the most formidable proposition that has ever been formulated; they are in strict training now, not for the Olympic Games, but for breaking some other and emphatically unsporting world records, and perhaps the world as well.' And yet, he added, 'there may be something to be made of them'.[52]

There were others too who, in the light of the Olympics, continued to hope for the best – a point taken up by London's *Evening Post*:

> Undoubtedly Germany has fulfilled her intention to impress visitors, but everybody has been surprised by the extraordinary impression visitors have created on their hosts as Germans have been taught for three years to suspect foreigners and at first greeted them courteously but coldly. Berlin people have now taken their visitors to their hearts with surprising warmth.[53]

The article went on to record how a long line of young people, mostly French, American and German, had been seen happily walking, arms linked, towards the stadium.

Not everyone left Berlin immediately after the Games. Basketball player Frank J. Lubin spent a further week in the city before travelling on to his native Lithuania. It was a week that was to leave him with a very different picture of the city. Despite the atrocious facilities offered his sport (Hitler was not interested in basketball and there was no German team), the Olympic experience had, in his words, 'all seemed so beautiful'. Now the scales fell from his eyes. When he and his wife chose a particular restaurant, their companion pointed out the Star of David in the window and led them quickly away. Then they went swimming, entering the baths under a large board inscribed '*Juden verboten*'. Lubin was puzzled, remarking that none of these signs had been there a few days before. 'No,' came the response, 'but now the Olympic Games are over.'

Three months earlier, the *Evening Post* had reported a jingle doing the rounds in Berlin:

> When the Olympic Games are done
> Then with Jews we'll have some fun[54]

The Olympics did not in the end attract as many visitors from overseas as the Nazis had hoped. Nevertheless, the influx of foreigners to Berlin was unparalleled. They were a disparate group, many of them visiting Germany for the first time. Naturally they carried away a wide variety of memories but the majority departed with an overriding impression of a thriving, efficient and friendly nation, albeit one obsessed with uniforms. However, African-American academic W. E. B. Du Bois, who was in Germany during the Olympics, and struggling to make sense of his own impressions, was right when he wrote, 'the testimony of the casual, non-German-speaking visitor to the Olympic Games is worse than valueless in any direction'.[55] This verdict was borne out by the likes of the Right Reverend Philip Cook, Protestant Episcopal Bishop of Delaware. On returning to the United States after the Games, the Bishop told the press that 'Germany was the most pleasant country for an American tourist of any abroad. If you conform to their customs and do what they tell you,' he said, 'they will take the best care of you.' His wife and seven children agreed.[56]

14

Academic Wasteland

Of all the foreigners who remained in Berlin after the Games, few can have cut a more curious figure than Professor William Edward Burghardt Du Bois. Based at Atlanta University, where he taught history, sociology and economics, Du Bois was already some weeks into a six-month sabbatical by the time the last Olympic visitors had departed. Like many other American academics (Ambassador William Dodd among them), he had first fallen under Germany's spell as a graduate student – in his case, at Berlin University in the 1890s. However, the sixty-eight-year-old professor differed markedly from his fellow Germanophiles for the simple reason that he was black. Having gained a PhD from Harvard – the first African-American to do so – he had gone on to become a prominent academic, civil rights activist and writer. Now, more than forty years later, he had returned to Berlin to investigate education and industry in the hope that American Negro industrial schools in the South might profit by pursuing the German model.

That an elderly black academic should have chosen to spend time in Germany at the height of the Third Reich, in order to examine ways to improve 'Negro' education, seems scarcely credible. Certainly Mr Victor Lindeman of New York thought so. After reading about the project in the press, he wrote to Du Bois saying that he was 'highly amused'. Then, having listed Nazi crimes against non-Aryans, Lindeman asked, 'What is there possibly that could be used from an educational point of view, that will further the possibilities of Negro education in any part of America?'[1] It was a reasonable question, to which Du Bois replied, 'I do not see why the search for truth by anyone under any circumstances should cause you amusement. My investigations in Germany do not commit me to any set conclusions or any attitude. 67 million people are always worth studying.'[2]

Du Bois's trip to Germany illustrates the ambiguities underlying many foreigners' travels in the Third Reich. At a crucial moment in his youth, Du Bois had discovered in Germany an intellectual treasure trove far beyond the reach of most African-Americans at that time – no matter how brilliant. Now, as he grew older, and with Europe's future looking increasingly fragile, he longed – despite Hitler – to return to the country that had offered him such rich cultural gifts. But beyond this intense personal motive, he was convinced that because 'Germany was a critical point where the fate of modern culture would be settled',[3] it was important to witness the unfolding drama for himself. The Oberlaender Trust, 'dedicated to fostering greater transatlantic understanding by sending intellectuals between the United States and Germany', offered him a grant of $1,600 to study industrial education. The founder of the trust, Gustav Oberlaender, was an emigrant from the Rhineland who had made a fortune manufacturing stockings in Pennsylvania before turning to philanthropy. Inevitably with the rise of the Nazis, the trust's noble intentions had become muddied – especially since the Führer and other leaders of the regime received Oberlaender warmly whenever he visited Germany. Although Oberlaender personally made clear to Hitler his dislike of anti-Semitism, there was still much in the Third Reich that he admired – particularly the Nazis' handling of industrial disputes.

The Oberlaender Trust's links with National Socialism were clearly an embarrassment to Du Bois. In a letter turning down an invitation to join the American Committee for Anti-Nazi Literature, he wrote:

> I have been given by the Oberlaender Trust a commission to make investigations in Germany for six months. At first I wanted to study race prejudice or the question of colonies directly, but that did not fit in with their objects, but they are allowing me to make a study of education and industry. Of course there is no limit set upon what I may say after I come back. It would not, however, be wise for me to publicly join any committee before I went otherwise I would probably not be allowed to study.[4]

Once in Germany, Du Bois chronicled his progress in a regular column for the African-American weekly the *Pittsburgh Courier*. In his first dispatch from Berlin he noted that by 1 September the Olympic decorations had all disappeared from the streets, and the cafés on Unter den Linden were half empty. Commenting on the black athletes, whose triumphs were still so fresh in the public mind, he wrote optimistically: 'They typified a new conception of the American Negro for Europe, and also a new idea of race relations in the United States.'[5] A few weeks later he told his readers how, at 9 o'clock one autumnal morning, he had presented himself at Siemens City – an immense industrial complex four miles north of the Olympic stadium – that employed 36,000. He had been treated with great courtesy and given a full tour of the Siemens school. Everything about it impressed him – the selection process, the classrooms, the equipment, the care taken to max-imise each student's potential and the far-reaching vision of the four-year course. 'The spirit is remarkable and no wonder,' he wrote. 'These students do not pay, they are paid to study … they are encouraged and enthused in every way: a clubhouse; fields for games, evening entertainment for their families and friends, the midday meal is served free.'[6]

However, despite Du Bois's enthusiasm for progressive education, for the fine housing he saw everywhere, the plen-tiful cheap food ('though I myself felt the lack of fats'), the perfect public order and general air of prosperity, there was nothing naïve in his assessment of Nazi Germany. When asked by a journalist, after his return to America, whether he thought the Germans were happy, he replied, 'Happy no, but full of hope.'[7] He was at pains to tell his readers how he had trav-elled the length and breadth of the country, read newspapers, listened to lectures, seen plays, been to the cinema and talked to all sorts of different people. He had watched 'a nation at work and play'. Even so, he still found it difficult to reach firm conclusions. 'One cannot really know 67 million people much less indict them,' he commented. 'I have simply looked on.'

About the evils of anti-Semitism, however, he was entirely unambiguous. 'The campaign against the Jews', he told his read-ers, 'surpasses in vindictive cruelty and public insult anything I have ever seen; and I have seen much.'[8] There had been no tragedy in modern times to equal this hounding of the Jews. 'It is an attack on civilization,' he wrote, 'comparable only to such horrors as the Spanish Inquisition and the African slave trade.'[9] This was, of course, a view shared by many returning travellers,

but Du Bois made an additional observation. It was impossible, he maintained, to compare the situation of the 'Negroes'
in America with that of the Jews in Germany because 'what is
happening in Germany is happening in a lawful way and openly,
even if it is cruel and unjust. But in the US, the Negro is persecuted and repressed secretly in flagrant violation of the laws.'[10]
Why, one wonders, did Du Bois not point out more robustly
the hypocrisy of Americans who, while expressing righteous
indignation at the treatment of German Jews, were content to
ignore the lynching and torture of African-Americans?

Although Du Bois detested the persecution of Jews, the
appalling propaganda, the censorship and many other unpleasant facets of Nazi Germany, this did not, as he explained to
his readers, 'mean that I have not enjoyed my five months in
Germany. I have. I have been treated with uniform courtesy
and consideration.' Then, echoing comments made by the
black Olympic athletes, he wrote: 'It would have been impossible for me to have spent a similarly long time in any part of
the United States, without some, if not frequent, cases of personal insult or discrimination. I cannot record a single instance
here.'[11] It was a powerful point to make publicly, but privately
Du Bois was under no illusion. 'I was not at all deceived by
the attitude of Germans towards me and the very few Negroes
who happened to be visiting them,' he wrote to the secretary of the Jewish American Committee. 'Theoretically their
attitude towards Negroes is just as bad as towards Jews, and
if there were any number of Negroes in Germany, would be
expressed in the same way.' Nevertheless, his trip had convinced him that, in contrast to their attitude to Jews, ordinary
Germans were not naturally colour prejudiced.[12]

Of all the reasons why Du Bois so passionately wanted to
return to Germany, none meant more to him than his love of

opera – particularly Wagner. Writing from Bayreuth during the 1936 festival, he revealed his addiction to *Pittsburgh Courier* readers in an unlikely article entitled 'Opera and the Negro Problem'. Aware that his admiration for a composer widely known for his racist views might raise a few eyebrows, he began, 'I can see a certain type of not un-thoughtful American Negro saying to himself, "Now just what has Bayreuth and opera got to do with starving Negro farm workers in Arkansas or black college graduates searching New York for a job?"' The answer, he suggested, lay in Wagner's own struggles – so similar to those of the Negro. Wagner had also had to fight for an education, been out of work and in debt. He too had known what it was to be an exile, to be spurned in his own country. 'The music dramas of Wagner', Du Bois argued, 'tell of human life as he lived it, and no human being, white or black, can afford not to know them if he would know life.'[13] It was a bold assertion and one spoken from the heart. Yet it is hard to believe that it carried much conviction with his readers.

Du Bois's arrival in Germany coincided with the 550th anniversary celebrations of the University of Heidelberg. Although the university – the oldest in Germany – had actually received its charter on 1 October 1386, the Nazis chose to mark the occasion on the last four days of June, exactly two years after Hitler's Night of the Long Knives. Unaware of all this, Sibyl Crowe,* at the time working on her PhD

* Sibyl Crowe was the daughter of Sir Eyre Crowe (whose mother was German), the Foreign Office's leading German expert in the run-up to the First World War.

at Cambridge University, arrived in Heidelberg early on the morning of 27 June to stay with friends. She had travelled out from England by train and had been much struck with a group of her fellow passengers, bound for a small town on the Mosel. 'They were a party of thirty from Manchester, mostly shopkeepers, shop assistants, typists and factory-hands – quite simple and poor persons,' noted Sybil. 'Some of them looked pathetically white and pinched but all were in the highest spirits at the prospect of their holiday.' To her surprise, she discovered that most of them had already travelled many times to Germany. 'One man, a draper, told me he had been there seven years running; he sang the praises of the Germans, said what nice people they were.' A young shop assistant from a Manchester department store had hiked all over the Bavarian Alps, staying in youth hostels. 'Others now joined in the conversation,' recorded Sibyl, 'and the compartment soon became a kind of buzzing ode of praise to the beauties of the German country, the German people, and the German character.'[14]

Just before 8 o'clock that evening, after a pleasant day's sightseeing, Sybil and her friend found themselves a good spot in University Square from which to watch the opening of the celebrations. Rows of flags belonging to the fifty-odd nations who had sent representatives stood in front of the university's fine new auditorium, built with money raised by an alumnus and former American ambassador to Germany, Jacob Gould Schurman. The inclusion of the Union Jack and Tricolore was wishful thinking since all the British and French universities had refused to send delegates. Their boycott was in protest against the sacking – purely on grounds of race, religion or politics – of forty-four Heidelberg professors; and because by destroying the university's academic freedom, the Nazis had destroyed its very credibility. This blatant denial of the Enlightenment did not deter everyone. No fewer than twenty American colleges and universities sent representatives, among them Harvard and Columbia. Despite the public furore surrounding Harvard's decision to attend, the university's president, James Conant, stuck to his guns. In a statement reminiscent of Avery Brundage's support for the Nazi Olympics, he maintained that 'the ancient ties by which the Universities of the world are united ... are independent of ... political condition'.[15]

Perhaps if Conant had been exposed to the kind of student literature that Swiss writer Denis de Rougemont (who was at the time still teaching at Frankfurt University) was reading that summer, he might have changed his mind. 'Nothing in France', de Rougemont wrote, 'can give any idea of the demagogic violence of these articles ... their offensiveness, the determination to chase the opposition and beat them down to the very last resort, even to their deepest inner life. They are no longer content with even an exemplary submission. Anyone who does not demonstrate a joyful ardour in the service of the Party is denounced.' To make his point, he quoted a Nazi litany published in Frankfurt University's party newspaper:

> I have followed my course with zeal,
> I have shone in the seminar,
> I have given half a sou to the desperate poor, and I have
>   not missed attending the SA service this evening,
> I have made my presence felt and I have read with
>   enthusiasm *Der Völkische Beobachter*,*

* The official Nazi newspaper that had appeared daily since 1923.

> I have paid today my subscription to the SA because I
> am a spirit of the order.[16]

Heidelberg University publications were full of the same depressing message. Certainly American alumni returning there for the anniversary scarcely recognised the place. Gone were the old uniforms and colourful sashes of the duelling corps, gone the convivial atmosphere of beer gardens like Seppl, where buxom waitresses had once served young aristocrats with foaming stone jugs and a merry '*Prost*'. Now students wore drab SA uniforms and spent their evenings discussing 'Germany's Racial Destiny', 'Nordic Science' or 'The Place of Woman in the National Socialistic State'.[17] These were the students who on the evening of 27 June lined the streets, forming a barrier with the leather straps that were normally slung across their shoulders as part of their uniform. Sybil noticed how young they were and how they broke their line 'with great good humour' whenever she and her friend wanted to cross a road.

As the two young women waited in the crowd for the dignitaries to appear, a squad of firemen lit the contents of four burnished braziers placed high above the square on giant pillars. Watching the great columns of smoke spiral into the clear evening sky, Sybil was mesmerised by 'the strange and barbaric splendour' of a scene that seemed to her to recall ancient sacrificial ceremonies. 'There was', she wrote, 'an almost religious hush, the crowd holding their breath, silent with admiration.' It was a typical piece of Nazi stagecraft, although on this particular occasion things did not go according to plan. Faulty fuel quickly caused the smoke to darken and thicken so that within seconds the golden evening light was entirely blotted out. 'An ominous darkness,' wrote Sybil, 'comparable to the shadowy gloom preceding an eclipse, filled the air. Torrents of soot began to rain down on everyone covering their heads, faces and clothes with black.' It was, she might have added, a perfect metaphor for the Third Reich. But before their mutterings of annoyance could turn to anger, the crowd's attention switched to the 400-odd foreign delegates assembling on the steps of the Schurman auditorium. Until recently a statue of Pallas Athene had graced its main entrance along with the inscription, 'To the Eternal Spirit'. Now a bronze eagle, its wings outspread, had displaced the Goddess of Wisdom, and the word 'Eternal' had been changed to 'German'. Little wonder that Jacob Schurman, whom the university had invited as chief guest of honour, chose to stay well away. As they left the square, Sybil and her friend peered through some railings into a courtyard where they could just make out the abandoned Athene 'sitting dejectedly, her hands clasped over weak and sagging knees'.[18]

The next three days were taken up with pageantry, processions, banquets and the inevitable fireworks. Sybil and her friends were invited to watch the display from a house with a view across the river to Heidelberg's picturesque castle. It was the home of one of the dismissed Jewish professors. Luckily he had private means as the tiny pension provided by the university was too small to live on, and the family had so far been unable to obtain a permit to leave the country. But apart from the fact that he was forbidden to employ an Aryan maidservant under the age of forty-five, Sybil could detect no social stigma attached to the professor's household. She noted that her hosts clearly thought it perfectly natural to socialise with their Jewish friends, 'and were not in any way afraid of the consequences'.[19] As for the firework display, Sybil had never seen anything like it. But in case anyone had forgotten what the Third Reich was really about, utter blackness descended after the display, followed by the terrifying, deafening roar of sustained 'bombardment'. This, so Sybil was informed by her friend, was 'in order that people would become accustomed to what they might one day have to bear in grim earnest'.

Despite the heat, which he found trying, Columbia University's delegate Arthur Remy, Villard professor of German philology, was having a splendid time at the Heidelberg celebrations. Along with all the other foreign guests, he had been invited to a magnificent 'sixteenth century reception' hosted by Goebbels at the castle, where even the waiters wore period costume. The Berlin Ballet's performance during dinner had been particularly memorable. 'It was a very enjoyable affair,' he reported, 'and cannot in any conceivable way be termed propaganda of any kind.'[20] But next day even the ingenuous Remy was taken aback by the minister of education's speech – obviously designed to be the centrepiece of the entire anniversary celebration. Every institution of higher learning throughout Germany, Herr Rust intoned, must shape itself in harmony with the Reich's social, political and racial ideals. 'We were frankly told', wrote Remy, 'that for men who cannot conform to this requirement there was no place on the staff of a German university and that the dismissal of certain professors was therefore necessary and justified.'[21] He noted that the minister's speech (lasting more than an hour) evoked a good deal of criticism among the overseas delegates, 'and I confess I think it was justified'. Remy implies that the speech came as a surprise to the foreigners. Yet how could they not have been aware of the purges taking place in German universities? And how could they not have known that many leading German academics, most prominently Martin Heidegger (considered by many to be the finest philosopher of the twentieth century) were willing supporters of National Socialism? Heidegger, who liked to lecture in Nazi uniform at Freiburg University (where he had been rector, 1933–1934), had been personally involved in the expulsion of Jews from his university. And yet, despite all this, Remy could still write: 'Neither Columbia, nor any one of the American universities that accepted the invitation to be represented, need offer any apology for its course.'[22]

It was not just the delegates who were privileged to hear the minister's oratory. Loudspeakers carried it for miles around, shattering Sybil's pleasure in the peace and beauty of Heidelberg on that ravishing June morning. 'Walking through the streets,' she noted, 'we saw that speakers were situated everywhere in the gardens and squares, with little knots of people gathered round them to listen.' Later, when she read newspaper accounts of the day's proceedings, she was disappointed to find no mention of any speech made by a foreigner. She soon discovered why: overseas delegates had been allotted only five minutes each. It was, as the *New York Times* reported, perfectly obvious that the festivities were entirely controlled by the Nazis from start to finish. Indeed, a special Propaganda Ministry office had been established in the town to run each event down to the last detail.[23]

For Sibyl, the anniversary had confirmed all her worst fears. The Nazis were even more unpalatable than she had been led to expect from the British press. There could be no hope for Germany, she decided, until they had been utterly destroyed. Yet Remy, in summing up his experience, wrote, 'I believe on the whole the celebration was dignified and impressive – also that it was primarily academic … the presence of black or brown uniforms can certainly not be construed as of sinister significance.' He left Heidelberg convinced that he had attended 'a notable academic event'.[24]

A few days after the anniversary celebrations, a party of girls from the George Watson's Ladies' College in Edinburgh posed for a group photograph before setting out on their school trip to Germany. 'I remember our excitement,' recalled Ida Anderson in her seventies, 'as wearing our maroon blazers and panama hats, we gathered in the Waverley station.' When they arrived in Cologne it was already dark. They set out in crocodile to walk to the youth hostel. '"There", cried Miss Thompson, "is Cologne Cathedral" and suddenly,' wrote Ida, 'as if it were for our benefit, it was illuminated by a great flash of lightning followed by a mighty crash of thunder and downpour of rain.' The brims of their panama hats quickly filled with rain, sending little cascades of water down their necks. When, a few days later, they visited Heidelberg, 'immaculate' storm troopers acted as their guides. Like Sibyl Crowe, Ida Anderson was impressed by their good manners. 'How charming and polite they were!' Moving on to the Black Forest, the girls seem to have been quite unperturbed when they saw 'what looked like a section of the woodland moving towards us, but what turned out to be soldiers with well camouflaged armoured tanks'. Making light of this encounter with the Nazi war machine, they laughingly agreed that now they knew how Macbeth felt.[25]

When Ji Xianlin* arrived in Germany as a graduate student in 1935, it was the fulfilment of a long-held dream. For him,

---

* One of the most brilliant Chinese scholars of his generation, Ji Xianlin was a specialist in Sanskrit and Indian history. He lived in Germany from 1935 to 1946.

Germany was the embodiment of an ideal, seen through a 'golden haze'. But by the time he arrived in Göttingen some months later, he admitted that his illusions had been 'somewhat shattered'. Despite this, he decided that he would stay two years to study for a PhD in Sanskrit. As it turned out, he was to remain a decade. All through this long period, Ji Xianlin lived in the same house. He described his landlady, of whom he was fond, as a typical *Hausfrau* – educated only up to middle school, conservative and an excellent cook. This all seemed perfectly normal to the young Chinese scholar, but there were other things that puzzled him. Why, for instance, would she fall out with her best friend simply because the latter had bought the same hat? 'Western women (and men too)', he noted, 'have an unaccountable dislike of others wearing the same hat or clothes. This is very hard to understand for a Chinese.'[26] For anyone accustomed to the filthy streets of urban China, the sight of old ladies scrubbing the pavements of Göttingen with soap was extraordinary. He loved the tall medieval houses with their overhanging roofs, and enjoyed sitting among the oak groves in the centre of town. Each Sunday he would go to the countryside with other Chinese exchange students. Sometimes they would climb the hill to the Bismarck 'pagoda' or picnic in the woods. Occasionally they went to a local restaurant to eat black bear – 'which tasted a lot like Chinese food'.[27] Ji never publicly discussed politics, although he noted how the Germans worshipped Hitler wildly 'like lunatics', and was shocked when a pretty young girl told him that to have Hitler's baby would be the greatest glory she could imagine.[28]

Ji and his Chinese friends grew accustomed to the 'bull bellowing' (Hitler speaking) on the wireless – especially during the Nuremberg rallies. In the wake of Germany's re-occupation of the Rhineland, the 1936 Reichsparteitag (8–14 September) was dubbed the 'Rally of Honour'. At first sight, it was not the sort of event likely to attract many academics – Du Bois, who listened to it on the wireless, thought the sabre-rattling rhetoric 'frightful' and likely to precipitate war. But Professor Charles C. Tansill, of the American University in Washington DC, was implacably both right wing and pro-German. He was also a devout Catholic. One of fourteen Americans 'honoured' that year with an official invitation to Nuremberg, he confided to a colleague how much he was looking forward to meeting Hitler and 'other outstanding men of the party'.[29] In addition to his university post, Tansill was employed as a historian at the US Senate, where he worked on key diplomatic documents. Although unashamedly revisionist, his published work won respect from fellow historians and was not without wider influence.

On 20 October 1936, at the request of the German authorities, he made a broadcast to the United States from Berlin.* After describing the wonders of Nazi Germany, he turned to the Führer. 'He is never extravagant in gestures, nor is he loud of voice or lurid in expression,' he explained to his listeners. 'There is a simplicity and restraint about the man that is most engaging, and a sincerity that few can deny.' The Nazis must have been delighted with their eloquent apologist, one, moreover, who, unlike so many other foreign visitors, perfectly understood two vital points – that their expanding military machine was 'truly an army of defence' and the fact that the Reich was playing a unique role in defeating communism.

* Tansill was at the time working on his best-known book, *America Goes to War* (1938), an analysis of America's role in the First World War.

'Even the most hostile American critics', Tansill informed his audience, 'will have to recognize that without the buoyant optimism of the Führer Germany would have lapsed into Bolshevism.'[30]

Du Bois saw things rather differently. He argued that it was entirely *because* of Hitler that Germany had in fact already 'lapsed into Bolshevism'. In his view, the Nazi government was copying the Soviet Union to such an extent that there was now almost no difference between their two systems. He cited 'its ownership and control of industry; its control of money and banking, its steps toward land ownership and control by government; its ordering of work and wages, its building of infrastructure and houses, its youth movement and its one party state at elections'.[31]

Twenty-four-year-old Barbara Runkle agreed. Although not herself an academic (she was studying voice and piano in Munich), she was steeped in university life, having grown up in Cambridge, Massachusetts, where her grandfather had been president of the Massachusetts Institute of Technology (MIT). She wrote,

> Politics is my biggest interest, of course, ever since I found out that communism was at its best in books. Slowly but surely I've grown to be a great enemy of National Socialism – oddly enough for practically the same reasons that turned me against communism; they're amazingly similar which makes it seem almost unbelievably stupid that the next war will be between Germany and Russia, each ostensibly protecting their respective 'religions'.[32]

Initially, as Barbara Runkle admitted, she had been sympathetic towards the Nazis. 'At first one does incline to be, particularly when one sees really how relatively more secure and hopeful the people feel.' Although she soon realised her mistake, her letters show her to have had a surprisingly mature understanding of ordinary Germans at this high point in Nazi fortunes – a moment when so many of them, perhaps for the first time in their lives, felt genuinely optimistic about the future. In this context her portrayal of the young German soldier Karl Maier, with whom she went out a few times, is worth quoting in full:

Outwardly, Karl was one of the most trustworthy numbers imaginable – absolutely moulded into his uniform, a clean, shapely head with crisp, closely cut chestnut hair, a straight little face, white teeth, and a darling, wide smile. His cap tilted over one of his green eyes was a sight. His character was no less trustworthy than his appearance. He was, actually, what they term here *ein einfacher Mensch* [a simple man] – that is, his parents live in the country, and he spoke a kind of Deutsch which at first I could scarcely understand – but his virtues were due largely to his ancestry. He was very proud, very sensitive, very amusing, very affectionate, could sing and play the guitar beautifully, was an expert shot and skier. In addition, he was of course for me a fascinating acquaintance because of his life and ideas. He was a typical soldier of the very best kind – quick, clean, brave, proud, and believed infinitely that Germany should be *wieder gross und stark* [once more big and strong], didn't want war, but said if it came he'd fight until he was killed. I had a most intriguing discussion with him about Jews and Communists. At first he wouldn't even let me mention them, but finally we got around to the fact that there really were some nice Jews and he even went so far as to say that in theory Communism had some good ideas.

> He adores every detail of a soldier's life, and will no doubt
> go far. He's just my age – unbelievable – and is already an
> *Unteroffizier* [corporal].[33]

It is a curiously touching portrait and a reminder that in 1936
not every young German wore a uniform in order to beat up
Jews.

~

If Barbara had wanted to seek the company of other young
Americans while she was in Munich, she would have had
no difficulty. The Junior Year Abroad programme had been
a staple of American undergraduate education ever since the
1920s and continued to send large numbers of students to
Germany (particularly Munich) throughout the Nazi period.
It was especially popular among the most prestigious women's
colleges, dubbed the 'Seven Sisters'.[34] Strangely, the flow of
female students going to study in Munich during the Third
Reich did not diminish despite the fact that German women
themselves were now strongly discouraged from seeking higher
education. It was considered far more important for a daughter
of the Reich to study midwifery in one of the thousands of
maternity schools that had mushroomed all over the country. A German woman's prime function, after all, was to bear
children for the Fatherland and to give unstinting support to
her husband. It was not, however, the shrinking opportunities
for German women that were uppermost in Lisa Gatwick's
mind when she reported back to Bryn Mawr on her foreign
escapade. She was having the time of her life. One of Lisa's
recent excitements had been to witness the 9 November
ceremony honouring the sixteen Nazis killed in the 1923
putsch:

There were crowds and crowds of people from all over Germany lining the sidewalks and so thickly packed by about midnight you actually couldn't even go across the street. In fact we stood on one corner for about four hours and even if we hadn't wanted to, we'd have been forced to by the mob. Troops and troops of soldiers, SS men, SA men, Hitlerjugend, veterans etc., filed by steadily for three hours in the dead of night – no drums, music or anything – all perfectly solemn and tragic, as those sixteen men are considered the heroes of today's Germany and these people had come, some of them from miles away, to honour them. Even when Hitler went by there was to be no 'Heil Hitler,' but one or two people couldn't restrain themselves from yelling and were quickly hushed.[35]

She was thrilled to report that she had seen Hitler 'quite close up four or five times'. Lisa's newsletter bubbles over with excitement but never once does it touch on Jewish persecution or any other Nazi horror. Rather she describes the opera audiences who 'clap and clap until you'd think their hands would drop off', the weekly dance at the Hofbräuhaus where 'everyone waxes very merry under the influence of that wonderful beer', and the family with whom she had her daily meals. 'Nearly every day Herr Klussmann gives us statistics (all very carefully and proudly worked out from his little notebook which has everything in it) about the relations between America and Germany – population, ancestry, temperature – *alles*!'

Lisa even enjoyed the food, although noting that they never had more than two courses and usually only one. 'Tonight we had some sort of pancakes with raisins in them and jam instead of syrup, tea and bread and butter sandwiches.

Yesterday we had thick vegetable soup for supper then cold rice mixed with apricots.' After supper, the family would sit round the wireless, 'quite a luxury', Lisa observed, chatting, sewing and reading. In fact, the radio had become such a vital propaganda tool that it was not as rare as Lisa had supposed. In 1934 a Frankfurt court ruled that bailiffs were no longer permitted to seize radios because they had become such indispensable items in the new Germany. 'It is of the utmost importance for the education of the citizen and for the struggle for the unity of the German people,' quoted the *Manchester Guardian* from a Nazi source.[36] At 9.30 the Klussmann wireless was switched off and the family went to bed. Hot baths were difficult to come by, Lisa reported, but at least the apartment was centrally heated. All in all, she concluded, 'it was a very fine life indeed'.[37]

Her uncritical account of Nazi Germany can be explained away as youthful naïveté. At a time when such travel was an unusual experience for the majority of young Americans, who could blame her for not wanting to let politics spoil her big adventure? But there can be no such excuse for the academics responsible for sending her (and her twenty-seven fellow students) to Munich at such a time. They must have known what was going on in Germany or, if they did not, they were not doing their job. Even allowing for hindsight, it is extraordinary that against such a repressive, anti-intellectual background, Professor Grace M. Bacon of Mount Holyoke College (professor of German and a director of the junior year in Munich programme) was able to maintain as late as 1938 that 'Study in Munich has resulted in a breadth of view, and a tolerance and understanding of another civilization which only direct contact can give.'[38]

There were of course professors like Tansill who genuinely sympathised with Nazi ideology and eagerly sought to identify with the regime. But many other academics chose to travel in the Third Reich because Germany's cultural heritage was simply too precious to renounce for politics, however unpleasant those politics might be. They allowed their reverence for the past to warp their judgement of the present. As a result they wilfully ignored the realities of a dictatorship that by 1936 – despite the Olympic mirage – was unashamedly parading itself in all its unspeakable colours.

15

Dubious Overtures

By the end of 1936, it was difficult for anyone in Britain who was not a recluse, an anti-Semite or a convinced National Socialist to claim ignorance of Nazi brutality. Jewish refugees, countless newspaper articles, surviving inmates of concentration camps and those persecuted for their religion provided ample proof that Hitler's dictatorship was anything but benign. Nevertheless the optimists – among them many establishment figures – hung on to their belief in the Führer's 'sincerity', arguing that if his more reasonable demands could in due course be met, all would be well. In consequence a number of distinguished individuals made their way to Germany during the late 1930s, confident that personal contact and rational dialogue would ultimately secure peace. Other travellers to post-Olympic Germany included anti-Semites, fascist sympathisers, celebrities, spies, royalty and the inevitable Mitfords. Meanwhile, despite what they read in the newspapers, most of the hundreds of ordinary American and British tourists who continued to holiday in Germany simply ignored the politics. True, they could not help noticing the Germans' curious addiction to uniforms and marching, but the overriding impression they carried home was still that of a cheerful, friendly people eager to give their foreign visitors the warmest possible welcome. The countryside remained beautiful, the medieval towns picturesque and the beer cheap. So why spoil a good holiday worrying about the Jews?

For Winifred Wagner the 1936 Bayreuth Festival brought with it the usual string of anxieties – plus, that year, an addition in the shape of Sir Thomas Beecham. Ribbentrop, as usual getting the wrong end of the stick, had reported to Hitler that the British conductor was an intimate friend of King Edward VIII; and because the king was sympathetic to the Nazis, ergo Beecham must be too. On the strength of this falsehood, Beecham had been invited to take the London Philharmonic Orchestra (LPO) on tour to Germany later that year at the regime's expense.

As Beecham was expected for the opening of the festival, Frau Wagner arranged a small lunch party so that he might meet Hitler informally. But just hours before Sir Thomas was due to appear, a telegram arrived: 'Sorry, cannot come. Greetings. Beecham.' This casual cancellation caused deep displeasure at Wahnfried as the Führer had particularly wanted Sir Thomas to sit with him in the Wagner box.[1] But only when Beecham was certain that Hitler had left Bayreuth and would not be returning, did he appear for the second half of the festival. Dispensing charm to all and sundry, the suave and immaculately dressed Beecham nevertheless made a point of leaving promptly after each performance so as to avoid having to speak to the likes of Göring's 'bourgeois and rather commonplace' sisters, alleged to be great gossips.[2]

It is clear that Beecham despised Hitler's regime. Yet, like so many others, in the end he found the lure of Germany too strong to allow the Nazis to derail his travel plans. The proposed LPO tour caused considerable controversy in

England, but for Beecham the temptation to show off his new orchestra (with all costs covered) in a country where, despite the Nazis, an orchestra still mattered, was too great. What is harder to understand is how Beecham – a man of such unfailing self-confidence – could have succumbed to German pressure to drop the Mendelssohn 'Scottish' Symphony from the programme simply because its composer was Jewish. But then, as Sir Thomas knew full well, the Nazis were paying the piper.

Hitler, accompanied by most of his government, was present at the opening LPO concert that took place in Berlin on 13 November 1936. After the first piece (Dvořák's Slavonic Rhapsody No. 3) he was seen applauding enthusiastically. The concert was broadcast far and wide – a fact that Beecham must have known when he famously remarked in range of a microphone – 'the old bugger seems to like it'.[3] Whatever Hitler may have thought of the performance, Goebbels judged it rubbish. 'The difference between Furtwängler and Beecham', he recorded in his diary, 'was like that between Gigli [the famous tenor] with Kannenberg [Hitler's accordion player].'[4] And, he added, 'embarrassing because you had to clap out of politeness'.[5] The next day a faked photograph appeared in newspapers, showing Beecham in Hitler's box during the interval chatting to leading Nazis. In fact he had never left the artists' room backstage.

Predictably, the full panoply of Nazi propaganda accompanied the LPO on its tour through Germany. But in the midst of all the receptions, swastikas and speeches, there was an occasional glimpse into the other Germany, one that still existed albeit in deep secrecy and torment. In Leipzig, an unsigned letter smuggled to Beecham informed him of how only a few days earlier the great bronze statue of Mendelssohn that had stood in front of the Gewandhaus had vanished. 'Nobody knows where it is,' wrote the despairing correspondent. 'It will probably be melted down for guns.' But, he went on, 'his music is immortal, and will continue to be played in all civilised countries with the exception of Germany where it is strictly forbidden. The whole cultural world of Germany thinks and feels as I do … It includes in its daily prayers the cry for help and freedom.'[6] If the LPO had brought even a flicker of hope to such people, then, Sir Thomas might reasonably have argued, the tour was justified. But what if, on the other hand, it had presented the Nazis with a massive propaganda coup that had only furthered their cause? This dilemma – to go or not to go – was one facing all thinking would-be visitors to the Third Reich who loved Germany and hated the Nazis. Whatever conclusions Beecham may have reached after the tour, as he journeyed towards Paris and the free world, Mendelssohn's 'Scottish' Symphony must have long reminded him of his own Faustian pact.

Opportunism took Beecham to Nazi Germany but in the case of David Lloyd George it is difficult to detect any real motive for his famous visit there in September 1936 other than hubris. At the age of seventy-three, Lloyd George was convinced that Europe's current problems stemmed from lack of strong leadership – the sort of leadership, in other words, that he had himself so brilliantly demonstrated as British prime minister during the Great War. Consequently, until such time as the nation would turn again to its former leader crying, as the *Western Mail* mischievously put it, 'Oh frabjous day: Come to my arms, my beamish boy',[7] dictatorships like Hitler's – at least in such vital matters as unemployment and infrastructure – would continue to outstrip any feebly led democracy like Britain.

It was against this background that Lloyd George arrived at the Vier Jahreszeiten hotel in Munich early on the morning of 3 September. With him were his daughter Megan and son Gwilym (both MPs), Dr Thomas Jones, deputy secretary to the Cabinet during Lloyd George's administration (now doing the same job for Stanley Baldwin), his personal secretary Arthur Sylvester, his doctor Lord Dawson of Penn and the ardently pro-appeasement editor of *The Times*, Geoffrey Dawson. Also in the party was the academic Philip Conwell-Evans, who three years earlier had witnessed the book burning at Königsberg University with such equanimity. Choosing to operate discreetly behind the scenes, Conwell-Evans had been instrumental in bringing together a number of influential British figures with leading Nazis. It was he, for instance, who, in December 1934, had been the driving force behind the first major dinner party Hitler ever hosted for foreigners and at which Lord Rothermere had been guest of honour. And it was now Conwell-Evans, in harness with his close friend Ribbentrop, who was masterminding the Lloyd George expedition. 'He is so blind to the blemishes of the Germans,' Dr Jones wrote of his fellow Welshman in his diary, 'as to make one see the virtues of the French.'[8]

Dinner with the Ribbentrops on the first evening was not a success. Much to Lloyd George's irritation, Germany's new ambassador to London stuck remorselessly to his favourite theme – Britain's inability to grasp the communist threat. However, the following day all was sweetness and light. At precisely 3.45 the Führer's car drew up outside the Grand Hotel Berchtesgaden, where the party was lodged, to whisk Lloyd George off to tea with Hitler in his mountain lair. Of the British contingent, only Conwell-Evans accompanied him, leaving the others to wait in suspense for his return. As the

car arrived at the entrance of the Berghof, Hitler descended
the great flight of stone steps to greet the Welsh statesman.
He then led Lloyd George through the arcade up to his personal sitting room where he seated his guest uncomfortably
on a backless sofa in front of a portrait of the young Frederick
the Great. When Lloyd George commented on the painting,
Conwell-Evans observed how the chancellor laughed and
looked at him 'his eyes brimming with benevolence and admiration'. Indeed, he noted, Hitler 'could hardly keep his eyes
away from him' throughout the whole visit.[9]

Their political talk covered familiar ground; the communist threat, Germany's desire for peace and need for
Lebensraum [living space], the return of its colonies, the
Spanish Civil War and so on. Then, with all that out of
the way, they moved down to the vast drawing room – 'like
some great hall in an old castle', commented Conwell-Evans.
A bust of Wagner stood on the Bechstein grand, a Gobelins
tapestry hung on the wall. But dominating the room, and occupying most of its north wall, was the famous window – 'quite
as large as a theatre curtain', noted Conwell-Evans. On fine
days the glass could be lowered through a groove to the floor
below, leaving Hitler's guests delightfully exposed to a great
expanse of sky and mountain. Salzburg, lying to the north
in Hitler's native Austria, was clearly visible in the distance.
'The dramatic beauty of the spectacle almost took one's breath
away,' remarked Conwell-Evans.[10]

Over coffee, Hitler animatedly discussed a favourite topic
– autobahn construction. He was delighted to learn that Lloyd
George had travelled from Munich to Berchtesgaden on one
of these splendid new roads, which, as he was keen to point
out, had done so much to alleviate unemployment. A surviving
film clip shows the British party's Mercedes driving along a

completely empty motorway towards the mountains. The only traffic they encounter is a solitary car and one bicycle. When a boiling radiator forces them to stop, an ox-cart, heavily laden with hay, can be seen slowly trundling across one of the bridges spanning the autobahn.[11]

The following afternoon Lloyd George returned again to the Berghof but this time accompanied by the entire British party. While Sylvester's cine camera whirred away in the background, Conwell-Evans made further notes:

> For some time there was general conversation, then suddenly we all found ourselves listening to a talk between Mr Lloyd George and Hitler. It is difficult to describe the atmosphere. It seemed to become all of a sudden almost solemn. One realised that the great War Leader of the British Empire and the great Leader who had restored Germany to her present position were meeting on a common ground. One seemed to be witnessing a symbolic act of reconciliation between the two peoples. Everybody listened intensely; it was a moving experience.[12]

And there was more bonding to come. 'If the War had been won by the Allies,' Hitler said quietly, 'it was not in the first place the soldiers to whom victory was due, but to one great statesman and that is yourself Mr Lloyd George.' With 'a tear in his throat',[13] the elderly politician replied that he was deeply touched by the Führer's personal tribute and was particularly proud to hear it paid him by 'the greatest German of the age'.[14]

After so much emotion, tea the following day with Rudolf Hess at his home on the outskirts of Munich was something of an anti-climax. Nevertheless, Lloyd George bombarded his

host with questions. But when he asked what was the difference between National Socialism and Italian fascism, the
deputy Führer could only reply that he had not the slightest
idea thus causing 'great laughter all round'.[15]

So eager were the Nazis to show off every last benefit
they had bestowed upon a regenerated Germany that there
was little time for any further merriment during the remaining ten days of the tour. Visits to factories, to Daimler-Benz, a
cotton mill and the Württemberg Dairy Company; to model
housing for agricultural workers, a country school and the
Labour Front headquarters, were accompanied by earnest discussion, endless statistics and many miles of motoring. At one
of several labour camps they visited, Conwell-Evans reported
that, when some of the men were lined up for questioning,
'Lord Dawson made them breathe deeply in order to check
their chest expansion.' The eminent physician (who had eight
months earlier hastened King George V's death in order that
its announcement might catch the early edition of *The Times*)
recommended that remedial gymnastics be introduced into
the camps to improve the various physical defects he had
observed in the young men.[16] Nazi reaction to this helpful
suggestion is not recorded.

Back in England, Lloyd George's praise of Hitler verged
on the ecstatic, as his notorious interview with the *Daily
Express* makes clear. 'He is a born leader of men. A magnetic,
dynamic personality with a single-minded purpose, a resolute
will and a dauntless heart ... He is the George Washington
of Germany – the man who won for his country independence from all her oppressors.' Even more to the point, Hitler
was unquestionably a man of peace. The idea, Lloyd George
told the newspaper, 'of a Germany intimidating Europe with
a threat that its irresistible army might march across frontiers

forms no part of the new vision ... they have learned that lesson in the war'.[17] This enthusiasm was echoed privately in a letter to Ribbentrop in which he described the trip as the most memorable visit he and the rest of the group had ever made to Europe. The admiration he had always felt for 'your wonderful Führer' had deepened and intensified. 'He is the greatest piece of luck that has come to your country since Bismarck,' wrote Lloyd George, 'and personally, I would say, since Frederick the Great.'[18]

Although his remarks were at the time widely derided, Lloyd George was not alone in expressing such views. Many of those who shared them were members of the Anglo-German Fellowship (AGF), founded towards the end of 1935. Conwell-Evans and Ernest Tennant (a prominent businessman who, in 1919, had served in Berlin with Lieutenant Colonel Stewart Roddie), together with Ribbentrop, were the chief instigators. From the start, the AGF set out to attract the rich and powerful and therefore numbered many politicians, businessmen and aristocrats among its membership. Some were fanatically pro-Nazi but others joined simply because they wanted to foster closer relations with Germany.

From November 1936 until July 1939 the AGF published a monthly magazine – the *Anglo-German Review* (*AGR*). Its pages are filled with glowing accounts of Germany written by travellers ranging from expert professionals to holiday tourists. Mrs Ursula Scott-Morris 'went to Germany expecting to be impressed by the rolling of drums, the flashing of medals and the sound of marching feet'. But instead 'found flowers – violets, pansies and roses at every street corner'.[19] Frank Clarke MP, one of the large British group that visited Germany in September 1937 to study autobahns, was touched by the welcome they received from the 'pretty children of Bayreuth'.

The children, 'in their dainty frocks and neat suits', went out to the autobahn to greet the delegation with salutes, cheers and songs. When the visitors returned to their coaches, they found on every seat a bag of tastefully prepared sandwiches, cakes and fruit. 'How they laughed at our surprise,' noted Clarke.[20] As for all the fuss about the Jews, Mr William Fletcher of Kensington, having just spent several months in Freiburg, was able to report that he had 'seen Jews flocking to their synagogues on a Friday evening without let or hindrance' and 'happy-looking Jewish children playing in front of the Jewish school'.[21]

While such comments may, in some instances at least, be put down to sheer gullibility, this was hardly a charge that could be levelled against Scottish lawyer Archibald Crawford KC. Yet the article he published in the 1937 January edition of the *AGR* – 'New Laws for Old' – is an astonishing panegyric to the Nazi legal system. Having watched a criminal trial while attending a conference in Munich, Crawford felt able to assure his English readers that in all his long court experience he had 'never witnessed justice being more patiently or more impartially administered'. He noted how the young men charged with manslaughter 'not only had every point brought out in their favour but when found guilty received sentences which I can affirm were lighter than ever came under my personal observation in the Scottish Criminal Courts'.[22] Crawford says nothing about the victim. Was he or she perhaps Jewish? And might the killers have been Nazi thugs? The article makes no reference to Dachau situated just 12 miles from Munich.

~

Despite all the efforts of the AGF to establish friendly relations with Nazi Germany, not to mention those of such eminent emissaries as the Marquesses of Lothian* and Londonderry, it was clear that, by the middle of 1937, a new coolness had entered Anglo-German relations. From the German side, the decline in approval was the result of Britain's persistent failure to go into partnership with the Nazis, Germany's increasing strength and the hostility of the British press. Sir Barry Domvile sensed the chill as soon as he arrived in Nuremberg for the 1937 Reichsparteitag. 'Thought the SS more truculent than usual,' he observed, and he was annoyed to find he had been given a room on the third floor – 'not nearly so good as last year'.[23] In fact, he was lucky to be in Nuremberg at all as not only were most of the British guests lodged in Bamberg forty miles away, but they had also been asked to contribute to the cost of their stay. At cocktails that evening, Domvile found Ernest Tennant and Philip Conwell-Evans in deep gloom. For men like them, who had invested so heavily in friendship with Hitler's Germany, this palpable change of mood was depressing. There was even an article in the *Daily Telegraph* highlighting the altered status of the British guests.[24]

Nevertheless, a frisson of excitement ran through their ranks† as they awaited Hitler's arrival at the tea-party that had

* Lord Lothian was a prominent appeaser who met Hitler in January 1935 and May 1937. He was appointed British ambassador to the United States in 1939.

† Among the more notable British guests attending the 1937 Nuremberg Rally were: anti-Semitic writer Gordon Bolitho; Colonel Sir Thomas Cuninghame DSO and Lady Cuninghame; Lieutenant Colonel John Blakiston-Houston; Robert Grant-Ferris MP; Sir Nevile Henderson, British ambassador; Diana Mosley; Unity and Tom Mitford; Professor A. P. Laurie; Lord Rennell; William Stourton, 22nd Baron Stourton, 26th Baron Segrave and 26th Baron Mowbray;

become an annual event for the foreign VIPs attending the Reichsparteitag. To underscore the importance of the occasion, guests had this year been invited to wear formal morning coat. Domvile did not approve, commenting, 'simplicity won't stand the test of success even in a National Socialist regime'.[25] And he was further disappointed when the Führer passed by him at the reception without a word. Indeed, as Hitler walked along the line of British guests, he remained stiff and expressionless until introduced to Francis Yeats-Brown, when he burst into smiles. Yeats-Brown's autobiography, *The Lives of a Bengal Lancer* (1930), had been made into a Hollywood movie (starring Gary Cooper) that had become a great favourite of Hitler's. He thought the film such a valuable demonstration of how Aryans should deal with an inferior race that he had made it compulsory viewing for the SS.[26]

For the first time, a British ambassador was also present at Nuremberg in what was surely one of Britain's more dubious overtures in 1937. Sir Nevile Henderson (who had replaced Sir Eric Phipps in April), together with his French colleague François-Poncet and the American chargé d'affaires, Prentiss Gilbert, attended for two days. The diplomats were lodged in railway carriages parked down a siding. As they breakfasted on the first morning, a Luftwaffe squadron flew twice over their train in tight swastika formation.[27] That night Henderson was impressed by the lavish *son et lumière*. The three-hundred-odd

Lady Snowden (widow of Labour Chancellor of the Exchequer, Philip Snowden); George Ward Price (*Daily Mail* correspondent); Lady Helen Nutting; Captain George Pitt-Rivers; Sir Assheton Pownall MP; Lady Hardinge, widow of Sir Arthur Hardinge; Sir Arnold Wilson MP; and Francis Yeats-Brown.

searchlights that met thousands of feet up in the air to form a square 'roof', struck him as both 'solemn and beautiful'. It was, he wrote, 'indescribably picturesque', like being 'inside a cathedral of ice'. And in terms of 'grandiose beauty', even the Russian ballet that he had so admired in Moscow could not compete with Nazi choreography.[28] But for one British visitor, the excitement was all too much. After the light show was over, the AGF's representative, Major Watts, who had watched it from a beer tent, had to be carried on to the bus over the shoulders of a strapping SS youth. To the horror of his fellow countrymen, the major spent the hour-long journey back to Bamberg sprawled over his seat before finally subsiding on to the floor.[29]

Despite his packed programme, Domvile found time to buy a print of the oil painting *In the Beginning was the Word* by Hermann Otto Hoyer depicting Hitler as 'The Bringer of Light'. He was so pleased with it that he returned to buy a second copy for a fellow guest. 'It is a wonderful bargain for DM 3.60,' he noted in his diary, adding, 'I am sure they intend to deify Hitler.'[30]

Although Reichsparteitag had been an uplifting experience, it had also been exhausting and Domvile was 'really glad to be off'.[31] Once back in England, he wrote a spirited account for the *AGR*. He had come away from Nuremberg, he told his readers, convinced yet again that if only people would go to Germany and 'see for themselves' instead of staying at home and writing about 'slaves and mass hysteria and all the other jargon of the peevish pen-pushers', they would be surprised at the gulf between imagination and reality. He ended with a warning. 'The German people want our friendship but are beginning to despair of getting it. A slight impatience at our inability or unwillingness to try to understand their point of view is creeping in as they regain their confidence and self-reliance ... Germany cannot be expected to wait forever.'[32]

Nor could Lord Londonderry, returning to England that September from his third visit to Germany in a few months, offer much comfort, having detected 'a distinct deterioration in our friendly relations with Germany'.[33] This time, instead of being feted by Göring at Carinhall, Londonderry had been packed off to a hunting estate on the Baltic where his host was fellow aristocrat Franz von Papen.* The Nazis, it seemed, had at last realised that the former air minister – even if he was a marquess – was not as influential as they had hoped. At least on this occasion Londonderry, in a notably non-Aryan gesture, had refused to shoot the elk offered him, explaining that he 'obtained as much pleasure in seeing the splendid animals as in shooting them'.[34]

Domvile had made the point that the Nazis would 'not wait forever' and when it came to preparing for war, the Nazis were certainly not waiting. Ji Xianlin, studying Sanskrit in Göttingen, recorded in his diary on 20 September that it was the first day of air-raid practice. 'No light allowed anywhere. All windows pasted with black paper. It lasts all week.'[35] The next day Kay Smith wrote to her daughter Kätchen, at school in Switzerland:

---

* It was von Papen who had urged Hindenburg to appoint Hitler as chancellor in the belief that the latter could be easily controlled. He narrowly escaped being assassinated during the Night of the Long Knives in 1934.

We have been having air raid week. We had to put black
paper over the windows in the kitchen and maids' rooms
and bathrooms, no light escapes. The street lights are out.
The cars have black over the headlights and only a tiny slit
of light allowed and half the red tail-lights. Last night was
full moon so it was bright anyhow. We went to dinner with
the Hungarian attaché and drove slowly safely there and
back. Tonight is raining so we stay home. It is very black
outside. No lights from any house. The planes fly overhead
and searchlights catch them and we hear machine guns in
the distance. No sirens have blown at night. But in the day-
time – yesterday morning twice – they blew and everything
stopped and people got out and ran into the cellars where
they stayed until the sirens blew again. Mrs Vanaman [wife
of the American air attaché] thought she had to go down
too, so she went into the cellar and said, although her husband had been a flyer for years, it was the first time it had
come home to her what bombing might mean and might
happen to her. They are getting along much better now.[36]

Once the sirens started, every car was required to stop wherever it was, while its occupants rushed to the nearest shelter.
To remain on the street during the 'air attack' was an offence
punishable by prison.[37] The American air attaché's wife cannot have been the only foreigner in Berlin that week (a full
two years before the outbreak of the Second World War) for
whom the sight of over a hundred aircraft 'bombing' the city
was a life-changing experience.

Yet despite the new frost in relations with Britain, despite
air-raid week, despite the persistent cry of 'guns before butter' and despite Hitler's relentless push for a free hand in
Eastern Europe, one distinguished foreigner after another

returned home from Germany convinced that war was the last thing on the Führer's mind. 'Hitler is a pillar of peace,' declared Sir Sultan Mohammed Shah, Aga Khan III, president of the League of Nations, following a visit to Berchtesgaden in October. 'Why? Because peace is an essential of all Hitler's plans for rebuilding the nation.' The Ismaili Muslim leader declared that he had never before seen such 'constructive and practical socialism' as in the new Germany. 'Everything is being organised for the greatest happiness of the greatest number,' he reported. 'Herr Hitler is a very great man, no one can deny that.'[38]

Although the Aga Khan's trip attracted a good deal of publicity, he could not compete with the Duke and Duchess of Windsor. In terms of celebrity and sheer inappropriateness, their visit, which also took place that October, was the most spectacular made by any foreigner to Germany in 1937. 'Arriving here early Monday morning for a twelve-day visit,' wrote the *Observer* Berlin correspondent, 'the Duke of Windsor faces a heavy programme.'[39] He did indeed. The former king's much feted interest in labour conditions and workers' housing gave the Nazis a perfect opportunity to showcase their social reforms. Boasting of how many foreigners visited Germany to study its institutions, the *Deutsche Allgemeine Zeitung* noted: 'Now the Duke of Windsor, too, has come to convince himself personally of the energy with which the new Germany has tackled her social problems.'[40] This was hardly the kind of copy that either King George VI (who had been crowned only four months earlier and had been given no warning of his brother's visit) or his government wished to read. Escorted by Dr Robert Ley, the peculiarly unpleasant head of the Labour Front, the Windsors toured factories, housing estates and, according to the Duke's equerry Dudley Forwood, even saw a concentration camp. It was an enormous concrete building that appeared deserted, Forwood recalled. 'When the Duke asked what it was, our hosts replied: "It is where they store the cold meat."'[41]

Forwood was probably right when he maintained that the Duke of Windsor's chief purpose in going to Germany was to make the Duchess feel like a queen. For what better way of doing that than by giving her a 'state' visit? Above all, Forwood remarked, 'he wanted to prove to her that he had lost nothing by abdicating'.[42] There was only one country where such a visit could be successfully carried off and that of course was Germany. The Nazis' wooing of the Duke acted as a soothing balm on his injured ego. And given his own family's obduracy on the matter, German insistence on addressing the Duchess as HRH was a source of particular pleasure. The Duke, who had always felt his German roots strongly and spoke the language fluently, clearly enjoyed the tour. He went drinking in a beer hall, wore a false moustache, joined in a singsong and played skittles.[43] The cheering crowds, fawning officials and endlessly whirring cameras must have made it easy for him to imagine that he was still king. Although the meeting with Hitler at Berchtesgaden produced nothing but platitudes, it did untold damage to the Duke's reputation, firmly fixing in the mind of the British public the perception that he was an enthusiastic supporter of Hitler. Furthermore, his evident delight in all that he saw encouraged the Nazis to believe that he would, in the words of Bruce Lockhart, soon return to the throne as 'a social-equalising king, inaugurate an English form of fascism and an alliance with Germany'.[44]

On 13 October 1937, as the Duke and Duchess of Windsor were nearing the end of their tour, Viscount Halifax, the Lord President of the Council (and more important in this context,

a master of foxhounds) received a letter from the German
Hunting Association inviting him to attend the International
Sporting Exhibition in Berlin the following month. It was an
unlikely pretext for what was to be the British government's
most serious overture to Hitler since Neville Chamberlain had
become prime minister in May. When Halifax agreed to go,
no one was fooled as to the real purpose. To avoid war by
dealing constructively with Hitler was, as he later wrote to
Henderson, 'easily the most important task before this generation'.[45] But first, to give credibility to his alibi, he toured the
Sporting Exhibition. It was, in the words of Halifax's biographer, 'a gruesomely Teutonic affair'. Hanging beside several
huge portraits of Göring was an equally vast map of Germany's
lost colonies.[46] Although the British contribution had been put
together only at the last moment, it won first prize in the big
game section, a success aided no doubt by the fact that several
of the beasts had been shot by King George VI and Queen
Elizabeth. Jack Mavrogordato, secretary of the British Falconers
Club, recalled how this triumph prompted snide remarks from
the Germans, keen to point out that the only reason they had
failed to challenge the British was because of the wrongful
confiscation of their African colonies.

Having visited the exhibition and duly admired the stuffed
giant panda, Halifax was free to embark on his real mission –
meeting the Führer. At Hitler's insistence their encounter was
to take place at Berchtesgaden, which meant an overnight journey to Munich on Hitler's special train. In order to maintain
the fiction that the visit was entirely 'private' and 'informal', the
Embassy's first secretary Ivone Kirkpatrick rather than
the ambassador accompanied Halifax. 'The servants on the
train', wrote Kirkpatrick 'evidently thought that Englishmen
lived on whisky, appearing every half hour or so with a tray

of whisky and soda.'[47] Met by a fleet of Mercedes, they were driven through the snowy landscape straight to the Berghof. 'As I looked out of the car window,' Halifax recorded in his diary, 'I saw ... a pair of black trousered legs, finishing up in silk socks and pumps. I assumed this was a footman who had come down to help me out of the car ... when I heard a hoarse whisper in my ear of "Der Führer, Der Führer"; and then it dawned upon me that the legs were not the legs of a footman, but of Hitler.'[48] If this was not a promising start, worse was to follow.

Lord Rennell (a former ambassador to Rome and Nancy Mitford's father-in-law) had several times met the Führer at Nuremberg. Keen to brief Halifax before he left, he had advised him to approach Hitler 'from his human side as man to man'. Then, Rennell wrote reassuringly, he would find Hitler 'really receptive'.[49] If Halifax had believed these words encouraging, he was to be in for a big disappointment. By the time the two men met, Hitler was in a 'peevish mood' and anything but receptive. After a couple of hours of unproductive talks (in Hitler's overheated sitting room) they went down to lunch. This, Kirkpatrick noted, was served in a 'hideous' dining room furnished with a long satinwood table and pink upholstered chairs. The food was indifferent and, from the social point of view, the lunch was 'a frost'. One topic of conversation failed after another – the weather, flying, the birth of Hess's son and the Sporting Exhibition. Hitler, who disliked all field sports, angrily condemned hunting with the memorable remark: 'You go out armed with a highly perfect modern weapon and without risk to yourself kill a defenceless animal.' Nor did things improve over coffee when Hitler's stated remedy for restoring order in India was to 'shoot Gandhi' and if that did not work 'to shoot a dozen leading members of Congress' and if that still did not work 'to shoot 200 and so on'. No wonder

Halifax (a former viceroy of India), as Kirkpatrick observed, 'gazed at Hitler with a mixture of astonishment, repugnance and compassion'.[50]

Diplomatically Halifax's visit marked a depressing close to a depressing year. But, although efforts by the good and the great to court Hitler met with increasingly negative results, most ordinary travellers, if fewer in number, continued to roam Germany with unfettered delight. Blinkered and naïve many may have been, but their philosophy, like that of the travel agencies who sent them, was simple – always look on the bright side.

16

Travel Album

As the regime tightened its grip on every aspect of German life, 'looking on the bright side' became ever more difficult. Nevertheless, in 1937, and even into 1938, there was still a surprising number of tourists (the great majority of them British and American) who were not only curious to experience Nazi Germany but keen to have a good time too. One of them was twenty-year-old Rhys Jones,* whose unpublished diary gives such a vivid impression that it is worth quoting at length:

> **Sunday 8th August 1937: Arrived Koblenz 12.15 p.m.**
> First impression – a sense of the massive and solid.
>
> People's physique definitely better than ours. Fitness put before personal looks. Girls often too fat by English standards.
>
> Hillsides covered in cabbages. No hedges.

---

* Jones was to become a lecturer in French at St David's University College, Lampeter, and editor of the journal *Trivium*.

Dress: Quite unassuming except for black shorts, peculiar plus fours etc. White shoes a novelty. Germans do *not* dress according to the weather. Absence of open cricket shirt. Berets unpopular – French!

Language: vigorous, almost militant.

Perturbed by thought of being taken for a Jew given my slightly aquiline features.

Discovered Woolworths.

Smell peculiar to each country (except our own). That of Germany a scented tobaccy [sic] smell mingled with fish.

Men walk upright, military fashion, keeping knees almost stiff. Impression of walking on heels and overbalancing. Nearly all close-shaven or glassily bald.

Very large families. Children clean and tidy if a little old-fashioned (frills etc.). Shop windows *full* of prams.

Fewness [sic] of cars. Germans too poor to buy more than a bicycle.

Women terribly plain. Carry packs in blazing sun. Would try any man! Little use of corsets.

Best proof of poverty found in cinemas. Only cheapest seats full. Solemnity would put many of our churches to shame. No smoking! No sweets! No whispering! No clapping. Strong silence. People like oysters. Don't know what to applaud, what not. No applause for Hitler! No national anthem at end! Little laughter. No mention in 'news' of England or France! Incidental music classical. Whole atmosphere like prison.

Lack of noise everywhere. No hooting of boats on the river, little of cars in streets. So orderly that accessories are needless, as are policemen. Feeling of absolute security.

No slums or slummy shops.

No French taught in school.

Passed famous Lorelei. No sign of nymphs, only Nazi flag on top!

Met Scotch fellows on boat. Told us Germans were friends of Scots and English, but as for the French – 'rat-tat-tat' within 3 years! Have heard not one word of French spoken here!

Books, posters etc. exceptionally moral. Very few 'birds' on streets.

Harmonicas, accordions everywhere. Love of folk music.

Cigarettes too full of saltpetre. Turkish.

Can get glorious mahogany tan here – unknown in England.

Do not stare at you like French.

Zimmersmann café – asked for rolls but no butter! Cakes instead.

No litter baskets yet no litter on roads.

Bought *Mein Kampf*. Shopkeeper quite suspicious but I paid so he said nothing.

Heard shooting at Ehrenbreitstein Fortress tonight.

People evidently doing all they can to curry favour with England.

Faces of people very kindly, rarely brutal.

People extremely honest. No need to count change. No tipping.

Saw Protestant church, closed and encircled by barbed wire like a fortress.

Have only seen one Jewish shop since I have been here and cannot say I have wittingly seen one Jew.

Sunday 15 August: Left Cologne 10.02 a.m.[1]

Arguably the most striking tourist attraction in Germany while Rhys Jones was there was the Exhibition of Degenerate Art in Munich. 'There is no place in the Third Reich', Hitler had declared at Nuremberg in 1935, 'for cubist, futurist, impressionist or objectivist babblers.'[2] It was in order to highlight the depravity of such artists that this famous exhibition was opened in July 1937. Works by the likes of Klee, Kokoschka, Kandinsky, Dix, Nolde, Grosz, Beckmann and Kirchner were haphazardly displayed with the sole purpose of inviting ridicule. A short distance away in the Haus der Deutschen Kunst (the monumental new art museum built by Hitler's favourite architect, Paul Troost) a Nazi-approved exhibition – Great German Art – also opened. However, when it came to a choice between chaste Aryan nudes and a spot of degeneracy, the public voted decisively with its feet.

In his book *Just Back from Germany* (1938), British writer J. A. Cole reflected a widespread view when he wrote, 'Some of the works I liked, some left me indifferent and some I was frankly unable to understand.' Everywhere, he noted, were labels, exclamations and question marks deriding the exhibits. 'It was almost as though the Nazis feared the visitors would not jeer enough.' The middle-aged man he spotted egging on visitors to poke fun at the art was almost certainly one of the actors hired by the gallery to do exactly that. In fact most people, Cole observed, showed no reaction at all. 'They just walked through dumbly, looking stolidly at pictures as they might have done in any art gallery on a wet Sunday afternoon, and then went out again.' Although Cole was not himself particularly avant-garde, halfway round the exhibition he experienced an odd exhilaration. 'The audacity of these pictures was infectious,' he wrote. 'It was like walking into a lunatic asylum and realizing that one had been trying to become a lunatic for years.'[3]

Truman and Kay Smith, together with Charles and Anne Lindbergh, were also among the thousands of visitors who poured through the Degenerate Art exhibition. Kay was horrified, commenting, 'The continuous viewing of ugly distorted faces and forms, with blood and vomit spewing from them – vulgar disgusting scenes – produced a definite physical reaction.' Once safely outside in the fresh air, Lindbergh admitted to needing a drink for the first time in his life. Kay, who had been reading articles in the American press condemning Nazi philistinism, was now, on this issue at least, entirely in sympathy with the Führer. 'I heartily supported the name Degenerate Art which Hitler had given it,' she wrote, 'and was delighted when he announced that "the era of the purple cow" was over.'[4]

After visiting the exhibition on 12 October 1937, the Smiths and Lindberghs dined with General von Reichenau. Anne Lindbergh was impressed:

> He is one of those completely rounded, charming, cultured men of wide experience, great strength, and concentrative ability, combined with fineness of perception and breadth of vision, delightful for dinner-party conversation. I do not think I have met more than two or three of his type in my life. Not that he gave you the impression of being a 'great' man, or a genius, or of great strength … it was something one felt gradually, increasingly through the evening: Here is a civilized man, as balanced and as well educated a man as one is likely to find.[5]

Exactly four years later, on 10 October 1941, when the German invasion of the Soviet Union had been underway several months, Anne Lindbergh's delightful host (by then a

Field Marshal) issued the 'Reichenau Severity Order' to the Sixth Army. 'The most important objective of this campaign against the Jewish-Bolshevik system', it ran, 'is the complete destruction of its sources of power and the extermination of the Asiatic influence in European civilization ... In this eastern theatre ... the soldier must learn fully to appreciate the necessity for the severe but just retribution that must be meted out to the subhuman species of Jewry.'[6] Von Reichenau's troops subsequently took part in the massacre of 33,000 Ukrainian Jews.

By the time Barbara Runkle (still studying music in Munich) wrote to her sister on 16 March 1937 describing an encounter with the high priest of anti-Semitism – Julius Streicher – any illusions she may have once harboured about Nazi achievement had long since been destroyed:

I had a quite exciting experience recently. I saw that Julius Streicher, the great Jew chaser of Germany, was going to speak in the Hofbräu House one evening. Klaus Lüttgens, the son of the house, and I decided to go. When we got there we found that our tickets wouldn't get us into the big main room, but only into one of the smaller rooms where the speech was to be relayed by radio. That was a pathetic substitute, so we decided by hook or by crook we'd get into the big room. I approached the dumbbell at the door with my passport and explained that I was an American very much interested in the Jewish question. He wouldn't believe that I wasn't German until finally a more intelligent bystander assured him that I was indeed a foreigner, and I was let in. That left Klaus outside, but he hopped through a pantry window while everybody else was busy *heiling* Herr Streicher as he entered. So there we both were in the gigantic smoke-and-noise filled hall. The speech which followed was the first of its kind I've ever heard in my life. I knew it was going to make me furious of course but I didn't quite realise that I'd be literally shaking with anger so that I didn't think I could stand up. First of all, he is a superb demagogue, who absolutely fascinates his audience. He knows just when to make them laugh and when to get sentimental, and how to fan the flames of race prejudice until the hearers are slavering for a Jew to attack. He told a long series of unbelievable lies: that there's no such thing as a decent Jew in the world, that they all have a certain bacillus in their blood which gives diseases to 'white' people; that they caused the world war, the downfall of Rome and heaven knows what else. He retailed gruesome stories of German girls defiled by marriage with Jews, and made every point clear with some vulgar joke. I really looked desperately around the room for one sane person who wasn't believing it all – but with the exception of Klaus, who, although a National Socialist, was also disgusted, they were all hanging on his words. Of course they were a very unintelligent, common crowd; the respectable people don't go to hear Streicher because they know what a devil he is – but if a few more of them did go, they might have a slightly more realistic view of the regime. Klaus hasn't been half so ardent since.

Klaus had been jotting remarks down on a piece of paper – points he wanted to discuss with me, and as we started to go out, a uniformed SA man came up to him and said he must go with him to the head man, because his wife (me) had obviously been so against the whole thing and hadn't heiled or sung, and he (Klaus) had been jotting things down on a pad. At this, all my pent up wrath and

nervousness burst forth in a torrent on the man in uniform. Actually I was terrified because I knew what Klaus
didn't, namely that on the same pad, which I had lent him,
was a half-finished essay by me on the Jewish question in
Germany. Klaus, quite jovial, joined me in a few minutes,
and explained that he'd been taken to an intelligent leader
who hadn't even asked to see the pad – thank heaven.
It was pretty thrilling, I can tell you. Anybody that talks
about a social system where the state is all-powerful and
thinks it will be paradise, had better keep still and thank
the lord that nothing like that has happened to us yet. He
just doesn't know his onions.[7]

A couple of months after Barbara Runkle attended the
Streicher meeting, Dr and Mrs William Boyle were brought
unexpectedly face to face with the reality of anti-Semitism.
They had recently married in Nairobi, where William practised medicine. His father-in-law, Brigadier-General Sir Joseph
Byrne, was Governor of Kenya. After returning to England
to visit their families, the couple decided to honeymoon in
Germany. They then planned to drive to Marseilles where they
would board a ship back to Kenya. Although they did not
(as recommended in an *AGR* article entitled 'Practical Advice
for Motor Travellers'[8]) fly a Union Jack on their car, they did
sport a large GB. Despite the cooling of relations between the
British and Nazi governments, this sticker remained a magnet
for ordinary Germans who, having sighted one, would go out
of their way to be friendly to its owners.

Nothing, however, could have prepared Eithne and
William for what was to happen one sunny day in Frankfurt.
They had just parked their car and were about to go sightsee-
ing when a Jewish woman and teenage girl approached them.

The child, limping badly, was about fifteen and wore a thick built-up shoe. The woman came straight to the point. She had seen the GB on their car and now implored the couple to take her daughter with them to England. It was Eithne who made the decision. Having seen enough on their holiday to realise that the outlook for a crippled Jewish girl in Nazi Germany was anything but rosy, she agreed on the spot. It was a remarkable act of charity on her part, and one of great trust on the mother's. It was also a sign of the woman's desperation when, on discovering that her daughter would not be going to England but to Africa, she did not change her mind. Only one thing mattered, getting her daughter out of Germany. Once the British Consulate had provided the necessary papers, Dr and Mrs Boyle resumed their holiday with the girl now in the back seat. A photograph of Greta taken several years later shows her in the Boyles' Nairobi garden, holding their new baby. She is smiling broadly.*

The Boyles were from a social class that regarded the increasingly popular package holiday with disdain. However, the *AGR*, aware of the potential of this relatively new form of travel, published several articles aimed at encouraging secretaries and shop assistants to travel to Germany this way. In 1938 the *AGR* recommended a two-week holiday (for a minimum of fifteen people) covering the Rhineland, Munich, Vienna, Innsbruck, Salzburg and Berchtesgaden. With everything

* Interview with William and Eithne's daughter, Alice Fleet (the baby in the photograph). Greta's subsequent history is unknown although attempts to track her down are currently under way.

included, the cost was £30 (about £500 in 2016).[9] In Germany, holidays for the workers were run by a state organisation with the catchy name of Strength through Joy – *Kraft durch Freude* (*KdF*). It was one of the Nazis' more successful enterprises, providing low-cost holidays, day trips and cultural events for some 25 million German workers between 1933 and 1939.

Because Archibald Crawford KC had proved himself such an enthusiastic apologist for Nazi Germany, he was one of four Britons invited in August 1937 to join 1,500 German workers and their families on board the *Wilhelm Gustloff** for a cruise to Madeira and Portugal. The ship, launched three months earlier, had been purpose built for the *KdF*. Crawford recorded how everything on board was done en masse – games, discussions, walks, songs and parades. 'We were more like a large boarding school than a collection of adults,' he wrote. 'Orders were given wholesale, but always accepted gladly and obeyed with a promptitude which astounded me.' Many Britons would have found such conduct unnerving, but Crawford looked for the positive. 'I came to the conclusion that Germans are born Socialists,' he observed, 'probably the only ones in the world.'

Socialist principles certainly governed life on board the *Wilhelm Gustloff*. As part of the Nazis' effort to stimulate social mixing, members of the middle class were included on the cruise but secured no special perks from their status. Cabins, for instance, were all allocated by lottery. There was plenty of

---

* The ship was originally named the *Adolf Hitler* but Hitler himself decided to name it the *Wilhelm Gustloff* after the Swiss Nazi leader, assassinated in 1936. It was sunk by a Soviet submarine in 1945. Some 9,400 Germans perished, making it the largest loss of life in a single ship in history.

opportunity for Crawford to speak to the passengers. Apart from resentment at the hostility of the British press to National Socialism and a fear that 'some of your Communists might create disturbance', it was clear that Britain was the place they most wanted to visit. Conceding that a holiday aboard the *Wilhelm Gustloff* might not be entirely to British tastes, Crawford was nevertheless impressed:

> This particular trip with its two weeks at sea on a luxury liner with its visits to Lisbon and Madeira, its six meals a day, its constant entertainments which included the best marionette troupe in the world, leading opera singers, several orchestras and pocket money in Portuguese currency when on shore, cost each of the workers but a fraction of what it would normally do under ordinary touring conditions.[10]

Although the great majority of passengers were only low-paid agricultural or industrial workers, thanks to *KdF* when it came to travelling the sky was now their limit. Indeed, some were already looking forward to rejoining the *Wilhelm Gustloff* for its world cruise to Tokyo in 1940.

To any non-believer visiting Germany in the late 1930s, it must have seemed as if National Socialism had permeated every last nook and cranny of human existence. Yet, as Sylvia Morris recalled, in Dresden (a city consistently hostile to Hitler), she somehow contrived to ignore the Nazis while at the same time extracting the best out of Germany:

> I went to Dresden in 1937 to study violin and singing. I lived with other girls in a *Töchterhaus* (girls' hostel). I was completely swept up in the music. Every night I went to

the opera and remember the joy of singing in the chorus under the baton of Richard Strauss. Nobody talked about Hitler or politics. Once a week I had to register with the police and once a week I went to *Brautschule* (bride school) where I learned to make clothes and soup (very useful in the war when I worked for MI5 and fed soup to German prisoners in Wandsworth jail). If I ever wanted to venture away from my normal route, a maid had to accompany me. Each month there was a dance but it was all very formal. We could only dance with a man if we had already been introduced. The chaperones sat round the wall. We were only supposed to speak when spoken to and expected to curtsey to our seniors. I met a fellow musician Fekko von Ompetda. Several times a week he went on bombing raids over Spain. I went to the Bayreuth Festival twice. The road up the hill to the Festspielhaus was lined with people waiting for Hitler. I can still remember the stench of sweat, feet and high leather boots.[11]

However, for seventeen-year-old Ursula Duncan-Jones, despatched in February 1938 to study German in Osnabrück, ignoring the Nazis was not an option. Her hosts, Dr and Mrs Heisler, were pro-Hitler but then, 'so was everyone'. Like a surprising number of her contemporaries, Ursula had been sent straight from the sheltered world of a girls' boarding school to Nazi Germany. In her case, the transition was all the more extraordinary since her father, Arthur Duncan-Jones, Dean of Chichester, had himself visited Germany three years earlier. Not only had he experienced the Nazis at first hand, but also throughout 1937 (in what Ursula called 'the year of the German invasion') given sanctuary to countless refugees at the Deanery. His cook and secretary were both Nazi victims.

Why, then, would the Dean and his wife consider Osnabrück a suitable place to send their innocent teenage daughter? The truth is that their love of Germany (visited regularly since their Munich honeymoon) and the German people was so deep-rooted that – as was the case with many other Britons – it had not only survived the Great War but was apparently impervious even to the Nazis.

Ursula, who despite her youth was an astute observer, found Dr Heisler tiresome – 'a roundabout, bouncy creature' with a silly sense of humour who 'as was the custom' was seriously over-indulged by his wife and family. Nor did she much like the two children, who spent most of their time attending Hitler Youth meetings and parades. However, Frau Heisler – small, squat and friendly – did all she could to make Ursula feel at home. Finally there was Tante Bertchen, who passed her days sitting in a corner of the kitchen knitting and listening to Nazi propaganda on the wireless. Despite her intense dislike of the regime, Ursula settled happily into the rhythm of the Heisler household. Then one day it was announced that Hitler would visit Osnabrück on a whistle-stop tour:

> The excitement was intense. The whole family trooped down to the station, along with what seemed to be the entire population of the town. And we waited and waited until finally the famous train drew in. Hitler made his way down the train, appearing at each window in turn making sure that everyone had a good look at him. The roaring response was indescribable. I couldn't believe it. For the rest of the day, probably the week, the family went on and on about how wonderful it had been to see our Führer, and how lucky it was for me to have seen him, and on and on and on. I adopted a fairly cool response – I refused to

acknowledge that it had been anything more than interesting and left it at that.[12]

Just as Ursula embarked on her German adventure, Barbara
Pemberton was enjoying an experience of a very different kind.
The daughter of an English father and a half-German, half-
Belgian mother, she had largely grown up in Hamburg. For
health reasons she used to spend the winters at Bad Oberdorf
in Bavaria. One afternoon, while supervising some children on
the nursery slopes, she was approached by a pleasant-looking
woman who asked if she would mind including a 'blonde
curly-haired little chap' in the group. The woman, Barbara
later learned, was Ilse Hess – wife of Hitler's deputy, Rudolf
Hess – the child was probably Hess's nephew. 'I got to know
Ilse well and actually liked her,' she wrote, 'even though she
was a totally dedicated Nazi.'

In February 1938 Ilse invited Barbara to stay with them
for the Munich Carnival – *Fasching*. Barbara was delighted,
her father less so. After much discussion he reluctantly gave
his permission but told his daughter that, should she fall for
Nazi doctrine, she would no longer be welcome at the family
home. With this warning ringing in her ears, Barbara arrived
at Munich station where she was met by SA men and driven
straight to the Hess house. It stood in a large park constantly
patrolled by SA and their guard dogs. After a warm welcome,
Barbara was offered a chair close to the wireless around which
the entire household had gathered to listen to the Führer's
annual speech, always given on 30 January, the day he had
become chancellor. 'I can see them now,' recollected Barbara,
'hanging on his every word.' The daughters of the Swedish
ambassador and an Italian countess also joined the party. On
one occasion everyone went for a walk, Hess leading the way.

'We all got a fit of the giggles,' wrote Barbara, 'as his bald patch was very prominent and someone suggested a piece of fur cut from one of our gloves would cover it nicely.'[13]

In Berlin, Emily Boettcher, an American concert pianist from South Dakota, struggled with the endless regulations inhibiting her efforts to develop her musical career. Since 1935 (when she was 28) she had spent long periods in Germany studying with some of the greatest pianists of the century – Wilhelm Kempff, Artur Schnabel and Edwin Fischer. Determined to succeed, she tried to ignore the unpleasantness around her by concentrating on her music and practising long hours each day. Finding a suitable room was not the least of her problems, as is clear from a letter written to her parents:

> Well, I've moved to my new place but I doubt very much if I'll be here long because the practising has already disturbed one of the roomers. I seem to be having terribly bad luck. Most people who sublet their rooms always take care to hide or not show the unpleasant things in their household. Usually it's the bathroom or perhaps the light plugs don't work. I didn't see anything wrong with this place when I first came – not until the noon meal was served and then I discovered what the Frau Doctor had been hiding from me – namely her roomers! She has three and with herself it makes 4 people in the house all over 70 years old. I feel as though I were in an old ladies' home.[14]

Shortly after this, and having moved to new quarters, she noted on 5 February 1938, 'Have bed bugs. Room will have to be sprayed. If that doesn't work, it will have to be gassed or I move out. Butter scarce, no eggs. Two months later she sat in yet another room taking stock:

I realise, for the first time, what a devastating effect the
Nazi propaganda machine has had on my nerves. Without
knowing it, I have succumbed, like thousands of others, to
fear of everything. Nevertheless, it is more than propaganda
that has driven me to this state. My telephone has been
tapped; I have been refused a meal when I went to a restaurant with a Portuguese friend who has Jewish features;
all my letters from abroad are censored.[15]

Given this not uncommon description of daily life in Germany,
how was it possible that as late as 1938 a steady trickle of ordinary tourists still chose to holiday there? Even more puzzling,
why, having been there and seen the regime for themselves,
did they not on returning home loudly condemn it?

Dr Jill Poulton's memories of family holidays in the late
1930s go some way to providing an answer. For Jill (a teenager)
and her older sister, Germany was paradise – the medieval
villages, the lack of traffic, the friendly hotels (which never
needed booking in advance) and numerous jolly beer gardens.
Best of all were the swimming pools in every village – not to
mention the 'beautiful adolescents' adorning them. It was quite
unlike anything Jill had experienced in England. Driving an
antiquated Rover, the family motored through Germany to
Austria at a leisurely pace, never covering more than 100 miles
in a day. Nor did they have any difficulty parking in the main
square of each town they visited. Everyone was polite and
charming – even the officials. On a path near Berchtesgaden
they met a group of youths in dirndls and lederhosen singing in perfect harmony as they strode up the mountain. The
family never discussed politics and never felt threatened.
The two girls were impressed by the smartness of the young
men in uniform. Medieval Frankfurt stood out as a particularly

fine memory for Jill. When their guide showed them Flea Street, narrow, dark and smelly, in the Jewish quarter, her mother (of German origin) made one of her frequent anti-Semitic remarks. It was only several years later that Jill and her sister discovered that their mother was herself Jewish.[16]

Equally, the writer J. A. Cole – who was no Nazi sympathiser – was able to comment after a prolonged stay in Germany in 1937–1938:

> I cannot see a German town for the first time on a sunny morning without a rising of the spirits, a feeling that here is a place delightfully foreign yet at the same time a place where one could live happily. The streets of Aachen are wide and tree-lined. Pavements, roadway and house steps bear the appearance of having recently been very thoroughly swept and washed. People's faces shine with soap and water. Carters crack their whips cheerfully, in contravention of the by-laws. Really poor people are difficult to find. The shops are smart and there is a cheering number of cafés. No hawkers or beggars stand in the gutters.[17]

It would seem that even those travellers fundamentally hostile to the Nazis instinctively looked beyond the regime to what they imagined to be the real Germany; a country that, despite everything, maintained its enduring power to beguile and entrance.

17

Anschluss

On 12 March 1938 Hitler annexed Austria – the Anschluss. While many foreigners were appalled by the ruthlessness of Hitler's latest move, others felt it to be a perfectly logical development that could only improve Austria's long-term prospects.

In Göttingen that day, Ji Xianlin answered the doorbell to find his friend Long Tongtian standing anxiously on the doorstep. 'I could never ever have imagined the shocking news he brought me,' he wrote in his diary. 'The German army has occupied Austria. War cannot now be avoided and I fear that I will not be able to return to China in the near future. I shall have to live abroad without money, perhaps even begging in the streets. Will I ever see the old country again?'[1] In Dresden, meanwhile, Sylvia remembered how everyone marked the Anschluss by eating lots of cream – 'particularly memorable given the food shortages'.[2] Lady Margaret Boyle, opera fan and daughter of the 8th Earl of Glasgow, was at a finishing school in Munich when Hitler marched into Austria:

> Unity Mitford asked if any of us would like to see him.
> So thinking it was rather a historic moment, some of us

said yes and went up in the train to stand in the street as
he drove past. There were soldiers lining the street and an
island in front of us so we were anxious as to which side of
the island he would drive. Of course it was the *far* side so
we pushed the soldiers aside and rushed up to his car. He
was standing up in that leather coat he always wore and
instead of smiling sweetly at us looked SIMPLY FURIOUS
that the soldiers had failed to hold us back. Anyway we *saw*
him. He looked just like his picture.[3]

Standing among the vast crowds in Linz awaiting the Führer's
triumphant arrival, was Kay Smith, who recorded that the
'*Sieg-heil Sieg-heil*' roar of the crowd 'was so repeated that it
sounded like a giant pulse beating in your ear'.[4]

The Anschluss horrified Ursula Duncan-Jones, who
summed it up as a 'despicable annexation by Hitler of a joyful
little country called Austria'. It was impossible, she complained,
to escape the endless propaganda on the wireless, 'on full blast
indoors and out'. She was puzzled. 'After all, these people, for
whom I had quite an affection, and who seemed intelligent
and balanced enough, were apparently hoodwinked by all the
propaganda. As an onlooker I kept quiet and thought my own
thoughts. I very soon ran out of suitable non-committal replies
to the eulogies tumbling from their lips.'[5]

Four days after the Anschluss, *The Times* published an article – 'Across Nazi Austria: A Traveller's Impressions':

The drive to the Vienna station was difficult and slow
because of the long columns of incoming German mecha-
nized units and the almost hysterical crowds. From the
windows of the train, journeying through the night, ghostly
processions of tractors, lorries and armoured cars were

continually seen moving towards Vienna, their headlights lighting up the countryside. In the towns the big hotels are in the possession of staff officers and their orderlies. The station restaurants are the monopoly of German soldiers, and the whole scene is reminiscent of Belgium in the Great War ... Trains to the frontier were packed mostly with Jews but also with a large number of English visitors from the winter sports resorts around Innsbruck who thought it better to leave Austria. The Jews were taken en masse to police headquarters in Innsbruck and searched to the skin for contraband currency. English visitors to the winter sports resorts were allowed to keep the money they had with them.[6]

It was this particular article, so seventeen-year-old Joan Wakefield noted in her diary on 28 March, which had provoked an intense political discussion between herself and a German girl over breakfast that morning. Uta, an enthusiastic member of the Bund deutscher Mädel (League of German Girls), the female branch of the Hitler Youth, had just returned to Berlin after six months in the countryside working with peasant families. 'Argued for 2 hours! In German!' wrote Joan, who was studying at Berlin University. On the day of Hitler's triumphant return from Vienna, she had accompanied her landlady, the Baronin von dem Bussche-Streithorst, to Wilhelmplatz to hear the Führer speak. Joan had stood by a fountain on which several Brown Shirts were sitting, swinging their legs. When she failed to salute they began kicking her head. That night the Baronin, fired up with patriotism, decorated the supper table with swastikas.

One month later, on 10 April, a plebiscite was held throughout the Reich seeking endorsement for the Anschluss.

The night before the vote Joan was on a train between Stuttgart and Munich. Out of the window, she could see massive fires blazing on all the hilltops and fireworks exploding above every village. When the results came through, 99.7 per cent of the electorate had allegedly approved. Ji Xianlin did not. His diary entry reads: 'Today is Election Day in Germany. All the Germans in the street are wearing badges. At the doors of the polling stations are lots of black dogs [SS] and yellow dogs [SA].' The next day he added:

> Last night I was suddenly woken up at midnight. Downstairs on the radio was the sound of a dog howling; no doubt it was Old Xi [Hitler] or perhaps someone else. After the howling there was thunderous applause, shrilly breaking the silence of the night like a banshee. The Germans have all gone mad. The day when it all falls apart cannot be far away.[7]

Undeterred by the political situation, the Charterhouse School hockey team set out in early April for a tour of Germany. A member of the team recorded their adventure for the school magazine:

> The Charterhouse hockey team was not, it must be admitted, the chief centre of interest on its arrival at Cologne. The reason for this was not difficult to find: Hitler had spent the whole day there, exhorting Germans for the 'Ja' in the coming plebiscite ... Every public building, from the humblest shop to the Opera House in Leipzig, was literally plastered with Nazi propaganda. At Cologne we stayed at a magnificent sports stadium, a splendid example of modern German architecture. This was the only place where we did

not stay with families. This was not due to the fact that we were not wanted, but every family had filled its house with friends and relations from the surrounding country, who had come to the city to see their leader ...

I think it is fair to say that most of the party enjoyed Leipzig best ... its atmosphere was more English, the spirit of Hitler did not brood so earnestly over the town as in the other parts of Germany we visited ... Everywhere we went was the same desire for friendship with England ... Their earnestness is almost tragic. They find it impossible to believe that we should prefer as an ally the French, the friends of Russia and Czechoslovakia, to them – fellow Saxons.[8]

Captain George Pitt-Rivers was equally perplexed. He utterly failed to understand why Britain showed such reluctance to join hands with Germany. By mid-1937 the number of British Nazi supporters had already diminished significantly, but of those now remaining, none was more fervent than Pitt-Rivers. The Anschluss, in his view, was a splendid achievement. On returning from one of his many trips to Germany, he wrote to congratulate the Führer: 'Allow me, an old British officer and sincere friend of Germany ... to express my sentiments of profound thankfulness that the Anschluss with Austria has been accomplished under your leadership without bloodshed and with the rejoicing of all the German and Austrian peoples.'[9]

On 6 July 1938, when Austria had been part of the Reich for three months, a train steamed its way slowly along a branch line from Fulda towards Hanover, stopping at every station no matter how small. Corvey (forty miles north-west of

Göttingen) was one such rural outpost and it was here that Joan Wakefield stepped on to the platform to begin what was to prove a memorable summer holiday. In Berlin she had met by chance the Duke of Ratibor at her German teacher's house. The Duke, who also held the titles of Prince of Corvey and Prince of Hohenlohe-Schillingsfürst, had taken a liking to the British girl and a few days later invited her to spend the summer with his family so that his younger children might improve their English. 'Drove straight to the Castle,' recorded Joan, 'the Duchess on the doorstep to meet me.'[10]

On that perfect summer's evening, the 'castle', a former Benedictine abbey, was bathed in golden light. The family may have been one of the oldest in Germany, 'the social equal of its Kings',[11] but the furnishings were sparse and modern comforts few. Two bathrooms served the entire household. Joan unpacked, the men returned from shooting and they all went in to dinner. Food shortages were now widespread throughout Germany but here the fare – all provided by the estate – was plentiful and delicious. Joan did not record their dinner conversation but it is unlikely that they discussed an important news item announced earlier that day, namely, that Jews were now prohibited from trading or providing certain specified commercial services. 'Felt at home and very happy after my first evening with the Ratibor family,' Joan wrote that night before falling asleep.

Her first week was spent canoeing down the Weser. A photograph taken in front of the Schloss, as they were about to set out, shows a group of attractive young people, beaming with excitement. The world was their oyster and not even the heavy grey skies that day could dampen their spirits. An album entitled – 'Paddel-Fahrt auf der Weser 9.VII. – 16.VII 1938. Münden bis Minden* [Canoeing trip on the Weser – Münden to Minden]' survives. Tiny faded black and white photographs (with frilly edges) show extraordinarily empty countryside stretching away on both sides of the river. Occasionally a curious child or a lone cyclist is caught in the frame. Half-timbered houses, churches and tranquil villages are all captured forming a backdrop to the friends' canoeing exploits. They survived thunderstorms, midges, a collision with a ferry, leaks, sunburn and a landlady who spied on them through a hidden peephole. When not drifting lazily downstream or paddling furiously against a headwind, they climbed the Bückeberg, shopped for clogs and ate vast quantities of Westphalian ham. The night spent at Kirchohsen (five miles south of Hamelin) was their merriest. The village mandolin band played while the Spanish cousins performed the tango and Joan a polka. By the end of the evening the entire village had joined in. It was, as Joan put it, 'all grand fun'.

A week later they arrived back at Corvey having hitched a ride on a vegetable lorry. As the weather grew hotter, each day dissolved delightfully into the next. They played tennis, shot buck, went riding and swam in the Weser. At night they danced to a gramophone, drank 'bowle' (a mixture of white wine and champagne) and discussed politics. A week after their canoeing trip, a party of them set off for the German Grand Prix. Thrilling though the races were, even more exhilarating for Joan was driving home with Viktor (the eldest Ratibor son and heir) in his Frazer Nash. 'A bit terrifying,' she wrote, 'but glorious light over the vineyards in the setting sun – romantic and lovely.' The following day it was announced that Jewish doctors were no longer permitted to practise medicine.

Schloss Corvey may have been grander than anything Joan had ever encountered but it was only the family's summer residence. The Ratibors' main seat was the imposing former

Cistercian abbey Schloss Rauden, in Upper Silesia. The Schloss, surrounded by its vast estates, was, in those pre-war days, only a few miles from the Polish border. On 3 August the whole household, including Joan, left Corvey for Rauden 500-odd miles to the east. The drive to Berlin, where they spent the night, was long and hot. Like all foreigners, Joan was impressed by the efficiency of the autobahns but found them monotonous. Arriving in Berlin, they quickly changed into tennis clothes, played a couple of sets and then spent the evening dancing at the Eden Hotel. 'Franz Albrecht was hopeless at the Jiggedy Jig,' noted Joan. She recalled how several months earlier she had danced in the same hotel with the Baronin's nephew Axel von dem Bussche-Streithorst. The tall handsome officer was to become a hero of the German resistance. In 1943, at the age of twenty-four, in what was intended to be a suicide mission, he planned to assassinate Hitler by hiding a grenade in the new Wehrmacht uniform that he had been asked to model for the Führer. In the event the meeting never took place because Allied bombs destroyed the train transporting the uniforms. Determined to have another go, Axel was again thwarted when a further planned meeting with Hitler was cancelled. Luckily for him, at the time of the 20 July bomb plot he was in hospital (having lost a leg), and was therefore above suspicion. Meanwhile Joan, on that hot August night in 1938, wrote wistfully in her diary, 'Thought of time when I dined at the Eden with Axel and we danced together. Divine!!'

The next day the whole party set off again to the immense Schloss Koppitz, complete with Gothic towers, flying buttresses and magnificent gardens. 'Not at all attractive,' commented Joan. It belonged to the Schaffgotsch family, whose great wealth was based on Silesian coalmines. The Ratibor party had been invited to stay at Koppitz for a

two-day tennis tournament. Organised with German preci-
sion, the tournament was a social event of the highest order.
'It was rather frightening,' Joan remarked. 'Had to walk up
to tennis pavilion under the inspection of a lot of people.'
For an unsophisticated English girl only months out of boarding school, it was a daunting experience. 'Didn't know a soul.
Count talked to me. Hundreds of servants etc. After tea we
changed quickly into tennis things and played for a short time.
I didn't play so badly which gave me confidence.' She was
introduced to Prince George of Denmark, also aged seventeen.
'A nice healthy young boy,' she noted. The Prince remarked to
her how much he detested the Germans and having to speak
their language. 'He told me it was terrible how the mothers
always pushed their daughters at him!!' Indeed, Joan could
not help noticing, his bedroom was 'discreetly' opposite that
of the prettiest Schaffgotsch daughter. The Prince may have
had an impressive pedigree but he was no good at tennis. 'He
was worse than useless,' complained Joan, having partnered
him in the mixed doubles. 'It was as much as I could do not to
laugh. He didn't even run to get the ball!'

The tournament was a splendid occasion. 'Drinks flowing, crowds of servants, ices and everything – marvellous,'
wrote Joan. But as tennis balls bounced around the Koppitz
courts that day on 8 August, 300 miles to the south at Linz,
Hitler's hometown, the new Mauthausen concentration camp
was being built. Intended for the Reich's most incorrigible
enemies – many of them drawn from the intelligentsia – the
plan was to exterminate them through slave labour in the local
quarries, mines and munitions factories. Meanwhile, back at
Koppitz, the prize-giving was followed by a great banquet.
'Prince George took me into dinner,' recorded Joan. 'We got
on well together. Afterwards I danced practically the whole

evening with him. Did the Lambeth Walk. Crowds of young people there. All very gay.'

The following day Joan and her friends set off for Schloss Rauden – an immense structure surrounded by forest. Three days later, on 12 August, Hitler mobilised 750,000 troops. That afternoon Joan went to Gleiwitz* to have a tooth filled. While the dentist, an enthusiastic Nazi, drilled away, he lectured her on the merits of National Socialism. On the road back to Rauden, they met 'hundreds' of tanks and lorries filled with soldiers. 'All a bit terrifying,' commented Joan. But anxiety melted away as she was absorbed once again into the daily pattern of riding, swimming in cold forest pools, parties, practical jokes and the inevitable tennis. Of particular delight to Joan were her shooting expeditions with the Duke. Each morning they would meet at 6 a.m. and set off in his battered old Ford with its bright orange mudguards and green upholstery. '*Wildschwein* [wild boar] – v. exciting. Saw them but not near enough to shoot,' reported Joan after one such outing. On rainy days she liked to walk the dogs deep into the forest, sometimes getting hopelessly lost. On 17 August she was rescued by local farmers. 'Talked to the peasants – all very poor but charming. I don't think they had ever spoken to a young English girl before.' It was on this same day that it became mandatory for Jews with non-Jewish names to identify themselves as 'Israel' if male and 'Sarah' if female.

---

* Almost exactly a year later, on 31 August 1939, the so-called 'Gleiwitz incident' occurred. Contrived by the Nazis, it provided Hitler with the pretext to invade Poland the following day, 1 September.

As September (and the Nuremberg rally) approached, Hitler's demands that the Sudetenland be detached from Czechoslovakia and incorporated into the Reich grew increasingly strident. The Sudetenland consisted of those parts of the country (on the borders of Moravia and Bohemia and Czech Silesia) that were mainly inhabited by ethnic German speakers and which before the First World War had belonged to Austria. But the more threatening the political situation, the more life at Rauden seemed to flourish in its own charmed bubble. Even so, it was arguably the sense of impending crisis that gave the young people's pleasures that summer an added edge. Few, though, can have foreseen the catastrophe that would soon overwhelm the powerful German families of Upper Silesia, destroying their way of life for ever. One evening at a neighbouring Schloss Joan met a doctor from Prague. 'He told me that the Czechs would fight whatever happened. They would fight against giving up one inch of their territory.' Such political comment is rare in her diary. Indeed, it would be hard to guess from reading it that Europe had been on the brink of war the whole time she was with the Ratibors. In the end, it was the Duke who decided that she must leave. But before she did, there was to be one last party.

On the evening of the ball, the Duke and his sons appeared looking resplendent in their bespoke Ratibor tails. Joan chose her black spotted dress – 'which everyone loved'. Sixty guests – in full evening dress – sat down to a five-course dinner. Afterwards the Duchess and Guido Henckel von Donnersmarck danced Tyrolean dances and Viennese waltzes 'quite marvellously'. The music, provided by a particularly jolly local band, continued until 4 a.m. 'The servants danced too,' observed Joan, 'but on the other side of the wall.'

Then came her last day – Wednesday 31 August:

Finished packing, my big trunks sent off. Bathed in pond, Duchess came too. Tennis – I beat Franz-Albrecht hollow. Duke etc. watching. All great fun. Then Franz-Albrecht and I had a long farewell ride through the forest. Leaves are turning – glorious colours. I felt sad. Cantered the whole way back as v. late and quite dark! One last time to the shooting lodge – lovely, lovely. Farewell dinner. Ate 4 coffee ice cream sodas. 10.30 all to bed. I said good night and goodbye to the Duke. Kissed the Duchess. Franz-Albrecht went to get the record I wanted. Duchess came back to say goodbye again, another kiss and she went. The others all said good night and goodbye. Franz-Albrecht last, quickly.

After some final packing, Joan listened to Big Ben on the wireless. She rose at 3 a.m. 'Tiptoed into FA's room! Left note and record.' The butler served her breakfast and escorted her to the car. Then it was 'goodbye Rauden and the Ratibors, two of the happiest months of friendship and development in my life!' Almost exactly one year later, on 18 September 1939, Lieutenant Viktor von Ratibor, hereditary Prince of Hohenlohe-Schillingsfürst, was burned alive in his tank at the battle of Brochów, forty miles west of Warsaw.

Joan left Rauden in a grey, drizzly dawn. The drive to Oderberg on the Czech border took an hour. She tipped the chauffeur, left a note for the Duchess and boarded a train for Vienna. On the Czech side, the grim concrete barriers and barbed wire were a stark reminder that war was expected any moment. She was surprised to see how many women were working in the stations and on the trains. As the train pulled away, it started to pour with rain. 'All grey and thoroughly depressing,' she wrote. She had left Rauden only two hours earlier but her life there already seemed utterly remote.

When the train stopped at the Austrian border Nazi officials came on board to check the passengers' documents. In her haste to leave Rauden, Joan had forgotten that she needed a re-entry visa for Austria. The guard slowly turned the pages of her passport, carefully examining each one. As he handed it back to her, he told her she must get off the train and go to Prague in order to obtain the correct visa before she would be allowed to enter Austria. It was a bleak moment. Joan had neither money (it was illegal to take more than 10 DM out of the country), nor any contacts in Czechoslovakia to whom she might turn for help. Sensibly she burst into tears. It worked. The guard muttered something about her probably not being much of a threat to the Reich and left the carriage.

In Vienna she had time to spare before catching a train to Salzburg where she was to stay with an American contact. She hired a taxi – 'expensive but saw everything'. The driver was delighted. 'He was very depressed,' wrote Joan, 'no foreigners, no good fares.' The railway station, she noted, was a profoundly sad place. 'Little groups of Jews tearfully waving farewell.' The train to Salzburg was equally grim – 'crowded with departing Jews'. But at least the scenery along the Danube was lovely – 'Linz etc. way of Hitler's march of triumph into Austria. Met crowds of troops on the trains going down to the frontier. Our train held up for ages. Had cheapest and best tea on railway station at Linz. Not feeling at all well. Had a large piece of wonderful cake and cup of coffee for 6d – Marvellous!'

Her host, Edith Keller, had lived in Austria for twelve years. When the Germans arrived five months earlier, as she explained to Joan over supper, they had been greeted with great joy – especially in Linz. The Austrians believed that the Germans would make their country prosperous without them having to put in any effort themselves. Now, despite working harder than ever before, they were still poor. As a result, Austria had lost all its gaiety and charm. Above all, Austrians hated to be organised. But although disillusionment with the Anschluss was widespread, there was no active resistance. Instead, according to Mrs Keller, in order to avoid joining the army or Hitler Youth, many Austrians had simply fled to the mountains. Foreigners had stopped coming and the best hotels were now forced to take *KdF* tourists at half the normal price.

It was a gloomy summary but it did little to spoil Joan's pleasure in the glorious scenery around Salzburg. Nevertheless, she knew that it was high time to leave. Early on 4 September, after checking the news to make sure war had not broken out overnight, she boarded a train for Munich. A few days later she was on another bound for Geneva. As the train crossed the border into Switzerland, she felt a great surge of joy and relief.

18

'Peace' and Shattered Glass

Joan Wakefield's departure from Germany on 6 September coincided with the first day of the 1938 Nuremberg Reichsparteitag. To mark the Anschluss, it had been dubbed 'The Rally of the Greater Germany'. Thelma Cazalet MP, unlike most of the other British 'honoured guests' attending, was strongly anti-Nazi and had accepted Ribbentrop's invitation only because she thought it important 'to be aware of what was going on'.[1] As she entered the dining room of the Grand Hotel on the first night, she immediately caught sight of Unity Mitford seated at the long 'British' table with her parents Lord and Lady Redesdale. 'Unity is alarmingly pretty,' she wrote in her diary, 'but I have never seen anyone so pretty with absolutely no charm in her face and a rather stupid expression.'

Thelma did not enjoy Nuremberg. She sat for hours in pouring rain watching the labour corps goose step past the Führer, their spades shouldered like guns; she shut her finger in a car door and disliked the second-rate opera to which they were all shepherded by their German minders. But her worst moment was opening *The Times* one morning and reading that the annexation of the Sudetenland was expected imminently. 'This was a bad day for the British table at Nuremberg,' she wrote. 'I hurried home as soon as I possibly could, and felt obliged to send a cable to President Roosevelt suggesting he fly to Europe in an effort to maintain Peace.'

In Truman Smith's view, Hitler's aggressive keynote speech on the last day of the rally (12 September) was 'one of the most important events since the World War'.[2] Three days later, Neville Chamberlain flew to Berchtesgaden to meet Hitler. Smith wrote to his daughter, setting the scene:

> On Wednesday evening, as I was sitting at supper in the hotel at Konigsberg in East Prussia, the newspaper boy brought around to every table a special edition which had just come from the press. The paper contained the most astounding news that the world has heard for many a year. It was that the Minister President Chamberlain [sic] of England had asked Hitler to receive him at the Berghof and that he was ready to fly to him the next day. I looked around at the many attachés and German officers at the surrounding tables. All were dumbfounded. Care was written on the face of many a foreigner and happiness on the faces of all the Germans. It was as if the fatal hour for Europe had struck.
>
> The interview the next day appears now to have been one of the most historical events of modern times. Chamberlain told Hitler that he was personally in favour of breaking up Czechoslovakia, but that he did not have the approval of his Cabinet or the French government and would have to return to London first ... On Sunday the 18th the British Cabinet approved Chamberlain's plan that the German districts of Czechoslovakia should be ceded to Germany ... A new meeting was scheduled for today, the 22nd, between Chamberlain and Hitler at Godesberg

on the Rhine which, you will probably remember, is that little sleepy town under the shadow of the Drachenfels within sight of Cologne Cathedral ... Chamberlain's visit is of course an indication that France and England would never fight for Czechoslovakia.[3]

At the time of these negotiations, the Swiss businessman Numa Tétaz was still working in Bavaria. His book *Ich war dabei, 20 Jahre Nationalsozialismus 1923–43* [*I Was There, 20 Years of National Socialism*] is a compelling read. But because it was published in 1944, he wrote under the pseudonym of René Juvet. Since Hitler first came to power, he had monitored the effect of National Socialism on his business colleagues with increasing pessimism. He noted how his boss, once a cultivated man with many Jewish friends, had transformed himself into a dedicated Nazi. He warned Tétaz that it would no longer be good enough for the Swiss just to keep his head down. From now on everyone must be seen actively supporting the Führer.

By 1938 half the management and a quarter of the firm's workforce had joined the Party. In the days leading up to Chamberlain's first meeting with Hitler, Tétaz wrote of the oppressive atmosphere in the office and of how their work had been at sixes and sevens. The most enthusiastic Nazi in the firm went round telling everyone that within eight days the Czechs 'would be in the bin'. Then came the bombshell. 'I cannot remember', wrote Tétaz, 'ever hearing a more sensational piece of news than the announcement of Chamberlain's meeting with Hitler at Berchtesgaden.'

'You'll see,' one colleague said to him, 'peace will be preserved and Hitler will achieve his goal without violence. If Germany and England were not already fundamentally united, old Chamberlain wouldn't have risked going to Berchtesgaden and becoming the scapegoat had the meeting failed.' The Nazi was triumphant. A division of the world between the two Germanic master-races – Germany and England – would, he claimed, give Germany *Lebensraum* in Europe and allow Britain to go on ruling the waves. Germany would at last get back its colonies, although that was now a less pressing concern since it would soon gain enough land in the East to keep its citizens going for generations.

The reaction of the workforce was very different. Many still clung to their Marxist principles. Because a Nazi spy had been planted among them, several had been sent off to concentration camps. They too regarded Chamberlain as a messenger of peace, but one who would liberate the German people from Hitler.

That September a number of the firm's employees were conscripted, including the accountant. 'He left looking troubled,' observed Tétaz. 'Things did not look good. He would have much preferred to stay at home nurturing his National Socialist ideals rather than have to defend them at the front with a gun in his hand.'

The Munich agreement, allowing Germany to annex parts of Czechoslovakia, was signed on 30 September 1938. That day Tétaz happened to be in Munich. Everyone, he noted, was trying to catch a glimpse of the big four – Hitler, Mussolini, Chamberlain and Daladier. It was a beautiful, warm autumn day, 'Hitler weather', people remarked. Flags were everywhere, flapping gently in the soft breeze. For once, the Union Jack and Tricolore were flying alongside the Swastika. Tétaz observed how – even before the news was released – no one seemed to doubt that there would be a successful outcome. Wherever the British prime minister turned up in Munich he was cheered by jubilant crowds. Unusually, so the Swiss noted,

Nazi propaganda was based on a genuinely spontaneous public response.

Later Tétaz had supper with friends who, although profoundly anti-Hitler, were also happy and excited because peace now seemed certain. Their disgust with the regime did not extend to wanting a war in order to destroy it. Then came the extraordinary news that Germany's demands regarding Czechoslovakia had been met in full. In Munich there was indescribable joy. Huge crowds gathered outside Chamberlain's and Daladier's hotels calling again and again for the statesmen to appear on their balconies. Tétaz went with his friends to the Oktoberfest celebrations. He had been often before but to none like this. Beer flowed endlessly, while in vast marquees happy, carefree people linked arms to form long lines that swayed all night to the music of brass bands. Hitler had achieved a Reich for his people without fighting, triumphed over the hated peace treaty, eliminated unemployment and turned yesterday's enemies into friends.

The firm's locksmith did not join the celebrations. Although by no means the only individual in Germany to be unmoved by all the excitement, he knew that on that day above all others it would have been suicidal to express his true feelings.[4]

~

By the middle of October life in Germany had more or less returned to normal. The director of the American 'Junior Year Abroad' programme, Edmund Miller, based in Munich, wrote to his executive council:

> Some days we fear that the Munich agreement is not
> producing the permanent results we had hoped for, while

on other days the world looks quite stable. One meets all
kinds of opinions here – from those who ascribe the peace
of Europe to Chamberlain to those who ridicule England's
weakness and boast of Hitler's achievement in bringing
the Western statesmen to heed his bidding. In our house
there is an old codger who laments that war was avoided!
But on the whole the German people are happy that war
did not come.[5]

Truman Smith was also able to reassure his daughter that
things had quietened down all over Europe:

The army is coming home from Czechoslovakia and the
Reservists are being released and the horses and automobiles turned back to their owners. We were down yesterday
in Dresden and coming home we got held up by long motor
columns moving in the same general direction we were
moving, that is, northward to their home stations. All the
automobiles and soldiers were decorated with flowers and
the artillery wheels had wreaths of flowers in the spokes. It
seemed very curious to see all the muddy flowers.[6]

His wife wrote, 'The change from imminent war to peace was
overwhelming … I was dazed and others with me. Bombs were
not going to fall within the next half hour! It was incredible.'[7]

But then, less than three weeks after Truman Smith's letter,
came the catastrophic news of Kristallnacht. On the night of
9 November Jewish shops across Germany were smashed to
pieces, a hundred Jews murdered and countless more beaten
and humiliated. Thousands were subsequently rounded up and
sent to concentration camps. For foreigners who had put their
money on Hitler's Germany, Kristallnacht came as a shocking

revelation. It destroyed any residual argument for appeasement and made plain that the Munich agreement – signed only six weeks earlier – had been a mirage.

Kay Smith wrote immediately to her daughter Kätchen to explain what had happened. 'Last night all over Germany they broke the windows of all the Jewish shops in retaliation, and as a future warning, for the death of Ernst vom Rath who was murdered in Paris at the German Embassy by a [German-born] Polish Jew.'[8] In Dresden, Sylvia Morris witnessed the ransacking of the Jewish department store – Etam's. 'Dresden had been peaceful and not pro-Nazi so this was a major event,' she recalled. 'We girls in the Töchterhaus made our terrified landlady go to the store to buy things. We opened all the windows and sang Mendelssohn songs as loudly as we could.'[9]

Margaret Bradshaw had not expected to find herself in Berlin on the night of 9 November. She should have been in Jodhpur with her husband, Colonel John Bradshaw of the Indian Political Service. But an accident to her eye had forced her to return to England for treatment. There she had been informed that there was only one doctor who could help her and he lived in Berlin. So, taking herself off to Berlin, she settled into an inexpensive hotel opposite a clothes shop. Displayed in the window was a scarlet frock she longed to buy. But not knowing how much her treatment would cost, she dared not. However, after two painful injections, she found to her great delight that she had just enough money left over to purchase it the next day before returning to England. She slept heavily that night but was dimly aware of a good deal of shouting and the sound of splintering glass. The next morning she rose early, eager to buy the dress. But when she drew back her bedroom curtains she saw the shop smashed to pieces and the dress gone.[10]

Samuel Honaker, American consul general in Stuttgart, reported on the burning of synagogues that night:

> Early on the morning of November 10th practically every synagogue at least twelve in number in Württemberg, Baden and Hohenzollern was set on fire by well disciplined and apparently well equipped young men in civilian clothes. The procedure was practically the same in all cities of this district, namely, Stuttgart, Karlsruhe, Freiburg, Heidelberg, Heilbronn, et cetera. The doors of the synagogues were forced open. Certain sections of the building and furnishings were drenched with petrol and set on fire. Bibles, prayer books, and other sacred things were thrown into the flames. Then the local fire brigades were notified. In Stuttgart, the city officials ordered the fire brigade to save the archives and other written material having a bearing on vital statistics. Otherwise, the fire brigades confined their activities to preventing the flames from spreading. In a few hours the synagogues were, in general, heaps of smoking ruins.[11]

Tétaz first became aware of the horror when, on 10 November, he drove past a burnt-out synagogue in Bayreuth. A happy, excited crowd looked on as firemen extracted charred furniture from the smouldering ruins. He had spent the previous night with Jewish friends in Nuremberg. It had been a civilised occasion, with music and wine. His elderly host had lost an eye and a leg in the Great War and been awarded the Iron Cross classes I and II. Worried about his friends, Tétaz turned his car around and drove straight back to Nuremberg. When he reached their house on the northern outskirts of the city, a scene of utter destruction confronted him. Doors torn off their hinges, furniture strewn all over the garden and taps left running. The magnificent Steinway that Tétaz had played only hours earlier had been smashed to pieces with an axe. Every painting had been slashed. The wife emerged covered in bruises. Her husband had been taken to hospital but died the next day.

Later, Tétaz discussed Kristallnacht with the firm's Nuremberg representative. Although the man was a member of the SA, Tétaz considered him a harmless and industrious individual. He told the Swiss how relieved he was that he had not been in Nuremberg that night, as he would have hated the violence. Tétaz then asked him whether, if he had been there, he would have taken part. 'Of course,' came the reply. 'Orders are orders.'[12]

Emily Boettcher, recently returned to Berlin, was practising hard for a concert tour in the coming spring. On 11 November she sent a letter to her English husband (they had met five weeks earlier on the SS *Washington*): 'I suppose you've heard and read about the plundering that went on here yesterday,' she wrote. 'It was a horrid experience. I went out just in time to see them stoning Newman's piano store and wrecking every instrument in the show window. All the Jewish stores in town are completely ruined and the synagogues burned ... Kurfürstendamm looks as if it had been through a minor air raid.' Yet two months later she was able to tell him, 'Berlin seems so quiet after London. The streets are practically empty except for people sauntering along window gazing. Most of the smashed windows have been replaced and the stores sold to Aryans. The former Jewish shops must be doing a thriving business because they had better goods for sale.'[13]

To the casual foreign traveller, Jewish anguish was largely

hidden from view in the weeks following Kristallnacht. Not only, as Boettcher pointed out, had cities soon regained their normal physical appearance, but there were now virtually no Jews to be seen on their streets. Restrictions governing their lives were so draconian that it was possible for a foreigner to remain weeks in the Reich without sighting even one of them. Twenty-three-year-old Manning Clark, however, was to witness the full force of Jewish misery within days of arriving in Germany. The future historian was visiting his girlfriend and fellow Australian, Dymphna Lodewyckx. He was at Oxford University after winning a scholarship to Balliol, while she, having spent a year at school in Munich in 1933, was now studying for a PhD at Bonn University.

On 11 December, almost exactly a month after Kristallnacht, the couple went to tea with the distinguished geologist and geographer, Professor Alfred Philippson – a Jew. 'His wife was very plaintive,' Clark wrote in his diary:

> Her voice and demeanour betrayed her awareness of a burden which she could scarcely bear. She was quite downcast with grief. Her daughter smoked cigarettes and tried to look composed. The man was very bitter. 'We live between these four walls and God knows how long it will last. Other countries have been full of words but no deeds.' His eyes were very lively but his words were clipped, short, almost scathing.

Far from expressing outrage at the elderly professor's predicament (he was seventy-four), Clark instead wrote: 'one could understand the criticism against the Jew: [Philippson] was so destructive in his criticism one felt afraid for what might be left. There was a maliciousness in his tone; a sneer was always lurking in the background. He was the personification of cleverness. The Jewish question is a very complex one.'*

On another occasion, a retired professor of physics at Bonn University made plain to Clark his strong disapproval of the recent pogrom but asked not to be quoted. He was convinced that Hitler had nothing to do with it. Had the Führer known about it beforehand, he would never have allowed it to happen. 'This was the first time I realised', noted Clark, 'that the person of Hitler was sacrosanct. He was never connected in any way with instances that were doubtful or likely to prove unpopular. It was always Göring or Goebbels. Hitler's reputation is unblemished and for the normal German there is a halo of infallibility around his head.'[14]

If Clark still regarded the 'Jewish question' as complex, any ambiguities Dr Edmund Miller may have once felt vanished with Kristallnacht. For him, it was the last straw. In a resignation letter sent shortly afterwards, he wrote, 'Mrs Miller and I have been in the Slough of Despond since the 10th November … The relentless thoroughness with which the anti-Jewish *Aktion* is being carried through and the abject slavery of the German people' had finally proved more than they could bear:

> There is much said for and against the current movement. Some say the Germans themselves are not behind it – but we know some who definitely are. The Catholics

* Manning Clark, Diary, 11 December 1938, National Library of Australia, Manning Clark papers, MS 7550, series 2, item 1. Four years later, at the age of seventy-eight, Philippson was sent with his wife and daughter to Theresienstadt concentration camp. The fact that they all survived was in part due to the intervention of Philippson's Swedish fellow geographer (and Nazi-supporter) Sven Hedin.

are reputedly in for similar treatment. Altogether we have
to admit that our American opponents who insist that it
is injurious to submit American youth to such a depressing environment are nearer right than heretofore. And if
it is not injurious, it is certainly unnecessary. There was
something idealistic about the Junior Year, and a love and
a joy of a Future Good. But we have temporarily lost all
that. We are not interested in importing the spirit of this
present regime into America. I haven't the courage to write
the promotion letters for 1939–40. The present letter is
to say that the Millers do not want to go back to Munich.
We don't want to be quitters, but we think we have served
our time there.[15]

Meanwhile, shortly after Kristallnacht, the American Friends
Service Committee (AFSC) met urgently in Philadelphia to
consider how best to respond to the shocking news. Worried
that starvation would follow the violence, their first concern
was how to provide enough food for the Jews. Those present
at the meeting were oppressed by a sense of déjà-vu. Was it
really possible that another Quaker feeding programme was
required in Germany only twenty years after the last? They
held a number of 'quiet' conversations before deciding to
send a small delegation to Germany as quickly as possible,
avoiding all publicity. Rufus Jones, an eminent writer and
historian, was chosen to lead the group. Accompanying him
were Robert Yarnall, a manufacturer who had been involved
in the 1919 child feeding in Germany, and a schoolmaster,
George Walton. Before they went, Jones put their mission in
perspective:

There must be no illusions in our mind about this venture of ours. The difficulties of space, of distance, of stubborn ocean stretches we can probably overcome. Mountains can be tunnelled; they can even be removed. Matter is no doubt stubborn, but nothing in the universe is so utterly unconquerable as a mind possessed by a set of ideas that have become entrenched and sacred … Whether we can influence minds or soften hearts or make spiritual forces seem real – that remains to be seen. We shall do our best and wisest and we shall go in the strength of God.[16]

It was an extraordinarily brave – if lunatic – undertaking. The three men had no idea how they would be received in Berlin or if indeed they would be received at all. There was a real risk that they might be physically harmed or arrested. The weather was bitterly cold and Jones was only weeks short of his seventy-sixth birthday. But on 2 December, full of faith, they sailed from New York on the *Queen Mary*. Yarnall spent the voyage reading *Mein Kampf*. He did not find it encouraging. Jones bought a beret and learned a ditty:

De Valera with his Green Shirts and his back against the wall
Mussolini with his Brown [sic] Shirts and riding for a fall
Hitler with his Black [sic] Shirts lording over all
Hurrah for Gandhi with no shirt at all!

Despite every attempt to keep their mission secret, Jones was summoned mid-ocean to take a call on the ship's radio-telephone from the *Philadelphia Record*. Although he gave nothing away, the next day sensational headlines announced that three Quakers were to intercede with Hitler on behalf of the Jews. Picked up in London, the story soon reached

Germany, prompting Goebbels to write a scathing article – 'The Coming of the "Three Wise Men" to "save" Germany'.[17] The little delegation had not even reached Europe and its mission was already in deep trouble.

After a quick transit through Paris, the valiant three boarded a sleeper for Berlin. At the frontier they had to dress hurriedly in order to deal with customs officials. Next morning, as they approached Berlin, Jones was engulfed in a crisis. He could not find his pyjamas. The other two joined in the search but with no success. Jones was so distressed (his wife had made them) that he wanted to send a telegram to the last railway station in the hope that they might have been left there. His colleagues, fearful that this would provoke the wrong kind of publicity, dissuaded him with difficulty by assuring him that as the train went on to Warsaw they would later telegraph the station there. Greeted in Berlin by a group of international Friends, the three men were soon installed in the Continental Hotel. Next morning Yarnall and Walton joined Jones at breakfast. He said quietly, 'I found them.' 'Where did thee find them Rufus?' 'I had them on.'[18]

The Quakers' first attempt to contact the authorities was made at the German Foreign Office. But when the German ambassador to the United States (recalled to Berlin) spotted them in a corridor, he fled. 'We never actually found him,' reported Jones, 'for he was always out when we called, which we did often.' After many fruitless visits, they decided to give up on the Foreign Office. Meanwhile in consultation with leading Jews, they learned that the greatest need was not for food but rather to find ways of facilitating emigration. 'It was soon clear', he wrote, 'that only the chiefs of the Gestapo could issue the permission we were seeking.' Having reached this daunting conclusion, it was the American consul-general, Raymond

Geist, who made the breakthrough. 'If ever there was a good man, he was one,' noted Jones. After failing repeatedly to reach Gestapo headquarters on the telephone, Geist 'seized his hat' and disappeared into the worst storm and coldest temperatures recorded in Berlin for eighty years.

Half an hour later Geist summoned the little band of Quakers. 'We leaped into a taxi and drove to the huge building,' wrote Jones. 'Six black-shirted soldiers with helmets and muskets escorted us to the great iron doors. We were given tickets and told that we did not need them to get in but we would need them to get out!' They were led through seven corridors, each one opening on to an uncovered square. They then climbed five flights of stairs to a room where Geist was waiting for them. He had achieved the impossible. Two senior Gestapo officers – Dr Erich Ehrlinger* and Major Kurt Lischka[†] – had been detailed to listen to the Quakers' plan. Through a window, Jones could see Reinhard Heydrich[‡] working at his desk in the next room.

George Walton described the leading actors in the ensuing scene. 'Rufus, clear, positive, brief, daring: Geist, crusty, clever direct, a magic open sesame: Lischka, tall, quick earnest, responsive, partly bald, punctilious.'[19] Jones handed the 'granite-faced' men a statement that he had already prepared. It was a reminder of the warm relationship the Germans had enjoyed with the Friends after the Great War; and of how

---

* Ehrlinger was later responsible for the mass murder of Jews in Russia and Belarus.
[†] In 1940 Lischka became head of the Gestapo in Cologne. He was later responsible for the largest single deportation of Jews from France.
[‡] Heydrich, known as 'hangman of the Reich', was one of the chief architects of the Holocaust. He was assassinated in Prague in 1942.

the Quakers had fed over 2 million children a day, importing hundreds of cows to supply milk to children in hospital, and coal to keep the hospitals heated. The document emphasised the fact that the Friends did not represent any government, international organisation, political party or sect. Nor did they have any interest in propaganda. As Jones watched the Gestapo men read the paper 'slowly, carefully and thoughtfully', he was convinced that it had 'reached' them, adding, 'We noted a softening effect on their faces – which needed to be softened.' There followed a long detailed debate before the two men announced that they would now discuss the Quakers' proposals with Heydrich and return in half an hour. 'During this awesome period,' Jones wrote, 'we bowed our heads and entered upon a time of deep, quiet meditation and prayer – the only Quaker meeting ever held in the Gestapo!'

To their astonishment, Heydrich agreed to everything in their plan. But when Jones asked for written confirmation, he was informed that, while the Gestapo never gave its decisions in writing, every word of their discussion had been taped. 'We were glad then', Jones wrote, 'that we had kept the period of hush and quiet and had uttered no words for the record.' Each police station in Germany, Lischka told them, would be telegraphed that night with instructions that the Quakers be permitted to investigate the sufferings of Jews and to initiate a relief programme. It seemed too good to be true. And, of course, it was. Even Jones – forever the optimist – did not believe that the message was ever sent. Nevertheless, he was convinced that their mission had not been totally unsuccessful. Two Quaker commissioners received permission to go to Germany and oversee the disbursement of Quaker relief funds and, in particular, to help those Jews not affiliated with a synagogue to emigrate. And for a brief period, at least, a new freedom was granted to the Quaker office in Berlin in their efforts to accelerate Jewish emigration. As Jones wrote,

> It will always be something of a mystery why the Gestapo, which was itself deeply involved in producing the tragic situation we went to relieve, should have received us respectfully, listened to our plea and finally have granted our unusual request to try to repair some of the damage they had done.

Certainly Jones continued to believe that they had touched the hearts of their cruel interlocutors. 'The gentleness of the men at the end of our meeting, the fact they went and got our coats and helped us put them on and shook our hands with goodbye wishes and with a touch of gentleness made me feel then and now in retrospect, that something unique had happened in their inside selves.' It was as well that Jones, who died in 1948, never knew that it was Lischka himself who, in the immediate aftermath of Kristallnacht, led the operation to incarcerate 30,000 Jews.

Kristallnacht prompted the American government to recall its ambassador, Hugh Wilson, in protest. His deputy, Prentiss Gilbert, now in charge of the Embassy, found life in Berlin confusing. In a report to the State Department, he described the 'peculiar character' of the German government, which, in his experience, had become a 'mass of inconsistencies'. Although new decrees were announced every day, many were never implemented. This, Gilbert suggested, was because there still existed 'just' and 'humane' officials, who took every opportunity to mitigate the unbearable situation in which Jews and

other Nazi victims found themselves. 'These men', reported
Gilbert, 'say repeatedly to us that they cannot put anything
in writing nor can they make any general statements of what
they can do but they will, and do, make marked and favourable
exceptions in specific cases.'[20]

Gilbert also commented on the behaviour of his fellow diplomats, post-Kristallnacht. No longer did they accept invitations
from the likes of Rosenberg and Goebbels. And, at those parties
they did attend, they hardly spoke to the Germans, preferring
to cluster together and discuss the latest excesses against the
Jews. Gilbert reported that the Italians were the most amusing
in discussing their relationship with the Germans:

> The wife of one of the secretaries who sat next to me asked
> me if I did not find Berlin very dull and rather difficult? I
> replied that there were naturally certain difficult features
> when the US and Germany are engaged in throwing rocks
> at each other. She replied that it was very much easier on
> the Americans here than on the Italians because the Italians
> had to see so much of these terrible people whether they
> wanted to or not.

There may have been the odd such lighter moment, but for
Gilbert, despite the professional kudos of being at the centre
of a global crisis, Berlin had become a distinctly undesirable
place. He spoke from the heart when he wrote to his ambassador, 'I imagine you are still in Bermuda for Christmas and I
repeat my envy of your being in the sunshine by the open sea.'[21]
As 1938 drew to a close, there can have been few foreigners
among the dwindling numbers still travelling to Berlin who
would have disagreed with Gilbert when he wrote to Wilson
two days before Christmas, 'It is still somewhat grim here.'[22]

19

Countdown to War

The year 1939 was not a good one for Germany's tourist trade. Naturally Kristallnacht did little to encourage what was still left of it, but then, only four months later, on 15 March, the world was forced to watch Hitler march into Prague – ripping up the Munich agreement as he went. Czechoslovakia ceased to exist; its territory now designated the 'German Protectorate of Bohemia and Moravia'.

Although the flow of tourists was drastically reduced, it did not, as the *AGR* makes clear, dry up completely. The magazine's July issue includes a photograph of young women in bathing suits on a North Sea beach (one of them vigorously exercising), entitled 'Laughter in the Sunshine'. 'Travellers who return from Germany just now', reads the caption, 'say that the deepest impression they bring back is of a land of smiles and peacefulness, full of gay music, and free from the cares and worries that beset the outside world. Crises may darken other horizons, but not those of Germany it seems.'[1] Nor was it just pro-German magazines like the *AGR* that were keen to promote holidays in the Reich. Thomas Cook published a brochure in 1939 urging people to come and see the 'new Germany' for themselves. 'All the old enchantment is there, much that is new will impress you tremendously and everywhere – everywhere, you will meet with that comfort, kindliness and good fare that are the first essential of an enjoyable holiday.'[2]

If, despite such glowing accounts, few foreigners chose to holiday in Germany, a number still continued to travel there for a host of different reasons. Professor Sir Frederick Hobday, for instance, lectured in Munich to bloodstock breeders on 'Thirty Years' Experience of the Ventricle Stripping Operation for Roaring'.[3] A number of distinguished figures, the historian Sir Arthur Bryant and Sir Evelyn Wrench among them, made futile attempts at last-ditch diplomacy, while groups with specialist interests or extreme right-wing views set off for Germany undeterred by the darkening scene. Ida and Louise Cook, two middle-aged ladies who still lived with their parents in suburban London, used their love of opera as cover for the numerous journeys they made to and from Germany, smuggling jewellery for would-be Jewish emigrants. Churchmen, musicians, businessmen, Quakers, teachers and spies – even Chinese peddlers [*Qingtian*] – were all travelling in the Reich during the last months of peace. That war now seemed both inevitable and imminent only gives their comments added spice.

On Christmas Eve 1938, Manning Clark and Dymphna Lodewyckx set off from Bonn to visit Munich where, five years earlier, Dymphna (then a schoolgirl) had witnessed the book burning. 'The train was almost unbearable,' wrote Clark. 'We were huddled together in a compartment, sitting on hard wood and freezing cold.' The 'icicles on the train, the notices in the carriage, and the very fact of being in Hitler's Europe, dashing through the night' appealed to his sense of adventure, but the 'ever-present discomforts' soon drove out 'sentiment and naïve reflections'.[4]

On Christmas Day they attended Mass in the Frauenkirche. 'The middle-aged and old were well represented,' Clark noted, 'but it was quite strange to see a young person.' A few soldiers were also in the congregation but 'seemed very out of place and gazed in a confused and embarrassed manner around the church as if they felt guilty about something'. The Australians were impressed by the courageous sermon. 'The priest was so enthused, his language so pure, so beautifully modulated and his subject matter so solid.'[5] Although the preacher avoided direct criticism of the Nazis, he made the Catholic position crystal clear, leading Clark to conclude that, despite everything, the Church was still strong.

They visited a number of Dymphna's former acquaintances. One of them, a Jew ('his wife was pure Aryan from Poland'), gave a harrowing account of his recent imprisonment in Dachau. Clark noted how their 'tragic position' was intensified by fear of their servant. 'Every few minutes his wife walked to the door to see whether she was listening to our conversation.'[6] Rather more cheerful was the evening the young couple spent at Munich's famous Hofbräuhaus [beer hall]. Seated at board tables in a long low room filled with smoke, they watched 'fat waitresses with red chubby cheeks and ugly-beautiful faces serve beer to the lower classes of Munich society'. Clark, always sensitive to the treatment of women, did not warm to the young couple at their table. 'The husband was almost animal in his bearing and his wife in mentality just the instrument of his possession.' More entertaining was the old peasant – 'a relic of the past' – who told them 'that man Hitler has more brains than all the rest of them'. There was, Clark reported, 'a good atmosphere'.[7]

A few days later they were back in Bonn where the impulsive Clark decided that they should marry at once. But because, even as foreigners, they could not do so without proof of their Aryan ancestry, the Anglican vicar in Cologne had no choice but to turn them down. Clark therefore returned to England, followed shortly by Dymphna, who, despite (as her fiancé put it) 'the rising tide of brutality, bestiality and barbarism', was reluctant to abandon her PhD. They married in Oxford on 31 January – as it so happened, almost six years to the day since Hitler had become chancellor.

Six weeks later, as German tanks rolled into Prague, Ji Xianlin was awoken in Göttingen by the national anthem blaring out of the radio. 'Germany has invaded Czechoslovakia,' his landlady announced. She then kept repeating, 'Hitler only wants peace, the Czechs were tyrannising the Germans – it's all the Jews' fault, just like the papers say.' 'I was so angry,' wrote Ji Xianlin, 'I didn't know whether to laugh or cry … the ordinary German bastards believe all this. I'll die unhappy if I don't see this whole German edifice collapse and them all reduced to slavery.' As he left the university that evening, he noticed how cheerful everyone looked, and that fresh flags hung outside every house. He went to the Schwarzer Bär to seek comfort with his friends, Long and Tian. 'We drank a little wine and discussed how we'd get back to good schools in China and do things properly. I walked home thinking – as the Germans sow today, tomorrow they shall reap.'[8]

On 25 March, Ward Price wrote to Lord Londonderry from the Adlon Hotel in Berlin. As correspondent for the *Daily Mail*, he had for many years been a Nazi toady and insider. His remarks therefore carried weight. 'I have had some long talks with Göring and Ribbentrop during this last week,' he wrote, 'and with several members of the personal staff of Hitler.' As a result of these conversations, he confidently confirmed that nothing would now deflect Hitler from realising his ambitions

in Eastern Europe. 'His greatest anxiety, during the days immediately before the occupation of Czech territory', Ward Price
reported to Londonderry, was 'lest the old gentleman should
get into an aeroplane again and come to try to talk him out
of it. Those close to Hitler say he formed the impression that
Chamberlain was a man with a bargaining type of mind, who
did not take large views of international questions. Daladier
made a better impression on him.'[9]

Robert Jamieson, a young English teacher in Essen, also
corresponded with Londonderry shortly after the rape of
Czechoslovakia. Referring to the guarantee Chamberlain had
made on 31 March (in the House of Commons) to Poland
and Rumania* that Britain and France would come to their
aid if Hitler invaded, he wrote: 'I think a good many people
must be shaken and uneasy here, for nearly everyone I have
spoken to since Chamberlain's promise to Poland has spontaneously told me how they don't want war. And they say it
with a depth of feeling I have never felt at home.' Jamieson,
an aspiring journalist whose stay in Germany was subsidised
by Londonderry, made sterling efforts to chronicle the reac-
tions of ordinary Germans to the unfolding drama. They
really believed, Jamieson informed his patron, that the Czech
government had voluntarily sought Hitler's protection, and
'that they would all starve if they do not get this living room
[*Lebensraum*] they talk about, and colonies. There is no real
food shortage but just sufficient of certain materials such as
dairy produce and green vegetables to lend weight to this
idea.'[10] Meanwhile, he added, every German was waiting on
tenterhooks for Hitler to annex Danzig; a move that he was

* 'Romania' became the accepted spelling circa 1975.

convinced would meet with universal approval – even from non-Nazis. One sunny weekend in June, Jamieson travelled on the back of a motorbike to the university town of Marburg where he met a professor of English. Despite the fact that the professor (an authority on Shakespeare) regularly read *The Times* and listened each night to the BBC, he too was utterly convinced that Germany was encircled by hostile countries and would starve if prevented from expanding to the East.

Some of Jamieson's most interesting information came via a group of British engineering inspectors headquartered in Essen. One of them related how he had been physically thrown out of a Polish post office the moment he started speaking German, although he had always spoken it there on previous trips. It seems extraordinary that these inspectors were able to travel all over Europe checking materials for foreign buyers until just a few weeks before the outbreak of war. No doubt their reports also landed on many a Whitehall desk. Another of Jamieson's German contacts asked him an intriguing question. Had he noticed the British newspapers discussing a possible pact between Russia and Germany? He only inquired because the German papers were currently saying such nice things about the Soviet Union that he felt there must be 'something in the wind'. Three months later, on 23 August, Ribbentrop and Molotov signed the German–Soviet Non-aggression Pact.[11]

Kristallnacht may have tempered Jamieson's latent anti-Semitism but it had by no means extinguished it. 'I am afraid I have learned enough about the Jews which is undoubted fact to have much sympathy with the Germans in their problem,' he wrote on 20 May, adding 'although nobody is going to condone the November business.'[12] After visiting a number of local villages around Marburg (where he was shown exquisitely embroidered wedding dresses), Jamieson established that the peasants 'are extremely glad to be rid of the Jews as at one time all the cattle markets of that part of the country were in their hands, and, as you can guess, the peasants were pretty badly treated in their trading'.[13]

Jamieson, a rather pompous young man of limited experience, was at least making a genuine effort to record grass-roots German opinion at a time of high tension. But what excuse was there for a seasoned churchman like the Reverend Henry Percival Smith to be travelling in Germany in the summer of 1939? Ostensibly it was to attend a conference in Berlin with the Anglo-German Brotherhood – a right-wing organisation founded in 1936 to promote understanding between British and German clergy. In an *AGR* article describing the trip, Percival Smith makes no bones about his admiration for Hitler's Germany:

> To spend ten days in Germany (personally I spent just over three weeks) and never to receive so much as a wry look but, on the other hand, to receive the utmost kindness and consideration from everybody is something, I think, that could not be guaranteed to a German visiting England at the present time. It seems there is a tremendous desire on the part of the average German to be friendly with the Briton … It is a chastening experience for an Englishman to see, in Durham or South Wales, men of 22 years of age who have not done a day's work since they left school at the age of 14, and then to see in Germany every young man being employed in some way or other … What it all means is that nothing short of the best will do for the German people, either in the services they give or in the privileges they receive.

In his article, Percival Smith referred neither to Kristallnacht
nor to the invasion of Czechoslovakia but he did stress German
admiration for Hitler's 'personal integrity', 'strength of character' and 'political sagacity'. Furthermore, he was keen to
point out (only a few weeks after German troops marched into
Prague) how 'they all ridicule the idea that [Hitler] seeks to
dominate over other nations though they have a lively apprehension of themselves being dominated by others, especially
by the Communist International'. The objective in attending
the conference, so the clergyman informed his readers, was
'to get below the political surface in our relationship with
the German people, and to endeavour to understand them'.
The current cancer of 'suspicion' and 'mistrust' could only
be cured in 'an atmosphere of goodwill and brotherhood'.[14]
Did the conference help him 'understand' such matters as
Dachau, the Jewish pogrom or the imprisonment of Christian
clergy? In any case, his enthusiasm for Nazi Germany did
nothing to damage his career. In 1956 he was promoted to
Archdeacon of Lynn at Norwich Cathedral.

When, in the spring of 1939, writer and Irish nationalist Francis Stuart received an invitation from the German
Academic Exchange Service to lecture in Germany, it offered
him a solution to several pressing problems. He badly needed
the money but he also wanted to escape an unhappy marriage.
Stuart was not an obvious choice for Germany since the fifteen
books he had so far published were quite unknown there. But,
given that no British author of repute was likely to accept such
an invitation at such a time, the Irishman was at least both
willing and available.

Stuart falls neatly into the category of those foreigners
who allowed personal political prejudice to fog their perception of the Nazis. While in Percival Smith's case (as with so

many other pro-Nazi foreigners) communism was the bogey that justified Hitler's regime, with Stuart it was loyalty to the Republican cause and a longing for a new world order. In Hitler he saw 'a kind of blind Samson who was pulling down the pillars of Western Society as we knew it, which I still believed had to come about before any new world could arise'.[15] In any case, Stuart was so wrapped up in himself that he seems to have viewed Germany on the eve of war almost exclusively in terms of his own life and internal development. He was not noticeably moved by the Jewish situation. 'I have heard something of the Jewish activities prior to 1933 here and in cooperation with the communists,' he wrote to his wife. 'They were in many instances appalling. As for the presence of Jews now, they are scarcely to be seen in this part of Berlin (central) or in the West End. But in the East End – beyond Alexanderplatz – where I penetrated one day there are still a good many.'[16] After his lecture tour was completed, Stuart was invited to return later in the year to teach English and Irish literature at Berlin University. His decision to accept the job was to have far-reaching consequences from which neither he nor his reputation would ever be entirely free.

The historian Sir Arthur Bryant was another notable foreigner whose benign view of the Nazis lasted longer than was decent. In his case, determination to see the best in Hitler's Germany was fuelled by his innate suspicion of left-wing intellectuals and their politics. On 9 July 1939 he flew to Berlin supposedly for a short holiday and to conduct research for his current book. In fact, he was on a mission, sanctioned by Neville Chamberlain, to explore the possibility – even at this late stage – of encouraging the Nazis in the direction of 'restraint' and 'delay'. Shortly after returning to England, he wrote about the trip (without, of course, referring to its true purpose) in his regular *Illustrated London News* column. In it he recalled how, when he had first flown over Germany in 1918, he had been greeted with 'white shell-bursts and the stutter of machine-guns'. But this time, as he looked down from the aeroplane on 'this fabulous country of marching armies and no butter, of parades, pogroms and concentration camps', it had seemed to him every bit as peaceful as England. 'A land of farms and homesteads and well-tilled fields and little ancient churches ... vestiges of a common civilisation: the neat ferry, glimpsed in the last slant of light, somehow recalled Bablock Hythe.' The thought that such a place could be soon a target for a bombing raid 'brought little pleasure'. As they flew into darkness, the pilot circulated a piece of paper with the names of the towns over which they were passing. 'Osnabrück and Minden,' wrote Bryant, 'where two hundred years ago, hungry English troops with an English monarch at their head fought and conquered to gain their breakfast; and Hanover, which gave us our Royal Family and old Handel.' His article was published on 5 August, less than a month before the outbreak of war. The sepia-tinted images he conjured up, set against the reality of the coming conflict, must surely have touched the hearts of any readers who cherished fond memories of Germany. 'Even before the marshalled lights of Berlin spun out of the darkness like a pageant,' Bryant wrote, 'the consciousness was strong on me of how much, for all its superficial differences, our European civilisation is a unity.'[17]

Two days later he met Walther Hewel in a Salzburg hotel. Hewel, a veteran of the 1923 putsch who had shared Hitler's subsequent imprisonment, was one of the Führer's few close friends. These facts, together with his low Party membership number, made him an indisputable member of the Nazi aristocracy. Because he spoke fluent English (he had worked as a coffee salesman for a British firm in the Dutch East Indies), he was often used to field Hitler's British visitors. The indefatigable Amy Buller (of the Student Christian Movement) had crossed swords with him in Berlin only a few months earlier when he tried to convince her that her delegation would learn more about National Socialism from autobahns than theology.[18] Now it was Bryant's task to take on Hewel. His main objective was to make clear that Britain's promise to Poland was binding. Hewel, who looked tired, having been up all night with Hitler in the Berghof (Berchtesgaden was less than twenty miles away), had only one response – Danzig must return to the Reich. He also spoke of Hitler's bitter disappointment that the friendly understanding he had reached with Chamberlain at Munich had been dishonoured in spirit. 'He referred', wrote Bryant in his report to the prime minister, 'to the violent and continuous attacks made on the Führer after Munich in the British press of all parties and on the wireless, which he said had reduced Hitler at the time to a state of almost uncontrollable fury, since he was utterly unable to believe that the British Government could not, had it wished, have controlled such attacks.'[19]

At first Bryant did not warm to Hewel, describing him as more 'the bolder kind of businessman than statesman', but he did feel that he was talking to 'a man of the world and a gentleman'.[20] In conclusion, he told Chamberlain, he thought that if his visit had not actually achieved much, at least it had not done any harm. He even believed that the 'slight bond of personal understanding and sympathy' that he had established with Hewel 'might conceivably be of some use in the future'.[21] In the light of history, the absurdity of Bryant's mission is summed up by his expenses claim of £28.[22]

Sir Evelyn Wrench – an equally prominent establishment figure – also travelled to Germany that summer, accompanied by his wife, Hylda. 'Our object', he wrote in his autobiography, 'was to ascertain on the spot whether there was still common ground between the Western democracies and the totalitarian states.' On 28 June the couple arrived in Constance. The first German they met after crossing the Swiss border (less than a mile from their hotel) was a girl – 'a porter who smiled at us in a very friendly way which we took to be a good omen'.[23] But an anti-British propaganda poster showing British soldiers blowing up an Arab village soon shattered their optimism. 'Not a very friendly welcome for a travelling Englishman,' remarked Wrench. Although the Insel was as pleasant as the couple had remembered from previous visits, there were few guests. 'Only about 25,' recorded Wrench, 'mostly German, two or three Dutch, I think we are the only English.' For a man of his breadth of experience (entrepreneur, journalist, founder of the English-Speaking Union and widely travelled advocate of the British Empire), he comes across as curiously naïve. 'The German waiters have not been to England,' he noted in his journal with apparent surprise, 'and don't seem to speak English.' This disappointment coupled with lowering clouds and peals of thunder, did little to lighten their mood. 'We went to bed with spirits rather weighed down.'

On 1 July they motored to Friedrichshafen, where they met Wrench's old friend Hugo Eckener, the highly successful manager of the Zeppelin airship project and former captain of the *Graf Zeppelin*. Wrench was relieved to find Eckener – a vocal critic of the Nazis – to be 'the same delightful human being', despite living under constant threat of arrest. At one time, Wrench recalled, there had even been talk of Eckener succeeding Hindenburg as president. This pleasant reunion and a sunset walk by the lake, 'its waters translucent aquamarine and pearl grey', were bright spots in an otherwise gloomy few days. 'Cold and raining,' recorded Wrench. 'I am wearing thick clothes; H is in her fur cape and glad of it.' They missed the 'old-time politicians of Germany' and were acutely aware of unfriendly stares. 'There is very much of the *Gott Straffe England* [May God Punish England] atmosphere in the air,' observed Wrench. 'We find it terribly oppressive.' Nor was there any comfort to be found in the hotel dining room. 'The coffee is very weak and the bread no longer crisp and made of poor flour. At dinner last night we asked for toast and butter and were charged 1/6 extra on our bill.' Worst of all, when they visited the cathedral, a group of well-dressed young men jeered at them, shouting 'oh, oh, oh, ja, ja, ja' – 'a thing that has never happened to me before,' noted Wrench sadly. They spent their last day in Constance sitting under pollarded trees by the lake watching passers-by. 'We were much impressed by the femininity of German women,' remarked Wrench. 'They look so charming in their national dress. Everywhere we see mothers with their children. It is very refreshing, after the depressed females we have noticed in other countries, to see the un-lipsticked and unpainted-nailed women here. The young girls all wear two long plaits that hang down in front.'

On 5 July they departed for Berlin on what was to be a gruelling thirteen-hour journey. 'Our train which left at 8 am passed by the Insel and our hall porters waved to us which was friendly of them.' After the disappointment of the hotel fare, breakfast on the train was a treat. 'Really crisp rolls. Plenty of butter.' Looking out of the window, they saw women and elderly men in their horse carts getting in the hay harvest. '*Women*', noted Wrench with astonishment, 'out in the fields everywhere and how they work!'

We saw hardly any young men. We did not see an untidy
human being or building right over the country and outwardly a look of prosperity and wellbeing. We practically
saw no soldiers. As far as we are concerned, we might have
been travelling through a peace-loving Utopia. Evidently
soldiers are not in central Germany. Very nice and well-
built modern workmen's dwellings with steep roofs. Many
swimming baths in wayside villages, on some of the balconies of the private dwellings bright large umbrellas, red
and white spots and yellow and blue. Saw no corrugated
iron roofs and of course no golf courses. We practically
never saw an unused acre on our whole journey. I thought
ashamedly of our derelict countryside at home. Their food
production must be enormous.

In Berlin, where they stayed at the Adlon, Wrench at once set
about arranging to meet old friends. When it came to fixing
an appointment with Herr Dieckhoff, still nominally German
ambassador to America, he succeeded rather better than had
the Quakers six months earlier. He found Dieckhoff 'disarm-
ingly frank'. The ambassador failed to understand why Britain
was suddenly taking such a 'frantic' interest in Poland. This, in
his view, had only resulted in stiffening Polish unreasonableness
and preventing Germany from making an amicable settlement. What Germany could not comprehend, Dieckhoff told
Wrench, was why Great Britain insisted on acting as the moral
godmother to the rest of the world. And why did the British
press and Parliament concentrate on Germany's supposed iniquities, and ignore the shortcomings of other countries such as
Russia? It was an uncomfortable interview, leaving Wrench
convinced that Germany was 'incapable of understanding the
wave of idealism which undoubtedly plays so strong a part in

the Anglo-Saxon world and which seeks to set up a collective system, with third party judgement when one's own interests are involved'. But when he made this last point, to Dieckhoff, the latter deftly turned the tables, asking the Englishman if he thought for one moment that Britain would be prepared to have problems involving its own national interests settled by a third-party judgement. As he left the building, Wrench gave a Nazi salute to a group of officials. It was an odd thing to do, but then, as he characteristically put it, 'when you are in Rome do as Rome does'.

One of the Wrenchs' more interesting Berlin encounters took place in a café over lemon tea with two senior women in the National Socialist Women's League. 'We had "an absolutely frank" talk,' reported Wrench. 'They were both so nice and *real idealists* but one comes up against a stone wall when Germany's interests are involved.'

> Nearly every German we have met excuses the rape of Czechoslovakia because its existence was a menace to Germany who must have 'security'. They are so living in the grievances of the past twenty years that they ignore the sufferings of other nations. You simply can't get them to look at things from a European viewpoint. They are really suffering from a resentment and inferiority complex. As one hard-minded German said to me 'my nation is at the moment mentally ill, they can't see straight'.

On 12 July, Wrench called on the British ambassador, Sir Nevile Henderson, whom he had not met since Eton where they had been good friends. He found him 'a little peppery in manner', and indignant with *The Spectator* (Wrench was chairman of the board) for advocating the inclusion of Winston Churchill in the government. The one thing Britain must do, Henderson intoned, was to rally round Chamberlain. 'He was very strong', Wrench noted, 'that we must be adamant if brute force was used, but simultaneously argued that we should try to get a fair settlement at Danzig.' Henderson thought it a pity that Danzig should have become the prime focus since there was 'quite a lot in the German case'. Nevertheless, since the rape of Czechoslovakia, the ambassador was clear that Britain 'must stand firm on the moral ground that no big nation has the right to impose its will on a weaker power'. Perhaps it had never occurred to Wrench, who spent so much of his life promoting the British Empire, or, indeed, to Henderson, that their own country had on occasion imposed its will on both smaller and bigger nations. But then, Wrench's conception of a non-racist empire, in which a free association of peoples cooperated to promote self-government and international stability, was rather different from Hitler's.

Wrench, who genuinely loved Germany and had visited it many times, reluctantly concluded that 'being in Germany these days is not a pleasant experience'. Any small kindness or politeness shown them now came as a surprise. In view of this, the couple decided to leave for Sweden earlier than planned. Acting on the advice of a German friend to 'get back to England by 1 September', they sailed from Gothenburg on 26 August. 'Our steamer was crowded with returning British holidaymakers and French reservists summoned to the Colours,' commented Wrench. 'We arrived at Tilbury on 28 August.'[24]

If more and more people were desperate to get out of Germany in 1939, there were some, like opera fans Ida and Louise Cook, who were equally determined to get in. It was in 1937 that the Austrian conductor Clemens Krauss and his wife Viorica Ursuleac (Richard Strauss's favourite soprano) had first alerted them to the Jewish crisis. From that time until just two weeks before the outbreak of war, the sisters travelled regularly to Germany helping Jews to organise their emigration documents, and smuggling their valuables back to England. It was a costly enterprise since, to remain credible in the eyes of the Nazis, it was essential that they stay in the best hotels. However, after her first book appeared in 1936, Ida's earnings as a romantic novelist (she was to publish over a hundred novels with Mills & Boon under the pseudonym of Mary Burchell) provided ample funds for their heroic venture.

Although Ida and Louise's genuine devotion to opera gave them perfect cover, the dangers they faced were far from negligible. Typically, Louise (having taken the Saturday morning off) would leave her mundane office job on a Friday evening and rush with her sister to Croydon airport, arriving just in time to catch the last flight to Cologne. They then boarded the night train for Munich. 'Either going or coming we would probably stop off at Frankfurt where most of our cases were,'[25] wrote Ida in her memoir.

Their smuggling operation became increasingly sophisticated. By flying in to Germany and returning home on the train, they were able to avoid meeting the same Nazi officials twice. This was vital because on the outward journey they dressed simply, wearing not a single item of jewellery – not even a wristwatch. On the return trip, however, these ordinary-looking women were transformed into fur-clad 'overdressed English girls with a taste for slightly too much jewellery'.[26] As neither of the sisters had pierced ears, they never carried that type of earring, knowing that this was precisely the sort of discrepancy the German officials had been trained to spot.

If questioned about their large amounts of jewellery, they planned 'to do the nervous British spinster act and insist, quite simply, that we always took our valuables with us, because we didn't trust anyone with whom we could leave them at home'.[27] They usually made their homeward journey through Holland, crossing to Harwich on the night boat. The early train up to London enabled Louise to arrive punctually at her office first thing on Monday morning.

While Ida and Louise were making their last trip to Germany in August 1939, the *AGR* was still churning out good news stories. Nancy Brown, for instance, gave a lyrical account of a recent fortnight in the Reich with the pro-Nazi organisation, the Link, in what was to prove the magazine's final issue. 'The Rhineland holiday has left me with such splendid impressions of modern Germany,' she wrote, 'that I should like to pass them on to other readers.'

> The sound of children's voices raised in a marching song, while we sat in a beer garden, gay with flowers, shady with sweet-smelling lime trees, watching the ripples on the lake. Presently the children came into sight from out of the dark forest, knapsacks on backs and swarmed into the garden for refreshment. One bright-eyed boy was playing the accordion, and as he played the shining plaits of the little girls around him gleamed in the sunlight like neat braids of gold.[28]

In that same August issue the following advertisement appeared: 'Young English girl, 20, seeks position as au pair in Germany during October.'

As August drew to a close, Sylvia Heywood was still studying music in Dresden. Her train ticket to England was dated 3 September but in view of the latest developments, it seemed prudent to bring her journey forward a week. However, not expecting to be away for more than a fortnight (surely there would be another 'Munich'), she left her two most precious treasures – her fur coat and her violin – in the safekeeping of her landlady. On 1 September German troops entered Poland; two days later Britain declared war on Germany. Sylvia eventually heard from her landlady (in a letter sent via the Red Cross) what had happened to her possessions. The fur coat was looted by soldiers and Sylvia hoped that it might later have brought comfort to some wretched young man fighting on the Eastern front. The violin suffered a different fate. When the bombs began falling on Dresden, her landlady had carefully wrapped it up, taken it to a nearby park, and buried it.[29]

20

War

In the first months it was hard to believe that there was a war on at all. True, rationing was more rigorous, but as it had already existed for so long in one form or another, people scarcely noticed. More worrying were the air raids, although, initially at least, even these inflicted relatively little damage. In other words, the 'good life' under National Socialism, so often depicted in the *AGR*, was surprisingly unaffected. On the other hand, the blackout and the endless notices warning 'The Enemy is Listening' were a constant reminder to citizens that their country was indeed at war. And, even if at its outset it appeared to change little outwardly, as American journalist Howard K. Smith noted, it nevertheless struck 'unmitigated fear'[1] into German hearts.

From January 1940, when Smith arrived in Berlin, up until 6 December 1941 when he boarded the last train to Switzerland before the United States entered the war, he made a point of monitoring public morale. The invasion of Russia in June 1941 was the turning point. Until then, people's hopes for a swift peace had swung wildly from one extreme to another. Any absurd piece of propaganda or the flimsiest rumour could spark joy or despair. But when the promised Eastern conquest consistently failed to materialise, it began to dawn on the average German that he had been duped. There would be no quick peace, no final victory. Meanwhile, journalists and diplomats, Nazi sympathisers, refugees, spouses and the odd businessman made up the majority of foreigners still able to travel in the Reich during the war. Individuals as diverse as the very British Princess 'Peg' of Hesse and the Rhine, and Erik Wallin, a Swede serving in the Waffen-SS, were among those to witness at first hand Germany's long descent into misery and defeat.

Biddy Macnaghten's memoir is a vivid account of the war as seen from a left-wing perspective. A rebel since childhood, Biddy was the daughter of a Northern Irish judge (and great granddaughter of social reformer Charles Booth). She went to live in Berlin in 1927 after studying art at the Slade School in London. By the time the war broke out, she was married to working-class Willi Jungmittag, a Bauhaus-trained photographer and technical draughtsman. Both were members of the Communist Party. As 3 September 1939 was a Sunday, they took their five-year-old daughter Clara (named after the communist Reichstag member Klara Zetkin) to the park and sat on the grass. 'They had a big white board like a cricket score board and the news was written up on it,' Biddy recalled. 'We saw England had declared war. That was it.'

Nearly three months later her second daughter was born. Lying in a hospital ward with eleven other women, there was no escaping the song '*Wir fahren gegen Engeland* [We are off to fight England]', broadcast loudly after each new sinking of a British ship. It was not an ideal time to have a baby. There were no extra rations for nursing mothers and, as Biddy could not produce enough milk, little Gerda survived on butter and wheat flour browned in a frying pan, mixed with milk and water. Just three weeks after the birth, Biddy was summoned to an interview with the Gestapo. It turned out that the woman who supplied their milk had implicated her in a recent attempt on Hitler's life. Fortunately the baby and Biddy's Irish connections convinced her interrogators that the accusation was groundless. Had the milk-woman succeeded, she would have collected a 1000-mark reward.[2]

Bridget Gilligan was also married to a German but one from a very different social caste. Count Hugo von Bernstorff belonged to a famous aristocratic family with strong links to Denmark. After their wedding in January 1939, the couple went to live at his ancestral home, Schloss Wotersen, thirty miles east of Hamburg. They might have married sooner had it not been for Bridget's difficulties in proving the purity of her blood. In November 1938 Hugo had written to her in England:

> My darling, if you should have the slightest suspicion that there was any non-Aryan blood in your family please do tell me. The worst thing that could happen would be to find out after we have been married because then we would have to be divorced. So clear everything as much as possible before. You must not say it is too expensive – nothing is too expensive to find out these things.[3]

Bridget's response was hardly reassuring. 'I think the Christening certificates on the Gilligan side are *never* going to be produced,' she replied, 'because, as they were all Wesleyan and the Wesleyan religion has long gone out of fashion, the churches have all been pulled down so I don't feel there is much hope.'[4]

It was as well that Bridget was both competent and tough. After war was declared, Hugo was sent with his regiment to Norway, leaving his English wife of eight months in charge of a complicated household and a large estate. It was not easy. In February 1940 she left for Garmisch and Haus Hirth where in peacetime the likes of Siegfried Sassoon and William Walton had stayed with such pleasure. On her way there she spent a couple of nights in Munich. Writing from the Regina Palast, she told her husband that now she had left Wotersen she could hardly bear to think of it. 'All those grumbling people, always quarrelling and wanting something more,' she complained, 'then the cook cheating us, it makes me sick. Come very *very* soon and leave your soldiers to build snowmen.'⁵ Meanwhile, it was 'bliss' to be in Munich where, unlike in Berlin or Hamburg, oranges could still be bought. Once she had settled into Haus Hirth it was even easier to forget the war. 'Masses of butter and real tea and chocolates after dinner and lovely pudding,' she wrote to Hugo in Norway. Nevertheless, the absence of young men in the village and the fact that there was nothing to buy in the shops ('not even a *Damenbinden* [sanitary towel]'⁶) were sharp reminders that the war was very much a fact of life.

Bridget was not entirely without British support. Several other Englishwomen who had married into grand German families were within easy reach of Wotersen, while, 350 miles to the south, Peg Hesse lived with her husband Prince Ludwig (Lu) in the equally beautiful Schloss Wolfsgarten, ten miles north of Darmstadt. The couple had first met while on holiday at Haus Hirth in 1936. They married the following year in London, where Prince Ludwig was working at the German Embassy. Peg and Bridget – one now a princess, the other a countess – corresponded regularly during the war, their letters, as we shall see, providing much mutual comfort and support.

A month after Bridget's trip to Munich, the Danish writer Karen Blixen, best known for her book *Out of Africa*, arrived in Berlin. She was on assignment for several Scandinavian newspapers and planned to stay a month. Her account of a visit to Bremen captures the curious blend of normality and angst that was so much a feature of the early months of the war. Bremen's medieval cathedral and city hall impressed her deeply, as did the city's patrician houses, a tribute, as she put it 'to the profound and vital culture of a widely-travelled citizenry'. Everywhere there were ships. 'Paintings and tapestries showing entire vast fleets of merchant ships – and in the great patrician halls, tall, monumental exactly proportioned models of the ships the families once owned, with every sail and hawser in place.' Yet set against this image of a great maritime city was the grim reality of March 1940. When Blixen arrived it was late at night and snowing hard. Because of the blackout it was also impossible to see anything. An elderly porter offered his help. 'We walked hand in hand through the dark streets,' Blixen recalled, 'from the train to the hotel, and to the police station [where every visitor had to register] and back again.' He had fought in the Great War and had two sons at the front. She noted how, like the Africans on her Kenyan farm, the old man expressed regret by making 'a clicking sound with his tongue and a little kiss'.[7]

In Berlin, peacetime projects now coexisted with the demands of war. Although the massive buildings, commissioned by Hitler in earlier years, continued to rise ('All the handicraft in stone, wood, or iron which I have seen here is beautifully executed,' observed Blixen), defence and camouflage structures mushroomed alongside them. However, this frenetic activity could not, in her view, disguise the fact that Berlin had lost its lustre – 'like some gorgeous bird in the moulting season'.[8] The streets, she noted, 'were everywhere dirty beyond description'. People walked 'cautiously' in last year's clothes and only the hotel porters looked as if they still belonged among the 'gold, marble, bronze and glass' of the Adlon.

She was surprised to find *King Lear* playing at the Deutsches Theater until she realised that Nazi Germany appropriated great foreign writers and artists in much the same way as it did other people's countries. 'Shakespeare, they say, is in reality Germanic, by virtue of his mighty humanity; Kierkegaard because of his depth of mind; Rembrandt, in his artistic earnestness and Michelangelo by virtue of his very size.'[9] Berlin's packed theatres puzzled Blixen, but, as Howard K. Smith pointed out, there was little else for people to spend their money on. And, unlike the propaganda-filled screens of the cinema, at least the familiar classics (contemporary plays were banned) took people's minds off the war for a couple of hours.[10]

The picture of wartime Germany as drawn by anti-Nazi American journalists was naturally in stark contrast to that so fondly depicted by foreign sympathisers. Swedish explorer Sven Hedin, a much-favoured guest of the Reich, was given regular access to Hitler and other leading Nazis. On 6 March, while Blixen was in Bremen, he lunched with Göring at Carinhall. 'Butter, real Gruyère cheese, caviar, lobster, fresh asparagus, hot dishes and delicacies of every sort' were on the menu. Afterwards, Göring's nineteen-month-old daughter Edda (for whom the wives of Italian diplomats 'were busy knitting tiny garments'[11]) 'tripped in and greeted the guests very prettily'. Despite petrol shortages and a ban on private motor travel, when Hedin needed to go from Berlin to Munich six months later, he was driven the whole way in an official car. His journey was very different from that endured by most wartime travellers, who were typically forced to stand for hours in overcrowded, cold, dirty trains that arrived hours late. Hedin's car, meanwhile, 'dashed through Potsdam, between Wittenberg and Dessau, between Leipzig and Halle and then at full speed along the endless autobahn that vanished like a white ribbon ahead of us'. He noted the wooden poles erected every thirty yards to prevent enemy aircraft landing on the autobahn's inviting smooth surface. They covered the 400 miles (half of it on ordinary roads) in exactly seven hours. 'We had travelled faster than an express train.'[12]

On 18 June 1940 Bridget wrote to Hugo from Wotersen, 'Isn't it wonderful that the war in the West is over? Just when the old man in Mecklenburg [a code name for Hitler?] said it would be.'[13] The war might have been going well but there were plenty of other problems. 'We still haven't got a house-maid which is dreadful,' she told her husband three days later. By July, the strain was beginning to tell. 'Please, darling, do come home *at once*. All these air raids are beyond a joke. I am so miserable, bombs crashing all around us and now they say that the troops in Norway will go to England. I'm so bored with this silly war.'[14] Pap, an elderly retainer, was particularly incensed that the British had bombed Bismarck's monument in Hamburg. A few weeks later, momentarily forgetting Bridget's nationality, he announced that 'he thought it a great pity that the German bombers had missed King George VI and his Queen in their train going up to Scotland the other day!!'[15] A disastrous potato harvest ('they are all rotting') and a huge tax bill did little to improve Bridget's morale.

By Christmas 1940, Harry Flannery, who had taken over William Shirer's CBS broadcasts, had been in Berlin about six weeks. He noted the increased rations of lentils, peas and beans, and the extra marmalade and sugar. Christmas trees were on sale and plenty of toys – bombers, submarines and soldier suits. Adding to the festive spirit, the newspapers published a poem by the Japanese ambassador:

> Look the morning is approaching over the Holy Shrine
> The Day of East Asia is coming.
> Merrily the swastika and the red, white, and green banner are
> Flying in the wind
> It will be Spring in Europe's countries[16]

Biddy and her family spent Christmas with Willi's brother on his farm near Bremen. The butcher had to be summoned in the middle of the night to slaughter a choking pig. 'We stood in the byre', Biddy recalled, 'by the light of an oil lamp to watch it. It was like a Rembrandt picture. The byre and the house were all under the same roof.' Killing a pig was a dangerous business. Only that September a farmer in Rostock had been beheaded for butchering one without permission.[17]

By New Year's Eve the family was back in Berlin where, close to midnight, Flannery was preparing a broadcast in the press office. William and Margaret Joyce, better known as Lord and Lady Haw-Haw, were also in the building and invited Flannery to join them in a bottle of champagne:

> [Haw-Haw] dodged under the roller shutters and went out on the balcony for a bottle. The radio was on. It brought the bells of Cologne Cathedral sounding the midnight hour, and then a Nazi radio band began the Horst Wessel song. Lady Haw-Haw stiffened, her expression became tense, and her arm came up in the Nazi salute. Haw-Haw came from under the shutters, noticed his wife, put down the bottle, clicked his heels together, and joined in the salute.[18]

Early in the New Year Flannery interviewed a German pilot who had flown some twenty raids over London. The pilot's flawless English surprised Flannery until the young man admitted that his mother was British, and that his grandparents lived in London. The American asked him if he had ever bombed their area. 'Yes, I have,' he replied. 'I try not to think about it.'[19]

If London was suffering from bombing, so too was Hamburg. On 13 March Bridget von Bernstorff was staying at the Vier Jahreszeiten – the city's best hotel. Apparently impervious to the war, it was still, according to Flannery, offering rare wines and real tea to its guests. Each afternoon in the restaurant, an orchestra played American favourites such as 'Carry Me Back to Old Virginny' and 'Chinatown'.[20] 'You can't imagine what a dramatic night we had,' Bridget wrote to Hugo from Dresden a couple of days later:

> In the cellar from 11–3 and again 4–5.30. Bombs were raining down. Left at 7 am to catch the train to Altona. The whole sky was full of red glows and most of the streets were shut. There were great columns of smoke all over town. The train was full of exhausted people with children who hadn't slept a wink. Travelling is certainly no pleasure cruise at the moment.[21]

She told him how glad she was that he was still in Norway as so many troops were now being sent to Africa; 'one sees them all the time on the train'.[22]

Certainly where bombing and food were concerned, life in the countryside was vastly better than in the cities. As Ji Xianlin put it, 'If anyone had contact with a peasant, others would drool with envy.' One day in the summer of 1941, he met a German girl who knew a farmer living some miles from

Göttingen. They bicycled out to his orchard where they spent the day picking apples. In addition to the fruit, they returned home with a bag of potatoes. 'When I got back,' Ji wrote, 'I boiled the potatoes, dipped them in the white sugar that I had saved up, and ate the whole lot. But I still didn't feel full.'[23]

Exactly one month after Easter, at 5.45 on the evening of 10 May, Deputy Führer Rudolf Hess climbed into his Messerschmitt and flew to Scotland. His futile attempt to open peace negotiations with Britain, through the Duke of Hamilton, came as a great shock to the German public. Bridget no doubt expressed widespread sentiment when, in a letter to Hugo she wrote, 'This Hess business seems to be rather one up for the enemy. Awfully stupid of Hess. Really he should have shot himself, not done a thing like that. I'm really very sorry for the Führer.'[24]

However, only six weeks later, Hess's act of derring-do paled into insignificance compared with the events of 22 June. On that day, as Ji learned from his landlady, Germany invaded Russia. To take his mind off things, the young scholar went on an expedition with two acquaintances, Frau Pinks and Herr Gross. 'Gross had brought an accordion and played on the way. From the ferry saw young girls bathing in the river – overwhelming.'[25] A short time later he wrote, 'Now whenever I hear of a German defeat I feel inexpressibly happy. But if Germany has occupied a city, I take a tranquilliser or I can't sleep. I don't love Russia and I don't love England and I don't really understand why I hate Germany so.'[26]

A few weeks before the invasion, while the Germans were busy subduing the Balkans, Howard K. Smith had realised something was up when a favourite Russian book of satirical short stories disappeared from the window of his local book-shop. This was noteworthy because it had been on display for a year. Smith entered the shop (which happened to be next to Alois – the restaurant owned by Hitler's half-brother) to inquire about books on Russia. When it became clear that the only ones now available were the likes of *My Life in the Russian Hell*, he knew for certain that the invasion of Russia must be imminent.[27]

Biddy also had advance warning. They lived right next to a railway station and for several weeks she had watched troop trains departing regularly for the East. On the first day of Operation Barbarossa, she met Frau Schroeder in the apartment-block garden where they both had allotments. 'Now,' said her neighbour tearfully, 'the war will never end.'[28] Bridget von Bernstorff, on the other hand, believed that it would all be over in three weeks. 'What will come next, I wonder?' She did not have to wonder long. Two months later she was writing to Hugo, 'In Hamburg one sees *so* many people in black, it's very depressing.' Felix von Schaffgotsche was just one of their many friends who had become a casualty. 'Felix has been shot in the lung and is lying in a cowshed in South Russia being eaten up by bugs.'[29]

That summer Biddy and Willi took their daughters on holi-day to a farm – an old watermill near Frankfurt an der Oder, sixty miles east of Berlin. It belonged to the cousin of a friend. 'I gave Friedel a shoe coupon,' recalled Biddy, 'and she arranged for us to go.'

There were no buses when they arrived at the station, so they had to walk the nine miles to the farm pushing the pram. On one side of the road was forest and on the other 'pale August fields'. Biddy made friends with one of the Polish slave workers on the farm. He had a damaged eye and a frostbitten foot. They gave him all their cigarettes. (These, like every-thing else, were rationed – twelve a day for a man and six for a woman, but only until she was fifty. After that she received none.) Two typists from Berlin, 'very smart in their sun suits, perms and glasses', were fellow guests. The sight of the bedrag-gled slave workers dressed in rags confirmed everything the young women had been told about the Poles being sub-human. After several attempts to enlighten them, Biddy gave up the task as hopeless.

The days passed pleasantly. They picked mushrooms and blueberries in the forest and Willi took Clara fishing on a 'silent and wind-blown' lake. When it was time to leave, a retired policeman offered to take them to the station. They trundled through the forest in the farm wagon drawn by two horses.[30]

Bridget's summer was less agreeable. Apart from the cease-less worry over friends fighting in Russia, the weather was atrocious. 'It's pouring and pouring and pouring every day, and icy cold,' she told Hugo. 'The harvest is completely ruined, far worse than last year.' By October things were no better. 'Darling, I'm so homesick. I long for home and cosy teas and Nanny and cinemas, and no rows and arrangements, and all my friends. How I long for it all.'[31]

While Bridget dreamt of the nursery, French author Jacques Chardonne, together with other foreign writers, was making a literary tour of Germany at the invitation of the Nazis. He was a true believer. 'The feeling I have when I con-sider German society as a whole', he subsequently wrote in a long essay, 'is aesthetic in nature. It is a question of moral beauty (courage, will, self-denial, decency, and various forms of health) and also of style and creativity.' The 'high-toned atmos-phere' of National Socialism was the hallmark of a reception he and the other writers attended in the Vienna Hofburg:

> This troop of foreigners … did not make a very good show-
> ing in the royal apartments. We were seated at about twenty
> round tables, each lit by a circle of red candles and deco-
> rated with a bouquet of autumn leaves, amidst splendid
> china from an earlier age. The electric light was extin-
> guished. We listened to a Bach chorale, a song hummed
> by children's voices; then a Mozart quintet, after which
> the pure song with its restrained resonances was repeated.
> The general silence, the half-darkness that shrouded the
> participants, the flickering of the red candles, the autumn
> foliage, and the really beautiful music united to create a sort
> of spiritual spectacle. There were no speeches that evening.

It was not just the quiet splendour of the occasion that impressed the Frenchman. He believed that the 'nobility' and 'good taste' of such Nazi events derived as much from 'a certain quality of mind' as from the music and beautiful surroundings. His view of the SS was equally romantic. He saw them as 'a new Germanic creation', but one drawn from an ancient past. He likened them to an order of 'militant monks', as they wandered through the streets, tall and elegant in their uniforms. 'They live ingenuously,' he wrote, 'in total self-denial … they do not seem to feel sorrow, or fear, or hunger, or desire: they are the angels of war come down for a moment from the heaven of Niflheim* to help people perform a task that is too difficult for them.'[32]

After nearly two years in Germany, Howard K. Smith's view of the Nazis was rather different. 'All the little things that make life pleasant have disappeared,' he wrote towards the end of 1941. 'All the things which are necessary to make physical

---

* A primordial, misty world found in Norse mythology.

life continue have deteriorated, and in some cases fallen below the level of fitness for human consumption.' He quoted the wife of a workman he knew. 'What', she had asked him, 'have we got to live for?'[33]

As the year drew to a close, Smith, in common with all the remaining American journalists in Berlin, longed to get out of Germany. Finally, late in the afternoon of 6 December, his exit visa was approved. Now that he actually had it, he was tempted to stay an extra day to say his goodbyes. Fortunately a colleague persuaded him that it would be madness to delay even an hour. Friends gathered at Potsdamer Station to see him off. They sang and drank champagne until it was time for him to board the train. At last he was on his way to Switzerland. Too stimulated for sleep, he removed the blackout curtains from the carriage window and stared into the blackness all night, listening to the 'rhythmic clicking of the wheels'. As dawn broke, the Rhine could be seen on one side of the train. Across it were 'the green bunkers of the Maginot Line, with their guns removed'. On the other side 'the grey bunkers of the Siegfried Line, the Westwal', were clearly visible. Daylight showed up the shabbiness of the carriage with its 'threadbare carpet spotted by brown cigarette burns', and the flaking varnish on scratched mahogany panels. When the train stopped at Freiburg, Smith got out to buy a newspaper. A notice issued by the Supreme Command caught his eye. It informed readers that due to the 'unprecedented' early winter, German troops would be shortening their lines on the Eastern front and preparing for winter defence. The newspaper was dated 7 December 1941. That evening, at 7.48 German time, the Japanese Imperial Navy began its attack on Pearl Harbor bringing the United States into the war.[34] Any American still in Germany now faced immediate internment – and a very uncertain future.

21

Journey's End

Accounts left by foreigners still able to travel independently in the Reich during the last three years of the war are both horrifying and touching. One theme links them all – bombing. For when it came to being trapped for hours in an overcrowded, stinking and often freezing cellar while the world above exploded into fire and rubble, it mattered little if you were a princess or a communist, a Nazi-lover, Nazi-hater, Russian, Swede, Sanskrit scholar or Irish nationalist. It was, as Bridget von Bernstorff put it, 'utter hell'.

By 1942, noted Numa Tétaz, the war had 'dug deep' into the national psyche. To be even a 'free' foreigner in Germany was increasingly unpleasant, especially for those who, like Tétaz himself, were known to have a ready means of escape. His Swiss passport – so recently an object of derision – had now become the cause of intense envy. The factory still functioned, despite having been bombed, although with so many German workers away at the war, it was largely in the hands of non-Germans. In fact, several million foreigners from every part of Nazi-controlled Europe were working in Germany – the great majority against their will. Women from the East were put to work in armaments factories while Hungarians and

Rumanians serviced hotels and restaurants. The Italians were generally employed clearing debris.[1] There were also millions of slave workers, many from Poland and Russia, forced to work under appalling conditions. For the native Aryans, this massive number of hostile aliens living so intimately among them was a source of ever-deepening anxiety.

Tétaz noticed that the French enjoyed greater freedom than other foreigners. They had, in consequence, taken over many of the better jobs vacated by Germans. To his surprise, rather than stoke their traditional enmity, this new contact had made the two nationalities realise how much they had in common.[2] If Tétaz was right, this was a rare example of something positive coming out of the war, for in general people were utterly fed up. The fact that, as 1942 dragged on, there was no end in sight depressed everyone, no matter what their politics.

Like Tétaz, the Swede Gösta Block, who broadcast for the Nazis from Berlin, was acutely aware of the growing animosity towards foreigners. It had become impossible, he maintained, to talk about Sweden to a German 'without being scolded'. The Dutch, Danes and Norwegians complained of the same problem. Having once been an avid National Socialist, Block had changed his mind. Indeed, he argued that most foreigners, however keen on the Nazis formerly, would now abandon Germany at the drop of a hat if given the chance. It was only their livelihood and fear for their families that kept them chained to a cause in which they no longer believed.[3]

Francis Stuart, who also broadcast for the Nazis, reacted differently. In March 1942 he wrote in his diary, 'Have been asked to give radio talks to Ireland ... for a time, at least, there are things I would like to say.'[4] As the months went by, he must surely have shared Block's urge to leave but was reluctant to admit it. Although like everyone else he was subject to constant air raids, his description of a solitary Russian aeroplane, seen one night from his apartment, is almost poetic:

> It shone like a soft star, and the flat shells burst always several points of white or reddish fire around it. It came from the East, passed behind the two poplar trees in front of the balcony, turned south and slowly disappeared. I got a strange impression. I had not before seen a raiding plane. But it was the fact that it was Russian and all alone and had come such an immense distance.[5]

Block cited food shortages as one of the main reasons why Germans had turned against foreigners. Certainly for Ji Xianlin, food – or rather lack of it – was becoming an ever more painful issue. On one occasion, when Ji was waiting in a queue to buy vegetables, an old woman mislaid her purse. 'She stared at me and asked if I had taken it. I felt as if I had been hit on the head and was struck dumb,' noted the outraged Ji. Judging from his diary, he spent more time hunting for food than he did studying Sanskrit. 'Went to eat at the Junkerschank. There wasn't a drop of oil in the pickled cabbage and boiled egg so although I was really hungry, I couldn't eat it. I'd always thought I could eat anything. Now I know I can't.' But a few weeks later his diary was full of the 'unspeakably lovely' fried lamb he had just consumed. 'After months of hunger suddenly to have a wonderful meal – my heart did not know how to respond.' On a rare visit to Berlin he visited a Tianjin restaurant having been tipped off that they were serving chicken:

> It was like entering a strange world. The room was full of my fellow countrymen, mostly businessmen with gold teeth. I felt that I had arrived in a region of demons, black

marketeers and crooks. Chinese students were also there, behaving like their brothers, dealing in the black market and playing mah-jong. Very few were concentrating on their studies. I felt frozen with fear for China's future.[6]

On 8 November 1942, Tétaz was lunching with his wife in the 'beautiful university town of Freiburg' when a brief radio announcement sent a ripple of apprehension through the restaurant. American and British troops had landed in North Africa.[7] As the days went by, the news grew steadily worse. By the end of the year even Stuart found it hard to maintain his customary detachment. 'For the last weeks have thought or felt little about my writing, nor indeed about anything else,' he wrote in his diary. 'The war is going badly for Germany with the North African Campaign and the Russian Stalingrad offensive.'[8]

On 2 February 1943, the German surrender brought the siege of Stalingrad to an end. A week later Peg Hesse travelled from Potsdam (where her husband was stationed at Krampnitz, the army tank school) back home to Wolfsgarten. It was, she wrote to Bridget, a 'plutocratic journey' complete with sleepers and 'porters waiting for a nod of my head'. The VIP treatment was not because she was a princess but because she was travelling with General von Lenski's wife, who at the time could not have known that her husband had just been taken prisoner at Stalingrad.

For Peg and Lu, a few days snatched leave at Wolfsgarten was to provide a regular respite from the stresses of war. 'Coffee, gin and the Widow Clicquot were blissful,' Peg wrote to Bridget that Easter, 'and Lu and I were happy again.' An 'excellent' production of The Taming of the Shrew in Darmstadt was an added treat.[9] It is curious that Shakespeare appears to have been such a staple of wartime Germany. Francis Stuart had just emerged from a performance of *Antony and Cleopatra* when, on 1 March 1943, 'the worst raid there has yet been on Berlin' began. Afterwards he walked home 'through smoking streets past many blazing houses'. Next morning these were still smouldering. Along the Kaiser Allée, furniture, pictures, pots, pans and books were all piled up in the 'misty rain'. None of this – or so he claimed – stirred him. 'In the midst of our destruction,' he wrote, 'one remains emotionally untouched.'[10]

Unlike Stuart, Knut Hamsun was emotionally devastated by the war. Not that the Nobel laureate had lost any of his admiration for Hitler or, more especially, for Goebbels. On 19 May 1943 he spent several hours with the literary-minded minister for propaganda at the latter's house in Berlin. Goebbels was so incensed to learn that Hamsun's *Collected Works* was no longer being read in Nordic countries that he at once decided to print an edition of 100,000 copies. Hamsun demurred, pointing out that it was hardly the right moment given Germany's severe paper shortage. This brief encounter must have left a deep impression on the Norwegian because, as soon as he reached home, he made the remarkable decision to send Goebbels his Nobel medal. 'I know of nobody, Herr Reichsminister,' he wrote in an accompanying note, 'who has unstintingly, year after year written and spoken on Europe's and humanity's behalf as idealistically as yourself. I ask your forgiveness for sending you my medal. It is of no use to you whatsoever, but I have nothing else to offer.'[11]

If Hamsun's admiration for the Nazi leadership was undiminished, so indeed was his hatred of England. This he made clear in a speech to an international conference of writers in Vienna just five weeks later. 'I am deeply and fervently anti-Anglophile, anti-British,' he told the 500 delegates. 'All the unrest, the troubles, the oppression, broken promises, violence and international conflicts have England as their source ... England must be brought to her knees.'[12]

Despite Hamsun's unswerving loyalty to the Nazis, he desperately sought a meeting with Hitler. The reason was his deep loathing for Josef Terboven, Reichskommissar for Norway. Hamsun maintained that his brutal regime was undermining any hope of persuading Norwegians to accept German supremacy. The longed-for interview with the Führer, at which Hamsun felt certain he would be able to persuade him to remove Terboven, took place at the Berghof on 26 June 1943. It was not a success. Hitler, no doubt briefed by Goebbels on Hamsun's genius, wanted to talk only about writing, Hamsun only about politics. The eighty-four-year-old (who had recently suffered a stroke and was deaf) refused to be deflected, even committing the gross sin of interrupting the Führer. At one point the old man wept openly as he unburdened his pain. 'The Reichskommissar's methods do not suit our country,' he told Hitler. 'His Prussian ways are intolerable. And then all the executions. We can't take any more.' Furious, Hitler responded by throwing up his arms in disgust and walking out on to the terrace.[13] For Hamsun, it was a disastrous outcome. Yet, as his biographer observes, he returned to Norway still believing in the Führer and the sacred mission of the Third Reich to create a new and better world.[14]

A month after Hamsun's unhappy encounter with Hitler, Operation Gomorrah was launched on Hamburg, virtually destroying the city. Bridget wrote to Hugo:

Such a tragedy as Hamburg *has* never been. Darling you don't know, you can't imagine there is nothing, nothing, nothing left. Every night the same – we are lucky to get out of the cellar alive. Every day the sky is black with smoke and the garden is black with ash. Today at 6 o'clock Hamburg must be entirely evacuated. Streets littered with blackened corpses and the heat is appalling. Typhus has broken out because there is no water and the people have drunk from the Elbe. There are about 90,000 wounded and ¼ million dead.[15]

Several days later Peg wrote to Bridget from Krampnitz. 'Thank God you are home. One feels one's heart will break and one only wants to creep into someone's arms and howl.' She had been in Mecklenburg when Rostock was bombed and it had taken two days to get back to Berlin – a distance of only 125 miles. 'I saw and lived through such scenes and saw so much stark tragedy,' she told Bridget, 'that I arrived here nearer hysterics than I have ever been.' But only three weeks later, she was writing from Wolfsgarten, 'I can't describe the bliss of being here. It is really like rubbing Aladdin's lamp when one gives up one's ticket at Langen station. There is not the slightest panic and my letters from Krampnitz now seem to me exaggerated and verging on the hysterical.'[16]

Meanwhile in Berlin that July, Biddy Jungmittag and her children were preparing to be evacuated:

The transport went from the Frankfurter Allee Ringbahn station. We had to be there at 9 a.m. There was a crowd of people round the train and Hitler Youth loading the baggage. We were late and the train was already full. There was an alarm but it was soon over and about eleven the train rumbled off slowly. It was an old train and the doors weren't very safe so we tied them up with string. We put the bigger children to sleep on the luggage racks.

Near dawn they crossed the Vistula. 'We were not supposed to raise the blind and look at it but I did,' wrote Biddy. As the train rolled over 'that great silver river' she found comfort in the thought that it would be there 'long after the Nazis and their insane crimes have been forgotten'.

Eventually they reached Kuckernese, a large village on the River Neman not far from the Russian border. Biddy put the heavy suitcases in the pram and pushed it to the town hall, where they sat while the local housewives 'came and picked the evacuees they thought would suit them'. Fortunately Biddy and her children ended up with the kind-hearted Frau Dregenus, whose father owned the village shop. 'She took us into the kitchen bade us sit down and have some potato soup,' Biddy remembered. 'The kitchen was wildly untidy and the two serving girls were bare footed. Biddy told her at once that she was English. 'In a way our skeletons in the cupboard cancelled out: one being English and the other having a mentally deficient child.' They were allotted two rooms but, as Frau Dregenus warned Biddy, they were so cold in winter that the potatoes she had stored there the previous year had frozen. Life in Kuckernese, however, was not unpleasant. There were evening walks along the river listening to nightingales and one of the teachers from Berlin organised a choir. 'We practised in a room over the bank where we had our sewing evenings,' wrote Biddy. Each Sunday they sang in the bare North German Lutheran church lit by its plain glass windows. When the village and local farm children were confirmed, Biddy recalled with pleasure how the choir sang Bach's Magnificat. 'It was a very moving service,' she wrote, 'with the girls in their white dresses and the boys in their first proper suits.'[17]

In October 1943 Peg told Bridget that their latest leave at Wolfsgarten had been 'too sad to be as wonderful as usual'.[18]

The reason was the death, in an air crash over the Appenines, of Prince Christoph of Hesse – great-grandson of Queen Victoria and nephew of the Kaiser. At the beginning of the war Prince Christoph, an SS Oberführer [Senior Leader], had resigned his post as head of the Forschungsamt [Göring's intelligence agency] in order to join the Luftwaffe. His widow, Princess Sophie, was the youngest sister of Prince Philip, the future husband of Queen Elizabeth II. Princess Sophie, or 'Tiny' as her friends called her, lived at Schloss Kronberg, twenty miles north of Wolfsgarten, with her four children (another was on the way) and her mother-in-law, the *Landgräfin* [Landgravine], Princess Margaret of Prussia – whom Colonel Stewart Roddie had befriended in 1919. Of the latter's six sons, two had died in the First World War and now a third had been killed in the Second.

'The day of the memorial service was like a Greek tragedy,' Peg reported to Bridget. 'Christoph's twin brother and two nephews who were expected from Kassel did not arrive and we didn't know if they were alive or dead.' After the service, Peg and Lu returned to Krampnitz in an agonisingly slow train. Their overcrowded carriage contained a child with whooping cough who was sick twelve times during the night. A few weeks later the chapel at Kronberg was bombed and the coffins of the Landgraf and his sons destroyed by fire. 'Very hard for the Landgräfin,' wrote Peg. 'Even the dead aren't left in peace.'[19]

But that autumn was not all gloom. Bridget danced on the table at Victor von Plessen's birthday party, while in Berlin a performance of Beethoven's Seventh Symphony conducted by Furtwängler 'swamped' Peg's soul 'with sound and emotion'. Then, back again at Wolfsgarten, where, having saved up lots of food, Peg and Lu hosted a house party for a group of close friends including the grieving Tiny. 'A wild boar arrived which tasted divine, we even managed 24 oysters!' It was a valiant attempt to forget the war for a few hours, but in reality, Peg told Bridget, 'we all have a lump of lead instead of a heart'.[20] As for Bridget, despite her privileged position, she surely spoke for Everyman when she summed up 1943. 'Apart from ammunition and children, no one creates anything anymore. Nothing beautiful is made and all the beauty that exists is being destroyed. There is no leisure, no romance.'[21]

Those words were written shortly before medieval Frankfurt, one of the cultural glories of Germany, was obliterated early in 1944. Frankfurt was only fifteen miles north of Wolfsgarten and on 29 March Peg wrote to Bridget, 'The town just doesn't exist anymore. In fact it is a Hamburg, Berlin or Kassel. A great many killed.'[22] After describing the full horror of the raid, she turned to the first signs of spring – revelling in the scyllas and crocuses, peach blossom and violets that had just appeared. 'But everything one touches', she added, 'is black with soot and ashes from Frankfurt and the garden is full of odd pages of English, German and Spanish books from the paper factory which got hit.'

As the world disintegrated around her, Peg adjusted her sights. 'A trip to Darmstadt is a weekend in Paris,' she told Bridget,

> the 'little' dressmaker in Egelsbach is Worth in London. I enjoy every second of every day because I feel this time next year my life won't be the same comfortable enjoyable life it is now. Any moment may be the last. Yesterday there was a huge droning in the air while we were on the train about ten kilometres from here. The train stopped so Lu and I got out and had a delightful walk home through the beautifully tilled fields and fresh green woods.[23]

Spring at Wolfsgarten may have meant sunshine and flowers but in Kuckernese, where Biddy had survived the winter with her daughters, there was still snow on the ground in May. 'All the time The Russians were advancing,' she wrote, 'and one mother after another got the news that their husbands were either fallen or missing. One of them was terribly worried because she had no black stockings to wear for the mourning.'

At the end of May Willi came from Berlin and they all set off to the Baltic for a holiday:

> We took the steamer from Kuckernese. We had to be there early, about six o'clock in the morning. We pushed the pram through the village. The sun had just risen and the shadows of the trees made diagonal stripes across the straight road that led down to the river. On the steamer were a group of *Arbeitsdienst Mädel* [girls from the women's labour service] in their blue linen dresses and embroidered aprons. They sang folk songs as the steamer puffed its way down the river to the Nehrung. They were going for a day's outing to the sea. We stayed in a little hotel in Nidden and went for walks across the dunes to the Baltic strand, silver and lonely by the blue sea. It was hot and the little pine trees and the flowers on the sandy dunes smelt sweet.[24]

It was the last time Willi saw his daughters. On his return to Berlin he was arrested. A snooping neighbour had discovered that he was harbouring an escaped prisoner and informed on him to the Gestapo.

On 6 June 1944 the Allies landed in Normandy. 'Well Bridget,' Peg wrote a few days later,

> What shall I say about the invasion? I just try not to think
> of it too much, all friends and a good many relations are
> fighting on both sides and the massacre must be quite
> beyond words. I feel as if my heart was locked up in a lead
> sound-proof box and only when I open the lid I feel as if I
> must stop breathing the pain is so great.[25]

A week after D-Day, on 13 June, the first V-1 flying bomb was
targeted on London. Francis Stuart was quick to record the
news, noting that the 'German secret weapon' had attacked
southern England. 'These are the most outwardly sensational
days in modern history,' he wrote. 'Though I hate the whole
war, I think the Germans are justified in using this weapon.
They are fighting back and that is always something which stirs
one's sympathy.'[26] However, on 9 July he recorded:

> Bad news for Germany from all the fronts. The Russians
> only 100 miles or so from Prussia, Caen about to fall. But
> even if I could, I would not like to leave here now. It is not
> my war but all the same, I cannot shake off what is still
> good in Germany as if it has nothing to do with me. In
> spite of all that is hateful, there is still a spark of fineness.[27]

Three weeks later his diary entry reads, 'the war is reaching
its climax. The Russians are on the border of East Prussia and
across the Vistula; in the south pushing on to Cracow and into
the mountain passes leading over into Slovakia and Hungary.'[28]
But despite the grim news, Stuart, like millions of Germans,
still hoped for a miracle. 'While things are certainly bad,' he
wrote on 17 August, 'they are not, I think, so bad for Germany
as they look. There is still a plan, which may be something
like this – an offensive against Russia with a new anti-panzer

weapon and when, and if, this achieves a limited success then a settlement there and a turning of all forces south and west.'[29]

To make things worse, the summer of 1944 was unbearably hot. At one point the thermometer outside Stuart's window stood at forty-five degrees centigrade. By September Stuart and his (Polish-born) German girlfriend, Madeleine, were desperate to leave Berlin. But as this was impossible without travel documents, they had no choice but to sit it out. 'Waiting,' he wrote on 4 September. 'Of all things, the hardest to accept is uncertainty.' He was finally granted a temporary travel pass and on 8 September the couple boarded a train for Munich. 'Tension, excitement and a certain amount of apprehension in the air,'[30] he wrote just before they left. The 'apprehension' was well justified for they were to spend the last months of the war wandering hopelessly from one dysfunctional hotel to the next – hungry, cold and very much alone.

Apart from fantasising about food, Ji spent the summer months of 1944 working on his thesis and keeping a meticulous record of air raids. Occasionally he turned his attention to women. 'Irmgard is typing her dissertation looking very pretty – disturbing to sit so close to her.'[31] But a conversation with Chinese friends a couple of weeks later soon put any thoughts of a European wife into perspective:

> 4 pm went to Mrs Hu's house, she had asked me for supper with some others. We talked about filial piety in China and how it didn't exist in Germany. Relations between German married couples aren't like Chinese either (and I include the British and Americans). Their relationships are based on extreme individualism: Think of yourself first and don't ever consider others. I think it would be unlucky for a Chinese man to marry a German girl. German girls are

pretty, lively, attractive but they are very ambitious. For a
Chinese who wants to succeed in his studies, a Chinese
girl is better.[32]

Their discussion was brought abruptly to an end by an air-raid
warning. That September, Ji recorded no fewer than seventeen
attacks, also noting that each night he was now taking four
different kinds of sleeping pill.

On Monday 12 September there was a catastrophic raid
on Darmstadt. 'Lu and I watched Darmstadt being bombed
and burnt to pieces,' Peg wrote to Bridget. 'We were in our
dugout, the very earth shaking and plane after plane roaring
over our heads. In about 3/4 of an hour it was over leaving
between 6,000 and 8,000 (some say 20,000 but I don't believe
that) dead* and 9/10ths of the town burnt to the ground.'[33]

Shortly after this Franz Wolfgang Rieppel, a Swiss economist who had received much of his education in Germany,
met a couple fleeing Darmstadt on the train. They wore only
nightclothes under their coats, and slippers on their feet. They
carried one small suitcase containing their documents and a
few precious objects salvaged from their bombed-out apartment. What most shocked Rieppel, was that no one seemed
to think this unusual.[34] Exactly why he was travelling around
Germany in September 1944 is unclear but the following
year he published a graphic account of his journey under the
pseudonym 'René Schindler'. On the train from Bregenz to
Munich, he noted that the conversation in his carriage centred
almost entirely on food. When the other passengers discovered
that he was Swiss, they questioned him closely about rationing

---

* About 13,000 were killed in the raid.

in Switzerland. They coveted the wide range of food available there and especially the unrationed alcohol and tobacco. But even more than food, they envied the Swiss their peaceful nights. The man sitting next to Rieppel stuffed his pipe and held a match to the bowl. A soldier asked him what he was smoking. '*Brust Tee* [breast tea],' he responded. 'I got it from a pharmacist. It tastes excellent and my wife assures me that it's very healthy.' When one of the passengers announced that the 'secret weapons were not a bluff', someone else informed them that the enemy had just broken through the southern front. As night fell, the compartment became pitch black, except for the occasional flare of a match.

When they arrived at Buchloe, forty-five miles west of Munich, they were unexpectedly told to get out. They waited for two hours before boarding another train – 'endlessly slow, stuffed full, absolutely dark'. When they were still some distance from Munich the train stopped, and again they were ordered out. 'We were "shoved into lorries",' recorded Rieppel, 'and driven through smouldering ruins before finally reaching the shattered city. The smell of burning permeated everything.'[35]

Surprisingly, even after the bombing of Frankfurt and Darmstadt, Peg was still able to telephone Tiny. 'She, poor soul, is going slowly dotty dragging all the children in and out of the cellar,' she reported to Bridget. On 29 September Peg and Lu bicycled to Kronberg to visit her – a round trip of forty miles. 'We went on the autobahn as it was the only way to get there. Every 50 metres or so, one biked over a spent firebomb. We were heavily camouflaged, dressed in dark green looking like bushes on bicycles (NB Macbeth for moving forests!). It was heaven seeing Tiny again – we at once drank up her last bottle of Vermouth and ate her last packet of Petit Beurre.'[36]

When Biddy first heard of Willi's arrest, she had at once returned to Berlin with the children to plead for him. But all appeals for clemency failed. Accompanied by Willi's mother, she went to the Brandenburg prison to see her husband for the last time. 'It was a beautiful autumn day,' she remembered. 'We were allowed to embrace and sat together. He looked haggard and told us he was chained all the time except for the interview. Oma [grandmother] had the presence of mind to bring some apples from Bremen. He ate them as we talked. We said good-bye.' On 20 November, Willi was guillotined.

Afterwards, with Clara evacuated to Saxony and four-year-old Gerda in a nursery, Biddy started looking for a job. She found one in a light engineering factory, but the endless electricity cuts prevented much work being done. Although her workmates initially regarded her with suspicion, she enjoyed the camaraderie. 'They made jokes about what would happen when the Russians came.' Then, after both the factory and Gerda's nursery were bombed, she stopped going. 'We just sat in our flat and ate cold potatoes.'[37]

There was no heating that winter, although the temperatures were rarely above freezing. But even in a situation as bleak as Biddy's there was the occasional reminder that beauty still existed in the world. Walking home one moonless, frosty night, after depositing Willi's clothes at a refugee centre, she was struck by the sheer loveliness of the night sky – enhanced by the blackout.[38] Ji, equally cold in Göttingen, found no such solace. 'Went into town to buy sausages,' he wrote on 19 December. 'Then went to the Sanskrit Institute where the heating was already off. I wore my overcoat, was wrapped in a rug and still cold. Freezing is as unpleasant as starving.'[39]

Princess Sophie (Tiny) was now looking after nine children but, despite this, was still expected to undertake war work. Peg reported to Bridget, how, after spending a night at Wolfsgarten, her friend had had to leave at dawn in order to get back in time for her job – 'nailing canvas caps on to wooden shoes'.[40] Peg, too, was working – at the local hospital and in an old people's home. By the autumn she was also supervising the dozens of refugees billeted in Wolfsgarten. 'The big event of the week', she wrote to Bridget in November, 'was when our girl doctor came in for a glass of wine and a potato biscuit. She is 22 years old and in charge of eighty patients here. She brought flowers, talked Frankfurtish without stopping and has twin sisters aged three.'[41] By December, with the Russians advancing from the East and the Allies from the South and West, no sane person could have been in any doubt about Germany's imminent defeat. Yet for Peg, despite all the human misery, this last Christmas of the war was not an unhappy one:

> A heavy frost painting the world white and silver; a strong sun in a cloudless blue sky set the trees a shining through the day, and a nearly full moon in a dark be-starred sky making the night a thing of beauty. Wolfsgarten sits so settled and snug into the landscape, smoke slowly rising from every chimney straight up into the sky.

Christmas Eve was spent at the hospital. The nurses stood round the candle-lit tree and sang traditional German carols. Then a small child dressed in white with a strip of silver (salvaged from a crashed aeroplane) recited a poem. 'Of course one felt rather weepy,' Peg wrote to Bridget, 'and men and nurses alike rather broke down in *Stille Nacht*. Three of the nurses' husbands have been killed, the men were all homesick and the "Christkind's" mother had died in the bombing etc. but one felt goodness, kindness and love being summoned up to fight down the powers of darkness.' Next day the 'powers of darkness' received a further blow in the shape of a Christmas feast made splendid with hoarded luxuries:

> Pigeons, goose, pork, curry (+ chutney!), real plum pudding (vintage 1930) + holly and brandy! Pineapple, tinned lobster, truffles and of course here a coffee, there a coffee, here a liqueur there a Champaggers, tea and cake being as nothing. *How* we've enjoyed it all and what pleasure it has brought us to eat once again in the olde style![42]

At midnight on 31 December 1944, Peg and Lu opened their window expecting to hear the bells ring in the New Year. 'We heard no bells,' wrote Peg, 'but only the dull thunder of the front.'[43]

Christmas for Francis Stuart and Madeleine was rather different. With great difficulty they had found a room in a seedy hotel in Munich named the Exquisite. As its pipes had frozen, there was neither heat nor water. After eating their Christmas lunch of mashed potato and gravy, they huddled in bed to keep warm. When an air raid destroyed the hotel's plumbing and electricity, they were allotted one candle a week. They decided to abandon the joys of the Exquisite and join the thousands of refugees hoping to cross into Switzerland. Travelling in trains with cardboard instead of glass in the windows, walking miles in sleet and snow and sleeping in filthy waiting rooms, they eventually found a room in a house in Tuttlingen about twenty-five miles north of the Swiss border. However, that lodging also ended in disaster. On Easter Monday (2 April), Stuart wrote in his diary: 'What a nightmare! These people want to put us out, shouting at us and now not speaking and we with nowhere to go.' Later he wrote, 'What a month of horror April was!' 'And yet,' he added, 'what a time for inner miracles, of revelation such as never before.'[44]

After several failed attempts to cross the border, the pair retreated to Dornbirn, a small Austrian town ten miles south of Bregenz. Here, on 3 May, Stuart wrote, 'Yesterday at half past one French troops occupied this town. For us the long years of war and one phase of life are over.'[45]

Like Stuart, Ji Xianlin also made a diary entry for 2 April. 'American tanks are only 40 km. away and their guns rattle the windows. Even I am worried. Now we just hope that the Americans will come quickly. And when they do come, every-one agrees that they will raise a white flag.' Three days later there was almost no bread and Ji had to walk into town each morning to fetch water in a bucket. But then, on 10 April, came joyous news. Not only were French soldiers amassing large quantities of food in a warehouse near the airport, but they were allowing the Chinese along with the other foreign-ers into 'this treasure house to stuff their bags full'.[46] After the surrender, there was still a long wait ahead for Ji. It was not until January 1946 that he was finally able to return to China.

After three years of fighting in the East, of which two had been in continuous retreat, Erik Wallin, a Swedish officer in the Waffen-SS, reached the outskirts of Berlin on 21 April. His company, relentlessly pushed back by Russian troops, was part of the 11th SS Volunteer Division *Panzergrenadier Nordland*, a division composed of foreign recruits, many of them from Scandinavia. He noticed how the forest gradually thinned until they found themselves fighting among the 'grocery shops, newsstands, post offices, cinemas and gardens' of Berlin's outly-ing suburbs.[47] To their surprise, they soon came across a group of civilians who, instead of fleeing like their neighbours, had decided to stay put and wait for the Russians. By now, although the defence of Berlin was little more than a desperate act of bravado, Wallin and his comrades stuck together fighting until the last. 'At important road junctions the blockades against Russian tanks were standing ready to be dragged into position with tractors or tanks,' he wrote. 'They were trams filled with paving stones and big freight wagons with well-known names such as *Knauer, Berliner, Rollgesellschaft* and *Schmeling*.'[48] He noted the old men, and young boys 'from the Hitlerjugend aged between eight and twelve or thirteen years old' manning the foxholes. 'These boys,' he commented, 'were just as hardened as frontline veterans.'

Eventually Wallin was badly wounded in the thigh. Somehow his comrades got him to a makeshift hospital where, on 1 May, his war finally ended with the arrival of the Russians. They announced the death of Hitler. 'Chitler kaputt! Bärrlin kaputt, Garmanija kaputt.' A German soldier lying next to Wallin silently wept.[49]

On Saturday 28 April, two days before Hitler shot himself, Bridget von Bernstorff was listening to the British artillery pounding Lüneburg. 'We thought now they are coming,' she later told Peg.

Sunday nothing, Monday nothing. Tuesday at midday I was lying on the floor of the living room studying the map of the surrounding villages, wondering where on earth they could be when artillery shells started crashing about us. The windows of Wotersen were all blown out. Wednesday I started knocking out the pieces of broken glass from the windows with a hammer and nearly cut my finger off. Later that morning tanks were reported by Frau Johns (she had a white sheet out). Everybody assembled. They took a few soldiers prisoner, gave us Gold Flakes [cigarettes] out of the

slits of the tanks and drove on. Just after lunch there was a
knock on the door. Who should it be but Dunstan Curtis
on his way to take Kiel, and, having got my address from
Mummy, had looked in!! I burst into tears.[50]

Throughout April Biddy could hear the Russian gunfire getting
closer. Then came the last air raid on Berlin. There was, however, no respite since after that the barrage began 'a sickening
noise that went on all the time and got on your nerves like
toothache'. She took Gerda down to the cellar where all the
occupants of her apartment block had gathered. They sat in
complete darkness, only lighting a candle when one of them
needed to find something. Every now and then Biddy would
go upstairs to her balcony to cook potatoes in a broken pail
with wood collected from bombed buildings. Suddenly they
heard soldiers running in the street. 'Then someone rattled
at the cellar door and it opened. We all sat as if we had been
turned to stone.' A Russian soldier entered the cellar and sat
down to bandage his finger. He gave Gerda a sweet and left a
message on a postcard that Biddy later had translated. 'Now
you are all safe and you will have democracy and the little girl
will learn Russian.' A week of chaos followed, in which, Biddy,
along with the whole street, went looting. Then, at last, the
miracle happened. The barrage ceased.

'We didn't really know what had happened. There were
no newspapers and I didn't have a wireless,'[51] she wrote. But
one thing was clear – the war had ended. Never again would
anyone travel in the Third Reich.

Afterword

In attempting to summarise all the impressions and experiences recorded in these pages, it is easy to sympathise with W. E. B. Du Bois. After months of travelling around the Third Reich in 1936, he wrote: 'It is extremely difficult to express an opinion about Germany today which is true in all respects without numerous modifications and explanations.'[1] That an intelligent observer like Du Bois should have found Nazi Germany so confusing comes as a surprise to anyone used to examining the period with the clarity of post-war hindsight. After all, Du Bois was a black academic and as such a prime Nazi target on two counts. Why did he not simply condemn Hitler's Germany outright? The truth is that many foreign visitors were similarly bewildered. Newspaper attacks on the Nazis from the earliest months of the regime, anecdotal evidence of street violence and repression, the opening of Dachau just a few weeks after Hitler became chancellor and, above all, the book burning, in May 1933, should have alerted all would-be travellers to the reality of the new Germany. But once they were actually there, the propaganda was so pervasive and truth so distorted that many found themselves uncertain about what to believe. In addition, there were at this early stage respectable reasons for giving Hitler the benefit of the doubt – belief that his revolution would evolve into responsible government, guilt over the Treaty of Versailles or simply the memory of a good German holiday. Many foreign visitors felt that it was not their business to comment on Germany's internal affairs, while many more were simply not interested.

But as the years passed, it became increasingly difficult for foreigners to remain agnostic. In the face of such events as the 1935 Nuremberg Laws (which deprived Jews of their citizenship), earlier assurances from moderate Germans that the Nazis would in time settle down and become civilised began to look utterly implausible. Foreigners were now either horrified by the ever-expanding catalogue of Nazi atrocities or impressed by the equally long list of so-called achievements. By the mid-1930s most visitors, even before they arrived, had made up their minds as to which camp they belonged. It is easy enough to see why those on the far right were drawn to Nazi Germany and why those on the left stayed away. Of more interest are the visitors who despised the Nazis but continued to love and admire Germany. Many in this category had travelled or studied in the country before the First World War and had found the experience transformative. It is not difficult to understand why. Even more enticing than Germany's physical beauty was its extraordinarily rich cultural and academic tradition – one that despite the First World War continued to play a key role in British and American intellectual life. The war had created despair among Germanophiles not only because of the human tragedy but because it had cut them off from such a significant part of their own lives. It was not that they were insensitive to Nazi horrors but they clung to the hope that Hitler would quickly fade and their Germany – the real Germany – would re-emerge in all its cultural glory. Others, who like Sir Thomas Beecham were in a position to make a public protest, ducked the opportunity because the professional rewards offered by Nazi Germany were in the end too tempting. In this respect, the American writer Thomas Wolfe emerges as a true hero.

It was this same admiration for German literature, music and philosophy that led so many liberal-minded parents to send their offspring to study in the Third Reich. For them, the importance of German culture and language far outweighed a transitory regime, however nasty. As for the British aristocracy, who also despatched their children to Nazi Germany in droves, many openly admired Hitler – for the way he had pulled his country up by its bootstraps and particularly for his determination to defeat Bolshevism. There were also more prosaic reasons to send your teenagers to Hitler's Germany. The exchange rate was good and there was always some impoverished Baronin willing to lodge them for a modest fee. But while it is nevertheless hard to find an entirely satisfactory explanation for the numbers of young British and Americans roaming around Germany right up to the eve of the Second World War, it is much easier to understand why First World War veterans put their money on Hitler. Many travelled repeatedly to Germany in their efforts, as they saw it, to prevent another war. What is less clear is why a significant number of these often much-decorated patriots became right-wing extremists. Certainly, having survived such a horrific war, many of them felt let down by the peace. In comparison with the orderly discipline and purposefulness they saw in Nazi Germany, their own democratic governments appeared hopelessly feeble and inadequate.

No foreign traveller in the Third Reich, whether casual tourist or seasoned diplomat, could escape the relentless propaganda. But how much were they influenced by it? At its most sophisticated – as at the Olympics, for example – it could be highly effective. But for the most part it was by the late 1930s too crude to leave much mark on overseas visitors – even those sympathetic to the Nazis. What impressed them far more were conversations held with individuals, particularly the young. Many travellers were astonished by the degree of idealism and patriotic devotion expressed by ordinary Germans, unmatched by anything they could cite in their own countries. It was this sense of purpose that many foreigners found inspirational – especially when they remembered the unemployed youths loitering aimlessly on street corners back home. 'Compare a Führerin to a French girl of the same age!' remarked Swiss academic de Rougemont, after hearing of an eighteen-year-old German girl who spent all her spare time organising her group's gymnastics, political sessions and visits to the poor.[2] Travellers' accounts expose another aspect of the Third Reich that might seem surprising – namely, the vulnerability of the man-on-the-street. His longing to be liked, understood and, above all, respected by foreigners – especially the British and Americans – is a constant theme. This neediness is at odds with the more familiar image of an aggressive, racist population eager for war. In fact, if the witnesses in these pages are to be believed, the great majority of Germans dreaded war just as deeply as those on whom they were about to inflict it.

Foreign visitors who concerned themselves with the plight of the Jews – and the majority did not – had to deal with an unanswerable question. How was it possible for these warmhearted, genial people, noted for their work ethic and devotion to family values, to treat so many of their fellow Germans with such contempt and cruelty? Any foreigner who travelled to the Third Reich determined to get beneath its surface was confronted by such contradictions at every turn. The similarities in method, for instance, between National Socialism and communism; Jews who were themselves anti-Semitic; the kindness and cruelty, the cosiness and street violence, the raucous singing and reverence for Beethoven ... No wonder that Du Bois, along with so many others, found it hard to come up with a comprehensive view.

To add to the confusion, there are surely few totalitarian states that welcome their foreign visitors with as much friendliness and enthusiasm as did Nazi Germany. Cruising on the Rhine, drinking beer in a sunlit garden or walking alongside a happy band of singing schoolchildren made it all too easy to forget tales of torture, repression and rearmament. Even in the late 1930s it was still possible for a foreigner to spend weeks in Germany and experience nothing more unpleasant than a puncture. There is, however, a difference between 'not seeing' and 'not knowing'. And after Kristallnacht on 9 November 1938, there could be no possible excuse for any foreign traveller to claim that they 'did not know' the Nazis' true colours.

Perhaps the most chilling fact to emerge from these travellers' tales is that so many perfectly decent people could return home from Hitler's Germany singing its praises. Nazi evil permeated every aspect of German society yet, when blended with the seductive pleasures still available to the foreign visitor, the hideous reality was too often and for too long ignored. More than eight decades after Hitler became chancellor we are still haunted by the Nazis. It is right that we should be.

Acknowledgements

As this long list of acknowledgements makes clear, *Travellers in the Third Reich* has been a collaborative effort. A book that is so dependent on fresh material relies heavily on the goodwill of a great many people. It is thanks to all those who allowed me access to private papers, and to the librarians and archivists around the world who sent me scans of documents, that this book exists.

Without Dr Piers Brendon's unbelievably generous and consistent support and his readiness to share with me his profound knowledge of the period, the book would be very much the poorer. I owe him a great debt. Hugh Geddes not only introduced me to the letters of his aunt HRH Princess Margaret of Hesse and the Rhine, but also pointed me in many other fruitful directions. I thank him for his time, enthusiasm and especially for the friendship that resulted from our joint explorations. My dear friend Angelica Patel, who has herself written about the Nazi period, contributed an essential German perspective to the project and suggested many improvements. Dr Frances Wood not only located obscure Chinese sources but also translated them. In a wider sense she has over many years given me consistent encouragement and much wise advice. Not all academics are as generous with their time and information as Dr Bradley Hart, who was also kind enough to let me read his book *George Pitt-Rivers and the Nazis* before publication. Sir Brian Crowe shared with me his extensive knowledge of Germany and its history. He generously read the book in manuscript and made countless helpful suggestions. At an early stage, Dr Barbara Goward and Camilla Whitworth-Jones gave me much-needed encouragement, raising many useful points. For years Phoebe Bentinck has been a long-suffering supporter of my writing efforts. In this instance, I thank her especially for leading me to a number of important sources.

The following individuals showed great trust in allowing me to study and quote from family papers. I am deeply grateful to them all: Viscount Astor, Brigid Battiscombe, Jonathan Benthall, Dominic Graf Bernstorff, Mary Boxall, The Hon. Lady Brooksbank, Sir Andrew Cahn, Sir Edward Cazalet, Randolph Churchill, Sebastian Clark, Miranda Corben, Sir Brian Crowe, April Crowther, Gloria Elston, Dr Richard Duncan-Jones, Francis Farmar, the late Sir Nicholas Fenn, Clare Ferguson, Diana Fortescue, Rosamond Gallant, George Gordon Lennox, Dr Joanna Hawthorne Amick, Francis Hazeel, Rainer Christoph Friedrich Prinz von Hessen, Rachel Johnson, Jackie and Mick Laurie, Lady Rose Lauritzen, Dr Clara Lowy, Judy Kiss, Colin Mackay, Richard Matthews, Joanna Meredith-Hardy, Keith Ovenden, Jill Pellew, Charles Pemberton, Lord Ramsbotham, David Tonge, Celia Toynbee, Evelyn Westwood, Camilla Whitworth-Jones, Anne Williamson and Patricia Wilson.

I was lucky enough to meet these women, all of whom – despite their advanced years – retained crystal clear memories of their time in Germany during the 1930s. The late Mary Burns, Alice Frank Stock, Marjorie Lewis, Sylvia Morris, the late Hilda Padel, the late Dr Jill Poulton and The Hon. Mrs Joan Raynsford. Alice Fleet told me the remarkable story of how her parents rescued a Jewish girl, and Annette Bradshaw that of her mother's Kristallnacht experience. I thank them both for letting me use these very personal accounts.

I am fortunate to have friends like Dr Nancy Sahli and Ken Quay, who undertook extensive research for me in America. Their efforts on my behalf cost them much time and effort – I am deeply grateful.

The following individuals have helped me in many and various ways. I offer heartfelt thanks to each and every one of them:

Bruce Arnold, Nicholas Barker, Professor Gordon Barrass, Ian Baxter, Lady Beecham, Professor Nigel Biggar, Embla Bjoernerem, Tony Blishen, The Hon. Lady Bonsor, Catherine Boylan, Alison Burns, Lady Burns, Sir Rodric Braithwaite, Georgina Brewis, Edmund and Joanna Capon, Joneen Casey, Professor C. C. Chan, Dr Peter Clarke, Harriet Crawley, Ronia Crisp, Lavinia Davies, Thomas Day, Professor Nicholas Deakin, Guy de Jonquières, Harriet Devlin, David Douglas, Lady Fergusson, Martin Fetherston-Godley, Dr Lucy Gaster, Sally Godley Maynard, Lord Gowrie, the late Graham Greene, Barbara Greenland, Jon Halliday, Sir Richard Heygate Bt, The Lady Holderness, Fiona Hooper, The Lady Howell, Elizabeth James, Linda Kelly, Professor James Knowlson, Beatrice Larsen, Barbara Lewington, Jeremy Lewis, Nigel Linsan Colley, The Lady Mair, Dr Philip Mansel, Jane Martineau, Christopher Masson, Charlotte Moser, Konrad Muschg, Dr Mark Nixon, Sir David Norgrove, The Dowager Marchioness of Normanby, James Peill, Matt Pilling, Dr Zoe Playdon, Catherine Porteous, David Pryce-Jones, Ambassador Kishan Rana, John Ranelagh, Clare Roskill, Nicholas Roskill, Daniel Rothschild, Lord and Lady Ryder, Professor Jane E. Schultz, Dr David Scrase, Kamalesh Sharma, William Shawcross, Michael Smyth, Dr Julia Stapleton, Dr Zara Steiner, Rupert Graf Strachwitz, Jean-Christophe Thalabard, Michael Thomas QC, Sir John and Lady (Ann) Tusa, Professor Dirk Voss, Sir David Warren, Brendan Wehrung, Joan Winterkorn, Dalena Wright, the late Melissa Wyndham, The Lady Young and Louisa Young.

I want to thank the following archivists and librarians who went well beyond the call of duty to provide copies of documents or to help me in numerous other ways:

Carlos D. Acosta-Ponce, Elaine Ardia, Julia Aries, Pamela Bliss, Bodil Børset, Lorraine Bourke, Jacqueline Brown, Christine Colburn, Mary Craudereuff, Kelly Cummins, Jayne Dunlop, Deborah Dunn, Angie Edwards, Jenny Fichmann, Susanna Fout, Neil French, Maggie Grossman, Alison Haas, Amy Hague, Ellie Jones, Christopher Kilbracken, Dr Martin Kröger, Brett Langston, Aaron Lisec, Dr Rainer Maas, Evan McGonagill, Duncan McLaren, Diana McRae, A. Meredith, Michael Meredith, Dr A. Munton, Patricia C. O'Donnell, Janet Olsen, Robert Preece, Carrie Reed, Susan Riggs, Andrew Riley, Steve Robinson, Emily Roehl, Dr Ingo Runde, Sabin Schafferdt, Florian Schreiber, Helge W. Schwarz, Wilfried Schwarz, Dr Joshua Seufert, Adrienne Sharpe, Paul Smith, Angela Stanford, Sandra Stelts, James Stimpert, Rachel Swanston, Susan Thomas, Kristina Unger, Debbie Usher, Anna van Raaphorst, Nathan Waddell, Katharina Waldhauser, Melinda Wallington, Jessica West, Madison White and Jocelyn Wilk.

I owe special thanks to Allen Packwood, director of the Churchill Archives Centre at Churchill College, Cambridge, and his exceptional team; to Spencer Howard of the Herbert Hoover Presidential Library; and to Andrew Lownie, my agent, who suggested the subject in the first place. Working with Jennie Condell and her team at Elliott & Thompson has been pure pleasure.

I am also deeply grateful to Zita Freitas, who has kept our household running for thirty years. Without her support I would be lost.

Lastly, I want to thank my very own live-in editor, translator, adviser, travelling companion and patient listener – my husband, John.

Bibliography

Adlon, Hedda, *Hotel Adlon: The Life and Death of a Great Hotel*, translated and edited by Norman Denny (London: Barrie Books, 1958)

Allen, Mary S., *Lady in Blue* (London: Stanley Paul, 1936)

Allen, Mary S., and Julie Heyneman, *Woman at the Cross Roads* (London: Unicorn Press, 1934)

Allen, Reginald Clifford, *Plough My Own Furrow: The Story of Lord Allen of Hurtwood as Told through his Writings and Correspondence* (London: Longmans, 1965)

Armstrong, Hamilton Fish, *Peace and Counterpeace: From Wilson to Hitler* (New York: Harper & Row, 1971)

Baranowski, Shelley, *Strength through Joy: Consumerism and Mass Tourism in the Third Reich* (Cambridge: Cambridge University Press, 2004)

Baring, Sarah, *The Road to Station X* (Bracknell: Wilton 65, 2000)

Bartlett, Vernon, *Nazi Germany Explained* (London: Victor Gollancz, 1933)

Bell, Anne Olivier (ed.), *The Diary of Virginia Woolf* (Harmondsworth: Penguin, 1983)

Benoist-Méchin, Jacques, *À l'épreuve du temps [Tested by Time]*, Édition établie, présentée et annotée par Eric Roussel (Paris: Julliard, 1989)

Bernays, Robert, *Special Correspondent* (London: Victor Gollancz, 1934)

Blakeway, Denys, *The Last Dance: 1936, the Year of Change* (London: John Murray, 2010)

Bolitho, Gordon, *The Other Germany* (London: Dickson, 1934)

Bonnell, Andrew G. (ed.), *An American Witness in Nazi Frankfurt: The Diaries of Robert W. Heingartner, 1928–37* (Bern and New York: Peter Lang, 2011)

Bowles, Paul, Miller Jeffrey (ed.), *In Touch: The Letters of Paul Bowles* (London: HarperCollins, 1994)

Breitman, Richard, Barbara McDonald Stewart and Severin Hochberg (eds.), *Advocate for the Doomed: Diaries and Papers of James G. McDonald* (Bloomington and Indiana: Indiana University Press, 2007)

Brendon, Piers, *Thomas Cook: 150 Years of Popular Tourism* (Secker & Warburg, new edition 1992)

Brendon, Piers, *The Dark Valley: A Panorama of the 1930s* (London: Pimlico, 2001)

Brendon, Piers, *Edward VIII: The Uncrowned King* (Allen Lane, 2016)

Brown, Daniel James, *The Boys in the Boat* (New York: Viking, 2013)

Brysac, Shareen Blair, *Resisting Hitler: Mildred Harnack and the Red Orchestra* (New York: Oxford University Press, 2000)

Bucknell, Katherine (ed.), *Christopher Isherwood: Diaries* (London: Methuen, 1996)

Buller, E. Amy, *Darkness over Germany* (London: The Right Book Club, 1945; first published 1943)

Burden, Hamilton Twombly, *The Nuremberg Party Rallies, 1923–39* (London: Pall Mall Press, 1967)

Burn, Michael, *Turned Towards the Sun: An Autobiography* (Norwich: Michael Russell, 2003)

Butler, J. R. M., *Lord Lothian, Philip Kerr, 1882–1940* (London: Macmillan, 1960)

Byron, Robert, *Europe in the Looking-Glass* (London: Routledge & Sons, 1926)

Cahn, Robert Wolfgang, *The Art of Belonging* (Lewes: Book Guild, 2005)

Carr, Jonathan, *The Wagner Clan* (London: Faber & Faber, 2007)

Cazalet-Keir, Thelma, *From the Wings: An Autobiography*, (London: Bodley Head, 1967)

Chandler, Andrew (ed.), *Brethren in Adversity: Bishop George Bell, the Church of England and the Crisis of German Protestantism, 1933–1939* (Woodbridge: Boydell Press, 1997)

Clark, Christopher, *The Sleepwalkers: How Europe Went to War in 1914* (London: Allen Lane, 2012)

Cole, J. A., *Just Back from Germany* (London: Faber & Faber, 1938)

Collomp, Catherine, and Bruno Groppo (eds.), *An American in Hitler's Berlin: Abraham Plotkin's Diary 1932–33* (Urbana and Chicago: University of Illinois Press, 2009)

Conwell-Evans, T. P., *None so Blind* (London: Harrison, 1947)

Cook, Ida, *Safe Passage* (London: Harlequin, 2016)

Cowles, Virginia, *Looking for Trouble* (London: n.p., 1942)

Cox, Geoffrey, *Countdown to War: A Personal Memoir of Europe, 1938–1940* (London: William Kimber, 1988)

Cox, Geoffrey, *Eyewitness* (Dunedin: Otago University Press, 1999)

Crittall, Ariel, *My Life Smilingly Unravelled* (Braintree: Braintree District Museum Trust Ltd, 2009)

D'Abernon, Viscountess, *Red Cross and Berlin Embassy, 1915–1926* (London: John Murray, 1946)

Dalley, Jan, *Diana Mosley* (New York, Alfred A. Knopf, 2000)

De Courcy, Anne, *The Viceroy's Daughters* (London: Weidenfeld & Nicolson, 2000)

De Courcy, Anne, *Diana Mosley* (London: Chatto & Windus, 2003)

De Courcy, Anne, *Society's Queen: The Life of Edith, Marchioness of Londonderry* (London: Phoenix, 2004)

De Rougemont, Denis, *Journal D'Allemagne* (Paris: Gallimard, 1938)

Dean Paul, Brenda, *My First Life: A Biography, by Brenda Dean Paul, Written by Herself* (London: J. Long, 1935)

De-la-Noy, Michael, *The Life of Edward Sackville-West* (London: Bodley Head, 1988)

Dodd, Martha, *My Years in Germany* (London: Victor Gollancz, 1939)

Dodd, William E., Jr. and Martha Dodd, *Ambassador Dodd's Diary, 1933–1938* (London: Victor Gollancz, 1941)

Domvile, Sir Barry, *By and Large* (London: Hutchinson, 1936)

Domvile, Sir Barry, *From Admiral to Cabin Boy* (London: Boswell, 1947)

Driberg, Tom, *The Mystery of Moral Re-Armament: A Study of Frank Buchman and His Movement* (London: Secker & Warburg, 1964)

Egremont, Max, *Forgotten Land: Journeys among the Ghosts of East Prussia* (London: Picador, 2011)

Elborn, Geoffrey, *Francis Stuart: A Life* (Dublin: Raven Arts Press, 1990)

Evans, Richard, *The Third Reich at War, 1939–1945* (London: Allen Lane, 2008)

Fergusson, Adam, *When Money Dies: The Nightmare of the Weimar Hyper-Inflation* (London: William Kimber & Co. Ltd., 1975)

Firchow, Peter Edgerly, *Strange Meetings: Anglo-German Literary Encounters from 1910 to 1960* (Washington, DC: Catholic University of America Press, 2008)

Fischer, Heinz-Dietrich, *Germany through American Eyes: Pulitzer Prize Winning Reports* (Berlin: Lit Verlag Dr. W. Hopf, 2010)

Flannery, Harry W., *Assignment to Berlin* (London: Michael Joseph, 1942)

Fortescue, Diana, *The Survivors: A Period Piece* (London: Anima Books, 2015)

Franck, Harry A., *Vagabonding through Changing Germany* (New York: Grosset & Dunlap, 1920)

François-Poncet, André, *The Fateful Years*, trans. Jacques LeClercq (London: Victor Gollancz, 1949)

Fussell, Paul, *Abroad: British Literary Traveling between the Wars* (Oxford: Oxford University Press, 1982)

Geissmar, Berta, *The Baton and the Jackboot* (London: Hamish Hamilton, 1944)

Gibbs, Philip, *European Journey: Being a Narrative of a Journey in France, Switzerland, Italy, Austria, Hungary, Germany and the Saar in the Spring and Summer of 1934* (London: William Heinemann, 1934)

Gilbert, Martin, and Richard Gott, *The Appeasers* (London: Weidenfeld & Nicolson, 1967)

Griffiths, Richard, *Fellow Travellers of the Right: British Enthusiasts for Nazi Germany* (London: Oxford University Press, 1983)

Griffiths, Richard, *Patriotism Preserved: Captain Ramsay, the Right Club and British Anti-Semitism* (London: Constable, 1998)

Guérin, Daniel, *The Brown Plague: Travels in Late Weimar and Early Nazi Germany*, translated by Robert Schwartzwald (Durham, NC, and London: Duke University Press, 1994)

Guinness, Jonathan, *The House of Mitford* (London: Phoenix, 2004)

Hamann, Brigitte, *Winifred Wagner* (London: Granta Books, 2005)

Hamilton, Cicely, *Modern Germanies* (London: Dent & Sons, 1931)

Harding, Brian, *Keeping Faith: The Royal British Legion, 1921–2001* (Barnsley: Pen & Sword Books, 2001)

Hart-Davis, Duff, *Hitler's Games: The 1936 Olympics* (London: Century, 1986)

Hattersley, Roy, *David Lloyd George: The Great Outsider* (London: Little, Brown, 2010)

Hawes, James, *Englanders and Huns* (London and New York: Simon & Schuster, 2014)

Heingartner, Robert W., *An American Witness in Nazi Frankfurt: The Diaries of Robert W. Heingartner, 1928–1937*, ed. Andrew G. Bonnell (New York: Peter Lang, 2011)

Hessen, Robert (ed.), *Berlin Alert: The Memoirs and Reports of Truman Smith* (Stanford: Hoover Institution Press, 1984)

Henderson, Nevile, *Failure of a Mission* (New York: G. P. Putnam's Sons, 1940)

Heygate, John, *Motor Tramp* (London: Cape, 1935)

Hillblad, Thorolf (ed.), *Twilight of the Gods* (Mechanicsburg, PA: Stackpole Books, 2009)

Hills, Denis, *Tyrants and Mountains: A Reckless Life* (London: John Murray, 1992)

Hitler's Winter Olympic Games 1936 (World Propaganda Classics, 2009)

Holtby, Alice and J. McWilliam (eds.), *Winifred Holtby: Letters to a Friend* (London: Collins, 1937)

Hutchison, Graham Seton, *Challenge* (London: Hutchinson & Co., 1939)

Isherwood, Christopher, *Christopher and His Kind* (London: Methuen, 1985)

Isherwood, Christopher, *The Berlin Novels* (London: Vintage, 1999)

Johnson, Gaynor, *The Berlin Embassy of Lord D'Abernon, 1920–1926* (Basingstoke: Palgrave Macmillan, 2002)

Jones, Thomas, *A Diary with Letters, 1931–1950* (London: Oxford University Press, 1954)

Juvet, René, *Ich war dabei… [I was there…]* (Zurich: Europa Verlag, 1944)

Kennedy, Richard S, and Paschal Reeves (eds.), *The Notebooks of Thomas Wolfe*, volume II (Chapel Hill: University of North Carolina Press, 1970)

Kent, Madeleine, *I Married a German* (New York: Harper & Brothers, 1939)

Kershaw, Ian, *Hitler, 1889–1936: Hubris* (London: Penguin, 1999)

Kershaw, Ian, *Making Friends with Hitler: Lord Londonderry and Britain's Road to War* (London: Allen Lane, 2004)

Kessler, Charles (ed./trans.), *Berlin in Lights: The Diaries of Count Harry Kessler (1918–1937)* (New York, Grove Press, 1999)

Keynes, John Maynard, *Collected Writings of John Maynard Keynes* (London: Macmillan, 1981)

Kirkpatrick, Ivone, *The Inner Circle: Memoirs* (London: Macmillan, 1959)

Knowlson, James, *Damned To Fame: The Life of Samuel Beckett* (London: Bloomsbury, 1996)

Knox, James, *Robert Byron* (London: John Murray, 2003)

Kolloen, Ingar Sletten, *Knut Hamsun: Dreamer and Dissenter* (New Haven: Yale University Press, 2009)

Lancaster Marie-Jaqueline (ed.), *Brian Howard: Portrait of a Failure* (London: Blond, 1968)

Laqueur, Walter, *Weimar: A Cultural History, 1918–1933* (New York: Putnam, 1974)

Larson, Erik, *In the Garden of Beasts* (New York: Crown Publishers, 2011)

Leitner, Maria, *Elisabeth, Ein Hitlermädchen: Erzählende Prosa, Reportagen und Berichte [Elisabeth, A Hitler Girl: Narrative Prose and Reports]* (Berlin und Weimar: Aufbau-Verlag, 1985)

Lewis, Jeremy, *Shades of Greene* (London: Jonathan Cape, 2010)

Lewis, Wyndham, *Hitler* (London: Chatto & Windus, 1931)

Lewis, Wyndham, *The Hitler Cult* (London: Dent, 1939)

Lindbergh, Anne Morrow, *The Flower and the Nettle: Diaries and Letters of Anne Morrow Lindbergh, 1936–1939* (New York: Harcourt Brace Jovanovich, 1976)

Lochner, Louis (ed. and trans.), *The Goebbels Diaries* (London: Hamish Hamilton 1948)

Lockhart, Robert Bruce, *The Diaries of Sir Robert Bruce Lockhart*, edited by Kenneth Young (London: Macmillan, 1973)

Lubrich, Oliver (ed.), *Travels in the Reich 1933–1945: Foreign Authors Report from Germany* (Chicago: University of Chicago Press, 2010)

Lucas, John, *An Obsession with Music* (Woodbridge: Boydell, 2008)

426   TRAVELLERS IN THE THIRD REICH

McKenna, Mark, *An Eye for Eternity: The Life of Manning Clark* (Melbourne: Miegunyah Press of Melbourne University, 2011)

Markham, Violet R., *A Woman's Watch on the Rhine: Sketches of Occupation* (London: Hodder & Stoughton, 1920)

Mears, John Henry, *Racing the Moon* (New York: Rae D. Henkle Co., 1928)

Melchior, Ib, *Lauritz Melchior: The Golden Years of Bayreuth* (Fort Worth: Baskerville, 2003)

Min, Shi, *Deguo youji*, Tao Kangde (ed.), *Ou feng mei yu*, 3rd edition (Shanghai: Yuzhou feng she, 1940).

Mosley, Charlotte (ed.), *The Mitfords: Letters between Six Sisters* (London: Fourth Estate, 2008)

Mowrer, Lilian T., *Journalist's Wife* (London and Toronto: William Heinemann, 1938)

Naess, Harald, and James McFarlane, *Knut Hamsun: Selected Letters*, 2 volumes (Norwich: Norvik Press, 1998)

Natwar-Singh, Kirpal, *The Magnificent Maharaja: The Life and Times of Bhupinder Singh of Patiala, 1891–1938* (New Delhi: Harper-Collins India, 1998)

Noakes, Jeremy, and Geoffrey Pridham (eds.), *Documents on Nazism, 1919–1945* (London: Cape, 1974)

Norwood, Stephen H., *The Third Reich in the Ivory Tower: Complicity and Conflict on American Campuses* (Cambridge: Cambridge University Press, 2009)

O'Keeffe, Paul, *Some Sort of Genius* (London: Jonathan Cape, 2000)

Parker, Peter, *Isherwood: A Life Revealed* (London: Picador, 2005)

Picton, Harold, *Nazis and Germans* (London: Allen & Unwin, 1940)

Pottle, Mark (ed.), *Champion Redoubtable: The Diaries and Letters of Violet Bonham Carter, 1914–1945* (London: Phoenix Giant, 1998)

Pryce-Jones, David, *Unity Mitford: A Quest* (London: Weidenfeld & Nicolson, 1976)

Rawson, Andrew, *Showcasing the Third Reich: The Nuremberg Rallies* (Stroud: History Press, 2012)

Reynolds, Rothay, *When Freedom Shrieked* (London: Victor Gollancz, 1939)

Rhodes James, Robert (ed.) *Chips: The Diaries of Sir Henry Channon* (London: Penguin, 1937)

Rhodes James, Robert, *Victor Cazalet: A Portrait* (London: Hamish Hamilton, 1976)

Roberts, Andrew, *The Holy Fox: The Life of Lord Halifax* (London: Head of Zeus, 1991)

Roddie, W. Stewart, *Peace Patrol* (London: Christophers, 1932)

Roskill, Stephen W., *Man of Secrets* (London: Collins, 1970–74)

Sachs, Harvey, *Reflections on Toscanini* (London: Robson Books, 1992)

Saikia, Robin (ed.), *The Red Book: The Membership List of the Right Club –
1939* (London: Foxley Books, 2010)

Schindler, René, *Ein Schweizer Erlebt Das Geheime Deutschland* [*A Swiss
experience of Secret Germany*] (Zurich and New York: Europa Verlag,
1945)

Seymour, Miranda, *Noble Endeavours: The Life of Two Countries, England and
Germany, in Many Stories* (London: Simon & Schuster, 2013)

Shapiro, James, *Oberammergau* (London: Little, Brown & Co., 2000)

Shirer, William L., *Berlin Diary* (New York: Alfred A. Knopf, 1941)

Smith, Howard K., *Last Train from Berlin* (London: Cresset Press, 1942)

Smith, Michael, *Foley, the Spy Who Saved 10,000 Jews* (London: Hodder &
Stoughton, 1999)

Spender, Stephen, *World within World: The Autobiography of Stephen Spender*
(London: Readers Union, 1953)

Spotts, Frederic, *Bayreuth: A History of the Wagner Festival* (New Haven and
London: Yale University Press, 1994)

Sylvester, A. J. and Cross, C. (eds), *Life with Lloyd George:
The Diary of A. J. Sylvester, 1931–45* (New York: Harper
& Row, 1975)

Sylvester, David, *The Brutality of Fact: Interviews with Francis Bacon*
(London: Thames & Hudson, 1987)

Taylor, D. J., *Bright Young People* (London: Chatto & Windus, 2007)

Tennant, Ernest, *True Account* (London: Max Parrish, 1957)

Tifft Fuller, Raymond, *The World's Stage: Oberammergau, 1934* (London:
Cobden-Sanderson, 1934)

Tobias, Fritz, *The Reichstag Fire: Legend and Truth*, translated by Arnold J.
Pomerans (London: Secker & Warburg, 1963)

Tuohy, Ferdinand, *Craziways Europe* (London: Hamish Hamilton, 1934)

Tusa, Ann, and John Tusa, *The Nuremberg Trial* (New York: Skyhorse
Publishing, 2010)

Tweedy, Owen, *Gathering Moss A Memoir of Owen Tweedy* (London:
Sidgwick & Jackson, 1967)

Urbach, Karina, *Go-Betweens for Hitler* (Oxford: Oxford University Press,
2015)

Van Til, William, *The Danube Flows through Fascism* (New York and
London: Charles Scribner's Sons, 1938)

Vansittart, The Rt Hon. Lord, *Lessons of my Life* (London: Hutchinson,
1943)

Vassiltchikov, Princess Marie 'Missie', *The Berlin Diaries, 1940–45* (London:
Pimlico, 1999)

Waddell, Dan, *Field of Shadows: The Remarkable True Story of the English
Cricket Tour of Nazi Germany 1937* (London: Bantam Press, 2014)

Waddy, Helena, *Oberammergau in the Nazi Era: The Fate of a Catholic Village in Hitler's Germany* (New York and Oxford: Oxford University Press, 2010)

Wagner, Friedelind, *The Royal Family of Bayreuth* (London: Eyre & Spottiswoode, 1948)

Waln, Nora, *The Approaching Storm: One Woman's Story of Germany, 1934–1938* (London: Creset Women's Voices, 1988)

Walters, Guy, *Berlin Games: How Hitler Stole the Olympic Dream* (London: John Murray, 2006)

Ward Price, George, *I Know These Dictators* (London: Harrap, 1937)

Wessling, Berndt W., *Toscanini in Bayreuth* (München: Desch, 1976)

Wheeler-Bennett, John, *Knaves, Fools and Heroes* (London: Macmillan, 1974)

Williamson, Anne, *Henry Williamson: Tarka and the Last Romantic* (Stroud: Alan Sutton, 1995)

Williamson, Henry, *Goodbye West Country* (London: Putnam, 1937)

Wilson, Arnold Talbot, *Walks and Talks Abroad, The Diary of a Member of Parliament in 1934–36* (Oxford: Oxford University Press, 1939)

Wolfe, Thomas, *You Can't Go Home Again*, 2 volumes (Gloucester: Dodo Press, 2008)

Woolf, Leonard (ed.), *A Writer's Diary: Being Extracts from the Diary of Virginia Woolf* (London: Hogarth Press, 1953)

Woolf, Leonard, *Downhill All the Way: An Autobiography of the Years 1919–1939* (London: Hogarth Press, 1967)

Wrench, John Evelyn, *Immortal Years (1937–1944): As Viewed from Five Continents* (London: Hutchinson, 1945)

Wrench, John Evelyn, *Francis Yeats-Brown* (London: Eyre & Spottiswoode, 1948)

Wrench, John Evelyn, *Geoffrey Dawson and Our Times* (London: Hutchinson, 1955)

Wright, Jonathan, *Gustav Stresemann: Weimar's Greatest Statesman* (Oxford: Oxford University Press, 2002)

Xianlin, Ji, *Zehn Jahre in Deutschland [Ten Years in Germany] (1935–1945)*, (Gottingen: Gottingen University Press, 2009); translated from *Ji Xianlin liu De huiyi lu [Memories of Study in Germany]* (Hong Kong: Zhonghua shuju, 1993)

Xianlin, Ji, *Ji Xianlin ri ji: liu De sui ye [Ji Xianlin Diaries: My Stay in Germany]*, (Nanchang Shi: Jiangxi Renmin Chubanshi, 2014) 6 vols

Youngday, Biddy, *Flags in Berlin* (published privately by Mary Brimacombe and Clara Lowy, 2012)

Ziegler, Philip, *King Edward VIII* (London: Collins, 1990)

Archives Consulted

UK
Archives of the National Maritime Museum, Greenwich
Beckett Archive, University of Reading
Bodleian Library, University of Oxford
Borthwick Institute, University of York
British Library
Cambridge University Library
Charterhouse School Archives
Churchill Archives Centre, Churchill College, University of Cambridge
Coleraine Library, University of Ulster
Cumbria Archive Centre
Eton College Archives
Exeter Cathedral Archives
Henry Williamson Literary Estate Archive (HWLEA)
Hull History Centre
Liddell Hart Military Archives, King's College, London
Middle East Centre Archive, St Antony's College, University of Oxford
Mitford Archives, Chatsworth House
National Archives
National Library of Wales
Parliamentary Archives
Public Record Office of Northern Ireland
Royal Academy of Music, London
Society of Friends Library, London
Thomas Cook Archives, Peterborough
University of Warwick Archives
West Sussex Public Record Office

USA
American University Archive, Washington, DC (AUA)
Archives and Special collections, Rembert E. Stokes Learning Resources
    Center, Wilberforce University

Beinecke Library, Yale University
Bryn Mawr College
Columbia University Archives
Harry Ransom Center at the University of Texas at Austin
Herbert Hoover Presidential Library
Lake Placid Olympic Museum
Library of Congress, Manuscript Division
Louis Round Wilson Special Collections, University of North Carolina
Northwestern University Archives
Rush Rhees Library, Department of Rare Books and Special Collections,
    University of Rochester
Sophia Smith Collection and Smith College Archives
Special Collections Research Center, Morris Library, Southern Illinois
    University
Special Collections University of Kentucky Library
Stanford Digital Repository
Swem Library Special Collections, College of William and Mary
United States Holocaust Memorial Museum (online)
University of Chicago Library, Special Collections
University of Massachusetts, Amherst Libraries Special Collections and
    University Archives
Virginia Historical Society

Germany
Auswärtiges Amt Politisches Archiv, Berlin
Hessisches Staatsarchiv, Darmstadt
Richard Wagner Museum

Australia
National Library of Australia, Canberra

New Zealand
Alexander Turnbull Library, Wellington

The Travellers

Aga Khan III, Sir Sultan Mohammed Shah (1877–1957). Leader of the Nizari Ismailis. He was president of the League of Nations when he met Hitler in 1937. Like many other distinguished visitors to Germany, he came away from the encounter convinced of Hitler's sincerity.

Allen, Mary (1878–1964). Pioneer British policewoman of extreme right-wing views. She narrowly missed being interned during the Second World War.

Anderson, Ida (née Watt; 1918–2013). A pupil at the George Watson's Ladies' College in Edinburgh, she went on a school trip to the Rhineland in 1936.

Auden, W. H. (1907–1973). It was the poet's ten-month stay in Germany (1928–1929) that first exposed him to the political and economic unrest that was to become such a central theme in his poetry. In addition, it provided him with an opportunity to explore his homosexuality.

Bacon, Francis (1909–1992). One of the most celebrated artists of the twentieth century. His powerful images focus on human trauma, alienation and suffering. As a teenager, he spent several months in Germany in 1927.

Barlow, Brigit (1916–2004). Writer and musician. She was married to Erasmus Darwin Barlow. Her autobiography, *A Family Affair*, covers her time in Germany as a teenager, life in England during the war and marriage into the Darwin clan.

Beckett, Samuel (1906–1989). Irish playwright and novelist. One of the most influential literary figures of the twentieth century. He travelled in Germany from September 1936 until April 1937. During the war he joined the French Resistance.

Beecham, Sir Thomas (1879–1961). Conductor. In 1932 he founded (with Sir Malcolm Sargent) the London Philharmonic Orchestra, which he took on a controversial tour of Germany in 1936. He employed Jewish refugee, Berta Geissmar, as his orchestra manager after she was forced to quit her job in Berlin with the conductor Wilhelm Furtwängler.

Benoist-Méchin, Jacques (1901–1983). Right-wing politician and journalist. As a young army officer he was stationed in the Ruhr during the French occupation. A Vichy government collaborator, he was imprisoned after the war.

Bernays, Robert (1902–1945). Journalist and politician. He was elected the Liberal MP for Bristol North in 1931. A consistent critic of the Nazis, he visited Germany a number of times during the 1930s. He was killed in an aeroplane crash over the Adriatic.

Bernstorff, Countess Bridget von (1910–1987). British born, she married Hugo von Bernstorff in 1939. Her letters give a vivid account of life in Germany during the war.

Birchall, Frederick (1871–1955). *New York Times* correspondent. In 1934 he won the Pulitzer Prize for his reporting on Nazi Germany.

Block, Gösta (1898–1955). Journalist, newspaper editor, public relations consultant and businessman. His right-wing sympathies led him to accept a broadcasting job in Berlin in 1942.

Boettcher, Emily (1907–1992). A concert pianist from South Dakota who studied in Berlin during the late 1930s.

Bogen, Dorothy (married name Farrington; 1905–1996). A seventeen-year-old Californian tourist who visited Germany in 1922 with her parents.

Bonham Carter, Lady Violet (1887–1969). A Liberal activist, she was the daughter of Herbert Asquith, British prime minister, 1908–1916.

Boyle, Lady Margaret (married name Stirling-Aird; 1920–2015). Daughter of the 8th Earl of Glasgow. Like many other upper-class girls of her generation, she went to a finishing school in Munich.

Boyle, Dr William (1903–1982) and Mrs Eithne (1911–1984). They rescued Greta, a disabled Jewish girl, while on honeymoon in Germany in 1936. They took her back to their home in Kenya.

Bradshaw, Margaret (1906–1996). A Cambridge history graduate, she married Colonel John Bradshaw of the Indian Political Service. By chance, she was alone in Berlin on Kristallnacht having gone there for medical treatment.

Brown, Ivan (1908–1963). American bobsledder. He won a gold medal at the 1936 Winter Olympics.

Bryant, Sir Arthur (1899–1985). Historian of right-wing views whose books won great acclaim during his lifetime. He was a regular columnist for the *Illustrated London News*.

Buchman, The Reverend Frank (1878–1961). Founder of the Oxford Group, also known as Moral Re-Armament, 1938–2001, and then subsequently Initiatives of Change. He attended the 1935 Nuremberg Rally.

Bulgaria, King Boris of (1894–1943). He attended the 1936 Berlin Olympics. During the war he personally halted the deportation of Jews from Bulgaria to the death camps.

Buller, Amy (1891–1974). Closely associated with the Student Christian Movement, she organised several conferences in Germany with the aim of better understanding the Nazis' approach to philosophy and religion. Her book, *Darkness over Germany*, records the numerous conversations she held with a wide range of Germans.

Burn, Michael (1912–2010). Soldier, journalist and writer. As a young man he was favourably impressed by Nazi Germany. He visited Dachau and attended the 1935 Nuremberg Rally.

Byron, Robert (1905–1941). Writer, art critic, historian and ardent critic of the Nazis. He was present at the 1938 Nuremberg Rally. He died when the ship in which he was travelling to Egypt was torpedoed.

Çambel, Halet (1916–2014). A member of the Turkish fencing team at the 1936 Berlin Olympics and the first Muslim woman to take part in the Olympic Games. She refused to meet Hitler.

Cazalet, Thelma (1899–1989). A keen feminist, she was Conservative MP for Islington, 1931–1945.

Cazalet, Victor (1896–1943). Elected Conservative MP for Chippenham in 1924, he travelled frequently to Germany in the 1930s. He was killed in an aeroplane crash in Gibraltar.

Chamberlain, Houston Stewart (1855–1927). British-born writer and philosopher who became a German citizen in 1916. Married to Richard Wagner's daughter Eva, he lived in Bayreuth. The Nazis revered his racist (and internationally acclaimed) book *Foundations of the Nineteenth Century* (1899).

Chamberlain, Sir Neville (1869–1940). Remembered chiefly for his appeasement policies, he was British prime minister, 1937–1940.

Channon, Sir Henry (1897–1958). Known as Chips, he was an American-born British Conservative MP, socialite and diarist. He attended the 1936 Berlin Olympics.

Chardonne, Jacques (1884–1968). Writer and Vichy collaborator. He was a member of the Groupe Collaboration that encouraged close cultural ties between France and Nazi Germany.

Christie, John (1882–1962). Founder of Glyndebourne Opera (1934), he was a regular visitor to Haus Hirth. This modest chalet near Garmisch-Partenkirchen was a favourite haunt of American and British literati between the wars.

Christie, Group Captain Malcolm (1881–1971). An air engineer who travelled extensively in Germany, 1933–1940, gathering information for the Foreign Office.

Clark, Manning (1915–1991). Australian historian and author of the six-volume *History of Australia*. In 1938 he visited his fiancé Dymphna Lodewyckx, then a PhD student at Bonn University.

Cole, J. A. (dates unknown). British writer whose book *Just Back from Germany* presents a graphic account of everyday life under the Nazis in the late 1930s.

Conwell-Evans, T. Philip (1891–1968). Historian and figure of mystery. Ostensibly a keen supporter of the Nazis (he was one of the founders of the Anglo-German Fellowship in 1935 and later editor of the *Anglo-German Review*), it is possible that he was in fact working for British Intelligence.

Cook, Ida (1904–1986) and Louise (1901–1991). Opera-loving sisters who made multiple trips to Germany in the late 1930s to rescue Jewish refugees and to smuggle out their valuables. Ida wrote romantic novels under the name Mary Burchell.

Cox, Sir Geoffrey (1910–2008). Before going up to Oxford University as a Rhodes Scholar in 1932, Cox spent the summer learning German in Heidelberg. After the war he became a pioneer television journalist.

Crowe, Dr Sybil (1908–1993). An Oxford academic who was working on her PhD at Cambridge University when she visited Germany in June 1936. Her father, the diplomat Sir Eyre Crowe, was the Foreign Office's foremost German expert in the years leading up to the First World War.

D'Abernon, Edgar Vincent 1st Viscount (1857–1941). The first post-First World War British ambassador to Germany (1920–1925). His wife Helen (1886–1954) disliked Berlin but supported her husband's efforts to restore Anglo-German relations.

De Margerie, Pierre (1861–1942). His term as French ambassador to Germany (1922–1931) encompassed the French occupation of the Ruhr.

De Rougemont, Denis (1906–1985). Swiss philosopher and writer. He spent a year teaching at Frankfurt University, 1935–1936.

Detzer, Dorothy (1893–1981). American Quaker involved with relief work after the First World War.

Dodd, Martha (1908–1990). Daughter of American ambassador, William E. Dodd. Initially supportive of the Nazis, she was later recruited as a Soviet spy.

Dodd, William E. (1869–1940). American ambassador to Berlin, 1933–1937. A liberal Democrat, he was a consistent critic of the Nazis. He found himself frequently out of step with the State Department.

Domvile, Vice Admiral Sir Barry (1878–1971). Director of Naval Intelligence, 1927–1930, and president of the Royal Naval College Greenwich, 1932–1934. His pro-Nazi sympathies led to his internment during the Second World War.

Du Bois, W. E. B. (1868–1963). African-American academic, Civil Rights activist, Germanophile and keen Wagnerian. He found his experience of Nazi Germany difficult to summarise. He was one of many foreign travellers to notice similarities between National Socialism and communism.

Duncan-Jones, Arthur (1879–1955). Dean of Chichester from 1924 until his death.

Duncan-Jones, Ursula (married name Baily; 1920–2007). Daughter of the Dean of Chichester, Arthur Duncan-Jones. In 1938 she spent some months living with a German family in Osnabrück. She served as a Wren during the war, later becoming active in Amnesty International.

Fairbank, Lucy (1892–1983). Yorkshire schoolmistress and cine-camera enthusiast. She went to the Oberammergau Passion Play in 1934 with her friend Clarice Mountain.

Fenn, The Reverend Eric (dates not known). Presbyterian theologian and college principal. At the time of his visit to Berlin in 1935, he was assistant director of the Student Christian Movement.

Finlayson, Horace (1885–1969). Financial adviser to the British Embassy in Berlin at the height of the hyperinflation crisis in 1923.

Flannery, Harry W. (1900–1975). American journalist and broadcaster. He was CBS correspondent in Berlin, 1940–1941.

Forwood, Sir Dudley, Bt (1912–2001). Equerry to the Duke of Windsor, he accompanied the Duke and Duchess on their tour of Germany in 1937.

Franck, Harry, A. (1881–1962). Travel writer. He served in the army during the First World War, and afterwards in the Rhineland with the American Expeditionary Forces.

François-Poncet, André (1887–1978). French ambassador to Germany, 1931–1938. The Germans imprisoned him for three years during the war.

Fry, Basil (dates unknown). Christopher Isherwood's cousin. On Isherwood's first visit to Germany in 1928 he stayed with Fry in Bremen, where the latter was British vice-consul.

Fry, Joan Mary (1862–1955). British Quaker campaigner for peace and social reform. She travelled all over Germany in the immediate aftermath of the First World War giving lectures and delivering aid. Her brother was the Bloomsbury artist and critic Roger Fry.

Gibbs, Sir Philip (1877–1962). Writer and war correspondent.

Gide, André (1869–1951). French writer and winner of the Nobel Prize for Literature 1947.

Gilbert, Prentiss (1883–1939). Diplomat. He attended the 1938 Nuremberg Rally. He died in Berlin while serving as American chargé d'affaires.

Glickman, Marty (1917–2001). American athlete. Chosen to compete in the 400-metre relay race at the 1936 Berlin Olympics, he was withdrawn at the last minute. It was generally assumed that this was because he was Jewish.

Goldberg, Herman (1915–1997). A member of the American baseball team that went to the Berlin Olympics. The team did not compete but played exhibition games to introduce the sport to the Germans.

Goodland, Mary (married name Burns; 1915–2016). After graduating from Oxford University, she taught social work and mental health at the London School of Economics.

Gordon Lennox, Diana (1908–1982). The daughter of an admiral, she took part in the Winter Olympics as a member of the Canadian women's skiing team.

Greene, Hugh C. (1910–1987). *Daily Telegraph* correspondent in Berlin from 1934 until he was expelled in 1939. Director-general of the BBC, 1960–1969, and younger brother of the novelist Graham Greene, who visited him in Berlin.

Griffin, Kenneth P. (1912–2002). American gymnast who took part in the 1936 Berlin Olympics.

Guérin, Daniel (1904–1988). French left-wing writer best known for his book *Anarchism: From Theory to Practice* (1970).

Halifax, Edward Wood, 1st Earl of (1881–1959). A former viceroy of India, he was foreign secretary, 1938–1940, and a key proponent of appeasement. He was ambassador to the United States, 1941–1946.

Hamilton, Cicely (1872–1952). Actor, novelist, journalist and feminist. She recounted her experiences of travelling around Weimar Germany in her book *Modern Germanies* (1931).

Hamsun, Knut (1859–1952). Norwegian writer. He won the Nobel Prize for Literature 1920. He admired the Nazis and hated the English in equal measure.

Hankey, Maurice, 1st Baron (1877–1963). Cabinet secretary to Lloyd George during the First World War, he remained in the post until 1928.

Hartley, Marsden (1877–1943). American artist influenced by German Expressionism.

Heingartner, Robert W. (1881–1945). American diplomat who served as a consular official in Frankfurt, 1928–1937.

Henderson, Sir Nevile (1882–1942). A supporter of appeasement, he succeeded Sir Eric Phipps as ambassador to Germany in 1937.

Hesse and the Rhine, HRH Princess Margaret of (1913–1997). She met her husband Prince Ludwig at Haus Hirth near Garmisch-Partenkirchen. They were married in London in 1937 while he was working at the German Embassy.

Heygate, Sir John, 4th Baronet (1903–1976). Journalist and novelist, he worked at the UFA studios in Berlin in the early 1930s. He attended the 1935 Nuremberg Rally with Henry Williamson.

Hill, Derek (1916–2000). An English portrait and landscape painter based in Ireland. He studied theatre design in Munich in 1934.

Hirschfeld, Dr Magnus (1868–1935). A German-Jewish physician and sexologist. His Institute for Sexual Research was opened in Berlin on 6 July 1919.

Howard, Brian (1905–1958). Described by Auden as the most desperately unhappy person he had ever known, he was a key member of the 'Bright Young Things' set. He hated Berlin, which he visited in 1927. He was a friend of Thomas Mann's children, Erika and Klaus.

Isherwood, Christopher (1904–1986). The writer who immortalised Weimar Germany in his *Berlin Stories* (1945) consisting of two novellas, *Goodbye to Berlin* and *Mr Norris Changes Trains*.

Jamieson, Robert (dates unknown). In 1939 he sent regular reports to Lord Londonderry from Germany where he was teaching English.

Ji Xianlin (1911–2009). One of the most distinguished Chinese scholars of his generation. He obtained his PhD in Sanskrit studies at Heidelberg University in 1941. Having initially intended to spend only a couple of years studying in Germany, he was trapped there by the war and did not return to China until 1946.

Jones, Gareth (1905–1935). A Welsh journalist who accompanied Hitler and Goebbels to an election rally in 1933. He was murdered in China.

Jones, Rhys (dates unknown). A Welsh teacher who, as a young man, kept a lively account of his 1937 holiday in the Rhineland.

Jones, Rufus (1863–1948). American Quaker, writer, philosopher and college professor. He led a delegation to Germany after Kristallnacht.

Jungmittag, Biddy (née Macnaghten, 1904–1987). The daughter of a Northern Ireland judge, she rebelled from her upper-class background by joining the Communist Party and marrying a working-class German photographer. She published her work under the name Biddy Youngday.

Kiaer, Alice (1893–1967). Captain of the American women's skiing team (the Red Stockings) at the Winter Olympics.

King, Michael (1899–1984). Father of Martin Luther King. He changed both his and his son's names to 'Martin Luther' on his return from Germany in 1934.

Kirkpatrick, Sir Ivone (1897–1964). First secretary at the British Embassy, 1933–1938. He accompanied Lord Halifax to the latter's meeting with Hitler in November 1937. After the war he was appointed British high commissioner for Germany.

Larkin, Sydney (1884–1948). Father of the poet Philip Larkin, he was appointed City Treasurer of Coventry in 1922. He and his family travelled regularly to Germany for their summer holidays throughout the 1930s.

Legge, Walter (1906–1979). Founder of the Philharmonia Orchestra, he attended the 1933 Bayreuth Festival as music critic for the *Manchester Guardian*. He was married to the soprano, Elisabeth Schwarzkopf.

Leitner, Maria (1892–1942). A Jewish Hungarian writer and journalist. She entered Nazi Germany illegally to report for the left-wing press. She died in Marseilles while trying to obtain a visa for America.

Lindbergh, Anne Spencer (1906–2001). Married to Charles Lindbergh, she too was an aviator and wrote books on a wide range of subjects.

Lindbergh, Charles (1902–1974). In 1927, he made the first non-stop flight across the Atlantic. The overwhelming publicity generated by the kidnapping and murder of his baby son in 1932 forced the family to take refuge in Europe. He and his wife Anne regularly stayed in Berlin with Truman Smith (military attaché to the American Embassy) during the 1930s.

Lindsay, Sir Ronald (1877–1945). He succeeded Lord D'Abernon as British ambassador to Germany, 1926–1928.

Lloyd George, David, 1st Earl Lloyd George of Dwyfor (1863–1945). Liberal politician and statesman. He was prime minister of the wartime coalition government, 1916–1922, and played a major role at the Paris Peace Conference of 1919.

Lodewyckx, Dymphna (1916–2000). Australian linguist and educator. She witnessed the 1933 book burning as a schoolgirl in Munich. She later returned to Germany to study for a PhD at Bonn University. She was married to the historian Manning Clark.

Londonderry, Charles Stewart Henry Vane-Tempest-Stewart, 7th Marquess of (1878–1949). A prominent supporter of appeasement, he travelled frequently to Germany in the 1930s where he was entertained by leading Nazis. The Londonderrys' teenage daughter Mairi accompanied them to the Winter Olympics.

Lubin, Frank J. (1910–1999). He played on the American basketball team at the 1936 Berlin Olympics.

Lunn, Sir Arnold (1888–1974). Skier, mountaineer and inventor of the slalom race. He was a judge at the Winter Olympics when his son Peter captained the British team. Both men refused to march in the inaugural parade.

McDonald, James Grover (1886–1964). American diplomat who was League of Nations High Commissioner for Refugees Coming from Germany, 1933–1935. After the war he was appointed ambassador to Israel, 1949–1951.

Mann, Tom (1856–1941). British communist and trade unionist who visited Berlin in 1924.

Markham, Violet (1872–1959). Writer, social reformer, administrator and granddaughter of the architect and gardener, Sir Joseph Paxton. She accompanied her husband (a colonel) on his posting to Cologne in 1919.

Marten, Dr Karl (dates unknown). A charlatan doctor who 'treated' many English upper-class men to 'cure' their homosexuality.

Martin du Gard, Roger (1881–1958). French writer who won the Nobel Prize for Literature 1937.

Melchior, Lauritz (1890–1973). Danish tenor famous for his Wagnerian roles. Early in his career he was financially supported by the English novelist Sir Hugh Walpole.

Miller, Dr Edmund (dates unknown). Director of the Junior Year Abroad programme, which provided American students with the opportunity to study in Europe. Based in Munich, Miller resigned his post soon after Kristallnacht.

Mitford, Diana (1910–2003). The fourth of Lord and Lady Redesdale's children, her first husband was Bryan Guinness. In 1936 she married Sir Oswald

Mosley in the Berlin home of Josef and Magda Goebbels. Her close association with the Nazis led to her internment during the war.

Mitford, Thomas (1909–1945). Lord and Lady Redesdale's only son. He was killed fighting the Japanese in Burma.

Mitford, Unity (1914–1948). Fifth child of Lord and Lady Redesdale, who became famously infatuated with Hitler.

Morris, Sylvia (née Heywood, 1920–). Professional musician who in later life became involved with the theatre. She was studying in Dresden until a week before the outbreak of war.

Mowrer, Lilian (1889–1990). A writer and theatre critic married to Edgar Mowrer, the *Chicago Daily News* correspondent in Berlin. He was forced by the Nazis to leave Germany in 1933.

Nicolson, Sir Harold (1886–1968). Diplomat, author, diarist, politician and husband of Vita Sackville-West. A devoted Francophile, he was posted to Berlin in 1928 but resigned from the Diplomatic Service the following year.

Patiala, Sir Bhupinder Singh, Maharaja of (1891–1938). He served as an honorary Lieutenant Colonel in the First World War, was an accomplished cricketer and the first man to own an aeroplane in India. From 1926 to 1931 he served as chancellor of the Chamber of Princes.

Paul, Brenda Dean (1907–1959). One of many young aspiring actors drawn to Berlin in the hope of finding work at the UFA studios.

Pegler, Westbrook (1894–1969). American journalist who reported on the 1936 Winter Olympics. His 'Fair Enough' column was widely syndicated.

Pemberton, Barbara (married name Lodge, 1921–2013). During the war she served in the WRAF 'Y' service, where her bilingual English and German was used to the full.

Phipps, Sir Eric (1875–1945). In 1933 he succeeded Sir Horace Rumbold as British ambassador in Berlin, remaining there until 1937 when he was posted as ambassador to France.

Pitt-Rivers, Captain George Henry Lane-Fox (1890–1966). Anthropologist, eugenicist and anti-Semite. His extreme pro-Nazi views led to his internment during the war.

Plotkin, Abraham (1893–1998). Born in the Ukraine, Plotkin emigrated with his Jewish family to America as a small child. He was a prominent activist in the Ladies' Garment Workers Union.

Pollard, Emily (1896–1972). Niece of the Governor of Virginia, John Garland Pollard. She left a diary account of her 1930 holiday in Germany.

Porritt, Arthur, 1st Baron (1900–1994). New Zealand physician, statesman and athlete. A member of the International Olympic Committee, he was present at the Berlin Olympics.

Poulton, Dr Jill (née Hunt, 1923–2017). As a teenager she went with her family on several motoring holidays to Germany in the late 1930s. After studying medicine during the war, she practised as a GP in Cambridge.

Prussia, Princess Margaret of (1872–1954). Married to Prince Charles Frederick of Hesse, she was a granddaughter of Queen Victoria and the younger sister of Kaiser Wilhelm II. She lived in Schloss Friedrichshof at Kronberg near Frankfurt. Two of her sons were killed in the First World War and another son (Prince Christoph of Hesse) was killed in the Second World War. Her daughter-in-law, Princess Sophie of Hesse, was the youngest sister of HRH Prince Philip, Duke of Edinburgh.

Remy, Arthur F. J. (c. 1871–1954). Villard professor of Germanic philology at Columbia University, NYC. He was present at the anniversary celebrations of Heidelberg University in June 1936.

Rieppel, Franz Wolfgang (1917–2000). A Swiss economist who wrote of his experiences in wartime Germany under the pseudonym René Schindler.

Rothermere, Harold, 1st Viscount (1868–1940). Owner of the *Daily Mail* and the *Daily Mirror*. Initially he was an enthusiastic supporter of Hitler whom he met on various occasions.

Rumbold, Sir Anthony, 10th Baronet (1911–1983). In 1935 he followed his father, Sir Horace, into the Diplomatic Service, ending his career as ambassador to Austria.

Rumbold, Constantia (1906–2001). Sir Horace and Lady Rumbold's daughter, whose description of life in Berlin is as vivid as her mother's.

Rumbold, Lady Etheldred (1879–1964). Wife of Sir Horace. She wrote delightfully unselfconscious letters to her mother throughout her time in Berlin.

Rumbold, Sir Horace, 9th Baronet (1869–1941). He succeeded Sir Ronald Lindsay as ambassador to Germany in 1928, where he remained until 1933. He was highly critical of the Nazis.

Runkle, Barbara (married name Hawthorne, 1912–1992). She studied piano and singing, first at the Juilliard School in New York and then in Munich. A talented writer and linguist, she married an Englishman in 1951 and settled in Cambridge.

Sackville-West, Edward, 5th Baron Sackville (1901–1965). Music critic, novelist and cousin of Vita Sackville-West. He first went to Germany in 1924 to undergo Dr Marten's 'cure' for homosexuality. He returned in 1927 to study music and German in Dresden.

Sackville-West, Vita (1892–1962). Writer, garden designer and wife of Sir Harold Nicolson. She disliked both Germany and the Germans.

Schiefer, Clara Louise (dates unknown). She visited Germany with an American school party in the summer of 1933.

Sefton Delmer, Denis (1904–1979). *Daily Express* correspondent in Berlin during the early 1930s. He witnessed the burning of the Reichstag.

Shirer, William (1904–1993). American journalist and war correspondent famous for his broadcasts from Nazi Germany.

Sinclair-Loutit, Kenneth (1913–2003). In 1934 he bicycled through Germany with a fellow student. After leaving Cambridge, he studied medicine and fought in the Spanish Civil War. Between 1961 and his retirement in 1973, he worked for the World Health Organization.

Smith, The Reverend H. K. Percival (1898–1965). A keen supporter of Nazi Germany, he gave a glowing account of his visit there in the spring of 1939. He was Archdeacon of Lynn, 1956–1961.

Smith, Howard K. (1914–2002). American journalist, broadcaster and political commentator. He caught the last train out of Berlin to Switzerland before America entered the war.

Smith, Katherine Alling Hollister (1898–1992). Known as Kay, she was the wife of Truman Smith. A woman of strong conservative views, she wrote 'My Life', an unpublished memoir of her time in Germany.

Smith, Colonel Truman (1893–1970). After serving in the First World War he was stationed in Koblenz with the American Expeditionary Forces. Appointed assistant military attaché at the American Embassy in Berlin, 1920–1924, then military attaché, 1935–1939. The first American official to interview Hitler (1922), he later became a close friend of Charles Lindbergh.

Spender, Stephen (1909–1995). The English poet who, like Auden and Isherwood, was strongly influenced by the months he spent in Germany during the Weimar Republic.

Stewart Roddie, Lieutenant Colonel William (1878–1961). He served in Berlin on the Inter-Allied Control Commission, 1920–1927. He personally knew many key military and political figures of the period, as well as members of the former German royal family.

Stuart, Francis (1902–2000). Irish writer. The years he spent in Nazi Germany led to much controversy but did not prevent him from being awarded Ireland's highest artistic accolade.

Tétaz, Numa (1926–2005). A Swiss businessman based in Munich between 1923 and 1943. Writing under the pseudonym René Juvet, he described his experiences in his book *Ich war dabei …* (1944).

Tonge, Joan (1916–2004). One of many upper-class English girls sent to finishing school in Munich during the 1930s.

Toscanini, Arturo (1867–1957). The great Italian maestro conducted twice at Bayreuth, in 1930 and 1931. But in protest at the Nazis' treatment of Jewish musicians, he refused to return in 1933 despite the pleadings of Winifred Wagner.

Toynbee, Antony (1913–1939). Son of the historian Arnold Toynbee, he studied at Bonn University in 1934.

Tresidder, Mary Curry (1893–1970). She attended the Winter Olympics with her husband Donald Tresidder, who served as president of Stanford University, 1943–1948.

Turville-Petre, Francis (1901–1941). British archaeologist who was friends with Auden and Isherwood in Berlin.

Tweedy, Owen (1888–1960). British soldier, civil servant and freelance journalist. He kept a detailed record of his 1933 visit to Germany in the weeks immediately after Hitler came to power.

Vane-Tempest-Stewart, Lady Mairi (married name Bury; 1921–2009). Youngest daughter of the 7th Marquess of Londonderry and his wife Edith, she visited Germany with her parents in 1936 and attended the Winter Olympics.

Vansittart, Robert, 1st Baron (1881–1957). Permanent under secretary at the Foreign Office, 1930–1938. He attended the Berlin Olympics. Vansittart and Sir Eric Phipps were brothers-in-law.

Wakefield, Joan (married name Raynsford; 1920–). After studying in Berlin during the spring of 1938 she spent the summer with a German family in Upper Silesia. She was again in Germany the following summer, returning to England only a couple of months before the outbreak of war.

Wall, Edward (1908–1988). Teacher, lawyer and politician. Having travelled extensively in Central and Eastern Europe in the late 1930s, he became an expert on Germany's minority populations. In later life he was appointed a judge at the Supreme Restitution Court in Germany.

Wallin, Erik (1921–1997). Swedish soldier who served as an officer in the Waffen-SS on the Eastern front, and fought in the battle of Berlin.

Waln, Nora (1895–1964). American novelist and journalist. She lived in Germany, 1934–1938.

Walpole, Sir Hugh (1884–1941). Celebrated British novelist. He accompanied the Danish tenor Lauritz Melchior to the Bayreuth Festival in 1925, where he met Hitler and became friends with Winifred Wagner.

Ward Price, George (1886–1961). As *Daily Mail* correspondent in Berlin, he formed close links with the Nazis and won the trust of Hitler.

Wasserman, Bradford (1918–1986). Fifteen-year-old Jewish Boy Scout from Richmond, Virginia. He kept a diary of his 1933 visit to Germany.

Westminster, Loelia, Duchess of (née Ponsonby, 1902–1993). She stayed with her friend Constantia Rumbold in Berlin in the early 1930s.

Wheeler-Bennett, Sir John (1902–1975). British historian who between 1927 and 1934 spent much of his time in Germany. He was on personal terms with many of the most significant politicians of the period.

Wildman, Herbert (1912–1989). American water-polo player who competed in the 1932 and 1936 Olympics.

Williams, Archie (1915–1993). African-American athlete who won gold in the 400 metres at the Berlin Olympics.

Williamson, Henry (1895–1977). First World War veteran, farmer and author of *Tarka the Otter* (1927). He accompanied John Heygate to the 1935 Nuremberg Rally.

Wilson, Sir Arnold (1884–1940). Soldier, writer and politician. Elected MP for Hitchin in 1933, he travelled extensively in Nazi Germany approving of much that he saw. However, at the outbreak of war, although aged fifty-five and an MP, he volunteered for the RAF. He was killed when his bomber was shot down.

Windsor, The Duchess of (1896–1986). Wallis Simpson, an American by birth and double divorcee. Her husband, the former King Edward VIII, abdicated his throne in order to marry her.

Windsor, HRH The Duke of (1894–1972). He became King Edward VIII in January 1936 but abdicated on 11 December in order to marry Mrs Wallis Simpson. As Duke and Duchess of Windsor, the couple made a controversial tour of Germany the following year.

Wolfe, Thomas (1900–1938). American novelist and Germanophile. He travelled extensively in Germany where his books were highly regarded.

Woodruff, John (1915–2007). African-American athlete who caused a sensation at the Berlin Olympics by coming from behind to win gold in the 800 metres.

Woolf, Leonard (1880–1969). Writer, political theorist and husband of Virginia Woolf with whom he founded the Hogarth Press in 1917.

Woolf, Virginia (1882–1941). Writer and leading member of the Bloomsbury Group. Mental illness led her to take her own life by drowning.

Wrench, Sir Evelyn (1882–1966). A dedicated advocate of the British Empire, he was founder of the Royal Over-Seas League and the English Speaking Union. He was editor of *The Spectator*, 1925–1932.

Wright, Dr Milton S. J. (1903–1972). African-American academic who gained a PhD in economics from Heidelberg University in 1932. While there, he had a meeting with Hitler lasting several hours. He became Dean of Wilberforce College, Ohio, in 1959.

Wyndham Lewis, Percy (1882–1957). Painter, novelist and founder of the Vorticist movement. After visiting Germany in 1930 he published *Hitler*, the first full-length study of the Führer.

Zamperini, Louis Silvie (1917–2014). American athlete. He ran in the 500 metres at the Berlin Olympics.

Notes

Introduction
1 Martha Dodd, *Through Embassy Eyes* (London: Gollancz, 1939), p. 25.
2 Pegler syndicated column, 'Fair Enough', 2 April 1936.
3 Quoted in Dirk Voss, 'Travel into the Heart of Evil: American Tourists in Nazi Germany, 1933–1939'; 'Ernst Schmitz Gives Talk on German Travel Facilities', *Daily Boston Globe*, 29 March 1938. For more detailed statistics regarding British and American travel to Germany, see Rudy Koshar, *German Travel Cultures* (Oxford and New York: Berg, 2000), p. 129.
4 Louis MacNeice, from *Autumn Journal*, IV (London: Faber & Faber, 1939).
5 Nancy Mitford, *Pigeon Pie* (London: Hamish Hamilton, 1940), p. 43.

Chapter 1: Open Wounds
1 W. Stewart Roddie, *Peace Patrol* (London: Christophers, 1932), p. 97.
2 Hedda Adlon, *Hotel Adlon: The Life and Death of a Great Hotel* (London: Barrie Books, 1958), pp. 74–75.
3 Harry A. Franck, *Vagabonding Through Changing Germany* (New York: Grosset & Dunlap, 1920), p. 172.
4 Ibid., p. 37.
5 Ibid., pp. 25–26.
6 Ibid., pp. 28–29.
7 Violet R. Markham, *A Woman's Watch on the Rhine* (London: Hodder & Stoughton, 1920), p. 181.
8 Franck, p. 74.
9 20 December 1918, Truman Smith papers (TSP), Herbert Hoover Presidential Library.
10 Ibid.
11 Ibid., 23 December.
12 'The American Watch on the Rhine by an American', Society of Friends Library, London, Friends' Emergency War Victims Relief Committee (FEWVRC) 1914–1924, 10/3/7.

13 Truman Smith to his wife Kay, 20 December 1918, TSP.

14 Markham, pp. 15–16.

15 Ibid., pp. 56–57.

16 Ibid., p. 71.

17 Alice Holtby and J. McWilliam (eds.), *Winifred Holtby: Letters to a Friend* (London: Collins, 1937), p. 280.

18 Truman Smith to his wife Kay.

19 Truman Smith to his mother-in-law, 16 March 1919.

20 Truman Smith to his wife Kay, 14 February 1919.

21 Ibid., 23 December 1918.

22 Franck, p. 114.

23 Stewart Roddie to Lord Stamfordhaven, 30 January 1920, Parliamentary Archives, Lloyd George papers, F/29/4/6.

24 Stewart Roddie, pp. 22–23.

25 Ibid., p. 1.

26 Franck, pp. 115, 130, 132–133.

27 Ibid., p. 102.

28 Stewart Roddie, p. 20.

29 Ibid., pp. 138, 139.

30 Franck, p. 19.

31 *The Friend*, 2 May 1919.

32 Joan Mary Fry, *In Downcast Germany* (London: James Clarke, 1944), p. 13.

Chapter 2: Deepening Pain

1 *The Friend*, 8 August 1919.

2 2 August 1919, Society of Friends Library, Relief Mission Germany, Joan M. Fry, FEWVRC/Missions/10/1/6/7.

3 Ibid., 2 August 1919.

4 Franck, pp. 190, 195.

5 Truman Smith to his wife Kay, 11 May 1919, TSP.

6 Stewart Roddie, p. 96.

7 Essen, 28 July 1919, Friends Library, FEWVRC/Missions/10/1/6/7.

8 Markham, p. 128.

9 Franck, p. 268.

10 Ibid., pp. 272–273.

11 Bonham Carter, Diary, 1–2 March 1923, vol. 15, University of Oxford, Bodleian Library (Bod.), Special Collections, MSS. Quoted in Mark Pottle (ed.), *Champion Redoubtable: The Diaries and Letters of Violet Bonham Carter 1914–1945* (London: Weidenfeld & Nicolson, 1998), p. 141.

12 Ibid. (not quoted in Pottle).

13 Ibid., 5 March 1923.

14 Viscountess D'Abernon, *Red Cross and Berlin Embassy, 1915–1926* (London: John Murray, 1946), p. 69.

15 Ibid., p. 83.

16 Ibid., pp. 68–69.

17 Ibid., p. 71.

18 Ibid., p. 78.

19 Bonham Carter, Diary, 3 March 1923.

20 Ibid.

21 D'Abernon, p. 112.

22 Ibid., p. 73.

23 Tom Mann to his wife, 2 April 1924, University of Warwick Archives, Tom Mann papers, MSS 334/3/6/14.

24 Bonham Carter, Diary, 3 March 1923.

25 Ibid., 5 March.

26 Ibid., 10 March.

27 Stewart Roddie, p. 50.

28 3 June 1921, Joan M. Fry papers, TEMP MSS 66/6.

29 Princess Margaret of Prussia to Lady Corkran, 21 October 1924, Bod., MSS Eng. Lett. d. 364.

30 Ibid.

31 25 July 1922, Fry papers, TEMP MSS 66/8.

32 Dorothy Detzer, 3 September, 1923, Society of Friends Library, FEWVRC 1914–24, 10/3/7.

33 Jacques Benoist-Méchin, *À l'épreuve du temps* [*The Test of Time*] (Paris: Julliard, 1989), p. 167.

34 Ibid., p. 164.

35 For contemporary evidence rebutting such allegations, see Sally Marks, 'Black Watch on the Rhine: A Study in Propaganda, Prejudice and Prurience', *European Studies Review*, vol. 13, no. 3 (1983), pp. 297–333.

36 Truman Smith, *Berlin Alert* (Stanford: Hoover Institution Press, 1984), p. 57.

37 Ibid., p. 46.

38 Benoist-Méchin, pp. 172–173.

39 D'Abernon, p. 117.

Chapter 3: Sex and Sun

1 Horace Finlayson, Diary, University of Cambridge, Churchill College, Churchill Archives Centre (CAC) GBR/0014/FLYN.

2 René Juvet, *Ich war dabei...* [*I was there...*] (Zurich: Europa Verlag, 1944), p. 5; René Juvet was the pseudonym of Numa Tétaz.

3   Dorothy Bogen, Diary, 26 September 1922, Farrington Historical Society, San José, CA.

4   *The Friend*, 22 February 1924.

5   John Wheeler Bennett, *Knaves, Fools and Heroes* (London: Macmillan, 1974), p. 21.

6   D'Abernon, 19 October 1923, p. 113.

7   Quoted in Jonathan Wright, *Gustav Stresemann: Weimar's Greatest Statesman* (Oxford: Oxford University Press, 2002), p. 505.

8   Wright, p. 271.

9   Charles Kessler (ed./trans.), *Berlin in Lights: The Diaries of Count Harry Kessler* (New York: Grove Press, 1999), 13 April 1926, p. 290.

10 Sir Ronald Lindsay to Sir Esmé Howard, 17 August 1926, Cumbria Archive Centre (CAC), Carlisle, Howard papers, DHW/4/2/17.

11 Christopher Isherwood, *Christopher and His Kind* (London: Methuen, 1985), p. 10.

12 Edward Sackville-West, commonplace book, 8 November 1927, British Library (BL) Add. MS 68906.

13 Sackville-West, Diary, 19 March 1924, BL, Add. MS 71871C.

14 Ibid., 6, 9, 10, 14 March 1924.

15 B. H. Fry, *Friends, Philosophers and Fishermen* (Oxford: Basil Blackwell, 1932), p. 15.

16 Peter Parker, *Isherwood* (London: Picador, 2005), pp. 153–154.

17 *Christopher and His Kind*, p. 10.

18 Ibid., p. 17.

19 Parker, p. 168.

20 *Christopher and His Kind*, pp. 19–20.

21 Ibid., p. 28.

22 Spender to Isaiah Berlin, n.d. 1931, uncatalogued letters, Bod.

23 *Christopher and His Kind*, p. 30.

24 Michael De-la-Noy, *The Life of Edward Sackville-West* (London: Bodley Head, 1988), p. 117.

25 David Sylvester, *The Brutality of Fact: Interviews with Francis Bacon* (London: Thames & Hudson, 1987), p. 186.

26 'Europe Revisited 1: The Rhineland', *The Spectator*, 20 September 1929.

27 Lilian T. Mowrer, *Journalist's Wife* (London: Heinemann, 1938), p. 194.

28 Emily Pollard, Diary, 29 July 1930, University of North Carolina, Louis Round Wilson Special Collections Library, vol. 7, folder 19.

29 10 October 1930, Spender to Isaiah Berlin.

30 October 1927, letters to James Stern from Brian Howard 1927–1955, BL, Add. MS 80860.

31 June 1931, Paul Bowles to Daniel Burns and Edouard Roditi, Jeffrey Miller (ed.), *The Letters of Paul Bowles* (London: HarperCollins, 1994), pp. 68, 72.

32 26 May 1928, CAC, RDCH 1/2/41.

33 De-la-Noy, pp. 112–113.

34 Lady Rumbold to her mother, Lady Fane, 17 December 1929. Unless otherwise stated, all Rumbold papers quoted are in a private collection (p.c.).

35 Kessler, 22 January 1929, p. 361.

36 Ibid., 10 May 1929, p. 362.

37 Peter Edgerly Firchow, *Strange Meetings* (Washington, DC: Catholic University of America Press, 2008), p. 134.

38 Piers Brendon, *The Dark Valley* (London: Pimlico, 2001), p. 90.

39 Cicely Hamilton, *Modern Germanies* (London: Dent & Sons, 1931), pp. 13–14.

40 'Europe Revisited 1', *The Spectator*, 20 September 1929.

41 Stephen Spender, *World within World: The Autobiography of Stephen Spender* (London: Readers Union, 1953), p. 92.

42 Kessler, 4 June 1930, p. 390.

43 Hamilton, p. 188.

44 Geoffrey Cox to his mother, 3 August 1932, p.c.

45 Mowrer, p. 169.

46 Pollard, Diary, 25 July 1930.

47 Hamilton, pp. 140, 145.

Chapter 4: 'The Seething Brew'

1 Pollard, Diary, 26, 28 July 1930.

2 Hamilton, pp. 160–161.

3 John Henry Mears, *Racing the Moon* (New York: Rae D. Henkle Co., 1928), p. 99.

4 Ibid.

5 Lady Rumbold to her mother, 11 September 1928.

6 Loelia, Duchess of Westminster, *Grace and Favour* (London: Weidenfeld & Nicolson, 1962), p. 135.

7 Martin Gilbert, *Sir Horace Rumbold* (London: Heinemann, 1973), p. 325.

8 Lady Rumbold to her mother, 16 October 1928.

9 Ibid.

10 Ibid., 11 January 1929.

11 Victor Cazalet, Diary, 1–12 January 1929, Eton College Archives, MS 917/2/4.

12 Lady Rumbold to her mother, 16 March 1929.

13 Lady Rumbold to a friend, 27 March 1929.

14 Lady Rumbold to her mother, 16 March 1929.

15 Ibid.

16 Victor Cazalet, Diary, first week September 1928.

17 *Berliner Zeitung*, 12 April 1929.

18 *Observer*, 28 April 1929.

19 Mowrer, p. 181.

20 Kessler, p. 353.

21 Mowrer, p. 221.

22 Lady Rumbold to her mother, 13 January 1929.

23 Brenda Dean Paul, *My First Life* (London: John Long, 1935), pp. 78, 80–81.

24 Loelia, Duchess of Westminster, p. 115.

25 Constantia Rumbold, 'Changing Night Haunts of Berlin', n.d., c. 1930.

26 Stephen Spender to Isaiah Berlin, 30 January 1930.

27 Mowrer, p. 210.

28 Rumbold to Harold Nicolson, 3 November 1930, Bod., MS. Rumbold dep. 38.

29 Kessler, 29 November 1931, p. 405.

30 Pollard, Diary, 25 July 1930.

31 *Christopher and His Kind*, p. 43.

32 *The Spectator*, 26 September 1930.

33 Rumbold to King George V, 31 October 1930, Bod., MS. Rumbold dep. 38.

34 Rumbold to his mother, 19 October 1930, ibid.

35 Quoted in Gilbert, p. 319.

36 Rumbold to Constantia, November 1928, Bod., MS Rumbold dep. 36.

37 Lady Rumbold to her mother, 27 February 1931.

38 John Maynard Keynes, 22 June 1926, *Collected Writings of John Maynard Keynes* (London: Macmillan, 1981), vol. 10, p. 383.

39 Hamilton, pp. 180–181.

40 W. H. Auden, Letter to Lord Byron Part V, quoted in Edward Mendelson (ed.), *The English Auden* (London: Faber & Faber, 1977), p. 198.

41 Wyndham Lewis, *Hitler* (London: Chatto & Windus, 1931), p. 42.

42 Ibid., p. 10.

43 Mowrer, pp. 229–231.

44 Lewis, p. 46.

45 Rumbold to Arthur Henderson, 31 October 1930, Bod., MS Rumbold dep. 38.

Chapter 5: The Noose Tightens

1 Rumbold to Sir Robert Vansittart, 29 May 1931, Bod., MS. Rumbold dep. 38.

2 *Observer*, 10 August 1930.

3 Kessler, 30 June 1930, p. 394.

4 Lady Rumbold to her mother, 18 June 1930.

5 Rumbold to Constantia, 7 January 1931, Bod., MS. Rumbold dep. 38.

6 Ibid., 10 March 1931.

7 *Time*, 23 March 1931.

8 Jewish Telegraphic Agency, 12 March 1931.

9 André François-Poncet, *The Fateful Years: Memoirs of a French Ambassador in Berlin 1931–1938* (London: Victor Gollancz, 1949), pp. 10–11.

10 Lady Rumbold to her mother, 28 June 1932.

11 Rumbold to Lady Rumbold, 30 July 1931, Bod., MS. Rumbold dep. 38.

12 Lady Rumbold to her mother, 27 September 1931.

13 Tom Mitford to Randolph Churchill, 19 November 1931, CAC, RDCH 1/2/41.

14 Lady Rumbold to her mother, 16 July 1931.

15 Spender, p. 111.

16 Bob Boothby to W. S. Churchill, 22 January, 1932, CAC, CHAR 1/398A/48–50.

17 Cox to his mother, 3 August 1932, p.c.

18 Geoffrey Cox, *Eyewitness* (Dunedin, New Zealand: Otago University Press, 1999), p. 71.

19 Cox to his mother, 11 August 1932, p.c.

20 Lady Rumbold to her mother, August 1932.

21 *Pittsburgh Courier*, 30 May 1942. Also material provided by the Archives and Special Collections, Rembert E. Stokes Learning Resources Center, Wilberforce University, Ohio.

22 Lady Rumbold to her mother, 11 August 1932.

23 Margaret Sanger to Havelock Ellis, 16 July 1932, *The Selected Papers of Margaret Sanger: Birth Control Comes of Age, 1928–1939*, vol. 2, Esther Katz, Cathy Moran Hajo and Peter C. Engelman (eds.) (Urbana and Chicago: University of Illinois Press, 2006), pp. 196–197.

24 Ibid.

25 Lady Rumbold to her mother, n.d. August 1932.

26 Ibid.

27 Thelma Cazalet MP, 6 October 1932, Eton College Archives, MS 917/2/8.

28 Kessler, p. 432–434.

29 Lady Rumbold to her mother, 15 October 1932.

30 Wheeler-Bennett, *Hindenburg* (London: Macmillan, 1967), p. 40.

Chapter 6: Monster or Marvel?

1 Isherwood, *Christopher and His Kind*, pp. 92–93.
2 Constantia Rumbold, n.d.
3 Ibid., and Mowrer, p. 247.
4 Constantia Rumbold, n.d.
5 Owen Tweedy, Diary, 16 February 1933, University of Oxford, St Antony's College, Middle East Centre Archive, GB165-0289, Box 3/4. All subsequent Tweedy quotations are taken from this source and are dated between 16 February and 31 March 1933.
6 'Reflections on the German Revolution', *The Nineteenth Century and After*, May 1933, p. 518.
7 Catherine Collomp and Bruno Groppo (eds.), *An American in Hitler's Berlin: Abraham Plotkin's Diary 1932–33* (Urbana and Chicago: University of Illinois Press, 2009), 6 February, p. 148.
8 Ibid., 11 February, p. 157.
9 Gareth Jones, Hitler-Diary, National Library of Wales, Gareth Vaughan Jones papers, B1/9.
10 Denis Sefton Delmer, *Daily Express*, 2 February 1933 and *Trail Sinister* (London: Secker & Warburg, 1961), pp. 185–200.
11 Lady Rumbold to her mother, 1 March 1933.
12 Philip Gibbs, *European Journey* (London: William Heinemann, 1934), p. 313.
13 Harold Picton, *From Republican to Nazi Germany* (Letchworth, 1938), p. 175.
14 Lady Rumbold to her mother, 22 March 1933.
15 *Christopher and His Kind*, pp. 96, 98.
16 2 April 1933.
17 Christopher Isherwood, *The Berlin Novels* (London: Vintage Books, 1999), pp. 488–489.
18 Richard Breitman, Barbara McDonald Stewart and Severin Hochberg (eds.), *Advocate for the Doomed: Diaries and Papers of James G. McDonald* (Bloomington and Indiana: Indiana University Press, 2007), 4 April 1933, p. 40.
19 Ibid., 7 April 1933, p. 48.
20 Ibid., 9 April, p. 50.
21 Karina Urbach, *Go-Betweens for Hitler* (Oxford: Oxford University Press, 2015), p. 300.
22 T. Conwell-Evans, 'Impressions of Germany', *The Nineteenth Century and After*, January 1934, pp. 72–82.
23 Robert Bernays, *Special Correspondent* (London: Victor Gollancz, 1934), p. 124.
24 Evelyn Wrench, 'What I saw in Germany', *The Spectator*, 13 April 1933.

25 University of Chicago Library, Special Collections, Martin Flavin papers, Box 1, Folder 9.
26 Quoted in Mark McKenna, *An Eye for Eternity: The Life of Manning Clark* (Melbourne: Miegunyah Press of Melbourne University, 2011), p. 133.
27 Conwell-Evans, 'Impressions of Germany', pp. 74–75.
28 Lady Rumbold to Lucy Wingfield, 11 May 1933.
29 Frederick Birchall, *New York Times*, 11 May 1933. Quoted in Heinz-Dietrich Fischer (ed.), *Germany through American Eyes: Pulitzer Prize Winning Reports* (Berlin: Lit Verlag Dr. W. Hopf, 2010), pp. 76–78.

Chapter 7: Summer Holidays

1 Daniel Guérin, *The Brown Plague*, trans. Robert Schwartzenwald (London: Duke University Press, 1994), p. 85. Banned in 1934, it was released in 1937, then published as *La Peste brune* (Paris: Spartacus, 1965).
2 Ibid., p. 90.
3 Quoted in Richard Griffiths, *Fellow Travellers of the Right: British Enthusiasts for Nazi Germany* (London: Oxford University Press, 1983), p. 157.
4 Letter from Sir Eric Phipps to Sir Maurice Hankey, 26 October 1933, CAC, Hankey papers, HNKY 5/5.
5 Nora Waln, *The Approaching Storm: One Woman's Story of Germany 1934–1938* (London: Cresset Women's Voices, 1988), pp. 42–43. First published as *Reaching for the Stars* (Boston: Little, Brown & Co., 1939).
6 Hankey to Phipps, ibid.
7 Ibid.
8 Guérin, p. 93.
9 Ibid., pp. 148–149.
10 Hankey to Phipps, ibid.
11 Marsden Hartley to Adelaide Kuntz, 27 May 1933, 'Letters from Germany', *Archives of American Art Journal*, 1985, vol. 25, no. 1/2.
12 Hartley to Kuntz, 12 July 1933, ibid.
13 *Manchester Guardian*, 26 May 1933.
14 Quoted in Kristen Semmens, *Seeing Hitler's Germany* (Basingstoke: Palgrave Macmillan, 2005), pp. 144–145.
15 Ibid.
16 Bradford J. Wasserman, Diary, 17 July–21 August 1933, Virginia Historical Society.
17 Clara Louise Schiefer, Diary, July–August 1933, Special Collections Research Center, Swem Library, College of William and Mary, Williamsburg, Virginia.

18 Louise Willson Worthington, Diary, 1 August 1933, University of Kentucky Library, Special Collections.
19 Interview with the late Mrs Mary Burns, London, 9 February 2015.
20 Constantia Rumbold, c. May 1933.
21 Ibid.
22 Andrew Chandler (ed.), *Brethren in Adversity*, Church of England Record Society, vol. 4 (London: Boydell Press, 1997), pp. 47–48.
23 'Memorandum by the Dean of Chichester on His Visit to Germany', ibid., pp. 52–58.
24 Gibbs, p. 323.
25 Duncan-Jones, draft letter to the Editor, *The Spectator*, 11 July 1937, West Sussex PRO, uncatalogued papers of Duncan-Jones in three boxes.

Chapter 8: Festivals and Fanfares

1 Houston Stewart Chamberlain, *Foundations of the Nineteenth Century* (London: John Lane, 1911), p. 542, translated by John Lees.
2 Quoted in Jonathan Carr, *The Wagner Clan* (London: Faber & Faber, 2007), p. 105.
3 Franck, p. 326.
4 Ibid.
5 Hugh Walpole, Diary, 23 July 1925, Hugh Walpole Collection, Harry Ransom Center, Austin, TX.
6 *John O'London's Weekly*, 11 October 1940; quoted in Rupert Hart-Davis, *Hugh Walpole: A Biography* (London: Macmillan, 1952), p. 264.
7 Walpole, Diary, 23 July 1925.
8 Hart-Davis, p. 264.
9 Walpole to Macmillan, 14 July 1925, BL, Add. MS. 54958–61.
10 Ibid., 1 August.
11 *Time*, 4 August 1930.
12 From documents in the Richard Wagner Museum, Bayreuth; quoted in Harvey Sachs, *Reflections on Toscanini* (London: Robson Books, 1992), p. 112.
13 Quoted in Brigitte Hamann, *Winifred Wagner* (London: Granta Books, 2005), p. 143.
14 Ibid., p. 159.
15 Ibid., p. 160.
16 Sachs, p. 119.
17 Ibid.
18 *Manchester Guardian*, 5 August 1933.
19 Friedelind Wagner, *The Royal Family of Bayreuth* (London: Eyre & Spottiswoode, 1948), pp. 99–100.

20 *Manchester Guardian*, ibid.

21 Waln, pp. 74–76.

22 *The Times*, 2 October 1933.

23 Konrad Warner, 'Harvest Festival 1935'; see Oliver Lubrich (ed.), *Travels in the Reich* (Chicago and London: University of Chicago Press, 2012), pp. 77–78.

24 Sir Eric Phipps to Sir Orme Sargent, 3 October 1934, CAC, PHPP, 2/10.

25 Lubrich, p. 78.

26 *The Times*, 2 October 1933.

27 Ibid., 1 August 1934.

28 *Traveller's Gazette*, April 1930, Thomas Cook & Son Archives.

29 *Observer*, 20 May 1934.

30 Quoted in Raymond Tifft Fuller, *The World's Stage: Oberammergau, 1934* (London: Cobden-Sanderson, 1934), p. 17.

31 *Manchester Guardian*, 30 May 1934.

32 Tifft Fuller, pp. 11, 12.

33 Sydney Larkin, Diary, 8 August 1934, Hull University Archives, Hull History Centre, U DLN.

34 *Hitler's Table Talk, 1941–44* (New York City: Enigma Books, 2000), 5 July 1942, p. 578.

35 *New York Times*, 30 September 1930.

36 *The Times*, 18 May 1934.

37 Lucy Fairbank, 1934 Travel Journal, p.c.

38 Ibid.

39 'Hitler at Oberammergau', letter to *The Times*, 26 March 1940.

40 The Rev. John W. Bradbury, *Watchman-examiner*, 13 September 1934. Quoted in Walter Wink, *Naming the Powers* (Philadelphia: Fortress Press, 1984), vol. 1, p. 116.

41 Wink, ibid.

42 10 August 1934 (from a summary of letters to his wife, Helga), Bod., Hugh C. Greene papers, dep. c. 888. Parts of the HCG quotations used here are quoted in Jeremy Lewis, *Shades of Greene* (London: Jonathan Cape, 2010), p. 153.

43 Phipps to Sir John Simon, 8 August 1934; quoted in Gaynor Johnson (ed.), *Our Man in Berlin: The Diary of Sir Eric Phipps 1933–37* (London: Palgrave Macmillan, 2008), p. 69.

44 *New York Times*, 22 August 1934.

45 Ibid.

46 Ibid., Frederick T. Birchall, 25 June 1935.

47 *Manchester Guardian*, 27 June 1938.

Chapter 9: Heiling Hitler

1 Andrew G. Bonnell (ed.), *An American Witness in Nazi Frankfurt: The Diaries of Robert W. Heingartner, 1928–37* (Bern and New York: Peter Lang, 2011), p. 235.

2 Michael Burn, *Turned Towards the Sun: An Autobiography* (Norwich: Michael Russell Publishing, 2003), p. 72.

3 Robert Byron, 'Nuremberg 1938', *The Spectator*, 22 August 1987.

4 *Manchester Guardian*, 9 September 1936.

5 Geoffrey Cox, *Countdown to War: A Personal Memoir of Europe, 1938–1940* (London: William Kimber, 1988), p. 21.

6 *Observer*, 3 December 1933.

7 David Pryce-Jones, *Unity Mitford: A Quest* (London: Phoenix Giant, 1995), p. 99.

8 Ibid., p. 132.

9 John Heygate, *Motor Tramp* (London: Jonathan Cape, 1935), p. 177.

10 Ibid., pp. 198–200.

11 John Heygate to Henry Williamson, 18 March 1934, from 'John Heygate: some notes on his life in the 1930s as gathered from documents in the Henry Williamson archive (HWLEA), compiled by Anne Williamson'.

12 Robert Byron to his mother, n.d. 1937, Robert Byron papers, Yale University, Beinecke Library, GEN MSS 605, Box 4, Folder 32.

13 Geoffrey Cox to his brother, 7 September 1934, p.c.

14 J. A. Cole, *Just Back from Germany* (London: Faber & Faber, 1938), pp. 124–125.

15 Jan Dalley, *Diana Mosley* (New York: Alfred A. Knopf, 2000), p. 186.

16 Anne de Courcy, *Diana Mosley* (London: Chatto & Windus, 2003), p. 135.

17 Joan Tonge, memoir, p.c.

18 Kenneth Sinclair-Loutit, *Very Little Baggage* (www.spartacus-educational.com, 2009). The author chose not to identify his travelling companion, instead calling him 'Matthew'.

19 Sinclair-Loutit, p. 20.

20 Edward Wall, Diary, 1935, p.c.

21 Ibid.

22 Ibid.

23 Sinclair-Loutit, p. 22.

24 Quoted in Jeremy Lewis, p. 140.

25 Cazalet, Diary, n.d. 1934, Eton College Archives, MS 917/2/5.

26 Arnold Talbot Wilson, *Walks and Talks Abroad, The Diary of a Member of Parliament in 1934–36* (London: Oxford University Press, 1939), p. 126.

27 Ibid., p. 83.

28 McDonald Stewart et al., p. 97.

29 Burn, pp. 76–77.

30 Bruce Arnold, *Derek Hill* (London: Quartet Books, 2010), pp. 29–30; Ariel Crittall, *My Life Smilingly Unravelled* (Braintree: Braintree District Museum Trust Ltd, 1988), pp. 35–36.

31 Tonge.

32 Crittall, p. 36.

33 Ibid., p. 32.

34 Sarah Baring, *The Road to Station X* (Bracknell: Wilton 65, 2000), p. 1.

35 Letter from Lady Margaret Stirling-Aird to David Pryce-Jones, n.d., p.c.

36 Baring, p. 2.

37 Dodo Lees, *Dodo* (Self Publishing Association Ltd, 1993), p. 39.

38 Baring, p. 4.

39 Hugh C. Greene papers, Bod., dep. c. 887.

40 De Courcy, pp. 144–145.

41 Shi Min, *Deguo youji*, Tao Kangde (ed.), *Ou feng mei yu*, 3rd edition (Shanghai: Yuzhou feng she, 1940), pp. 162–184. Bod., HD Chung Chinese Studies, translated by Frances Wood.

42 Cox to his brother, 7 August 1934, p.c.

43 Cox, p. 137.

44 *The Spectator*, 1 November 1934.

45 Antony Toynbee, Diary, 5 November 1933, p.c.

46 Ibid., 14 February 1934.

47 Ibid., 1 November 1934.

48 Brigit Barlow, *A Family Affair* (Lewes: Book Guild Ltd, 1990), p. 46.

49 Ibid.

Chapter 10: Old Soldiers

1 Kirkpatrick to R. F. Wigram, 17 September 1935, NA, FO/371/18858.

2 Truman Smith, *An Estimate of the Inner Political Situation 1935–1936*, TSP, Box 2, Folder 1.

3 Yencken report to Foreign Office, 6 October 1935, NA, FO/371/18858.

4 Ibid.

5 Katherine (Kay) Smith, *My Life*, 11, TSP, Box 3.

6 Yencken report, ibid.

7 Ibid.

8 Reproduced in Nina Boyd, *From Suffragette to Fascist: The Many Lives of Mary Sophia Allen* (Stroud: The History Press, 2013).

9 Mary Allen, *Lady in Blue* (London: Stanley Paul, 1936), p. 148.

10 Ibid., p. 149.

11 Ibid., p. 150.

12 Conversation between the author and Lady Normanby.

13   Phipps to Vansittart, 8 January 1935, CAC, PHPP 2/17.

14   William L. Shirer, 28 November 1934, *Berlin Diary* (New York: Alfred A. Knopf, 1941), p. 25.

15   Gaynor Johnson (ed.), *Our Man in Berlin*, p. 56.

16   Ibid., pp. 56–57.

17   Ibid., p. 57.

18   Ibid., p. 58.

19   Graham Seton Hutchison to Ezra Pound, 15 June 1934, BL, ADD MS 74270.

20   Graham Seton Hutchison, *Challenge* (London: Hutchinson & Co., 1939), pp. 195–196.

21   Pitt-Rivers papers, CAC, PIRI Box 3, 17/3.

22   Karl Astel to Heinrich Himmler, 14 June 1937, quoted in Günter Grau (ed.), *The Hidden Holocaust: Gay and Lesbian Persecution in Germany 1933–45*, (London: Cassell, 1995), p. 119.

23   Astel to Pitt-Rivers, 31 December 1935, CAC, PIRI 17/3.

24   This photograph is published in Brian Harding, *Keeping Faith: The Royal British Legion 1921–2001* (Barnsley: Pen and Sword Books, 2001), p. 152.

25   Quoted in Iain Kershaw, *Hitler, 1889–1936: Hubris* (London: Penguin, 1999), p. 558.

26   *Regimental Chronicle of Prince of Wales Volunteers (South Lancashire)*, vol. X, 4 October 1935, pp. 305–306.

27   Ibid.

28   Ibid.

29   The Reverend Professor Eric Fenn, unpublished memoir, p.c.

30   Buller's book, *Darkness over Germany* (first published in 1943), records the many interviews she had with a wide range of Germans during the 1930s.

31   S. C. Carpenter, *Duncan-Jones of Chichester* (London: A. R. Mowbray, 1956), p. 88.

32   Carpenter memoir, Exeter Cathedral Archives.

33   Fenn.

34   Ibid.

35   Admiral Sir Barry Domvile, Diary, 4 August 1935, Archives of the National Maritime Museum, Greenwich, Dom 52.

36   Ibid., 5 August.

37   Ibid.

38   Kirkpatrick to Wigram, 17 September 1935, NA FO/371/18858.

39   Domvile, Diary, 7–14 August 1935, Dom 52.

40   Quoted in K. Natwar-Singh, *The Magnificent Maharaja: The Life and Times of Bhupinder Singh of Patiala – 1891–1938* (New Delhi: HarperCollins, 1998), pp. 273–274.

Chapter 11: Literary 'Tourists'

1   1 August 1935, HWLEA. A summary of this letter was provided by Anne Williamson. By 1935 Heygate had published *Decent Fellows* (1930), *White Angel* (1934) and *Talking Picture* (1935).
2   Henry Williamson, *Goodbye West Country* (London: Putnam, 1937), p. 228.
3   Williamson, p. 235.
4   Letter from Frank Buchman to Garth Lean, 29 November 1936, Moral Re-Armament Collection, Manuscript Division, Library of Congress, Box 54.
5   Ibid.
6   *Time Magazine*, 14 October 1935.
7   19 September 1935, NA, FO/371/188858.
8   Williamson, p. 255.
9   Broadcast on 11 October 1969.
10 *New Yorker*, 'In From the Cold', Jeffrey Franks, 26 December 2005.
11 21 June 1938, quoted in Robert Ferguson, *Enigma* (London: Hutchinson, 1987), p. 338.
12 Hamsun to W. Rasmussen, 11 March 1934, Harald Naess and James McFarlane, *Knut Hamsun Selected Letters*, vol. 2, 1898–1952 (Norwich: Norvik Press, 1998), p. 209.
13 Hamsun to his daughter, 8 February 1934, Harald Naess, *Knut Hamsuns Brev* (Gyldendal: Norsk Forlag, 2000), vol. 6, 1934–50, letter 2368.
14 Ibid., 29 September 1934, letter 2399.
15 Ibid., Hamsun to his son, October 1934, letter 2406.
16 Richard S. Kennedy and Paschal Reeves (eds.), *The Notebooks of Thomas Wolfe*, vol. II (Chapel Hill: University of North Carolina Press, 1970), p. 748.
17 Katherine (Kay) Smith, p. 2.
18 Martha Dodd, *My Years in Germany* (London: Victor Gollancz, 1939), p. 81.
19 Kennedy and Reeves, p. 745.
20 Thomas Wolfe, 'I Have a Thing to Tell You', *New Republic*, 10 March 1937, pp. 132–136.
21 Ibid.
22 *New Republic*, 24 March 1937, pp. 202–207.
23 Ibid.
24 Denis de Rougemont, *Journal d'Allemagne* (Paris: Gallimard, 1938), p. 19.
25 De Rougemont, p. 17.
26 Amy Buller, *Darkness over Germany* (London: The Right Book Club, 1945; first published 1943), p. 4.
27 Katherine Smith, p. 24.

28 Interview, 2015.

29 Nancy Mitford to Deborah Mitford, 25 September 1939, Charlotte Mosley (ed.), *The Mitfords: Letters between Six Sisters* (London: Fourth Estate, 2008), p. 152.

30 De Rougemont, pp. 24–25.

31 Leonard Woolf, *Downhill All the Way: An Autobiography of the Years 1919–1939* (London: Hogarth Press, 1967), p. 185.

32 Ibid., p. 191.

33 Anne Olivier Bell (ed.), *The Diary of Virginia Woolf*, vol. IV, 1931–1935 (Harmondsworth: Penguin, 1983), 12 May 1935, pp. 311–312.

34 Ibid.

35 Leonard Woolf, p. 193.

36 De Rougemont, pp. 26–27.

37 Maria Leitner, *Elisabeth, ein Hitlermädchen: Erzählende Prosa, Reportagen und Berichte*, 'Dorfschule im Dritten Reich' [*Elisabeth, A Hitler Girl: Narrative Prose and Reports*, 'Village Schools in the Third Reich'] (Berlin und Weimar: Aufbau-Verlag, 1985), p. 226.

38 Ibid., 'Die Stummen von Höchst', p. 212.

39 Ibid., 'Besuch bei Heinrich Heine', p. 224; see Lubrich: 'A Visit to Heinrich Heine', p. 165. Originally published in *The Word* (Moscow), 3 January 1938.

40 Beckett to Thomas MacGreevy (TM), 18 January 1937. Quoted in James Knowlson, *Damned to Fame: The Life of Samuel Beckett* (London: Bloomsbury, 1996), p. 238.

41 Samuel Beckett, German diaries (GD), Beckett Archive, University of Reading, notebook 2, 6 December 1936. Quoted in Mark Nixon, *Samuel Beckett's German Diaries 1936–1937* (London: Continuum, 2011), p. 28.

42 GD, notebook 6, 9 March 1937.

43 GD, notebook 4, 13 January 1937; quoted in Knowlson, p. 244.

44 Knowlson, p. 244.

45 Quoted in Nixon, p. 90.

46 GD, notebook 2, 24 November 1936.

47 GD, notebook 4, 2 February 1937; quoted in Knowlson, p. 251.

48 GD, notebook 1, 29 September 1936; quoted in Knowlson, p. 231.

49 GD, notebook 4, Leipzig, 22 January 1937.

50 GD, notebook 3, Berlin, 31 December 1936; quoted in Nixon, p. 33 and Knowlson, p. 233.

51 Beckett to TM, 7 March 1937; quoted in Knowlson, p. 256.

52 GD, notebook 1, 6 October 1936; quoted in Nixon, p. 7.

53 See letter from Beckett to TM, 18 January 1937, 'I shan't be in Germany again after this trip'; quoted in Nixon, p. 7.

54 See Lubrich, pp. 33–35.

55 Summary of letter dated August 1934, Hugh C. Greene papers, Bod., dep. c. 888, 18.63.

56 Jean Genet, 'A Race of Thieves', *The Thief's Journal* (New York: Grove Press, 1964), trans. Bernard Frechtman, pp. 123–124, ; see Lubrich, pp. 157–158.

57 Pryce-Jones, p. 62.

Chapter 12: Snow and Swastikas

1 François-Poncet, p. 203.

2 Nicholas Howe, 'Alice Kiaer and her Red Stockings', *Skiing Heritage Journal*, June 2006, vol. 18, no. 2, pp. 22–28.

3 Quoted in Jim Ring, *How the English Made the Alps* (London: Faber & Faber, 2011), pp. 253–254.

4 Shirer, *Berlin Diary*, pp. 46–47.

5 Westbrook Pegler, 'Fair Enough' column, *Evening Independent*, 14 February 1936, Pegler papers, Hoover Presidential Library.

6 Ibid., 25 February.

7 Shirer, pp. 46–47.

8 Mary Curry Tresidder, Diary 1936, Stanford Digital Repository.

9 *Ottowa Evening Citizen*, 8 February 1936; *Canadian Amateur Ski Association Year Book 1936*; conversation with Diana's son George Gordon Lennox.

10 Howe.

11 Tresidder, Diary.

12 Ibid., 13 January.

13 Ibid., 7 February.

14 Lady Mairi Vane-Tempest-Stewart, Diary, 7 February 1936, PRONI, Londonderry papers, D4567/1/5.

15 Ibid., 31 January.

16 Ibid., 4 February.

17 Quoted in Lawrence Whistler, *Laughter and the Urn* (London: Weidenfeld & Nicolson, 1985), p. 136.

18 Quoted in Max Egremont, *Siegfried Sassoon* (Oxford: Picador, 2005), p. 326.

19 John Christie, 5 January 1959, Hessisches Staatsarchiv, Darmstadt, Haus Hirth papers, D26.

20 Lady Mairi Vane-Tempest-Stewart, Diary, 16 February 1936.

21 Pegler, 17 and 20 February 1936.

22 Lady Londonderry to Hitler, D3099/3/35/1/1; partly quoted in Kershaw, *Making Friends with Hitler: Lord Londonderry and Britain's Road to War* (London: Allen Lane, 2004), p. 145.

23 Shirer, p. 48.
24 Katherine Smith, p. 84.
25 De Rougemont, pp. 44–45; quoted in Lubrich, p. 84.
26 Katherine Smith, p. 85.
27 De Rougemont, ibid.
28 Katherine Smith, ibid.
29 *The Carthusian*, 1936, p. 295, Charterhouse School.
30 Anne Morrow Lindbergh, *The Flower and the Nettle: Diaries and Letters of Anne Morrow Lindbergh, 1936–1939* (New York: Harcourt Brace & Co., 1976), pp. 80–81.
31 Katherine Smith, p. 95.
32 Quoted in Truman Smith, *Berlin Alert*, p. 95.
33 Anne Lindbergh, p. 86.
34 Katherine Smith, pp. 98–99.

Chapter 13: Hitler's Games

1 Kennedy and Reeves, vol. II, p. 232.
2 Frederick T. Birchall, *New York Times*, 2 August 1936.
3 *Manchester Guardian*, 3 August 1936.
4 Ibid.
5 *New York Times*, 25 July 1936.
6 Soundtrack from *Olympia-Zeitung*, quoted in Karl Lennartz, 'I had the Cup of Spiridon Louis in my Hand', *Journal of Olympic History*, 2012, vol. 2, p. 25.
7 Birchall, ibid.
8 Arthur Porritt, Diary, 1 August 1936, Alexander Turnbull Library, MS. Papers-9608-01-14.
9 Louis S. Zamperini, interview with George A. Hodak, June 1988 (http://library.la84.org/6oic/OralHistory/OHZamperini.pdf).
10 Archie Williams, interview with George A. Hodak, June 1988 (http://library.la84.org/6oic/OralHistory/OHWilliams.pdf).
11 Herbert A. Wildman, interview with George A. Hodak, October 1987 (http://library.la84.org/6oic/OralHistory/OHWildman.pdf).
12 Ibid.
13 Ibid.
14 Ibid.
15 Herman Goldberg, interview, 15 May 1996 (https://collections.ushmm.org/search/catalog/irn504462).
16 Wildman.
17 Kenneth P. Griffin, interview with George A. Hodak, August 1988 (http://library.la84.org/6oic/OralHistory/OHZamperini.pdf).

18 Ibid.
19 John Woodruff, interview (https://collections.ushmm.org/search/catalog/irn504460).
20 Obituary, *Daily Telegraph*, 23 January 2014.
21 Katherine Smith, p. 108.
22 *New York Times*, 7 August 1936.
23 Ibid.
24 *San Francisco Chronicle*, 12 June 1984.
25 Marty Glickman, interview, 1966 (https://collections.ushmm.org/search/catalog/irn504463).
26 *Evening Post*, vol. CXXII, issue 34, 8 August 1936, Alexander Turnbull Library, Wellington.
27 Iris Cummings Critchell, interview with George A. Hodak, May 1988 (http://library.la84.org/6oic/OralHistory/OHCummingsCritchell).
28 Vansittart, 'A Busman's Holiday', 10 September 1936, CAC, Vansittart papers, VNST 1/17.
29 Ibid.
30 Ibid.
31 Ibid.
32 Joachim von Ribbentrop, *The Ribbentrop Memoirs* (London: Weidenfeld & Nicolson, 1954), p. 65.
33 Vansittart, 'A Busman's Holiday'.
34 Ibid.
35 Goebbels, Diary, 2 August 1939. *The Goebbels Diaries*, ed. and trans. Louis P. Lochner (London: Hamish Hamilton 1948).
36 Vansittart, 'A Busman's Holiday'.
37 Ibid.
38 Goebbels, Diary, August 1936.
39 *New York Times*, 7 August 1936.
40 Ibid.
41 *Sydney Morning Herald*, 17 August 1936.
42 *Milwaukee Sentinel*, 3 November 1936.
43 *Chicago Tribune*, 6 August 1936.
44 François-Poncet, pp. 206–207.
45 Robert Rhodes James, *Chips: The Diaries of Sir Henry Channon* (London: Penguin, 1970), p. 137.
46 *Ribbentrop Memoirs*, p. 64.
47 François-Poncet, p. 206.
48 James, p. 140.
49 Ibid., p. 141.
50 Vansittart, 'A Busman's Holiday'.

51   *New York World Telegram*, 26 August 1936; quoted in Tom Driberg, *The Mystery of Moral Re-Armament: A Study of Frank Buchman and His Movement* (London: Secker & Warburg, 1964), pp. 68–71.

52   Vansittart, 'A Busman's Holiday'.

53   *Evening Post*, vol. CXXII, issue 34, 8 August 1936.

54   Ibid.

55   *Pittsburgh Courier*, 5 December 1936.

56   *Brooklyn Daily Eagle*, 15 September 1936, and *New York Times*, 16 September 1936.

Chapter 14: Academic Wasteland

1   Victor D. Lindeman to Du Bois, 26 March 1936, W. E. B. Du Bois papers (MS 312), University of Massachusetts Amherst Libraries, Special Collections and University Archives.

2   Du Bois to Lindeman, 31 March 1936, ibid.

3   Du Bois, unpublished paper, 'Russia and America: An Interpretation', ibid.

4   Du Bois to American Committee for Anti-Nazi Literature, 5 May 1936, ibid.

5   'Fact and Forum', *Pittsburgh Courier*, 19 September 1936.

6   Ibid., 7 November 1936.

7   'Man of color tours Nazi Germany', *Staatszeitung und Herold*, February 1937, Du Bois papers.

8   *Pittsburgh Courier*, 5 December 1936.

9   Ibid., 21 November 1936; quoted in Werner Sellors 'W. E. B. Du Bois in Nazi Germany: A Surprising, Prescient Visitor', *Chronicle of Higher Education*, 12 November 1999.

10   *Staatszeitung und Herold*, ibid.

11   *Pittsburgh Courier*, ibid.

12   Du Bois to Stein, 10 March 1937, Du Bois papers.

13   *Pittsburgh Courier*, 31 October 1936.

14   Sibyl Crowe, Travel Journal, p.c.

15   Quoted in Stephen N. Norwood, *The Third Reich in the Ivory Tower: Complicity and Conflict on American Campuses* (Cambridge: Cambridge University Press, 2009), p. 63.

16   De Rougemont, pp. 22–23.

17   *New York Times*, 28 June 1936.

18   Crowe.

19   Ibid.

20   'A Report of the Celebration of the 550th Anniversary of Heidelberg University, June 27th–July 1st, 1936', by Arthur F. J. Remy, Columbia University Archives, Central Files, Box 549, Folder 13.

21 Ibid.

22 Ibid.

23 *New York Times*, 28 June 1936.

24 Remy.

25 Mrs Ida Anderson, unpublished memoir, George Watson's College, Archive.

26 Ji Xianlin, *Zehn Jahre in Deutschland* [*Ten Years in Germany*] *(1935–1945)*, (Göttingen: Göttingen University Press, 2009), p. 60; translated from *Ji Xianlin liu De huiyi lu* [Memories of Study in Germany] (Hong Kong: Zhonghua shuju, 1993).

27 Ji Xianlin, *Ji Xianlin ri ji: liu De sui ye* [*Ji Xianlin Diaries: My Stay in Germany*], (Nanchang Shi: Jiangxi Renmin Chubanshi, 2014) 6 vols., p. 482, pagination runs right through.

28 Ji Xianlin, *Zehn Jahre in Deutschland*, p. 159.

29 Quoted in Norwood, p. 137, Tansill to Ernest S. Griffiths, 7 September 1936, Tansill personnel file, American University Archive (AUA).

30 Transcript of Tansill's radio talk, 'Impressions of Germany', 20 October 1936, Hoover Presidential Library, Tansill papers.

31 Du Bois, 'America and Russia: An Interpretation'.

32 Runkle to Mrs Robert C. Withington, 16 March 1937, p.c.

33 Runkle to her sister, 14 November 1936.

34 Vassar, Smith, Mount Holyoke, Wellesley, Bryn Mawr, Radcliffe and Barnard.

35 *Bryn Mawr College News*, 15 January 1936.

36 *Manchester Guardian*, 10 April 1934.

37 *Bryn Mawr College News*.

38 Grace M. Bacon, 'German Department Report to the President', 1 June 1938; quoted in Norwood, p. 106.

Chapter 15: Dubious Overtures

1 Berta Geissmar, *The Baton and the Jackboot* (London: Hamish Hamilton, 1944), p. 211.

2 Ibid., p. 215.

3 Multiple sources, including the *Guardian*, 6 April 2001.

4 Quoted in Hamann, pp. 258–259.

5 Goebbels, Diary, 14 November 1936.

6 Geissmar, pp. 238–239.

7 *Western Mail*, 30 September 1936. The quote is from Lewis Carroll, Jabberwocky.

8 Thomas Jones C. H., *A Diary with Letters 1931–1950* (London: Oxford University Press, 1954), p. 242.

9   National Library of Wales, Sylvester papers, B1990/42, B55.

10 Ibid.

11 Lloyd George 'Visiting Germany 1936' (https://www.llgc.org.uk/blog/?p=12184).

12 Sylvester papers.

13 Jones, p. 250.

14 Sylvester papers.

15 Ibid.

16 Ibid.

17 *Daily Express*, 17 September 1936.

18 Sylvester papers.

19 *AGR*, October 1937.

20 Ibid., December 1937.

21 Ibid., September 1937.

22 Ibid., January 1937.

23 Domvile, Diary, 6 September 1937, Dom 54.

24 Ibid., 9 September 1937.

25 Ibid.

26 Ivone Kirkpatrick, *The Inner Circle: Memoirs* (London: Macmillan, 1959), p. 97.

27 *The Times*, 11 September 1937.

28 Nevile Henderson, *Failure of a Mission* (New York: G. P. Putnam's Sons, 1940), pp. 66–67.

29 Pitt-Rivers, 28 September 1937, and Catherine Sharpe, 28 June 1938 to Raymond Beazley, Pitt-Rivers papers, PIRI 25/2, 25/3.

30 Domvile, Diary, 10 September 1937, Dom 54.

31 Ibid., 11 September.

32 *AGR*, October 1937.

33 Londonderry papers, 28 September 1937, D3099/2/19/36.

34 Ibid., D3099/2/19/37A.

35 Ji Xianlin, Diaries, 20 September 1937, p. 534.

36 Kay Smith to Kätchen Smith, 21 September 1937, TSP.

37 Truman Smith to Kätchen Smith, 21 September 1937, ibid.

38 *AGR*, May 1938.

39 *Observer*, 10 October 1937.

40 Quoted in the *Manchester Guardian*, 13 October 1937.

41 Obituary, Sir Dudley Forwood Bt, *Daily Telegraph*, 27 January 2001.

42 Ibid.

43 Philip Ziegler, *King Edward VIII* (London: Collins, 1990), p. 391; *Daily Express*, 15 August 1938; *Manchester Guardian*, 13 October, 1937.

44 Bruce Lockhart, Diary, 22 November 1937, vol. 1, p. 403; quoted in Ziegler, p. 392.

45 Viscount Halifax to Henderson, 24 November 1937, Halifax papers, Borthwick Institute, A4.410.3.2 (i).
46 Andrew Roberts, *The Holy Fox: The Life of Lord Halifax* (London: Head of Zeus, 1991), p. 96.
47 Kirkpatrick, p. 94.
48 19 November 1937; quoted in The Earl of Halifax, *Fulness of Days* (London: Collins, 1957), p. 185.
49 Lord Rennell to Halifax, 14 November 1937, Halifax papers, A4 410.3.2 (ix).
50 Kirkpatrick, pp. 95–97.

Chapter 16: Travel Album

 1 Rhys S. Jones, 'Impressions of Germany 1937', Rhys S. Jones papers, National Library of Wales.
 2 Speech given at the 1935 Nuremberg Rally.
 3 Cole, pp. 138, 142–143.
 4 Katherine Smith, p. 104.
 5 Anne Lindbergh, p. 184.
 6 Quoted in William Craig, *Enemy at the Gates: The Battle for Stalingrad* (New York: Penguin, 2000), pp. 10–11.
 7 Runkle to her sister, 16 March 1937.
 8 *AGR*, May 1938.
 9 *AGR*, April 1938.
10 *AGR*, May 1938.
11 Interview with Sylvia Morris (née Heywood), 2015.
12 Ursula Duncan-Jones, unpublished memoir, p.c.
13 Barbara Pemberton, unpublished memoir, p.c.
14 Letter from Emily Boettcher to her parents, 9 January 1938; unpublished, undated biography edited by Elsa Heald, compiled from letters and other sources; Northwestern University Archives, Emily Boettcher Papers, Box 1, Folder 1, series 19/3/6.
15 April 1938, ibid.
16 Jill Poulton, interview, March 2016.
17 Cole, p. 16.

Chapter 17: Anschluss

 1 Ji Xianlin, Diaries, 12, March 1938, p. 638.
 2 Sylvia Morris, interview, 2015.
 3 Lady Margaret Stirling-Aird (née Boyle) to David Pryce-Jones, n.d., p.c.
 4 Katherine Smith, p. 269.
 5 Ursula Duncan-Jones, unpublished memoir.

6   'Across Nazi Austria: A Traveller's Impressions', *The Times*, 16 March 1938.

7   Ji Xianlin, Diaries, 10–11 April 1938, p. 657.

8   *The Carthusian*, 1938, Charterhouse School archives, pp. 904–7.

9   2 June 1938, CAC, PIRI 17/4.

10 Joan Wakefield, Diary, 6 July 1938, p.c. All J. W.'s quotations are from this source.

11 Margaret Lavinia Anderson, *Practicing Democracy* (New York: Princeton University Press, 2000), p. 69.

Chapter 18: 'Peace' and Shattered Glass

1   Thelma Cazalet, Diary, 6–10 September 1938, Eton College Archives, MS 917/2/8.

2   Truman Smith to his daughter, 23 September 1938, TSP.

3   Ibid.

4   Juvet, pp. 67–75.

5   Edmund Miller to Executive Council of Junior Year Abroad, 17 October 1938, Smith College Archives, Sophia Smith Collection, Office of the President.

6   Truman Smith to his daughter, 21 October 1938, TSP.

7   Katherine Smith, p. 228.

8   Kay Smith to her daughter, 10 November 1938, TSP.

9   Sylvia Morris, interview.

10 Interview with Mrs Bradshaw's daughter, Annette Bradshaw.

11 German Historic Documents and Images, vol. 7. Nazi Germany, 1933–1945: Description of Anti-Semitic Persecution and Kristallnacht and its after effects in the Stuttgart Region (12, 15 November 1938).

12 Juvet, pp. 78–82; quoted in Lubrich, pp. 176–178.

13 Boettcher papers.

14 Ibid., 2 December 1938.

15 Miller to Professor Diez, 27 November 1938, Sophia Smith Collection, Office of the President.

16 Rufus Jones, 'The Day of Broken Glass', Rufus M. Jones papers, Quaker Collections, Haverford College Library, n.d. Box 81, 1130.

17 Ibid.

18 Quoted in Elizabeth Gray Vining, *Friend of Life: The Biography of Rufus M. Jones* (London: Michael Joseph, 1959), p. 288.

19 Quoted in Vining, p. 293.

20 Prentiss Gilbert to Pierrepont Moffat, 10 December 1938, University of Rochester, Rush Rhees Library, Department of Rare Books and Special Collections, Box 1, Folder 5.

21 Ibid., 23 December 1938.
22 Ibid.

Chapter 19: Countdown to War

1   *AGR*, July 1939.
2   Thomas Cook brochure, 1939, Thomas Cook Group archives.
3   Ibid., June 1939.
4   Manning Clark, Diary, 23 December 1938.
5   Ibid., 25 December.
6   Ibid., 28 December. When Dymphna returned to Munich in 1964, she could find no trace of the couple or their family.
7   Ibid., 27 December.
8   Ji Xianlin, Diaries, 15 March 1939, pp. 845–846.
9   Londonderry papers, D3099/2/19/214.
10 Jamieson to Londonderry, 8 April 1939, Londonderry papers, D3099/2/19/280.
11 Ibid., 20 May 1939, D3099/2/19/297.
12 Ibid.
13 Ibid., 19 June 1939, D3099/2/19/B.
14 *AGR*, July 1939.
15 Quoted in Geoffrey Elborn, *Francis Stuart: A Life* (Dublin: Raven Arts Press, 1990), p. 114.
16 Ibid., p. 113.
17 *Illustrated London News*, 5 August 1939.
18 Buller, pp. 76–77.
19 Bryant report to Chamberlain, 13 July 1939, King's College, Liddell Hart Military Archives, Bryant papers, C66, 8.
20 Ibid., C66, 12.
21 Ibid., C66, 19.
22 Letter to A. N. Rooker, 1 August 1939, C68.
23 Wrench, Journal, 28 June, British Library, Add. MS 59594/40.
24 Wrench, *Immortal Years (1937–1944): As Viewed from Five Continents* (London: Hutchinson & Co., 1945), p. 17.
25 Ida Cook, *Safe Passage* (London: Harlequin, 2016), p. 121; first published by Hamish Hamilton in 1950 under the title *We Followed our Stars*.
26 Ibid., p. 135.
27 Ibid., p. 184.
28 *AGR*, July 1939.
29 Interview with Sylvia Morris.

Chapter 20: War

1 Howard K. Smith, *Last Train from Berlin* (London: The Cresset Press, 1942), p. 66.

2 Biddy Youngday, *Flags in Berlin* (published by Mary Brimacombe and Clara Lowy, 2012), pp. 53, 56–57.

3 Hugo von Bernstorff to Bridget Gilligan, 21 November 1938, Bernstorff papers (BP) BL, Add. MS 71515.

4 Gilligan to Bernstorff, 1 December 1938, ibid., 71516.

5 Bridget von Bernstorff to her husband, 2 February 1940, ibid.

6 9 February, ibid.

7 Isak Dinesen (alias Karen Blixen), *Daguerretypes and other Essays* (Chicago: University of Chicago Press, 1979), p. 101. Originally published in 1948 as *Letters from a Land at War* in the Danish journal *Heretica*.

8 Ibid., p. 113.

9 Ibid., p. 130.

10 Howard K. Smith, p. 114.

11 Princess Marie 'Missie' Vassiltchikov, *The Berlin Diaries 1940–45* (London: Pimlico, 1999), p. 7.

12 Sven Hedin, *Sven Hedin's German Diary* (Dublin: Euphorion Books, 1951), pp. 82, 144.

13 18 June, 1940, BP 71516.

14 4, 10 July, ibid.

15 27 August, 3 September 1940, ibid., 71517.

16 Quoted in Harry W. Flannery, *Assignment to Berlin* (London: Michael Joseph, 1942), p. 95.

17 Howard K. Smith, p. 100.

18 Flannery, p. 95.

19 Ibid., p. 98.

20 Ibid., p. 295.

21 15, 19 March 1940, BP, 71516.

22 21 March 1941, ibid., 71517.

23 Ji Xianlin, *Zehn Jahre in Deutschland*, p. 117.

24 15 May 1941, BP, 71517.

25 Ji Xianlin, Diaries, 22 June, 1941 p. 1210.

26 Ibid., 14 August 1941, p. 1231.

27 Howard K. Smith, pp. 46–47.

28 Youngday, p. 62.

29 12 August 1941, BP, ibid.

30 Youngday, pp. 62–64.

31 6, 12, 22 August 1941, BP, 71518.

32 Jacques Chardonne, *Le Ciel de Niflheim* (self-published, 1943); quoted in Lubrich, pp. 266–268.

33   Howard K. Smith, p. 100.

34   Ibid., pp. 261–264.

Chapter 21: Journey's End

1   René Schindler, *Ein Schweizer Erlebt Das Geheime Deutschland* [*A Swiss Experience of Secret Germany*] (Zurich and New York: Europa Verlag, 1945), p. 44.

2   Juvet, p. 121.

3   Reichssicherheitshauptamt, report on Gösta Block's *Tyskland inifran* [*Germany from Inside*], 18 June 1943, Bundesarchiv R58/1091; quoted in Lubrich, p. 286.

4   Francis Stuart, Diary, n.d. March 1942, Southern Illinois University, Special Collections Research Center, Morris Library, 1/4/MSS 167.

5   Ibid., 30 August 1942.

6   Ji Xianlin, Diaries, 19 January 1942, p. 1298; 20 April, p. 1366; 19 August, p. 1388; 2 January 1943, p. 1447.

7   Juvet, p. 121.

8   Stuart, Diary, 25 November 1942.

9   Letters between HRH Princess Margaret (Peg) of Hesse and the Rhine and Bridget, Gräfin von Bernstorff, Hessisches Staatssarchiv, Darmstadt (HStDA), D26 Nr. 41/1, 21 February, 28 April 1943.

10   Stuart, Diary, 2 March 1943.

11   Hamsun to Goebbels, draft, 17 June 1943; quoted in Ingar Setten Kolloen, *Knut Hamsun: Dreamer and Dissenter* (New Haven: Yale University Press, 2009), p. 279.

12   Hamsun speech in Vienna, 23 June 1943, printed in the NS party newspaper *Fritt Folk*, 24 June; quoted in Kolloen, p. 280.

13   The account of Hamsun's meeting with Hitler is based on Ernst Züchner's notes sent to the Office of Norway's Chief of Police, 25 June 1945; see Kolloen, pp. 282–286.

14   Ibid., p. 288.

15   BP, 71520, Bridget to Hugo, 30 July 1943. In fact, the death toll was closer to 45,000.

16   D26 Nr. 41/4, Peg to Bridget, 2, 23 August 1943.

17   Youngday, pp. 71–77.

18   D26 Nr. 41/1, Peg to Bridget, 30 October 1943.

19   Ibid., 29 November 1943.

20   Ibid.

21   D26 Nr. 40/3, Bridget to Peg, 9 October 1943.

22   D26 Nr. 41/2, Peg to Bridget, 29 March 1944. About 5,500 were killed.

23   Ibid., 13 May.

24 Youngday, pp. 78, 80.
25 D26 Nr. 41/2, Peg to Bridget, 14, 22 June 1944.
26 Stuart, Diary, 18 June 1944.
27 Ibid., 9 July.
28 Ibid., 1 August.
29 Ibid., 17 August.
30 Ibid., 4, 8 September 1944.
31 Ji Xianlin, Diaries, 18 July 1944, p. 1669.
32 Ibid, 11 August 1944, p. 1679.
33 D26 Nr. 41/2, Peg to Bridget, 17 September 1944.
34 Schindler, p. 17.
35 Schindler, pp. 8–10.
36 D26 Nr. 41/2, Peg to Bridget, 24 September 1944.
37 Youngday, pp. 92, 94–96.
38 Ibid., p. 95.
39 Ji Xianlin, Diaries, 19 December 1944, p. 1730.
40 D26 Nr. 41/2, Peg to Bridget, 23 October 1944.
41 Ibid., 13 November.
42 Ibid., 26 December.
43 D26 Nr. 41/3, Ibid., 12 January 1945.
44 Stuart, Diary, 3 May 1945, Francis Stuart papers, Coleraine Library, University of Ulster.
45 Ibid.
46 Ji Xianlin, Diaries, 2 April 1945, pp. 1774, 1779.
47 Erik Wallin, *Twilight of the Gods*, ed. Thorolf Hillblad (Mechanicsburg, PA: Stackpole Books, 2002), p. 72. First published 1945.
48 Ibid., p. 82.
49 Ibid., p. 99.
50 D26 Nr. 40/5, Bridget to Peg, 7 July 1945.
51 Youngday, p. 100.

Afterword

1 Du Bois to Stein, 10 March 1937, W. E. B. Du Bois papers.
2 De Rougemont, p. 27.

Index

ABOUT THE AUTHOR

Julia Boyd is the author of *A Dance with the Dragon: The Vanished World of Peking's Foreign Colony*, *The Excellent Doctor Blackwell: The Life of the First Woman Physician* and *Hannah Riddell: An Englishwoman in Japan*. An experienced researcher, she has scoured archives all over the world to find original material for her books. As the wife of a former diplomat, she lived in Germany from 1977 to 1981. Previously a trustee of the Winston Churchill Memorial Trust, she now lives in London.